T0295847

The Data Economy

The Data Economy

TOOLS AND APPLICATIONS

ISAAC BALEY AND
LAURA VELDKAMP

PRINCETON UNIVERSITY PRESS
PRINCETON AND OXFORD

Published by Princeton University Press
41 William Street, Princeton, New Jersey 08540
99 Banbury Road, Oxford OX2 6JX

press.princeton.edu

Library of Congress Cataloging-in-Publication Data

Names: Baley, Isaac, author. | Veldkamp, Laura, author.
Title: The data economy : tools and applications / Isaac Baley and Laura Veldkamp.
Description: Princeton : Princeton University Press, [2025] | Includes
    bibliographical references and index.
Identifiers: LCCN 2024018670 (print) | LCCN 2024018671 (ebook) |
    ISBN 9780691256726 (hardback) | ISBN 9780691256740 (ebook)
Subjects: LCSH: Economics—Data processing. | Economics, Mathematical. |
    BISAC: BUSINESS & ECONOMICS / Economics / Macroeconomics |
    COMPUTERS / Data Science / General
Classification: LCC HB143.5 .B35 2025 (print) | LCC HB143.5 (ebook) |
    DDC 330.0285/63—dc23/eng/20240715
LC record available at https://lccn.loc.gov/2024018670
LC ebook record available at https://lccn.loc.gov/2024018671

British Library Cataloging-in-Publication Data is available

Editorial: Joe Jackson and Emma Wagh
Production Editorial: Mark Bellis
Jacket Design: Wanda España
Production: Danielle Amatucci
Publicity: William Pagdatoon
Copyeditor: Susan Matheson

Jacket Credit: iunewind / Shutterstock

This book has been composed in Arno and Sans

Printed in the United States of America

10 9 8 7 6 5 4 3 2 1

To Moisés and Laura Baley
and
Wilfrid and Mary Veldkamp

CONTENTS

FIGURES

ACKNOWLEDGMENTS

Our work featured in the book is a joint venture with many coauthors. Isaac thanks Andrés Blanco, Ana Figueiredo, Cristiano Mantovani, Ali Sepahsalari, Javier Turén, and Robert Ulbricht. Laura thanks Nina Boyarchenko, Jan Eeckhout, Maryam Farboodi, David Lucca, Adrien Matray, Roxana Mihet, Thomas Philippon, Dhruv Singal, Venky Venkateswaran and especially Stijn Van Nieuwerburgh for his constant support and encouragement throughout the project. We both thank Mike Waugh.

For incredibly useful feedback, we thank Vladimir Asriyan, Hassan Afrouzi, Pau Belda, Rudi Bachmann, Alessandro Bonatti, Giacomo Candian, Gaetano Gaballo, Alex Kohlhas, Albert Marcet, Bartosz Maćkowiak, Roxana Mihet, Guillermo Ordoñez, Luigi Paciello, Elena Pastorino, Pau Roldan-Blanco, Mirko Wiederholt, Mike Woodford and two anonymous reviewers.

We are also thankful to the graduate students who helped us with many aspects of the book. At Columbia University, Kirsten Burr, Kaiwen Hou, Jianye (Jerry) Hua, Angélica Muñoz Rodríguez, Junjun Quan, Dayou Xi, and Yuqi Zhang. At Universitat Pompeu Fabra, Nicolás Oviedo, Alejandro Rábano, Alessandro Pompa, Ricardo Tallini, Santiago Gamba, and Janick Klink.

The Data Economy

1

The Data Economy

The most valuable firms in the global economy are valued largely for their data. Amazon, Google, Apple, and other highly prized technology firms have market caps that exceed the total assets of many small countries. Historically, high-value firms were ones with high-value physical assets: factories, offices, or equipment. Today, a firm with high-precision equipment and prime office real estate can still reap value from those assets. But neither confers the competitive advantage of a good data set. As data storage has become cheaper and data science has improved, the value of data has risen.

Data helps firms find customers, select new products, manage inventory, and choose suppliers. A firm that consistently makes these decisions well has a competitive advantage over those that do not. Such a data-rich firm raises its revenues and cuts its costs. It will profit more, grow more, sell more, and accumulate more data. More data begets more data. This is the data feedback loop. The self-reinforcing nature of data in a competitive market can explain trends in market power and the rise of superstar firms.

Despite the growing importance of data as a strategic asset, modern textbook theories of macroeconomics and finance neglect its role. The tools of macroeconomics describe an industrial economy: physical capital and labor combine to make goods or services that can be used by only one consumer at a time. These models do not describe a modern knowledge economy. An economy where workers use data to add value behaves quite differently from one in which value added comes from combining work with physical capital. Firms built on data compete, grow, and price goods and services differently. In the aggregate, the data economy grows and fluctuates differently. When vast amounts of data can be collected, mined, and traded, what agents know may be less important than where they direct their attention or what data they decide to analyze. When data-intensive firms offer products or services for free or at a discount in exchange for data—bartering for data—then gross domestic product (GDP) will fail to capture an important share of economic activity. Adopting new tools that reflect modern uses of data can offer fresh

1

insights into every corner of macroeconomics and new ways of measuring economic activity.

In finance, data is an important asset to price: it changes firm valuation, and it is a key consideration for entrepreneurs starting new firms. The rise of the data economy is changing sources of both revenue and risk. The industrial-age measurement and valuation tools commonly used in finance need updating for a new era. Furthermore, data may constitute a significant barrier for entrepreneurs and an impediment to business dynamism.

At its essence, data is digitized information. According to information theory pioneer Claude Shannon, information is that which reduces randomness or uncertainty. New data science tools, like machine learning and artificial intelligence, use data to make more precise predictions, making the future more predictable and less uncertain. This book starts from the premise that data is something that facilitates prediction and thereby reduces uncertainty. This definition distinguishes data from ideas and technologies, from knowledge and human capital, and from physical capital. Data helps firms forecast or predict uncertain outcomes, such as which products, suppliers, investments, and advertisements would be most profitable. A hallmark of data-informed choices is that they covary with outcomes like demand, returns, and sales.

Since data is information, the tools of information economics are valuable inputs for data economy research. Therefore, this book collects many information-related tools from macroeconomics and finance that can be used for modeling and measuring data economies. The following chapters teach a mix of old and new tools, many of which were not originally intended to describe a data economy. When discussing existing tools from other topics, we describe how they might be repurposed to model or measure data economies. The tools are primarily theoretical, with careful attention to how these theories can inform or enable measurement.

Data economics research is in its infancy. It will take decades for competing theories to be developed, measurements to be executed, and controversies to be resolved. Answering the many questions posed by the data economy will be a research journey. The role of this book is to facilitate new research about the data economy, its welfare consequences, and optimal data policy.

1.1   Why Theorize About Data?

Research on the data economy is exploding. This book is not a comprehensive summary of that research. Instead, this book teaches a set of modeling tools and describes how the resulting models can inform measurement and policy. Many of the questions in this area cannot be answered without theory. Empirical evidence alone cannot teach us what will happen if we enact a data privacy policy that has never been tried. Often the interpretation of a covariance or parameter estimate is not clear. Theories guide measurement and the interpretation of what is measured. Even within the set of data economy theories, we are not comprehensive. Our focus is on aggregate theories. These are not theories about how one firm uses data, although that is often an ingredient in the model. These are theories designed to think about a market or an economy as a whole. Most models have many agents and balance supply with demand. While many books teach the reader the microeconomics of data, which is a worthy field of study, this book takes a macro perspective to study the data economy.

Macro models always miss important details. They are like maps of the world that are missing most roads. They do not have the detail one would need to drive somewhere. At the same time, a local map is useful for a commute but lacks the perspective of a globe. Both are imperfect. Each is more useful for some purpose. As we build macro models, or maps, of the data economy, a reader is sure to feel dissatisfied at some point with an ingredient that feels essential but is missing. This is the point at which we sincerely hope you will take out a pencil or open a laptop and get to work adding the important details to build out these models. These models are simple structures. Think of them like an artist's canvas on which to project creative ideas. They are not an end product but rather a beginning.

1.2   Essential Features of Data

The modern data economy arose from computing, data storage, and data science innovations. Recorded data has been around for millennia. Data, accounting, and bookkeeping are some of the most basic building blocks of modern human civilization. However, while this data was essential for organizing human activity, it was not a valuable, traded asset or a key input into firm production until recently. Headlines like "Data Is the New Oil" appeared in response to a surge in the storage, use, and value of economic data.

Data moved to the forefront of economic debates because we became capable of storing large data sets at low cost and using them to compute estimates and, most of all, because of new data science algorithms that used big data to make better predictions. Artificial intelligence (AI) and machine learning are two names for these new prediction algorithms. While AI research has been going on since the 1950s, it is only recently that breakthroughs in deep neural networks have enabled these algorithms to be useful for most prediction tasks. In 2012, AI algorithms could finally classify photos of cats and reliably identify them as such. A few years later, these algorithms could identify most human faces or species of birds. Of course, identifying images is not what most businesses do with data. But, because that task is challenging, it is an indicator of the progress of algorithms that take a set of data, like the pixels in a large collection of images, and make predictions about what these data points might mean. In the last decade, data scientists have made immense progress in using large data sets to make predictions.

1.2.1   An Input into Predictions

Since the data science advances that have made data a valuable asset are inherently prediction technologies, most of the tools we introduce in this book treat data as something used to predict uncertain outcomes. Data is an input into this prediction. Data might need to be combined with labor input; capital input, such as computer equipment; or other complementary inputs. But the output is a prediction with higher accuracy than was previously possible. More data enables better, meaning more accurate, predictions.

Thus, one feature distinguishing data from technology, human capital, and other intangible capital is that it improves prediction. Because firms with bigger data sets can predict which ads, products, or procurement sources will be most profitable, they can make choices that covary more with the realized return on each choice. Firms with more data can place ads that are more likely to result in sales, produce goods that are more likely to be in high demand, or choose suppliers that are more likely to offer consistently low costs. By facilitating better predictions, data improves firms' decision-making and lowers their uncertainty about the payoffs of their decisions.

Chapter 2 describes statistical tools used for prediction. Many are applications of Bayes law. Survey evidence and "information-provision experiments" confirm that economic agents revise their beliefs in response to new information in ways broadly consistent with Bayes' Law.[1] Bayes' Law is the foundational tool of most models in this book.

Other prediction tools in Chapter 2 are more like machine learning and artificial intelligence in that they are non-Bayesian. None of the estimation tools we present are as sophisticated as modern data science algorithms. This book contains tools for models. Models are caricatures or simplifications of reality. Our objective is not to estimate outcomes as precisely as possible but to characterize types of estimates firms might make with data. We distill the approaches to their essence in order to gain economic understanding.

---

1. See, for instance, Coibion, Gorodnichenko, and Weber (2019); and Coibion et al. (2021) for the case of households and, for firms, Coibion, Gorodnichenko, and Kumar (2018); and Chapter 14 of the *Handbook of Economic Expectations* (Bachmann, Topa, and van der Klaauw, 2022).

1.2.2 A By-Product of Economic Activity

Most new prediction technologies require vast troves of data. The tool becomes powerful only when combined with a large quantity of training data. While data can come from many sources, large data sets arise naturally as the digital footprint is left by the multitude of daily economic transactions that firms, consumers, suppliers, and governments do. Almost every economically relevant action leaves a digital trace in the modern economy. That action could be buying something, making a payment with a credit or debit card, driving over a bridge, parking in a lot, searching the web, browsing a store either online or in person, or even checking the weather on one's phone. All of these activities generate data as a by-product of the action, even if the data was simply that someone drove, visited, or parked. If every action leaves a trace, then the volume of data generated in the aggregate is stunningly large.

Because digital footprints of economic activity naturally generate so much data that is relatively easy to harvest, it is the primary source of most business data. This sort of data is also naturally relevant for businesses. Evidence of demand, search behavior, traffic patterns, or attention all help firms forecast demand, target advertising, manage supply chains, and predict costs. Thus, data is not produced separately from goods or services. Unlike physical capital and most intangible capital, and unlike new technologies, data does not require a separate investment to produce. Unlike human capital, data does not require a person's time to cultivate it. Of course, an investment might be required to structure, store, and analyze data. But the data itself is a by-product of economic activity. It is generated in the process of buying or selling goods and services. This form of data production is important because large firms that produce and sell lots of goods and services will naturally acquire more data assets. This gives a natural advantage to large firms.

1.2.3 Nonrivalry

Consider a physical good, like a pencil. If Alice sells Bob a pencil, Bob now has the pencil. Alice cannot use that pencil, as only one person can write with the pencil simultaneously. Data is very different. Data fundamentally differs from physical goods because of its nonrival nature. Nonrivalry means that one party can use data at the same time as another party is using the same data. A seller can sell data and still keep the same data.

The nonrival nature of data distinguishes it from human capital acquired through learning by doing, for example. However, the nonrivalry of data is similar to the nonrivalry of ideas. Recognition of the nonrival nature of ideas or technologies revitalized growth theory in the 1980s and 1990s (e.g., Romer,

1990) because models with the production of nonrival ideas could produce sustained growth in a way that goods production could not.

Nonrivalry does not mean that sharing data is without cost. When competing firms use the same data set, they may reduce the value of the data to each other. Both firms can make use of the same data at the same time. But doing so can still make both parties worse off. The idea that one firm's use of data reduces the value of that data to other firms is central to the competitive equilibrium in the data market and the goods market.

1.2.4 Increasing and Decreasing Returns

Data can have both increasing returns to scale and diminishing marginal returns. Returns to scale in data refers to the idea that when an economy is scaled up, meaning that all its inputs or endowments are multiplied, the value of data rises. For example, data has returns to scale in a portfolio problem because it can be used to evaluate one share of an asset or many shares of that asset. When a decision-maker has lots of an asset, data about that asset's payoff is more valuable.

The increasing return to scale in data has important aggregate consequences. There are returns to scale in data because information is expensive to discover but cheap to replicate. If the first copy of a piece of data is much more expensive than the hundredth, there is an incentive to buy the data that others are buying because it is less expensive. This is complementarity in data acquisition. When agents acquire the information others acquire, it leads them to take similar actions. Such mimicking actions resemble fads, herds, or frenzies. Returns to scale also means that big firms extract more value from data than small ones. Evidence from Eckert, Ganapati, and Walsh (2022) supports the finding that large firms benefit more. This force creates gains from merging firms and their data sets. Thus, the data economy may favor large firms and disadvantage small ones.

Data also has decreasing marginal returns. A small amount of data greatly improves prediction. The millionth piece of data has a minute effect. When a firm has an enormous data stock, it can make close to the best possible prediction. At that point, the gains from additional data are small.

While the data economy naturally generates increasing returns to firm size, the decreasing data value for prediction produces decreasing returns. These two forces compete. Increasing returns may dominate early in a firm's life while it is still small and data-poor. Unless the prediction problem changes over time, decreasing returns will dominate and slow growth in the long run.

1.2.5 An Asset of a Firm

The value of economic data has exploded in the past decade. The global market for big data and related technology and analytics was valued at $130 billion in 2017 and grew to over $200 billion by 2020 (Kolanovic and Krishnamachari, 2017). Data is an enormously valuable resource with some durable value, but it also depreciates. Because data used in one period can also be used in the next period, we will need the tools of recursive macroeconomics to model and value it. At the same time, data is used to forecast outcomes in a changing world, so old data is typically less relevant than new data. The loss of relevance shows up as rapid depreciation.

As of today, US data is primarily owned by firms. It is possible to enact a legal framework so that consumers have ownership and control over their data. However, since the current legal framework makes that challenging, in practice, firms own data. Therefore, we model data as an asset that firms own, buy, sell, and extract value from, recognizing that it is possible that another regime could arise, requiring new models.

Because it is difficult to quantify, not typically observed, and often unreported on firms' balance sheets, data is an especially challenging asset to measure and value. The book will discuss these challenges and offer various tools to overcome them.

1.3 How Do Firms Profit from Data?

1.3.1 Buying and Selling Data

The data economy has brought about new business models. At some large firms like Facebook and Google, most revenue does not come from their primary products—search and information sharing. Instead, they harvest the data of product users and earn most of their revenue from selling that data or selling services derived from it.

Other firms acquire data by intermediating trades. Amazon and eBay allow sellers to offer products on their digital platforms. They earn revenue partly through seller fees and partly through data. This business model is similar to that of financial intermediaries or dealers, who have long benefited from seeing the information in clients' order flow.

Not all data is sold directly. Some data is monetized through advertising services. Data-rich firms use their data to target ads to customers with particular characteristics that make them likely to purchase the advertised product. Placing ads is like investing capital in a risky portfolio of assets. The firm is investing advertising funds in a risky portfolio of ads. Just like mutual fund managers (should) use data to invest capital in high-return assets on behalf of their clients, data intermediaries use data to invest a firm's advertising budget in purchasing ads that are predicted to have a high customer conversion rate. The primary difference between these two problems is that a high-return asset conveys a high return to all who invest in it, but a promising customer for one firm is not necessarily promising for another. So, while financial assets are risky common-value assets, advertising invests in an asset portfolio with a large private-value component.

Chapter 3 explores sources of data. It offers tools to capture data revealed in the production process and to describe data choices. Data choices might involve the choice of what to buy or sell or the choice of what data to structure, process, or analyze. Such choices are subject to costs or constraints. Modeling costs or constraints requires measures of data. Thus, the chapter explores different measures and cost functions for data in order to enable the investigation of data choices.

1.3.2 Prediction and Data-Driven Decisions

Firms use data to enhance profits by predicting their costs and revenue shocks and acting to anticipate or mitigate their effect on profits. Brynjolfsson and McElheran (2016) and Goldfarb and Tucker (2019a) give examples of and describe the mechanics of such data-driven decision-making. They orient their analysis around what sorts of firm shocks the data is used to predict, such as sales, advertising, procurement, or hiring.

For a given firm, what to predict and how to use the prediction are central. Whether firms better anticipate costs, revenues, or inventories may not matter as much for aggregate economic outcomes. What matters for the economy as a whole is the way in which data is used to make the prediction. Chapter 4 catalogs and dissects types of prediction problems. Firms could use data to track and forecast a changing economic state, like consumer tastes or the price of raw materials. They might also use data to distinguish short-term fluctuations from long-term economic trends. Alternatively, a firm might use data to decipher what part of an economic shock or trend is firm-specific and what part is aggregate. Is demand generally surging, or did the firm produce a hot product? When solving these problems, firms might buy or choose what data to use in their forecast. The chapter explores data choice and traces its consequences for the aggregate economy.

Data has strategic uses as well. It can be useful to infer what others know or forecast what others will do. Chapter 5 explores the use of data and data choices in settings where firms' or agents' choices depend on what they believe others will do. Since the book focuses on aggregate outcomes, the strategic games it analyzes are ones with many players, often called "mean-field games." A subset of such models is global games. Data can reduce inertia or dampen volatility depending on the strategic motives in the mean-field game. The chapter classifies economic settings, describes the effect of data in each class, and offers economic examples, highlighting the role and effect of data and data choice.

1.3.3 Resolving Risk

Data also reduces risk. Data, at its core, is digitized information, and information is a technology used to reduce uncertainty. Firms use prediction technologies such as machine learning and AI. These technologies aim to predict whether an observation belongs to one set or another. Machine learning can be used in making better predictions about uncertain consumer demands for various products, costs to make certain products, or returns to a portfolio of assets one will buy. Thus, not only can data increase returns, but it can also decrease uncertainty.

Chapter 6 introduces the benefits of risk reduction in the context of an investment allocation problem. Data is often used to allocate resources in an uncertain environment. A salient example of this is the choice of a financial asset portfolio. An investor who can use data to predict the future returns of risky assets can choose to buy more of the profitable assets and earn more. Portfolio problems typically include an aversion to risk or a price of risk. Data not only increases the expected profit but also helps to reduce the utility and financial costs associated with bearing risk. The chapter explores varieties of investor choice problems, the prices that result when many investors solve a data choice and investment choice problem, and the price inelasticity that can arise from investors' use of data.

A simple calculation suggests that risk matters enormously for firm and data valuations. Of the 10% expected returns on firms, about 3% is the riskless return, and 7% is the risk premium, the compensation for risk. This suggests that, for the average firm, risk matters twice as much as the expected value that most economists model and measure. For financial data, Farboodi et al. (2022b) compute the value originating from each component. They break out the part of data value that comes from increasing the expected return and the part that comes from reducing uncertainty. In most cases, far less than half of the value comes from a higher expected return. Most of the value of financial data comes from its ability to resolve risk, making forecasts less uncertain.

Risk also matters in firms' decisions. Corporate finance classes teach potential firm managers to price risk and scale back investment in the face of risk. Corporate finance research finds abundant evidence that this risk adjustment does, in fact, take place throughout the economy. Thus, firms making real output decisions price risk. This implies that they should value data for its risk-reduction properties and its use as an asset. Neglecting the risk component of data's value could lead to a substantial undervaluation of its financial value and its welfare benefit.

1.3.4 Market Power

One of the greatest concerns about using big data is the potential market power it engenders. Data could allow firms to grow larger and take a larger market share. It could function as an entry barrier. And, data could allow firms to compete aggressively on exactly the new products offered by new entrants. All of these are uses of data that will maximize the long-run revenue of the incumbent firm. Chapter 7 explores ways in which firms may use data to create market power. Much of the chapter builds on the investment choice problem. Instead of considering what risky assets to buy, firms choose what products to produce when those products have uncertain demand. A portfolio of assets becomes a portfolio of attributes in a product the firm might design. Investment research is similar to using data for product innovation. The end of the chapter explores the ways in which customer relationships, often called customer capital, might function as data to create and sustain market dominance.

1.4 Distinguishing Features of a Data Economy

The uses of data described above are ways that individual firms use data to profit. Most of these uses have been described in other texts. This book contributes to the formal mathematical modeling tools that can enable structural measurement and inform policy choices. These models can structure our thinking about the aggregate consequences of firms' data choices. While many others have explored the microeconomics of data, this book is about the macro view. It considers equilibrium. Adding the macroeconomic perspective is essential for understanding economic growth, business cycle fluctuations, price-setting, investment, measurement, and sound policymaking.

1.4.1 Platforms and Data Brokers

Intermediaries who connect buyers and sellers have been around for a long time. But data has given them a new business model. Traditional intermediaries were typically compensated by commissions. Either the buyer, seller, or both paid the matchmaker a fee. Household investors paid stockbrokers, property sellers paid real estate agents, and hiring firms paid for job postings in the newspaper. Today, many intermediaries do not earn most of their revenues from fees. Instead, their revenue comes from the data they observe. The intermediary sees the buyers' and the sellers' actions. They have data about multiple parties in the market that no other single agent can know.

Some intermediaries now offer their services at a zero monetary price. For example, Robinhood, the digital platform for trading financial assets, offers free trading. However, they will sell information about your trades to other financial market participants. Order execution is being bartered for order flow data. But because intermediation is data-rich—it exposes both sides of the trade—the barter trade is particularly beneficial to the data platform or intermediary.

Furthermore, some intermediaries are also market participants. Amazon sees which products are profitable and introduces its own brands in that space. Zillow used its house price data to bid for and sell houses. Many regulatory questions surround this type of behavior. Structural models can assist policymakers in assessing its welfare consequences.

Chapter 8 explores models of data platforms. It focuses on equilibrium models with market clearing prices because they are compatible with the macro orientation of the book. Some of the models build on matching tools taken from macroeconomics of labor markets. Some of the models are from industrial organization. But some of the models are an extension of the framework of production allocation choice with market power, built up in the previous two chapters. It adds an intermediary who observes the trades of agents who use their platform. But in return, the intermediary may advise the buyer and/or seller about what to produce, what to purchase, or what other platform participants are buying or selling. Buyers and sellers who choose to trade through the platform barter data for data: they barter the data about their trades for aggregate data provided by the platform. While data platforms are typically associated with sales of goods, they also describe the behavior of financial intermediaries who observe client order flow and provide information or just execution services in return. The data platform model for the goods market is a novel framework, not previously published, written for this book.

1.4.2   A Data Feedback Loop

The data feedback loop refers to the self-reinforcing growth dynamic that arises when firms produce data as a by-product of economic activity. Suppose that having more transactions or getting more customers generates more data. Firms find out a wealth of information about their customers, such as what they like to buy, what kind of credit card they have, where they live, their zip code, and so forth. Firms use this data to generate higher-quality or better-matched goods for customers, and they become more efficient. Firms may use data to appropriately stock their shelves and inventory or hire the right workers to be more profitable. Becoming more efficient or having higher-quality goods allows a firm to attract more customers and transact more. Higher efficiency also incentivizes the firm to invest more and grow larger. Thus, a firm with more data has greater efficiency and more customers, and it gathers even more data.

Amazon's notion of a flywheel captures the spirit of this dynamic. Agrawal, Gans, and Goldfarb (2018) describe Amazon's strategy: By launching sooner, the Amazon flywheel can get ahead, as better predictions will attract more shoppers, and more shoppers will generate more data to train the AI prediction algorithm. As more data improves predictions, the product will be more successful, creating a virtuous cycle.

Chapter 9 builds a dynamic, recursive model where firms produce goods, taking account of the data that will result from their future production. The chapter shows how a slight lead in data allows a company to collect more and better data, reinforcing its lead and generating market dominance over time. Data feedback from production can also change the shape of business cycles, speeding up recessions and slowing booms. Finally, data feedback can make economies and markets fragile, when agents do not know the structure of the economic environment.

1.4.3 Data Barter

A new feature of the modern data economy is that many digital goods and services are given away at zero price. These products were costly to develop. This sort of behavior is difficult to rationalize in a classical production economy. However, when data is a valuable asset generated by economic transactions, this pricing behavior makes sense. Firms develop products to attract users. Selling the products at zero price is profitable because the value of the data that is generated from each sale of the product is valuable enough to compensate the firm for the product development.

In short, these zero-price goods are not free; they are part of barter trade. The digital product is bartered for the user's data at zero monetary price. Some economists and policymakers have called for users to be paid for using their data. In a data-barter view of the world, consumers are paid: they are paid with the zero-price digital service.

The data feedback model formalizes the logic, the value, and the consequences of this barter trade. Structural models of this barter phenomenon are useful because the magnitude of the barter trades has yet to be carefully measured. This barter value is missing in GDP and will likely grow over time. It could lead us to underestimate aggregate growth.

Pure barter trades with zero-price services are still relatively rare. What is potentially much more common is partial barter trades. Consider a firm that recognizes that data from transactions is quite valuable. Such a firm should be eager to do lots of transactions. How does the firm achieve more transactions? They lower their price to lure more customers. A firm that values its customers' data should charge a price below the no-data optimal price. The difference between the price with data and what the price would be without data is the data discount. Now, when a customer buys a product, they are paying a fraction of the true cost with money and a fraction with their data. The true value of the transaction is the posted price plus the value of the data transferred.

Another version of the barter trade is bartering a product for the consumer's attention. For a long time, this was the business model of commercial television. Viewers got zero-price entertainment. In return, they were served with ads. Viewers bartered the entertainment for their attention. The attention allocation tools in Chapter 3 could be used to speak to this slightly different form of barter.

Measuring the value of data barter is not easy. Data-free prices are rarely posted. Perhaps customer loyalty card discounts represent payments for data, although some data can still be collected without using the loyalty card. But it is likely that economists will want structural models to help fill in for counterfactual prices that are never observed.

1.4.4   Superstar Firms

Data favors large firms. Returns to scale in data and the data feedback loop are two separate forces, both of which advantage large firms over smaller ones. Because of returns to scale, a large firm values a piece of data more than a smaller version of the same firm would. The large firm can use the information in that data to produce many units more efficiently or profitably. The small firm can only use the data at a limited scale. Thus, large firms are more likely to make the investments needed to gather, process, and act on data efficiently.

Because of the data feedback loop, not only does a large firm benefit more from a given piece of data, but it also gets more data from its customers. Working together, these forces make large firms more efficient data collectors and more efficient producers than small firms.

Data encourages and enables large firms to grow larger. It makes mergers or acquisitions more valuable. A merger not only merges two firms but also merges two data sets. With a larger data set, both original businesses can become more profitable.

Thus, one of the hallmarks of the data economy is a change in the optimal size of firms. Large firms dominating their market is to be expected when the returns to size increase with the advent of new data technologies. This is not proof that the increase in market concentration observed in the US economy is because of data technology. It simply means that improvements in data technology should explain some increase in concentration, either now or in the future. The magnitude of this effect remains to be seen. Another open question is whether these large firms represent mostly a gain for consumers from greater efficiency or a loss from the greater use of market power to extract consumer surplus.

1.4.5 Growing Covariance of Payoffs and Choices

When a given firm has more data, it uses that data to align its choices more closely with profit opportunities. In other words, data increases the covariance between actions and the uncertain states that data is used to predict. This growing covariance can take many forms and have important aggregate consequences.

For example, Chapter 4 considers firms that are uncertain about monetary policy and are choosing prices for their goods. More data would allow these firms to align their prices more precisely with monetary policy. This would reduce the efficacy of monetary policy and bring us closer to monetary neutrality. Chapter 5 considers settings where agents want to coordinate. Perhaps they have a preference to behave like others. Perhaps these are firms in a supply chain that want to coordinate; for example, they may want to produce more laptop keyboards when the makers of laptop screens produce more screens for them to connect their keyboards to. In any case, data allows them to coordinate more effectively. More data might show up as more synchronized supply chains. As a final example, if firms can predict which product will be in high demand, they can produce more of these products. In an imperfectly competitive market, high-demand products are typically high-markup products. If data helps firms predict demand, they can skew their product mix toward high-markup goods to generate more profit.

Chapter 10 uses this insight and many others to propose ways of measuring and valuing data. While the book is primarily about presenting theoretical tools, the success of these theoretical tools will depend, in large part, on their ability to make contact with data and policy. Measuring data is a challenging task, and different tools are needed for different contexts.

1.4.6 Privacy Concerns

Another feature that makes data different from other intangible assets is that data is personal. Data is often about people, their characteristics, and their actions. Many people would prefer that their actions and characteristics were not widely known. This gives rise to a concern for data privacy. Privacy preferences could encompass concerns about financial theft, identity theft, physical safety, harassment, price discrimination, or a feeling of being violated. Until the last chapter, this book will neglect these concerns. This is not to say they are not important. But the tools of macroeconomics and finance are not yet integrated with tools to model or measure privacy costs. We acknowledge that privacy is a serious concern. The little attention given to the topic reflects that work on the aggregate value of privacy is in its infancy.

Chapter 11 studies the welfare implications of the data economy and points to policy challenges. It describes data externalities, labor market effects, public and private data, risk-sharing, as well as privacy.

1.5 Goals

This research area is nascent. The models are incomplete descriptions and imperfect tools; they need improvement. The data measures should be refined and applied to suitable data sets. Since new papers on this topic continuously appear, our literature reviews are surely incomplete. We apologize to the authors we have omitted. This book aims to quickly bring the reader to a frontier of this research area, to enable them to advance this frontier, and to facilitate new theory, measurement, and policy analysis of the growing data economy.

2

Statistical Tools

This book starts from the premise that data is digitized information used for prediction. It is something that reduces uncertainty about an economically relevant outcome. This chapter explores different ways in which data predicts outcomes and how to quantify the uncertainty reduction it achieves. Tools like Bayes' Law and the Kalman Filter lie at the core of the following chapters. The set of statistical tools used for forecasting could fill many textbooks.[1] The tools we describe here are most commonly used in macroeconomics and finance theories because they are analytically tractable and produce interesting effects.

In what follows, a model is what an agent knows about the structure of a problem, and a parameter is what they might not know. A state is a moving object, and a parameter is a fixed object. If the agent does not know the form of the model, families of models can be indexed by parameters. A parameter could even be an indicator for one of two nonnested models. The point is that model uncertainty can be represented as parameter uncertainty.

2.1 Bayes' Law

Bayes' Law is a tool for assessing the probability that an event will occur, given observed data. Forecasting or predicting involves assessing probabilities of possible future events. Bayes' Law uses data to form these probabilities and predictions.

1. For derivations of Bayes' Law, the Kalman Filter, and hidden Markov models, see Elliott, Aggoun, and Moore (1995); see Mamon and Elliott (2007) for applications of these tools to finance. For the probability and measure theory underlying the expectations, variances, and covariances, see Billingsley (1995). To learn more about filtering in continuous time see Karatzas and Shreve (1991), Lipster and Shiryaev (2001), Øksendal (2007) and Øksendal and Sulem (2010).

One who uses Bayes' Law to form expectations is "Bayesian." A Bayesian starts with some prior belief about a probability or a probability distribution. That prior belief may be 50-50 odds, or it could be the belief that all outcomes on the real number line are equally likely. That initial belief is called a "prior." Then, a Bayesian typically observes new information or data. Using that new information to form a new belief is called "updating" or "Bayesian updating." The belief that results from combining the prior belief and the new information is called a "posterior."

Bayes' Law for Events   The probability of event A occurring, given the observation of event B, is

$$P(A|B) = \frac{P(B|A)P(A)}{P(B)}, \quad \text{with} \quad P(B) \neq 0. \tag{2.1}$$

This law comes from the definition of a conditional probability: $P(A|B) = P(A \cap B)/P(B)$. Likewise, $P(B|A) = P(A \cap B)/P(A)$. Rearranging both of these expressions yields $P(A|B)P(B) = P(A \cap B) = P(B|A)P(A)$. Dividing both sides by the unconditional probability $P(B)$ delivers Bayes' Law. Here, the unconditional probability $P(A)$ is the prior, and the conditional probability $P(A|B)$ is the posterior.[2]

Bayes' Law for Continuous Random Variables   For continuous random variables with smooth distributions, the probability of any point realization is zero. However, Bayes' Law can also be applied to probability densities. Let f be a continuous random variable with a smooth distribution. Then the probability density of event A, given that event B occurred, is

$$f(A|B) = \frac{f(B|A)f(A)}{f(B)}, \quad \text{where} \quad f(B) = \int_{-\infty}^{\infty} f(B|A)f(A)\,dA \neq 0. \tag{2.2}$$

When prior $f(A)$ and posterior $f(A|B)$ distributions are in the same probability distribution family, we say that they are "conjugate distributions." Working with conjugate distributions is very tractable. Normal, binomial-beta (used in section 2.3) and normal-gamma (used in section 2.5) are conjugated families.

2.1.1   Bayes' Law for Normal Random Variables

For normal random variables and signals with normally distributed noise, there is a handy shortcut for Bayesian updating. We will exploit this shortcut extensively throughout the book.

---

2. See Elliott, Aggoun, and Moore (1995), Lipster and Shiryaev (2001), or Bernardo and Smith (2009) for technical conditions and rigorous derivations of the various forms of Bayes' Law.

Suppose there is an unknown random variable θ. According to an agent's prior beliefs,

$$\theta \sim \mathcal{N}(\mu_\theta, \tau_\theta^{-1}). \qquad (2.3)$$

In other words, before observing any additional data, θ was believed to be μ_θ on average, with a precision of τ_θ. Note that the precision is the inverse of the variance (not the standard deviation). We will work with precisions because doing so often simplifies solutions.

Assume an agent sees a noisy signal:

$$s = \theta + \eta, \quad \eta \sim \mathcal{N}(0, \tau_s^{-1}). \qquad (2.4)$$

The signal is an unbiased piece of data about θ with precision τ_s and is *conditionally independent* of $\mu_\theta - \theta$. That means signals and priors are related only because they are both informative about θ, but their errors are independent. Independence implies that $\mathbb{E}[(\mu_\theta - \theta)(s - \theta)] = 0$. Given the prior information and the signal, the agent forms a posterior belief, also called a conditional belief, about the value of θ using Bayes' Law:

$$\hat{\theta} \equiv \mathbb{E}[\theta|s] = \frac{\tau_\theta \mu_\theta + \tau_s s}{\tau_\theta + \tau_s}. \qquad (2.5)$$

With normal random variables, the posterior mean is simply a weighted average of the prior mean and the signal. Each piece is weighted by its relative precision. If a signal contains no information about θ, it would have zero precision. In this case, the posterior mean would be the same as the prior mean. The posterior (or conditional) variance also has a simple form:

$$\hat{\Sigma}_t \equiv \mathbb{V}ar[\theta|s] = \frac{1}{\tau_\theta + \tau_s}. \qquad (2.6)$$

The posterior precision (the inverse of the variance $\hat{\Sigma}^{-1}$) is the inverse of the expected squared forecast error if one uses $\mathbb{E}[\theta|s]$ to forecast θ. It equals the prior precision τ_θ plus data precision τ_s. Every additional piece of independent data adds precision to the estimation.[3]

Multivariate Normals   The formulas above also apply to multivariate normals as long as the division is replaced with a matrix inverse. If θ is an $N \times 1$ vector of random variables, μ and s are $N \times 1$ vectors, and τ_θ^{-1} and τ_s^{-1} are $N \times N$

---

3. The precisions of nonnormal variables are not additive and may not always increase. For instance, when agents learn about Bernoulli random variables (e.g., learning a proportion), additional observations may increase variance and reduce precision.

variance-covariance matrices, then

$$\mathbb{E}[\theta|s] = (\tau_\theta + \tau_s)^{-1}(\tau_\theta\mu + \tau_s s), \tag{2.7}$$

$$\mathbb{V}ar[\theta|s] = (\tau_\theta + \tau_s)^{-1}. \tag{2.8}$$

This version of Bayes' Law works for correlated outcomes and data signals. The variance matrices need not be diagonal.

2.1.2 Bayesian Updating of Normals and Ordinary Least Squares

With normal variables and a linear, unbiased, and uncorrelated signal, the formula for the Bayesian posterior belief $\mathbb{E}[\theta|s]$ in (2.5) is nothing else than the prediction obtained from an OLS regression of θ onto the signal s. To see this, add and subtract the term $\tau_s\mu_\theta$ in the numerator and rewrite precisions in terms of variances:

$$\mathbb{E}[\theta|s] = \mu_\theta + \frac{\tau_\theta^{-1}}{\tau_\theta^{-1} + \tau_s^{-1}}(s - \mu_\theta). \tag{2.9}$$

Since the signal is unbiased and uncorrelated, we have $\mu_\theta = \mathbb{E}[\theta] = \mathbb{E}[s]$, $\tau_\theta^{-1} = \mathbb{V}ar[\theta] = \mathbb{C}ov[\theta, s]$, and $\tau_\theta^{-1} + \tau_s^{-1} = \mathbb{V}ar[s]$. Substituting these expressions and collecting terms, we recover the standard expressions for the constant β_0 and slope β_1 coefficients of an ordinary least squares (OLS) regression:

$$\mathbb{E}[\theta|s] = \underbrace{\left(\mathbb{E}[\theta] - \frac{\mathbb{C}ov[\theta, s]}{\mathbb{V}ar[s]}\mathbb{E}[s]\right)}_{\beta_0} + \underbrace{\frac{\mathbb{C}ov[\theta, s]}{\mathbb{V}ar[s]}}_{\beta_1} s. \tag{2.10}$$

In section 2.2, we show that the equivalence between Bayesian updating and OLS regression for normal random variables also holds when considering correlated information and richer signal structures.

2.1.3 Biased Data

When data s is biased, its mean is shifted away from θ. Before being observed, nature draws data from the distribution

$$s|\theta \sim \mathcal{N}\left(c\theta + d, \tau_s^{-1}\right). \tag{2.11}$$

In other words, $s = c\theta + d + \eta$ where $\eta \sim \mathcal{N}(0, \tau_s^{-1})$. In this case, we can construct new unbiased data $\tilde{s}$ simply by linearly manipulating the original data as follows

$$\tilde{s}|\theta \equiv \frac{s|\theta - d}{c} \sim \mathcal{N}\left(\theta, \frac{\tau_s^{-1}}{c^2}\right). \tag{2.12}$$

In doing such a transformation, note that we scale the variance by $1/c^2$.

2.1.4 Law of Total Variance

The law of total variance states that if θ and s are random variables on the same probability space, and the variance of θ is finite, then

$$\mathbb{V}ar[\mathbb{E}[\theta|s]] = \mathbb{V}ar[\theta] - \mathbb{E}[\mathbb{V}ar[\theta|s]]. \tag{2.13}$$

For normal variables, the conditional variance $\mathbb{V}ar[\theta|s]$ is not stochastic. So, we could drop the last expectations operator.

Imagine there are three dates. At date 1, data s is not yet observed. The uncertainty about the state θ is $\mathbb{V}ar[\theta]$. At date 2, the data s will be observed. At date 3, the state θ will be realized and observed. At date 3, the variance of θ will be zero because it is known. Thus, the total amount of variance about θ to be resolved between date 1 and date 3 is $\mathbb{V}ar[\theta]$. At date 2, the uncertainty about θ is $\mathbb{V}ar[\theta|s]$. That is the amount of uncertainty resolved between date 2 and date 3, when uncertainty drops to zero. If the total amount of uncertainty is $\mathbb{V}ar[\theta]$ and the amount resolved between dates 2 and 3 is $\mathbb{V}ar[\theta|s]$, then the amount of uncertainty resolved between dates 1 and 2 must be the difference $\mathbb{V}ar[\theta] - \mathbb{V}ar[\theta|s]$. The uncertainty that will be resolved at date 2 is the uncertainty about what one will believe at date 2, $\mathbb{V}ar[\mathbb{E}[\theta|s]]$. The conditional expectation is unknown at date 1 but becomes known when s is observed at date 2. Figure I illustrates how uncertainty about future expectations and posterior variance add up to prior variance.

Later, this law will be helpful in computing the expected utility of data. One of the inputs into expected utility will be the uncertainty one has about what one will learn. Uncertainty about what will be learned is uncertainty (variance) of what one will believe after learning (the conditional expectation $\mathbb{E}[\theta|s]$). If working out this variance directly is messy, one can use the prior minus the posterior uncertainty about the state.

2.2 Untangling Correlated Data

In many contexts, outcomes and/or data noise are correlated. When data about one outcome is informative about another, language to describe the information content of data can be helpful. For example, if a price aggregates the information of a finite number of agents, then each agent's signal will affect their choice and affect the price. Thus, signal noise is part of price noise. Both private signals and prices are still informative, but these two pieces

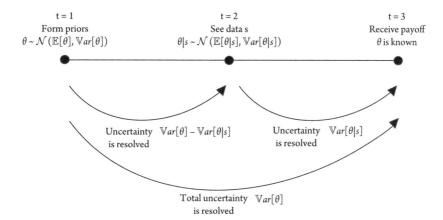

FIGURE I. The Law of Total Variance. *Notes:* This figure illustrates the law of total variance. The total uncertainty or prior variance, $\mathbb{V}ar[\theta]$, equals the sum of the uncertainty resolved between dates 2 and 3, $\mathbb{V}ar[\theta|s]$, and the uncertainty resolved between dates 1 and 2,– $\mathbb{V}ar[\theta|s] - \mathbb{V}ar[\theta]$.

of information cannot be simply weighted by their relative precisions and added up. Extracting independent information or solving for all covariances can be difficult. The following tools can simplify data choice and belief updating when states and data are normally distributed with complicated linear relationships.

2.2.1 Correlated Outcomes and Orthogonal Risk Factors

This section aims to put forth a language for describing the information content of signals when risks are correlated. If a signal can pertain to multiple outcomes, we need language to describe what information each signal has.

The idea of the solution methods outlined below is to form linear combinations of correlated variables, such that the linear combinations are independent of each other. After reexpressing the problem in terms of the newly formed independent variables, we can solve any linear model as if the outcomes were independent. This means that any model that is solvable with independent risks can also be solved with correlated risks.

Using Principal Components Suppose we have an $N \times 1$ vector of normal random variables $\theta \sim \mathcal{N}(\mu, \Sigma)$ with a $N \times 1$ vector of means μ and an $N \times N$ prior variance-covariance matrix Σ that is not diagonal. Thus, the realizations of the N elements of θ are correlated. Because Σ is real, square, and symmetric ($\Sigma = \Sigma'$), one can do an eigendecomposition that splits Σ into a diagonal matrix of eigenvalues Λ and an orthonormal matrix Γ of eigenvectors ($\Gamma' = \Gamma^{-1}$) that satisfies the following relationship (see appendix A.5

for rules about eigendecomposition):

$$\Sigma = \Gamma \Lambda \Gamma'. \tag{2.14}$$

The linear combinations $\Gamma'_i \theta$, for $i \in \{1, 2, \ldots, N\}$, are independent random variables. They are called principal components, risk factors, or synthetic payoffs. Each diagonal element of the matrix Λ (denoted Λ_i) is the prior variance of the principal component i. The ith column of matrix Γ (denoted Γ_i) gives the loadings of each random variable on the ith principal component.

Consider the following normally distributed signals s_i about θ's principal components:

$$s_i = \Gamma'_i \theta + \epsilon_i, \quad \forall i \in \{1, 2, \ldots, N\}. \tag{2.15}$$

Since realizations of principal components $\Gamma'_i \theta$ are independent, a signal about principal component i would contain no information about principal component j. This allows an unambiguous description of the information content of a signal. Signal noise ϵ_i is uncorrelated across components i. In other words, the $N \times 1$ vector of noise terms is distributed $\epsilon \sim \mathcal{N}(0, \Lambda_s)$, where Λ_s is a diagonal matrix of signal noises. The assumption that Λ_s is diagonal simplifies the problem greatly because it reduces its dimensionality. It allows us only to keep track of the N diagonal entries of Λ_s, rather than the $N(N+1)/2$ distinct entries of a symmetric variance-covariance matrix. However, the reduced number of choice variables is a restriction on the problem.

If signals about principal components are independent, then the variance of posterior beliefs has the same eigenvectors as prior beliefs: $\mathbb{V}ar[\theta|s] = \Gamma \hat{\Lambda} \Gamma'$. (The proof of this is left as an exercise.) The diagonal matrix $\hat{\Lambda}$ contains the posterior variance of principal component forecasts. According to Bayes' Law, the posterior precisions are the sum of prior and signal precisions: $\hat{\Lambda}^{-1} = \Lambda^{-1} + \Lambda_s^{-1}$. Learning about risk i lowers $\hat{\Lambda}_i$ relative to the prior variance Λ_i. The decrease in risk factor variance $\Lambda_i - \hat{\Lambda}_i$ captures how much an agent learned about risk i.

Signals with Same Risk Structure as Payoffs   To use this technique, data does not have to be about principal components. It can be a signal directly about the state. As long as the signal noise has the right variance-covariance structure, the tools just described can be applied.

Define $\nu \equiv \theta + \Gamma \epsilon$. Since $\Gamma \epsilon$ has a mean of zero, ν is an unbiased signal about θ. The variance of the signal noise in ν is $\Gamma \Lambda_s \Gamma'$, which has the same eigenvectors (same risk structure) as the prior beliefs about θ.

Notice that the signal just defined is the same as defining $\nu = \Gamma s$ where s is the signal vector defined by (2.15). Since one can always premultiply the signal by Γ^{-1}, this is effectively the same signal as (2.15). Therefore, this information structure results in an equivalent problem.

With either information structure, simply solve the problem as if all payoffs and signals were independent. Take the solution for the independent state and independent signal case, then premultiply the solution by the eigenvector matrix Γ' to get the solution for the original correlated state problem.

Example: Correlated Asset Payoffs Suppose assets A and B have unknown but positively correlated payoffs. An investor observes a signal about asset A, suggesting its payoff is likely high. Knowing that the payoff of asset B is positively correlated, the investor infers that B's payoff is also likely to be high. How can we describe the information content of this signal? Or how can one value data that is about both assets?

Principal component analysis has a long tradition in finance. It can also help to clarify the content and value of data. In Chapter 6.3.2, we use this technique to create linear combinations of assets—call them portfolios or synthetic assets—that one can learn about, buy, and price, just as if they were the underlying assets. Given an optimal portfolio $\tilde{q}$ and equilibrium price $\tilde{p}$ that solve this independent asset and signal problem, we will simply premultiply these solutions by the eigenvector matrix to obtain solutions to the original problem: $q = \Gamma'\tilde{q}$ and $p = \Gamma'\tilde{p}$.

Other Orthogonal Decompositions Principal components or eigendecomposition are not the only way to recombine correlated events or data into orthogonal events. Cholesky decomposition, triangular decomposition or simply premultiplying by the inverse square root of the variance-covariance matrix ($\Sigma^{-1/2}$) can achieve a similar goal. In fact, there are infinite ways to orthogonalize a set of N correlated, normal random variables. When data has a different covariance structure from payoffs, one rotation typically will orthogonalize both. See the appendix of Kacperczyk, Van Nieuwerburgh, and Veldkamp (2016) for how to compute this rotation.

2.2.2 State-Space Updating

When data is correlated, a state-space method can often simplify belief updating. This is called a state-space method because the procedure first defines a set of orthogonal shocks or states. Then, we describe each signal and each outcome (payoff) as a linear combination of these states. This is the state-space representation of payoffs and data. Once payoffs and data are represented this way, there are simple formulas for the conditional expectation and variance.

Suppose we have a model with payoff-relevant states (payoffs for short) θ and data s. That data may be a vector of many signals. The state could also be a vector. The idea is to find a set of orthogonal states z, so the payoffs θ and signals s can be expressed as a linear function of z. Define the linear coefficients for the payoffs to be A_0 and A_1 so that

$$\theta = A_0 + A_1 z. \qquad (2.16)$$

If θ is an $N \times 1$ vector of payoffs and there are m states, then A_0 is $N \times 1$, and A_1 is a $N \times m$ matrix. Define the linear coefficients for the data to be B_0 and B_1

$$s = B_0 + B_1 z. \qquad (2.17)$$

From the model's structure, we need to know the prior mean and variance of the states in the vector z. Call these μ_z and Σ_z, where Σ_z is a diagonal matrix. Without loss of generality, we can set the mean of the state z to be zero. If the mean was not zero, we could subtract the mean μ_z from the state, create a new state z, and redefine the linear coefficients A_0 and B_0 accordingly.

Why doesn't the data representation in (2.17) explicitly contain a noise term? If data is a deterministic function of the state, isn't the state and, thus, the payoff fully revealed? The answer is that the state z should include the data noise. For example, if a piece of data is an unbiased signal of the $N \times 1$ payoff vector θ, plus an $N \times 1$ vector of independent noise ϵ, then the state z should contain both the payoff and the noise. In this example, the state is $z = [\theta', \epsilon']$. Thus data is the sum of these two: $s = 0 + [I_N, I_N] z$, where I_N is an $N \times N$ identity matrix. In this simple example, $B_0 = 0$ and $B_1 = [I_N, I_N]$, because multiplying the $2N \times 1$ vector z times the identity matrix placed horizontally next to itself results in an $N \times 1$ vector of signals that adds together each element of θ with the corresponding element of the data noise ϵ.

This representation then allows us to form three important moments that will be input into Bayes' Law: the variance of the data, the variance of the state, and the covariance of the data with the state. By assumption, the variance of the state vector is Σ_z. The variance of the data vector s is simply the linear coefficient B_1 squared, times the variance of the state: $\mathbb{V}ar[s] = B_1' \Sigma_z B_1$. Finally, if s is a linear function of z, then the covariance is $\mathbb{C}ov[z, s] = B_1' \Sigma_z$.

Finally, we use these moments to form conditional means and variances of the state z. We can use the linear function that expresses the payoff θ to map these beliefs about z into beliefs about payoffs θ. Optimal state-space projection theorems (Luenberger, 1997) tell us that

$$\mathbb{E}[z|s] = \mathbb{C}ov[z, s]' \mathbb{V}ar[s]^{-1} (s - B_0), \qquad (2.18)$$

$$\mathbb{V}ar[z|s] = \mathbb{V}ar[z] - \mathbb{C}ov[z, s]' \mathbb{V}ar[s]^{-1} \mathbb{C}ov[z, s]. \qquad (2.19)$$

If we substitute in the expressions we derived for these moments, we get

$$\mathbb{E}[z|s] = \Sigma_z B_1 (B_1' \Sigma_z B_1)^{-1} (s - B_0), \tag{2.20}$$

$$\mathbb{V}ar[z|s] = \Sigma_z - \Sigma_z B_1 (B_1' \Sigma_z B_1)^{-1} B_1' \Sigma_z. \tag{2.21}$$

We can easily convert these into means and variances of the payoff:

$$\mathbb{E}[\theta|s] = A_0 + A_1 \mathbb{E}[z|s], \tag{2.22}$$

$$\mathbb{V}ar[\theta|s] = A_1 \mathbb{V}ar[z|s] A_1'. \tag{2.23}$$

Notice that, in the special case where payoffs are independent, and data has independent signal noise, (2.18) collapses back to the Bayesian updating formula that weights each signal by its relative precision and adds them up with the prior. The only difference is that it returns both the expectation of the payoffs and the expectation of the signal noise. If each signal is an unbiased predictor of payoffs, then $B_0 = 0$ and $B_1 = [I_N, I_N]$. The variance of the signal noise is represented by the entries on the diagonal of the lower-right quadrant of the matrix Σ_z. The prior variance is represented by the entries on the diagonal of the upper-left quadrant of the matrix Σ_z. Multiplying $(B_1' \Sigma_z B_1)$ effectively adds together the prior variance and the signal variance. The first N entries of $\mathbb{E}[z|s]$, which represent the expectations of the payoffs, average the prior 0 with the signal s. The signal is weighted by $\mathbb{V}ar[\theta](\mathbb{V}ar[\theta] + \mathbb{V}ar[\epsilon])^{-1}$, which is the same as weighting by relative precision $\mathbb{V}ar[\epsilon]^{-1}(\mathbb{V}ar[\theta]^{-1} + \mathbb{V}ar[\epsilon]^{-1})^{-1}$.

Equivalence between State-Space Updating and OLS   Notice that expressions in (2.18) and (2.19) take the same form as ordinary least squares estimators. In econometrics, one might learn that the formula for an estimated coefficient is $(X'X)^{-1}X'Y$, where X is the independent variable and Y is the dependent variable. In our case, the data s plays the role of the independent variable. We are using data points s to predict the outcome z. In OLS, the variance of the independent variable is approximated by $(X'X)$. Since we divide by that variance, we have $(X'X)^{-1}$. The OLS expression $X'Y$ estimates the covariance of the independent and dependent variables. In OLS, one would transpose and multiply this estimator by the data realization s. Our expression for $\mathbb{E}[z|s]$ has the order of the covariance and variance reversed because that is the transpose of the expression equivalent to $(X'X)^{-1}X'Y$. This is multiplied by the signal or independent variable s. Similarly, (2.19) takes the same form as the expression for OLS expected squared forecast errors.

The parallel arises because Bayes' Law for normal variables is the optimal linear projection, as is ordinary least squares. The only reason we express the estimates differently is that when solving theories, the variances and covariances are known to the model-builder. Therefore, when solving theories, we use the true moments. Econometricians do not know these moments. Given the data at hand, the OLS estimator is expressed as the best estimate of the variance and covariance.

In section 2.1.2, we showed that in univariate, linear-normal environments with uncorrelated signals, Bayesian updating and OLS are equivalent. This is true even with a richer correlated signal structure.

This tool can be applied in many settings. Hellwig, Kohls, and Veldkamp (2012) apply these insights to study coordination games with correlated signal structures. It is particularly useful in that setting because agents care about forecasting the state and the noise in public signals. Data sales, sharing, or platforms are easy to handle because they simply change the weights that each agent's information places on each state in the economy (see Chapter 8). Chapter 10 uses this equivalence between OLS and Bayesian updating to value data that other market participants may know, like data purchased from a platform.

2.3 Non-Gaussian Bayesian Updating

In many economic applications, risks are more accurately or conveniently represented as Bernoulli or Uniform. We describe Bayesian updating for such variables next.

2.3.1 Bernoulli Variables: Learning the Probability of Success

Consider a random variable θ that takes the value 1 with probability p (a success) and 0 with probability $1 - p$ (a failure). It can be thought of as the outcome of an experiment that asks a "yes or no" question or the realization of a variable that can only take two values, say high and low, such as a country's unemployment rate or a firm's demand elasticity. Therefore, θ follows a Bernoulli distribution with parameter p:

$$\theta \sim Bernoulli(p) \quad \Longleftrightarrow \quad \Pr[\theta = x] = p^x(1-p)^{1-x}, \quad x \in \{0, 1\}.$$
$$(2.24)$$

Suppose the value of p is unknown and is learned by observing data. There are two ways to set up the Bayesian updating problem to learn about p that depend on the type of prior assumed, either discrete or continuous.

Updating with a Discrete Prior　　In the discrete case, we consider a prior belief p_0 consisting of a set of K values $\{\pi_1, \pi_2, \ldots, \pi_K\}$ for the probability $p = \Pr[\theta = 1]$ and the corresponding probabilities assigned to each value

$\{\omega_1, \omega_2, \ldots, \omega_K\}$. The ω_k's are probabilities about the probability p, are non-negative, and sum up to 1.

We observe N independent data points $\mathcal{I} = \{\theta_n\}_{n=1}^N$, that take on the values 0 or 1. We let $s = \sum_{n=1}^N \theta_n$ denote successes and $f = N - s$ denote failures. To save on notation, we use $\Pr[\pi_k|\mathcal{I}]$ to denote the conditional probability (or posterior belief) $\Pr[p = \pi_k|\{\theta_n\}_{n=1}^N]$.

By Bayes' Law, the posterior belief is a discrete probability distribution with K mass points

$$\Pr[\pi_k|\mathcal{I}] = \frac{\omega_k \Pr[\mathcal{I}|\pi_k]}{\sum_{l=1}^K \omega_l \Pr[\mathcal{I}|\pi_l]} = \frac{\omega_k \pi_k^s (1 - \pi_k)^f}{\sum_{l=1}^K \omega_l \pi_l^s (1 - \pi_l)^f} \quad \forall k \in \{1, 2, \ldots, K\}.$$

(2.25)

Each posterior probability is constructed as the product of the prior belief ω_k and the likelihood of observing the data set $\Pr[\mathcal{I}|\pi_k] = \binom{N}{k}\pi_k^s(1 - \pi_k)^f$, which follows a binomial distribution (note that the binomial coefficient $\binom{N}{k}$ cancels out because it appears in the numerator and denominator). Finally, we divide by the sum of all posteriors so that they sum up to one.

Updating with a Continuous Prior Alternatively, one may consider a continuous prior p_0 that places positive probability density on a continuum of probabilities p. A conjugate prior is a formula for expressing the prior with a similar data structure to the likelihood. In this case, a conjugate prior for the binomial likelihood is the Beta distribution, which is proportional to

$$p_0 \sim Beta(a_0, b_0) \propto p_0^{a_0 - 1}(1 - p_0)^{b_0 - 1}, \quad p_0 \in [0, 1].$$

(2.26)

The parameters (a_0, b_0) control the shape of the distribution and encode the prior beliefs. For instance, its mean equals $a_0/(a_0 + b_0)$, and its variance is $a_0 b_0/((a_0 + b_0)^2(a_0 + b_0 + 1))$. Therefore, if prior beliefs are very confident on a particular value p_0, then pick $a_0 = b_0 p_0/(1 - p_0)$ and a large b_0 to yield a prior mean of p_0 with a small prior variance. The similarity between the formulas for the binomial and Beta functions makes the Beta a conjugate prior to the binomial likelihood. It is bounded between 0 and 1, and it is self-conjugate.

As before, suppose we observe N independent data points $\mathcal{I} = \{\theta_n\}_{n=1}^N$. Then the posterior density is $\hat{p} = p|\mathcal{I} \sim Beta(a_n, b_n)$, with shape parameters

$$a_n = a_0 + s, \quad b_n = b_0 + N - s,$$

(2.27)

where $s = \sum_{n=1}^N \theta_n$ is the number of successes.

2.3.2 Uniform Random Variables

In other settings, working with uniform random variables makes a model more tractable. Updating with uniform variables is conceptually easy. But one must carefully avoid problems at the bounds of uniform intervals.

Suppose that the prior belief is that $\theta \sim \mathcal{U}[-b, b]$ and an agent observes a signal

$$s = \theta + \eta, \qquad \eta \sim \mathcal{U}[-a, a]. \tag{2.28}$$

The simplest case is $s - a \geq -b$ and $s + a \leq b$. This means that for every value of θ that the signal assigns a positive probability density, the prior beliefs also assign a positive probability density to θ. Under the prior beliefs, the probability densities of the state θ and the signal s are both $1/(2b)$. The probability density of the signal given the state θ is $f(s|\theta) = 1/(2a)$. Applying Bayes' Law:

$$f(\theta|s) = \frac{1}{2a}\frac{1/2b}{1/2b} = \frac{1}{2a}, \qquad \forall \theta \in [s - a, s + a]. \tag{2.29}$$

If θ is outside of that range, then $f(s|\theta) = 0$, thus Bayes' Law dictates that $f(\theta|s) = 0$ as well. In other words, $\theta|s \sim \mathcal{U}[s - a, s + a]$.

What if the signal s is close to one of the bounds of the prior distribution? For example, suppose that $s - a < -b$. Then the set of values that both the prior and the signal place positive probability mass on is $[-b, s + a]$. The posterior will be uniform over this smaller interval: $\theta|s \sim \mathcal{U}[-b, s + a]$. In sum,

$$\theta|s \sim \mathcal{U}[\max(-b, s - a), \min(b, s + a)]. \tag{2.30}$$

2.3.3 A Diffuse Prior

One way to specify uniform prior beliefs is the so-called diffuse prior. This assumption represents an agent who knows absolutely nothing about the value of a random variable. A diffuse prior for a variable θ is a uniform distribution over the entire real line: $\theta \sim \mathcal{U}[-\infty, +\infty]$. Since the probability density of a continuous uniform interval $[a, b]$ is $1/(b - a)$, the density of a variable with a diffuse prior is zero. If an agent with a diffuse prior gets a signal, the posterior is the distribution of the random variable conditional on that signal.

For example, suppose the signal is $s = \theta + \eta$ where $\eta \sim \mathcal{U}[-a, a]$. Applying Bayes' Law for uniform variables (2.30) and taking the limit as $b \to \infty$, delivers $\theta|s \sim \mathcal{U}[s - a, s + a]$. In other words, the posterior probability density $f(\theta|s)$ is $1/(2a)$ over the interval $[s - a, s + a]$ and 0 everywhere else.

The fact that $f(\theta|s)$ and $f(s|\theta)$ take the same form when the prior belief is diffuse does not depend on the assumption of a uniform signal. If the prior is diffuse, but the signal is normally distributed, this same result holds. One consequence of this property is that the following two modeling assumptions are equivalent: (i) agent i has a diffuse prior, observes signal s_i and updates, or (ii) agent i has a prior belief given by $f(\theta|s_i)$.

2.4   Filtering

Filtering is updating beliefs about a state in a dynamic environment. When the state is changing, an agent's beliefs about that state are constantly trying to catch up with the new state. When applied in dynamic models, the formula for Bayesian updating with normal variables becomes the Kalman Filter. Filtering applies when agents know the form of the model but not the realization of the state variable.

2.4.1   The Kalman Filter

The Kalman filtering formulas can be applied whenever there is a problem that can be written in the following form. An unknown or "hidden" state variable θ_t has a known linear evolution over time

$$\theta_{t+1} = D\theta_t + Fe_{t+1}, \quad e_{t+1} \sim \mathcal{N}(0,1). \tag{2.31}$$

In each period t, there is a data signal about θ_t, which takes the form

$$s_t = G\theta_t + H\eta_t, \quad \eta_t \sim \mathcal{N}(0,1). \tag{2.32}$$

Shocks to the state e_t and data noise η_t are assumed independent and identically distributed (i.i.d.) standard normal variables across time and shocks.

While the dynamic problems we study in this book typically have an unknown state that is a scalar, in principle, the Kalman Filter applies to vectors as well. If θ_t is an $N \times 1$ vector of states and s_t is an $M \times 1$ vector of signals, then D and F are $N \times N$ matrices, G is $M \times N$, H is $M \times M$, $e_t \sim \mathcal{N}(0, I_N)$ is $N \times 1$, and $\eta_t \sim \mathcal{N}(0, I_M)$ is $M \times 1$.

Constructing the Filter   State realizations $\{\theta_t, \ldots, \theta_0\}$ are never observed, but we use the data set $\{s_t, s_{t-1}, \ldots, s_0\}$ and the structure in (2.31) and (2.32) to generate predictions.

To start out, we specify prior beliefs. It is natural to assume a normal prior so that posterior beliefs will be normal. Suppose that $\theta_0 \sim \mathcal{N}(\hat{\theta}_0, \hat{\Sigma}_0)$.

For all $t > 0$, let $\hat{\theta}_t$ be the expectation of θ_t conditional on all the signals s observed up to, but excluding time t: $\hat{\theta}_t \equiv \mathbb{E}[\theta_t|s_{t-1}, \ldots, s_0]$. Similarly, let $\hat{\Sigma}_t$ be the conditional variance of θ_t: $\hat{\Sigma}_t \equiv \mathbb{V}ar[\theta_t|s_{t-1}, \ldots, s_0] = \mathbb{E}[(\theta_t - \hat{\theta}_t)(\theta_t - \hat{\theta}_t)']$.

In essence, the Kalman Filter consists in running at each date t an ordinary least squares regression of the hidden state on the data observed until t, correcting on both sides by what is already known up to date $t - 1$ and reflected in $\hat{\theta}_t$:

$$\theta_t - \hat{\theta}_t = \beta_t(s_t - G\hat{\theta}_t) + \nu_t. \tag{2.33}$$

Here, ν_t is the least square residual, and therefore, it satisfies the orthogonality condition $\mathbb{E}[\nu_t(s_t - G\hat{\theta}_t)'] = 0$. Substituting ν_t from (2.33) into this condition

$$\mathbb{E}\left[(\theta_t - \hat{\theta}_t)(s_t - G\hat{\theta}_t)'\right] = \beta_t\mathbb{E}\left[(s_t - G\hat{\theta}_t)(s_t - G\hat{\theta}_t)'\right]. \tag{2.34}$$

To compute these expectations, note that $s_t - G\hat{\theta}_t = G(\theta_t - \hat{\theta}_t) + H\eta_t$ by replacing s_t from (2.32). Next, use this fact on the left-hand side, transpose and multiply the matrices, substitute in $\hat{\Sigma}_t$ and set the linear term $\mathbb{E}[(\theta_t - \hat{\theta}_t)\eta_t'H']$ to zero (because the estimator is unbiased) to get:

$$\mathbb{E}\left[(\theta_t - \hat{\theta}_t)(G(\theta_t - \hat{\theta}_t) + H\eta_t)'\right]$$
$$= \mathbb{E}\left[(\theta_t - \hat{\theta}_t)(\theta_t - \hat{\theta}_t)'G' + (\theta_t - \hat{\theta}_t)\eta_t'H'\right] = \hat{\Sigma}_t G'. \tag{2.35}$$

Similarly, compute the expectation on the right by transposing and multiplying the matrices, substituting $\hat{\Sigma}_t$ and setting the last two linear terms to zero to get:

$$\mathbb{E}\left[G(\theta_t - \hat{\theta}_t)(\theta_t - \hat{\theta}_t)'G' + H\eta_t\eta_t'H' + G(\theta_t - \hat{\theta}_t)\eta_t'H'\right.$$
$$\left. + H\eta_t(\theta_t - \hat{\theta}_t)'G'\right] = G\hat{\Sigma}_t G' + HH'. \tag{2.36}$$

Substitute back the expectations into (2.34) and solve for the regressions coefficient β_t:

$$\beta_t = \hat{\Sigma}_t G'(G\hat{\Sigma}_t G' + HH')^{-1}. \tag{2.37}$$

Conditional Mean We have now an estimate of θ_t, but we would like to predict its value at $t + 1$. To do that, start from (2.31), then add and subtract $D\hat{\theta}_t$

to write it as

$$\theta_{t+1} = D\hat{\theta}_t + D(\theta_t - \hat{\theta}_t) + Fe_{t+1}. \tag{2.38}$$

Substitute $(\theta_t - \hat{\theta}_t)$ using (2.33), take expectations conditional on date t information, and replace the expression for β_t to obtain:

$$\hat{\theta}_{t+1} = D\hat{\theta}_t + \underbrace{D\hat{\Sigma}_t G'(G\hat{\Sigma}_t G' + HH')^{-1}}_{\equiv K_t \ \text{Kalman gain}} \underbrace{(s_t - G\hat{\theta}_t)}_{\text{news}}. \tag{2.39}$$

The term K_t is called the *Kalman gain*. It represents how much weight is put on the innovation or "news" term $s_t - G\hat{\theta}_t$ relative to the old information in the prior belief $D\hat{\theta}_t$ when forming the posterior belief $\hat{\theta}_{t+1}$. The Kalman gain is the analog of the term $\tau_s/(\tau_\theta + \tau_s)$ in (2.5) that dictates how much weight the signal is given relative to the prior belief. In that formula, this weight is written in terms of the precision of the prior τ_θ and the precision of the signal τ_s.

Conditional Variance   Finally, we derive the conditional variance $\hat{\Sigma}_{t+1}$. The trick is to subtract $\hat{\theta}_{t+1}$ in (2.39) from θ_{t+1} in (2.38), transpose and multiply matrices, take expectations to replace $\hat{\Sigma}_t$ and set all linear terms to zero, and rearrange to deliver

$$\hat{\Sigma}_{t+1} = \mathbb{E}[(\theta_{t+1} - \hat{\theta}_{t+1})(\theta_{t+1} - \hat{\theta}_{t+1})'] \tag{2.40}$$

$$= \mathbb{E}\Big[(D(\theta_t - \hat{\theta}_t) + Fe_{t+1} - K_t(s_t - G\hat{\theta}_t))(D(\theta_t - \hat{\theta}_t)$$
$$+ Fe_{t+1} - K_t(s_t - G\hat{\theta}_t))' \Big]$$

$$= \underbrace{D\hat{\Sigma}_t D' + FF'}_{\text{prior variance}} - \underbrace{K_t(G\hat{\Sigma}_t G' + HH')K_t'}_{\text{data resolves uncertainty}}.$$

This expression for the conditional variance is known as a Riccati difference equation. Note that the variance changes deterministically. According to the law of total variance in section 2.1.4, we know that the posterior variance $\hat{\Sigma}_{t+1}$ must equal the prior variance minus the uncertainty resolved by observing data. The prior variance comes from taking the variance of the left and right sides of equation (2.31).

To summarize, the following three recursive formulas describe how to update beliefs $\hat{\theta}$ and Σ using the Kalman Filter (note that here we provide an alternative expression for the variance):

$$\hat{\theta}_{t+1} = D\hat{\theta}_t + K_t(s_t - G\hat{\theta}_t) \tag{2.41}$$

$$K_t = D\hat{\Sigma}_t G'(G\hat{\Sigma}_t G' + HH')^{-1} \tag{2.42}$$

$$\hat{\Sigma}_{t+1} = (D - K_t G)\hat{\Sigma}_t(D - K_t G)' + FF' - K_t HH' K_t'. \tag{2.43}$$

Special Case: Univariate, First-Order Autoregressive Process   As a useful case, we consider a univariate state θ_t that follows a first-order autoregressive process or AR(1) process. Let s_t be an unbiased signal about θ_t. The system consists of two equations, one for the hidden state and one for its noisy observation:

$$\theta_{t+1} = \rho\theta_t + \varepsilon_{t+1}, \quad \varepsilon_{t+1} \sim \mathcal{N}(0, \tau_\theta^{-1}), \tag{2.44}$$

$$s_t = \theta_t + \eta_t, \quad \eta_t \sim \mathcal{N}(0, \tau_s^{-1}). \tag{2.45}$$

To describe how to update the mean and variance of beliefs, we use the three recursive formulas in the system (2.41), (2.42), and (2.43) with $D = \rho$, $G = 1$, $F = \tau_\theta^{-1/2}$ and $H = \tau_s^{-1/2}$. We also provide three alternative ways to write these expressions that are useful in certain cases.

$$\hat{\theta}_{t+1} = \rho\hat{\theta}_t + K_t(s_t - \hat{\theta}_t), \tag{2.46}$$

$$K_t = \rho\frac{\tau_s}{\hat{\Sigma}_t^{-1} + \tau_s}, \tag{2.47}$$

$$\hat{\Sigma}_{t+1} = \rho^2\frac{1}{\hat{\Sigma}_t^{-1} + \tau_s} + \frac{1}{\tau_\theta}. \tag{2.48}$$

The Kalman gain K_t shows that the higher the signal precision τ_s, the higher the weight placed on the news. The conditional variance $\hat{\Sigma}_{t+1}$ can be interpreted as the recursive analog of the Bayesian updating formula for the posterior variance in (2.6). It is the inverse of the posterior precision, which equals the sum of the prior and signal precisions (the additional term $1/\tau_\theta$ is due to the state dynamics).

2.4.2   The Kalman-Bucy Filter

Now we consider a continuous time setup and derive the Kalman-Bucy Filter. The key result for solving Bayesian updating problems in continuous time comes from theorem 12.1 in Lipster and Shiryaev (2001).

Suppose there is an unobserved state process θ_t that is a continuous-time diffusion process:

$$d\theta_t = (a_0 + a_1\theta_t)\,dt + \sigma_1\,dW_t + \sigma_2\,dZ_t \tag{2.49}$$

where W_t and Z_t are Wiener processes (also called standard Brownian motions, see appendix A.6). The diffusion's drift is a linear function of the state variable's level. There are two random innovation terms because the signal will contain information about one of these innovations (Z) but not the other (W). An agent observes the signal, which is also a continuous-time diffusion process:

$$ds_t = (A_0 + A_1\theta_t)\, dt + \gamma\, dZ_t. \tag{2.50}$$

Then, if the agent forms expectations that minimize the mean squared error of the forecast, those expectations will be normally distributed with a mean that follows a continuous-time diffusion process: $\theta_t | \{s_{t'}\}_{t' \le t} \sim \mathcal{N}(\hat{\theta}_t, \hat{\Sigma}_t)$ where

$$d\hat{\theta}_t = (a_0 + a_1\hat{\theta}_t)\, dt + \frac{\sigma_2\gamma + \hat{\Sigma}_t A_1}{\gamma^2}\left(ds_t - \left(A_0 + A_1\hat{\theta}_t\right)dt\right) \tag{2.51}$$

$$d\hat{\Sigma}_t = \left[2a_1\hat{\Sigma}_t + \sigma_1^2 + \sigma_2^2 - \left(\frac{\sigma_2\gamma + \hat{\Sigma}_t A_1}{\gamma}\right)^2\right]dt. \tag{2.52}$$

Given some exogenous time-0 prior beliefs $\hat{\theta}_0$ and $\hat{\Sigma}_0$, (2.51) and (2.52) describe the evolution of the mean and variance of beliefs. In equation (2.51), the first term is just the expected drift of $\hat{\theta}$. The second term adjusts that drift for information incorporated in the signal s_t. The information that the agent wants to extract from s_t is knowledge of Z_t, because that enters in equation (2.49) for θ_t, and information about θ_t directly. Thus, they construct $dZ_t + A_1(\theta_t - \hat{\theta}_t)\, dt/\gamma = \left(ds_t - \left(A_0 + A_1\hat{\theta}_t\right)dt\right)/\gamma$. The term $\sigma_2 + \hat{\Sigma}_t A_1/\gamma$ is the analog of the Kalman gain in discrete time. It is the weight that the agent puts on the new information. That weight is higher if σ_2 is higher because the state is more sensitive to the shock Z. The weight on the new signal is also higher if the agent has a more uncertain prior belief ($\hat{\Sigma}_t$ is higher). The remaining term A_1/γ accounts for the fact that if $A_1 > 0$, then θ_t enters in s_t and thus s_t provides information about the level of θ_t, beyond just revealing its innovation dZ.

The Kalman-Bucy Filter can be generalized by allowing all the coefficients in both the state and the signal process to be deterministic functions of time and of the signal s_t, as long as these functions satisfy some integrability conditions.

Special Case: Driftless Brownian Motion   Suppose the unobserved state θ_t follows a diffusion process with zero drift and volatility σ:

$$d\theta_t = \sigma\, dW_t, \quad W_t \sim \textit{Wiener}. \tag{2.53}$$

This process is the continuous-time analog to a discrete-time random walk. Data signals also follow a diffusion process, with drift θ_t and noise volatility γ:

$$ds_t = \theta_t\, dt + \gamma\, dZ_t. \tag{2.54}$$

Then, if the agent forms expectations that minimize the mean squared error of the forecast, those expectations will be normally distributed with a mean that follows a continuous-time diffusion process: $\theta_t | \{s_{t'}\}_{t' \leq t} \sim \mathcal{N}(\hat{\theta}_t, \hat{\Sigma}_t)$ where

$$d\hat{\theta}_t = \frac{\hat{\Sigma}_t}{\gamma} d\hat{W}_t, \tag{2.55}$$

$$d\hat{\Sigma}_t = \left(\sigma^2 - \frac{\hat{\Sigma}_t^2}{\gamma^2} \right) dt. \tag{2.56}$$

The innovation process, defined as $d\hat{W}_t \equiv \gamma^{-1}(ds_t - \hat{\theta}_t \, dt)$, reflects the news and is a Wiener process under the agent's information set. Given some exogenous time-0 prior beliefs $\hat{\theta}_0$ and $\hat{\Sigma}_0$, (2.55) and (2.56) describe the evolution of the mean and variance of beliefs.

Uncertainty Dynamics in the Long Run   According to the Riccati equation (2.56), the posterior variance or belief uncertainty $\hat{\Sigma}_t$ continuously and deterministically decreases until it reaches a minimum value in the long run. In particular, when agents learn about a fixed characteristic ($\sigma^2 = 0$, $d\theta_t = 0$), uncertainty eventually disappears and the state is perfectly revealed:

$$\hat{\Sigma}_\infty \equiv \lim_{t \to \infty} \hat{\Sigma}_t = 0. \tag{2.57}$$

In the less extreme case in which learning is about a stochastic state that follows a Brownian motion, as in (2.53), uncertainty converges in the long run to a constant minimum level equal to the product of the state and noise volatilities:

$$\hat{\Sigma}_\infty \equiv \lim_{t \to \infty} \hat{\Sigma}_t = \sigma \gamma. \tag{2.58}$$

Uncertainty Dynamics in a Cross Section   What do the deterministic dynamics of uncertainty imply for a cross section of agents? Imagine an economy populated by many agents engaging in the same estimation problem. The fact that belief uncertainty eventually settles to a number implies that any differences in uncertainty across agents also disappear. This may not be a desirable feature in some setups—especially if the objective is to explain time variation and cross-sectional differences in idiosyncratic uncertainty observed in forecast data from surveys (see section 10.4).

2.4.3   The Kalman-Bucy Filter with Jumps

A simple way to introduce stochastic uncertainty dynamics is by assuming that the state's volatility σ_t or the signal noise γ_t are time-varying. Next, we explore two additional ways for generating time-varying uncertainty in a steady state, which we label *upward* and *downward* uncertainty cycles.

Upward *Uncertainty Cycles* Baley and Blanco (2019) propose estimating fat-tailed risk as a way to generate time-varying uncertainty. Assume the true state θ_t follows a jump-diffusion process (Øksendal and Sulem, 2010):

$$d\theta_t = \sigma_f \, dW_t + \sigma_u u_t \, dQ_t, \tag{2.59}$$

where Q_t is a Poisson process with intensity λ—the rate at which jumps arrive—and the innovation $u_t \sim \mathcal{N}(0, 1)$ is the size of the jump. Jumps capture regime changes. The agent observes the arrival of a Poisson shock but not the size of the innovation u_t. Knowing the timing of a regime switch preserves the normality assumptions required for the Kalman-Bucy Filter.[4] At all times, the agent observes noisy signals $ds_t = \theta_t \, dt + \gamma \, dZ_t$ as in (2.54). With these assumptions, the information set is given by $\mathcal{I}_t = \sigma\{s_r, Q_r; \, r \leq t\}$, where $\sigma\{\cdot\}$ denotes the generated σ-algebra. The filtering dynamics resemble those in the diffusion case in (2.55) and (2.56) except for the evolution of uncertainty that now includes positive jumps of size σ_u^2:

$$d\hat{\theta}_t = \frac{\hat{\Sigma}_t}{\gamma} \, d\hat{Z}_t \tag{2.60}$$

$$d\hat{\Sigma}_t = \left(\sigma_f^2 - \frac{\hat{\Sigma}_t^2}{\gamma^2} \right) dt + \underbrace{\sigma_u^2 \, dQ_t}_{\text{upward jumps}}. \tag{2.61}$$

Here, $d\hat{Z}_t$ is a Wiener process under $\mathcal{I}_t$. Observe that (2.60) and (2.61) imply *upward* uncertainty cycles, in which uncertainty features a saw-toothed profile: when the Poisson shock arrives, uncertainty jumps up and then falls over time with learning until the arrival of the next Poisson shock (see panel A in Figure IV in section 4.4). The belief $\hat{\theta}$ still follows a diffusion with uncertainty $\hat{\Sigma}_t$ that never settles down.

   In a cross section of agents facing this filtering problem with i.i.d. shocks, uncertainty cycles generate a steady-state distribution of uncertainty. Heterogeneous uncertainty may have important aggregate implications. For instance, Baley and Blanco (2019) introduce uncertainty cycles in a price-setting model to explain the real effects of monetary policy. Senga (2018) uses (discrete-time) uncertainty cycles to explain the cyclicality in the cross-sectional dispersion of sales growth; and Baley, Figueiredo, and Ulbricht (2022) endogenize

---

4. Without observing the time of a regime switch, the filtering problem is more complicated. See Hamilton (2010) for filtering of hidden regime-switching models.

uncertainty cycles in a model of occupational choice to explain features of
labor market dynamics in the United States.

Downward *Uncertainty Cycles*   A second alternative assumes that agents perfectly learn their idiosyncratic state at random times, while at other times, they
only observe noisy signals. This learning process combines *inattentiveness* and
signal extraction that we review in section 3.4. The state θ_t follows a diffusion
process: $d\theta_t = \sigma_f\, dW_t$. A Poisson process $\tilde{Q}_t$, with intensity λ, determines the
dates the firm observes the true state. At other dates, the firm observes a noisy
signal: $ds_t = \theta_t\, dt + \gamma\, dZ_t$. The information set is given by $\mathcal{I}_t = \sigma\{s_r, \tilde{Q}_r,$
$r \leq t;\ \theta_k$ if $d\tilde{Q}_k = 1\}$. The filtering equations that describe beliefs are

$$d\hat{\theta}_t = \frac{\hat{\Sigma}_t}{\gamma}\, d\hat{Z}_t \qquad + \hat{\Sigma}_{t-}\,\epsilon_t\, d\tilde{Q}_t \qquad (2.62)$$

$$d\hat{\Sigma}_t = \left(\sigma_f^2 - \frac{\hat{\Sigma}_t^2}{\gamma^2}\right) dt - \underbrace{\frac{\hat{\Sigma}_{t-}}{\gamma}\, d\tilde{Q}_t}_{\text{downward jumps}} \qquad (2.63)$$

where $d\hat{Z}_t$ is a Wiener process under $\mathcal{I}_t$; $\epsilon_t \sim \mathcal{N}(0,1)$ captures the difference between the current, unbiased estimate and its true value; and
$\hat{\Sigma}_{t-} = \lim_{\Delta\to 0^+}\hat{\Sigma}_{t-\Delta}$ is the level of uncertainty "immediately" before period
t. Equation (2.63) encodes *downward* uncertainty cycles: with a Poisson
arrival of perfect information, uncertainty collapses to zero and then grows
over time. The estimate in (2.62) follows a diffusion process, but at the arrival
dates of perfectly informative data, the estimate is corrected (upwards or
downwards) by its difference from the truth. Downward uncertainty cycles
also generate heterogeneous uncertainty in a steady state.

2.4.4   Continuous Time Filtering of Bernoulli Random Variables

Suppose an agent wants to learn about a Bernoulli random variable that
takes a high or a low value, $\theta \in \{\theta^H, \theta^L\}$, with unknown probability p and
$1-p$. In section 2.3.1, data about p arrived at discrete time intervals. Here,
data arrive continuously. We assume signals follow a Brownian motion with
(unknown) drift θ and noise volatility γ:

$$ds_t = \theta\, dt + \gamma\, dZ_t, \quad Z_t \sim Wiener. \qquad (2.64)$$

We can write the drift in terms of the unknown probability p as

$$ds_t = [p\theta^H + (1-p)\theta^L]\, dt + \gamma\, dZ_t, \quad Z_t \sim Wiener. \qquad (2.65)$$

Following the results in Wonham (1964), the posterior belief $\hat{p}_t = p_t | \mathcal{I}_t$ is a diffusion

$$d\hat{p}_t = \hat{\Sigma}_t \, d\hat{Z}_t, \qquad (2.66)$$

with volatility $\hat{\Sigma}_t = \hat{p}_t(1 - \hat{p}_t)h$. The constant $h \equiv (\theta^H - \theta^L)/\gamma$ is the signal-to-noise ratio, and the innovation process $\hat{Z}_t$ is a standard Brownian motion under the information set of the agent, equal to the normalized difference between the signal, and the expected state

$$d\hat{Z}_t \equiv \gamma^{-1} \left(ds_t - [\hat{p}_t \theta^H + (1 - \hat{p}_t)\theta^L] \, dt \right). \qquad (2.67)$$

When filtering Bernoulli variables, the conditional variance $\hat{\Sigma}_t$ does not always drop as data accumulates, contrasting with the Kalman Filter formula for the variance for normal variables (2.56). Uncertainty is highest at $\hat{\Sigma}_t = h/4$ when $\hat{p}_t = 1/2$ (equal odds) and falls toward zero at the extremes $\hat{p}_t = 0$ and $\hat{p}_t = 1$. Data that move the belief $\hat{p}_t$ towards $1/2$ increase uncertainty.

2.5   Estimating the Distribution of the State

In many setups, agents know the true probability distribution of all economically relevant outcomes. However, for some applications, the distribution of random variables has to be estimated. We start with a simple case in which an agent knows that the distribution is normal and learns the mean, the variance, or both, observing a sample of independent draws from that distribution.

2.5.1   Estimating the Mean

Assume that the true distribution of the state is $\theta \sim \mathcal{N}(\mu_\theta, \tau_\theta^{-1})$. Suppose an agent knows the precision τ_θ but not the mean μ_θ. Prior beliefs about the mean are normal: $\mu_\theta \sim \mathcal{N}\left(\mu_0, \tau_0^{-1}\right)$. After observing an i.i.d. sample of t draws of the state θ, the date-t information set is $\mathcal{I}_t = \{\theta_r | r \leq t\}$. The posterior belief is normal, where $\theta_t \equiv \mathbb{E}[\mu_\theta | \mathcal{I}_t]$ is a weighted average of the prior mean μ_0 and the sample mean: $\bar{\theta}$.

$$\theta_t = \frac{\tau_0 \mu_0 + t \tau_\theta \bar{\theta}}{\tau_t}, \qquad \tau_t = \tau_0 + t \tau_\theta, \qquad \bar{\theta} = \frac{1}{t} \sum_{r=1}^{t} \theta_r. \qquad (2.68)$$

This is like Bayesian updating in section 2.1.1. As before, the posterior precision $\tau_t = \mathbb{V}ar[\mu_\theta | \mathcal{I}_t]^{-1}$ is the sum of the prior precision τ_0 and the sample precision $t\tau_\theta$, which grows linearly with the number of observations. As the number of observations increases $(t \rightarrow \infty)$, the posterior belief converges to the sample mean $\theta_t \rightarrow \bar{\theta}$, and precision goes to infinity (uncertainty disappears). The truth is eventually revealed. Section 4.2, uses this structure to model agents who estimate a fixed characteristic (e.g., a worker's ability) over time.

2.5.2   Estimating the Precision

Next, suppose the variance or precision of the state is not known. With an i.i.d. data sample $\mathcal{I}_t = \{\theta_r | r \le t\}$, an agent now simultaneously learns about the mean and the precision of $\theta \sim \mathcal{N}(\mu_\theta, \tau_\theta^{-1})$. The standard way to formalize this problem is to use a joint normal-gamma distribution. The precision is gamma distributed $\tau_\theta \sim Gamma(\alpha, \beta)$, with density

$$f(x|\alpha, \beta) \propto (\beta x)^{\alpha-1} e^{-\beta x}. \tag{2.69}$$

This distribution has mean α/β and precision β^2/α. Conditional on the precision, the state, and its mean are normally distributed. This formulation is convenient because when a normal mean and a gamma precision are updated with data drawn from that same type of distribution, the posterior beliefs will also involve a normally distributed mean and a gamma-distributed precision.

Given prior beliefs $\mu_\theta | \tau_\theta \sim \mathcal{N}\left(\mu_0, (\kappa_0 \tau_\theta)^{-1}\right)$ and $\tau_\theta \sim Gamma(\alpha_0, \beta_0)$, the posterior belief about the mean is $\mu_\theta | (\mathcal{I}_t, \tau_\theta) \sim \mathcal{N}\left(\theta_t, (\kappa_t \tau_\theta)^{-1}\right)$, with

$$\theta_t = \frac{\kappa_0 \mu_0 + t\bar{\theta}}{\kappa_t}, \qquad \kappa_t = \kappa_0 + t, \qquad \bar{\theta} = \frac{1}{t} \sum_{r=1}^{t} \theta_r. \tag{2.70}$$

In turn, the parameters that govern the precision's posterior distribution $\tau_\theta | \mathcal{I}_t \sim Gamma(\alpha_t, \beta_t)$ evolve according to

$$\alpha_t = \alpha_0 + \frac{t}{2}, \qquad \beta_t = \beta_0 + \frac{1}{2}\left[\sum_{r=1}^{t} (\theta_r - \bar{\theta})^2 + \frac{t\kappa_0 (\bar{\theta} - \mu_0)^2}{\kappa_t}\right], \tag{2.71}$$

and the conditional moments are

$$\mathbb{E}[\tau_\theta | \mathcal{I}_t] = \frac{\alpha_t}{\beta_t}, \qquad \mathbb{V}ar[\tau_\theta | \mathcal{I}_t]^{-1} = \frac{\beta_t^2}{\alpha_t}. \tag{2.72}$$

As the sample size increases ($t \to \infty$), the posterior belief about the mean θ_t in (2.70) converges to the true value μ_θ and belief uncertainty converges to zero $\kappa_t^{-1} = 0$. Regarding the beliefs about the precision, both α_t and β_t in (2.71) go to infinity. However, the ratio α_t/β_t, equal to the conditional mean, converges to the true precision τ_θ, while belief uncertainty goes to zero.

The normal-gamma approach is implemented by Cogley and Sargent (2005) to estimate the parameters of central bank policy rules and by Weitzman (2007), Bakshi and Skoulakis (2010), and Collin-Dufresne,

Johannes, and Lochstoer (2016) to study asset-pricing puzzles. Ghofrani (2021) shows that this framework generates persistent impacts of tail-event shocks.

2.5.3 Estimating Skewness and Tail Risk

One of the challenges models of data frictions face is that means and variances are easy to estimate. Unless data is excessively noisy, a few observations quickly shrink uncertainty to near zero. What is harder to learn are the higher moments of a distribution, like skewness or tail probabilities.

When agents estimate the skewness of a random variable, they may experience (i) cyclical fluctuations in uncertainty driven by tail events and (ii) small sample biases. We discuss these ideas in the following example, which features two crucial ingredients: parameter uncertainty and skewness in the distribution.

A Skewed Forecasting Model Consider a state-space model for a random variable y_t

$$y_t = c + bg(\theta_t) \tag{2.73}$$

$$\theta_t = m_t + \sigma_\epsilon \epsilon_t \tag{2.74}$$

$$m_t = \rho m_{t-1} + \sigma_\eta \eta_t, \tag{2.75}$$

where $\epsilon_t, \eta_t \sim \mathcal{N}(0, 1)$ are i.i.d. random variables. The hidden state θ_t is the sum of a persistent component m_t, with autoregressive parameter ρ and volatility σ_η, and a transitory component ϵ_t with volatility σ_ϵ. The function g is a *nonlinear* one-to-one mapping, which renders y_t a skewed random variable.[5] Due to Jensen's inequality, if g is concave, then y is negatively skewed; if g is convex, then y is positively skewed (see appendix A.2 for Jensen's inequality and appendix A.4 for skewed transformations of normal variables). For example, let us consider g to be concave, $g(\theta_t) = -\exp(-\theta_t)$. In this case, a given amount of uncertainty about θ creates more uncertainty about y when θ is low than when θ is high (the opposite is true when g is convex).

Agents observe y_t every period (but not θ_t or m_t). However, they do not know the distribution from where it is drawn; that is, the parameter values $(c, b, \rho, \sigma_\epsilon, \sigma_\eta)$ are unknown and are learned in a Bayesian way. This additional source of uncertainty, parameter uncertainty, is reflected in y's conditional variance $\mathbb{V}ar[y_t | \mathcal{I}_t]$.

---

5. While here the function g is exogenously assumed, it can also result from modeling the economic environment. For instance, Straub and Ulbricht (2023) microfound a concave mapping from fundamentals θ to economic activity y_t through a model of financial frictions.

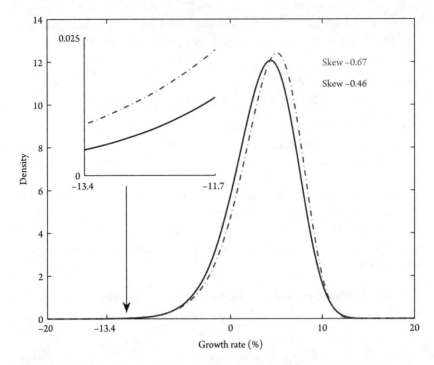

FIGURE II. Subtle Changes in Skewness Create Big Shifts in Tail Risk. *Notes*: This is an example of the perceived distribution of the growth rate of GDP y_t from the data generating process in (2.75), where the agent observed real GDP data from 1947 onward and estimated the model parameters in 1971 Q2 or 1973 Q1. A small difference in the skewness parameter in the growth distribution (from -0.46 to -0.67) raises the conditional probability of a 5-standard deviation tail event from 0.46% to 0.93%. The upward shift in the probability of the tail event is illustrated in the top left subfigure that zooms into the left tail of the distribution. (Orlik and Veldkamp, 2014.)

Uncertainty Shocks   Uncertainty about skewness can cause uncertainty shocks. Uncertainty about the future state y_{t+1} may exhibit large and asymmetric fluctuations. The reason is that small changes in estimated skewness cause tail event probabilities to rise or fall by orders of magnitude. Figure II shows how a small change in the skewness parameter can boost the probability of the left-tail event by more than 50%. This is a powerful force because just a few data points can easily shift a skewness estimate like this. Skewness estimates are easily revised because higher moments like skewness are difficult to estimate. Difficult-to-estimate moments are a headache for econometricians but are fertile ground for theorists looking for ways in which beliefs might fluctuate.

Reestimating skewness wags the tail of the distribution. Because tail events are far from the mean and uncertainty depends on the squared distance from the mean, changes in tail probabilities have an outsized effect on uncertainty.

Orlik and Veldkamp (2014) show this idea using real-time GDP growth and estimating parameter uncertainty using Markov Chain Monte Carlo methods. Estimates reveal that revisions in parameter estimates, especially those that affect tail risk, explain most uncertainty variability. Moreover, uncertainty shocks are countercyclical.

Negative Skewness and Downward Bias   Parameter uncertainty and skewness also create bias in small samples. This is a Jensen inequality effect from a concave change of measure. Appendix A.4 shows how a negatively skewed distribution can be created from a concave function of a normal distribution. See Orlik and Veldkamp (2014) for a proof of estimation bias.

2.5.4 Nonparametric Estimation of a Distribution

Finally, consider a case where the functional form of the probability density is unknown. Agents in the model use an i.i.d. data sample $\mathcal{I}_t = \{\theta_r | r \leq t\}$ to construct a frequentist (not Bayesian) estimate $\hat{f}_t$ of the true density f. A drawback of this non-Bayesian approach is that agents who use this procedure ignore the uncertainty about their estimated distribution. The advantage of this procedure is that it is easy to compute.

A simple approach is to use a normal kernel density estimator:

$$\hat{f}_t(\theta) = \frac{1}{tZ_t} \sum_{s=0}^{t-1} \phi\left(\frac{\theta - \theta_{t-s}}{Z_t}\right). \tag{2.76}$$

Here $\phi(\cdot)$ is the standard normal density function, and Z_t is the bandwidth parameter. The Gaussian kernel is just one of many options. Greene (2003) provides a comprehensive list of other commonly used kernels.

As new data arrives, agents add the new observation to their data set $\mathcal{I}_t$ and update their estimates, generating a sequence of beliefs $\{\hat{f}_t\}$. Belief changes tend to be very persistent, even if the θ_t shocks that caused the beliefs to change are transitory. This persistence arises from the martingale property of beliefs: On average, expected future beliefs are the same as current beliefs. As a result, any changes in beliefs induced by new information are approximately permanent. This persistence feature is common to any problem with learning about a fixed parameter. The nonparametric approach made a complicated model computationally feasible. Kozlowski, Veldkamp, and Venkateswaran (2020) use this mechanism to generate belief scarring that explains the persistent effects of the Great Recession.

2.6 Beyond Rational Expectations: Machine Learning

Recent breakthroughs in machine learning are algorithms that are not fed any information about the problem's structure. They learn from observations of outcomes without building an underlying model to rationalize those outcomes. Machine learning creates models that are predictive and may optimize predictions, but they do not incorporate an understanding of others' optimizing behavior. The details of machine learning algorithms are beyond the scope of this book. Economic models are caricatures of reality. In this case, we caricature complex algorithms with simple ones that capture the spirit of modern machine learning.

To show the connection between the rational methods that most of the book focuses on and a machine-learning approach, we discuss this topic in three steps. First, we describe a canonical cobweb model and its rational expectations outcome as a point of departure for the following discussion. Then for the next two steps, we consider two models with nonrational expectations.[6] In one, the mapping from fundamentals to prices is the correct functional form. However, agents must estimate the parameters of this relationship. They forecast optimally, given their information sets. In the second model, agents do not know the model structure or parameters. They learn about equilibrium prices only from observing past prices. In section 9.9, we revisit these ideas in the context of asset pricing models and discuss how the theory of internal rationality has been fruitful in explaining several asset pricing puzzles.

The Cobweb Model   As a guiding model for the discussion, we consider the cobweb supply and demand model in Muth (1961). Demand D_t depends negatively on the market price

$$D_t = d_0 - d_1 p_t + v_{1t}, \qquad (2.77)$$

where d_0, d_1 are parameters and v_{1t} is a demand shock. There is a time lag in production so that supply Y_t depends positively on the expected market price and an exogenous shock θ_{t-1}. Let $\mathbb{E}[p_t | \mathcal{I}_{t-1}]$ be the expectation of p_t conditional on the information set $\mathcal{I}_{t-1} = \{p_r, \theta_r | r < t - 1\}$, which includes the history of observations up to time $t - 1$. Then, supply is given by

$$Y_t = y_0 + y_1 \mathbb{E}[p_t | \mathcal{I}_{t-1}] + y_2 \theta_{t-1} + v_{2t}, \qquad (2.78)$$

where y_0, y_1, y_2 are parameters and v_{2t} is a supply shock. The expected market price can be interpreted as the average expectation across a continuum of firms. Demand v_{1t} and supply v_{2t} shocks are white noise. Imposing market

---

6. See Evans and Honkapohja (2001) for a comprehensive treatment of this literature.

clearing $Y_t = D_t$ yields

$$p_t = \frac{d_0 - y_0}{d_1} - \frac{y_1}{d_1}\mathbb{E}[p_t|\mathcal{I}_{t-1}] - \frac{y_2}{d_1}\theta_{t-1} + \frac{v_{1t} - v_{2t}}{d_1}. \qquad (2.79)$$

Letting $\bar{p} \equiv \frac{d_0 - y_0}{d_1}$, $\alpha \equiv -\frac{y_1}{d_1}$, $\kappa \equiv -\frac{y_2}{d_1}$ and $\eta_t \equiv \frac{v_{1t} - v_{2t}}{d_1} \sim \mathcal{N}(0, \sigma_\eta^2)$, yields a simple expression for how price p_t depends on expected price, a known state θ_{t-1} and an innovation η_t:

$$p_t = \bar{p} + \alpha\mathbb{E}[p_t|\mathcal{I}_{t-1}] + \kappa\theta_{t-1} + \eta_t. \qquad (2.80)$$

Many economic models can be framed as (2.80). The aggregate supply model in Lucas (1973) is one example.

What Does Rational Expectations Mean? Rational expectations impose the consistency condition that each agent's choice is the best response to the choices of others.[7] This approach assumes that agents understand the structure of the model and, in particular, the mapping from fundamentals θ_{t-1} to equilibrium prices p_t, which in the case of the cobweb model in (2.80) implies knowing that the mapping is linear and knowing the parameter values $(\bar{p}, \alpha, \kappa, \sigma_\eta^2)$. We start by solving the rational expectations model and then contrast it to cases where agents do not know and must use data to estimate the probabilities of outcomes.

First, we consider full-information rational expectations, where the state θ is known in real-time. Section 2.5 included models where a parameter governing the θ_t process is unknown and must be estimated. This is also considered rational expectations because, while the state process is unknown, the mapping from the state to the equilibrium outcome p_t is known.

The Full-Information Rational Expectations Solution Under full-information rational expectations, the expectation $\mathbb{E}[p_t|\mathcal{I}_{t-1}]$ is computed, given knowledge of the true model and its parameters. To solve the cobweb model with full-information rational expectations, take the conditional expectation of both sides of (2.80), using $\mathbb{E}[\theta_{t-1}|\mathcal{I}_{t-1}] = \theta_{t-1}$ and $\mathbb{E}[\eta_t|\mathcal{I}_{t-1}] = 0$ yields

$$\mathbb{E}[p_t|\mathcal{I}_{t-1}] = (1 - \alpha)^{-1}\left(\bar{p} + \kappa\theta_{t-1}\right). \qquad (2.81)$$

Substituting (2.81) back into (2.80) delivers the unique full-information rational expectations equilibrium—a linear mapping between fundamentals and

---

7. See Guesnerie (2011) and Belda, Heineken, and Ifrim (2023) for a discussion of rational expectations as a Nash Equilibrium and not a dominant strategy in the case of heterogeneous beliefs.

prices with constant parameters:[8]

$$p_t = a + b\theta_{t-1} + \eta_t, \quad \text{with} \quad a \equiv \bar{p}/(1-\alpha) \text{ and } b \equiv \kappa/(1-\alpha).$$
(2.82)

2.6.1 Estimating Coefficients of Equilibrium Outcomes

Agents often use data to estimate equilibrium outcomes, like prices, returns, or payoffs. Models of agents who use data in this way are referred to as *adaptive learning* models. While agents are still rational in that they may maximize a standard utility function, this is not a rational expectations model because the mapping from the state to the equilibrium outcomes is unknown.

Suppose that agents know that prices follow the linear process in (2.82) but do not know the value of the coefficients a and b. Agents form a price forecast p_t^e, given their estimates $(\hat{a}_{t-1}, \hat{b}_{t-1})$:

$$p_t^e = \hat{a}_{t-1} + \hat{b}_{t-1}\theta_{t-1}.$$
(2.83)

Agents use an OLS regression of past observations of prices $\{p_r\}_{r=0}^{t-1}$ on the state $\{\theta_r\}_{r=0}^{t-1}$ and an intercept to estimate $(\hat{a}_{t-1}, \hat{b}_{t-1})$. These parameters are updated every period with the arrival of new information. Let $x_r = [1 \; \theta_r]'$, then the OLS estimates are:

$$\begin{pmatrix} \hat{a}_{t-1} \\ \hat{b}_{t-1} \end{pmatrix} = \left(\sum_{r=1}^{t-1} x_{r-1} x_{r-1}' \right)^{-1} \left(\sum_{r=1}^{t-1} x_{r-1} p_r \right).$$
(2.84)

Substituting (2.83) into (2.80) yields the realized price:

$$p_t = \bar{p} + \alpha[\hat{a}_{t-1} + \hat{b}_{t-1}\theta_{t-1}] + \kappa\theta_{t-1} + \eta_t$$
$$= [\bar{p} + \alpha\hat{a}_{t-1}] + [\alpha\hat{b}_{t-1} + \kappa]\theta_{t-1} + \eta_t.$$
(2.85)

Equations (2.84) and (2.85) constitute the adaptive learning solution.

2.6.2 When Is Least Squares Learning Rational and Optimal?

Least squares learning is rationalized when it corresponds to the rational expectations price $\mathbb{E}[p_t|\mathcal{I}_{t-1}]$. For p_t^e to be equal to $\mathbb{E}[p_t|\mathcal{I}_{t-1}]$, the coefficients multiplying 1 and θ_{t-1} in (2.83) and (2.85) must match: $\hat{a}_{t-1} = \bar{p} + \alpha\hat{a}_{t-1}$ and $\hat{b}_{t-1} = \alpha\hat{b}_{t-1} + \kappa$. This implies $\hat{a}_{t-1} = \frac{\bar{p}}{1-\alpha}$ and $\hat{b}_{t-1} = \frac{\kappa}{1-\alpha}$.

8. Evans and Honkapohja (2001) argue that rational expectations is an equilibrium concept. The process followed by prices in (2.82) depends on the agent's forecasting rule, which is conditional on the choice of others. The consistency can be seen by substituting the expectations implied by (2.82) into (2.80), which yields again (2.82).

These are the rational expectations coefficients. For $\alpha < 1$, the adaptive learning scheme converges to the rational expectations equilibria.

To show convergence, reformulate the problem recursively, as in Marcet and Sargent (1989). Let $\phi_t = [\hat{a}_{t-1} \quad \hat{b}_{t-1}]'$ be the vector of coefficients and $x_t = [1 \quad \theta_t]'$. Then the least squares formula is:

$$\phi_t = \phi_{t-1} + t^{-1}R_t^{-1}x_{t-1}(p_t - \phi_{t-1}'x_{t-1}) \tag{2.86}$$

$$R_t = R_{t-1} + t^{-1}(x_{t-1}x_{t-1}' - R_{t-1}) \tag{2.87}$$

with the adequate initial conditions ϕ_0 and R_0. Since $p_t^e = \phi_{t-1}'x_{t-1}$ by definition, the term $(p_t - \phi_{t-1}'x_{t-1})$ in the first equation must be the forecast error. Evans and Honkapohja (1996) show convergence to rational expectations when $\alpha < 1$. Evans et al. (2013) characterize convergence with parameter uncertainty. Intuitively, least squares learning converges to rational expectations when agents stop learning (in the limit, $\lim_{t\to\infty} t^{-1} = 0$, so ϕ_t and R_t become a constant) and the process about which they are learning does not explode (which happens if $\alpha < 1$).

Some applications of adaptive learning include Bullard and Mitra (2002) in a New Keynesian setting and Eusepi and Preston (2011) and Mitra, Evans, and Honkapohja (2013, 2019) in a real business cycle setting.

Microfounding Least-Squares Learning   Adam and Marcet (2011) and Adam, Marcet, and Nicolini (2016) develop a decision-theoretic framework in which agents learn about market behavior, providing a microfoundation for models of adaptive learning. Agents are "internally rational": they maximize discounted expected utility under uncertainty given dynamically consistent subjective beliefs about the future. Still, agents may not be "externally rational" as they may not know or are unable to deduce the true equilibrium stochastic process for payoff-relevant variables beyond their control (for example, prices). If agents do not know the equilibrium mapping from fundamentals to prices, as in (2.80), then agents have *imperfect market knowledge*.

2.6.3 Machine Learning: Model-Free Estimates of Equilibrium Outcomes

In economics, machine learning has been called "adaptive expectations." Adaptive expectations refer to any mechanical rule for directly extrapolating equilibrium outcomes from past observed data (Nerlove, 1958). Although adaptive learning and adaptive expectations share the adjective "adaptive," they differ greatly. Agents with adaptive expectations learn prices without any presumption that others behave optimally.

Suppose agents form a price forecast p_t^e,

$$p_t^e = p_{t-1}^e + \lambda(p_{t-1} - p_{t-1}^e) = \lambda \sum_{i=0}^{\infty}(1-\lambda)^i p_{t-1-i}, \qquad (2.88)$$

for any constant $\lambda > 0$. This is similar to Bayesian learning, which weighs new information $(p_{t-1} - p_{t-1}^e)$ according to the relative precision of that new information, which in this case is time-varying. However, the weight λ on new information is constant in adaptive expectations. For this reason, it is also known as *constant gain learning*.

Substituting in the price p_{t-1} from (2.80), shows that price expectations p_t^e follow an AR(1) process:

$$p_t^e = (1 - \lambda(1-\alpha))p_{t-1}^e + \lambda\bar{p} + \lambda\kappa\theta_{t-2} + \lambda\eta_{t-1}. \qquad (2.89)$$

This process is stationary for $|(1 - \lambda(1-\alpha))| < 1$.

The second equality in (2.88) shows that adaptive expectations consist of a distributed lag with exponentially declining weights. Substituting the distributed lag into the equilibrium price formula (2.80) yields a stochastic process for the realized price under machine learning:

$$p_t = \bar{p} + \alpha\lambda \sum_{i=0}^{\infty}(1-\lambda)^i p_{t-1-i} + \kappa\theta_{t-1} + \eta_t. \qquad (2.90)$$

The expectations implied by (2.90), when substituted into the equilibrium price (2.80), yields $p_t = (1+\alpha)\bar{p} + \alpha^2\lambda \sum_{i=0}^{\infty}(1-\lambda)^i p_{t-1-i} + \kappa(1+\alpha)\theta_{t-1} + \eta_t$. This law of motion for the price is inconsistent with the perceived law of motion agents use to forecast the price. This is because the machine learning algorithm ignores the equilibrium structure of the model.

2.7 Prediction versus Matching

In this book, we primarily consider data used for prediction. However, a popular alternative approach models data as something that enables more or better (more directed) matches to form. Data allows customers to access products that were otherwise unknown to them. Data can bring products to the customer's attention, workers to a firm, or assets to an investor and change the decision-maker's choice set.

These two ways of approaching data have many similarities. Predictive information also improves matching. The more a customer knows about all the shirts that are out there, the more likely a customer is going to get the one that is the best match for them. Data as information and data as an ability to access something both increase revenue. They should both boost market power for a firm.

The key difference is that noisy signals also resolve risk. One thing we rarely see in matching settings is that matching changes uncertainty. Unmatched entities do not face uncertainty; they simply behave as though the unmatched counterpart does not exist. Matched entities are assumed to know all relevant information about each other. This makes matching like the extremes of learning; matching is all information or nothing. The all-or-nothing approach of matching simplifies many models. However, ignoring risk often misses important insights or effects. Risk matters. It creates an inefficient wedge in every transaction that hurts both parties. There is no upside to risk. It is a downside for the customer, having to bear it, and it is a downside for the firm that gets less revenue from it.

Finance gives us some insight into how much risk matters. Of the 10% expected returns on firms, about 3% is the risk-less return, and 7% is the risk premium that is compensation for risk. This suggests that risk matters more than twice as much as a riskless return for firm values. Corporate finance teaches us that when firms face uncertainty, they scale back real investment projects. When considering data choices and data valuations, risk is also a key consideration. For financial data, 80% of the value of financial data comes from uncertainty reductions (Farboodi et al., 2022b). Much of the value of data is derived from its ability to resolve uncertainty.

The book will use the tools of matching from time to time. In sections 4.2.1 and 5.5, we consider how predictive data interacts with matching in a labor market setting. In section 7.9, we use matching to describe customer acquisition and customer capital. Finally, in section 8.4, we explore the idea of data platforms as matching technologies for firms and their customers. While we acknowledge the importance of matching in the data economy, matching tools are also well-understood. Most of this book will focus on a new set of models that incorporate the way in which predictive data resolves uncertainty and risk.

Key Ideas

- Bayes' Law is a tool to incorporate data in predictions. For normal variables, Bayesian forecasts average the prior belief and the unbiased signals derived from data, each weighted by their relative precision.
- In dynamic models, the Kalman Filter is an application of Bayes' Law that shows how to update beliefs about a changing state.
- Tools from adaptive expectations can capture the spirit of economic uses of machine learning in practice.

Practice Questions

In questions 2.1 to 2.4, assume that all signals and prior beliefs are conditionally independent.

2.1. Suppose the prior belief is that $\theta \sim \mathcal{N}(\mu_\theta, \tau_\theta^{-1})$ and the signal is $s|\theta \sim \mathcal{N}(\theta, \tau_s^{-1})$. Prove carefully that the posterior density is also normal, that is, that the mean $\mathbb{E}[\theta|s]$ and variance $\mathbb{V}ar[\theta|s]$ are, in fact, the mean and variance of a normal distribution.

2.2. Suppose the prior belief is that $\theta \sim \mathcal{N}(\mu_\theta, \tau_\theta^{-1})$ and the signal is $s|\theta \sim \mathcal{N}(\theta, \tau_s^{-1})$. If instead the prior was $\theta \sim \mathcal{N}(s, \tau_s^{-1})$, and the signal was $s|\theta \sim \mathcal{N}(\theta, \tau_\theta^{-1})$, would the posterior be the same or different?

2.3. Suppose that the prior is diffuse, meaning that $\theta \sim \mathcal{N}(\mu_\theta, \zeta^{-1})$, and take the limit as $\zeta \to 0$, but the agent then observes two signals, $s_1|\theta \sim \mathcal{N}(\theta, \tau_1^{-1})$ and $s_2|\theta \sim \mathcal{N}(\theta, \tau_2^{-1})$. What is the posterior in this case? Are posterior beliefs fundamentally different from signals?

2.4. Suppose the prior belief is that $\theta \sim \mathcal{N}(\mu_\theta, \tau_\theta^{-1})$, and two signals are observed: $s_1|\theta \sim \mathcal{N}(\theta, \tau_1^{-1})$ and $s_2|\theta \sim \mathcal{N}(\theta, \tau_2^{-1})$. What is the posterior belief?

2.5. Derive the posterior variance when the prior has a Beta distribution $Beta(a_0, b_0)$ and the signals are binomial (Bernoulli). Show that, in contrast with Bayesian updating of normal variables, more data may reduce precision when updating Bernoulli variables.

2.6. Suppose there is a $N \times 1$ random variable $\theta \sim \mathcal{N}(\mu, \Sigma)$, where $\Sigma = \Gamma \Lambda \Gamma'$. Agents receive signals $s = \Gamma'\theta + \epsilon$, where $\epsilon \sim \mathcal{N}(0, \Lambda_s)$ and Λ_s is a diagonal matrix. Prove that the variance of the posterior beliefs has the same eigenvectors as prior beliefs.

2.7. Let θ follow a random walk with unknown drift $\theta_t = \mu_\theta + \theta_{t-1} + u_t$, with $u_t \sim (0, \sigma_u^2)$. Estimate the drift μ_θ using the Kalman Filter.

2.8. Let a sequence of signals $s_i \sim_{iid} \mathcal{N}(\theta, \tau_s^{-1})$ have an unknown mean θ and a known precision τ_s. Under the prior that $\theta \sim \mathcal{N}(\mu_\theta, \tau_\theta^{-1})$, show the posterior $\theta|s_1 \cdots s_n$ is also normal, and compute its mean and variance.

2.9. Let a sequence of signals $s_i \sim_{iid} \mathcal{N}(\theta, \tau_s^{-1})$ have an unknown mean θ and an unknown precision τ_s. Consider the normal-gamma prior $\theta \mid \tau_s \sim \mathcal{N}\left(\mu_\theta, (\kappa\tau_s)^{-1}\right)$, $\tau_s \sim \Gamma(\alpha, \beta)$. Show the posterior $(\theta, \tau_s) \mid s_1 \cdots s_n$ is also normal-gamma, and derive its distributional parameters.

3

Data Sources

Collecting and processing data is an integral part of the data economy, but where do firms source their data from? Generally, we can distinguish between first-party data, which is collected directly from a firm's users, customers, and employees; second-party data, which is shared by or bought from other firms; and third-party data, which is data aggregated by the market or collected and traded by intermediaries, such as data platforms.

This chapter begins by defining data stocks and data flows and establishing a connection between these two concepts through the data law of motion. Then, we formally define knowledge as the posterior precision of beliefs. While most of the book (and the majority of the literature) treats data and knowledge as equivalent, in certain situations, it is important to draw a distinction between them.

With these definitions at hand, we discuss different ways researchers have modeled data collection and processing. We distinguish between passive data acquisition and active data acquisition. In section 3.2, we review passive data models, where firms are endowed with data or learn as an unintended consequence. Firms could learn unintentionally by observing data from other firms, market prices, or quantities bought or sold. Passive learning is usually tractable, as one's data is independent of one's choices. While passive learning is a tool to answer some questions, the data feedback loop at the core of the data economy requires that firms engage in active learning.

Active learning means that agents make choices, taking into account the effect of those choices on their future information sets. Data depends on one's own choices. Choices involve purchasing data, choosing when to update one's data set, or producing a good and observing the amount sold. Alternatively, in the case of social learning, agents may actively choose the network of people from whom they learn (Herskovic and Ramos, 2020). Active data collection can be costly. The cost varies with the data type, the frequency with which it is gathered, the recording technology, and the processing capacity. Firms balance the cost of data collection with the benefits of better prediction. For example, a firm that runs a customer survey may pay the cost of adding more questions or increasing the sample size to improve its data quality. Even a firm that observes its own sales or prices may need to hire workers to analyze their data. Section 3.3 discusses active learning models that differ in the cost structure of collecting and processing data.

One reason to work with a more complicated active learning model is that active learning models can be more quantifiable and testable. In a passive learning model, the nature of an agent's data is assumed. Results typically depend on this assumption. Since data is rarely observed by an economist, measuring and testing such models can be a challenge. An active learning model predicts what data will result from the agent's choices. These data-relevant choices often depend on features of the model that an economist can measure. Thus, active learning models begin and end with variables that an economist can measure. By using observable outcomes to predict information, which, in turn, predicts observable actions, active learning models generate testable hypotheses and lend themselves to estimation and calibration. Thus, active learning models may be quantifiable and empirically testable in ways that their passive learning counterparts are not.

3.1   Data and Knowledge Accumulation

We begin by setting up language to distinguish between information sets, data stocks and flows, and knowledge.

Information Set   We use the term information set, denoted by $\mathcal{I}_{i,t}$, for the collection of data signals received by agent i between dates 0 and t:

$$\mathcal{I}_{i,t} \equiv \{s_t, s_{t-1}, \ldots, s_0\}. \tag{3.1}$$

This is the information available to an agent when making their decision. The signals may be informative or not and may come from exogenous or endogenous sources.

Data Stock   Agent i's stock of data is the history of all digitized signals i has observed. In some of the models we explore, there is a sufficient statistic that summarizes what we need to know about this history to solve the model. That sufficient statistic is the time-t conditional precision (the inverse of the conditional variance) of the forecast of a random state θ_t:

$$\Omega_{i,t} \equiv \mathbb{V}ar[\theta_t|\mathcal{I}_{i,t}]^{-1}. \tag{3.2}$$

This precision represents the accuracy of beliefs about the state at time t. A lower conditional variance or more accurate estimate means we know more about the state θ_t and make smaller expected forecast errors. We use the conditional precision of the posterior beliefs $\Omega_{i,t}$ to keep track of the amount of data a firm has and refer to the precision $\Omega_{i,t}$ as a measure of the stock of data.

Data Flow   In a standard production economy, economists distinguish between the stock of capital in an economy or owned by a firm and the flow of new capital, typically referred to as investment. Data economics does not have a separate term for the stock and flow of data. We will use the term data stock $\Omega_{i,t}$ to refer to the total amount of data in a firm or economy. We will use the term data flow $\delta_{i,t}$ to refer to new data being added to the data stock.

In a static model or one where data depreciates fully each period, the stock and flow of data are identical: $\Omega_{i,t} = \delta_{i,t}$. If data does not depreciate fully, it should be cumulated and depreciated. The data law of motion is given by:

$$\Omega_{i,t+1} = \underbrace{(1-\zeta)\Omega_{i,t}}_{\text{undepreciated data stock}} + \underbrace{\delta_{i,t}.}_{\text{new data}} \tag{3.3}$$

This is like a capital accumulation equation in a standard business cycle model, where capital depreciates, and new investment flows in. For most of the book, we treat the depreciation rate ζ as a parameter between 0 and 1. In section 10.1, we will develop a method to determine the speed of data depreciation ζ that depends on how fast the relevant state changes.

The inflows of new data are the data investment. The data flow $\delta_{i,t}$ consists of the effective number of signals, that is, scaled by their precision. If we normalize the precision of each signal to one $(\tau_s = 1)$, then $\delta_{i,t}$ is just the number of signals or data points received. If we do not normalize precision, the data flow is $\tau_s \delta_{i,t}$.

Knowledge   We interpret knowledge as actionable information. More knowledge is a more accurate action recommendation, with a smaller expected distance to the optimal action. Thus, throughout most of the book, we equate data and knowledge. However, in sections 10.8 and 11.5, we distinguish between raw data, structured data, and knowledge. We dig deeper into the process of knowledge creation. We discuss how raw data and structured data are paired with different types of labor and information-technology capital to generate knowledge.

3.2   Exogenous Data Sources and Passive Learning

Consider a firm that wants to collect data to learn about a random state θ. For example, θ could be the firm's long-run profitability. The simplest way to model data collection about θ is to assume it is completely exogenous. That is, the content and the arrival speed of information are not under a firm's control.

Information may be an endowment at a fixed date, or it may arrive stochastically. Endogenous information can also be learned passively. For example, the behavior of others or market prices could convey information. This is still passive learning because agents are not exercising any control over the information they observe.

3.2.1 Data Endowments: Every Period or Infrequent

In some settings, a firm receives data, every period, in the form of a noisy signal about an unobserved state θ, with exogenous signal noise:

$$s_t = \theta + \epsilon_t, \qquad \epsilon_t \sim \mathcal{N}(0, \sigma_\epsilon^2). \tag{3.4}$$

The information set $\mathcal{I}_t$ grows as data points accumulate over time:

$$\mathcal{I}_t = \mathcal{I}_{t-1} \cup \{s_t\} = \{s_t, s_{t-1}, \ldots, s_0\}. \tag{3.5}$$

Due to the tractability of data endowments, a large literature reviewed in Chapter 4 studies signal extraction problems with data endowed every period.

In other settings, firms get an intermittent information flow. Data collection may happen at fixed time intervals of T periods. Information sets remain unchanged between those fixed intervals. We can represent this as

$$\mathcal{I}_t = \begin{cases} \mathcal{I}_{(k-1)T} & \text{if } (k-1)T < t < kT \\ \mathcal{I}_{(k-1)T} \cup \{s_{kT}\} & \text{if } t = kT, \end{cases} \tag{3.6}$$

where $k \in \mathbb{N}^+$ is a counter. For example, if investors observe public firms' annual balance sheet data and the unit of time is a month, then $T = 12$ and k counts the number of years observed.

Data collection may also happen on random dates. Mankiw and Reis (2002) model "sticky information" that arrives at an exogenous constant rate $\lambda > 0$. Observing this data perfectly reveals the state.[1] On dates when information does not arrive, information sets stay the same:

$$\mathcal{I}_t = \begin{cases} \mathcal{I}_{t-1} & \text{with prob. } 1-\lambda \\ \mathcal{I}_{t-1} \cup \{\theta_t\} & \text{with prob. } \lambda \end{cases} \quad \text{with} \quad \lambda \in (0, 1]. \tag{3.7}$$

Random data collection dates resemble the Calvo (1983) "fairy" assumption, in which firms may update their price with a constant probability and keep it constant otherwise. It is used in New Keynesian frameworks to describe nominal price-setting frictions (see section 5.4.1).

---

1. The assumption of perfectly revealing data can be relaxed and observe a noisy data point s_t instead of the truth at the observation dates.

3.2.2   Social Learning and Networks

Firms, consumers, and other economic agents may observe the behavior of others. Agents with data may reveal that data to others through their actions. This is social learning. Social learning may generate rational herds, bubbles, booms, and crashes. For a comprehensive discussion of social learning and its consequences, see Chamley (2004) and Goyal (2011).

A Model of Local Learning   In certain settings, it is natural to observe the behavior of other agents who are geographically, culturally, socially, or economically "close." The local learning that emerges generates similar beliefs and actions for members of the same group but heterogeneous beliefs and actions across different groups.

Consider an economy with many firms, partitioned into J locations or traits, indexed by j. For instance, j may represent an industry, a region, or a social group. From here on, we will refer to j as a location, keeping in mind that this might not be a geographic location but rather a location in some characteristic space.

Firms want to learn about a parameter θ. For example, θ could be the investment return in novel technology. Their prior beliefs are $\theta \sim \mathcal{N}(\mu_\theta, \tau_\theta^{-1})$. Firms in each location j observe second-party data on the profits of other firms that have invested in this technology and are colocated in j. Profits $s_{i,j}$ from an investing firm i in location j are a noisy signal about the return to investment θ:

$$s_{i,j} = \theta + \epsilon_{i,j}, \qquad \epsilon_{i,j} \sim \mathcal{N}(0, M_j \tau_\epsilon^{-1}), \qquad (3.8)$$

where profit shocks $\epsilon_{i,j}$ are i.i.d. across firms and locations, and $M_j \geq 0$ governs the noisiness of the data originating in location j. Locational differences in information quality could capture size effects from larger average investments, the heterogeneity of the population, or the population of that location, among other features. However, what is common to all locations is that only firms that invest generate data. Data is a by-product of investment. Let α_j be the fraction of investing firms in location j.

In Fajgelbaum, Schaal, and Taschereau-Dumouchel (2017), larger locations have more firms, with more noise. In this case, M_j represents the number of firms in location j. This assumption causes firms in large and small locations to learn at a rate independent of market size. The learning rate depends on the fraction of firms that invest. Size invariance may be a desirable feature, depending on the application.

Because data noise and priors are normally distributed, the average profit of investing firms in location j is a sufficient statistic for the information gathered by all firms in location j. This signal is public for all firms in j. Since α_j is the fraction of investing firms in location j, then $\alpha_j M_j$ is the number of observations gathered by firms in that location. This public signal s_j equals

$$s_j = \frac{1}{\alpha_j M_j} \sum_{i=1}^{\alpha_j M_j} s_{i,j} = \theta + \epsilon_j, \quad \text{with} \quad \epsilon_j \sim \mathcal{N}\left(0, (\alpha_j \tau_\epsilon)^{-1}\right). \tag{3.9}$$

Public signal noise in location j is given by $\epsilon_j \equiv \frac{1}{\alpha_j M_j} \sum_{i=1}^{\alpha_j M_j} \epsilon_{i,j}$. The variance of this noise is

$$\mathbb{V}ar[\epsilon_j] = \frac{1}{(\alpha_j M_j)^2} \alpha_j M_j \mathbb{V}ar[\epsilon_{i,j}] = \frac{1}{(\alpha_j M_j)^2} \alpha_j M_j M_j \tau_\epsilon^{-1} = (\alpha_j \tau_\epsilon)^{-1}.$$

This setting delivers location-specific public signals, with signal precision that increases with the share of investing firms α_j in the location. Thus, the partition and the spatial allocation of investing firms determine the data precision.

Finally, consider how firms use average profit data to form their beliefs. By Bayes' Law, the posterior mean $\hat{\theta}_j \equiv \mathbb{E}[\theta|s_j]$ and the posterior variance $\hat{\Sigma}_j \equiv \mathbb{V}ar[\theta|s_j]$ in location j are:

$$\hat{\theta}_j = \pi_j \mu_\theta + (1 - \pi_j) s_j, \quad \text{with} \quad \pi_j = \frac{\tau_\theta}{\tau_\theta + \alpha_j \tau_\epsilon}, \tag{3.10}$$

$$\hat{\Sigma}_j = (\tau_\theta + \alpha_j \tau_\epsilon)^{-1}. \tag{3.11}$$

The crucial result is that the higher the proportion of investing firms α_j, the larger the data precision. In turn, larger precision leads to stronger belief updating after observing data. While our simple example considers the proportion α_j to be exogenous, it is an endogenous outcome in many setups. In that case, a feedback loop arises between data and choices.

Applications of Local Learning   The following papers examine local learning mechanisms as the one just described. In Conley and Udry (2010), farmers learn a new agricultural technology from nearby farmers; in Fogli and Veldkamp (2011), women learn the effects of maternal employment on children by observing nearby employed women; in Buera, Monge-Naranjo, and Primiceri (2011), countries learn the impact of market-oriented policies from the experience of similar countries; in Galenianos (2013), firms learn an applicant's suitability for a job or match quality when the applicant is referred to the firm; in Fernandes and Tang (2014), exporters learn the returns to export in foreign markets from neighboring firms' export performance; in Figueiredo (2020), high-school students learn the college premium from the wages of

college-educated workers in their neighborhood; in Boerma and Karabarbounis (2021), households learn the returns to entrepreneurship from their
family's entrepreneurial experience; in López-Moctezuma (2023) and López-
Moctezuma and Johnson (2023), committee members learn about optimal
policymaking from the choices of other members in the context of sequential
deliberation by central bankers and sequential voting by US Supreme Court
justices, respectively. The use of social networks for learning in the labor market is widespread and the subject of extensive literature; see, for instance, Topa
(2001, 2011). Section 9.8 discusses environments that use social learning to
generate economic fluctuations.

3.2.3   Data from Market Outcomes

Market prices are another exogenous source of data. In centralized markets, prices simultaneously aggregate information about market participants
and reveal information to participants. For example, Chapter 6 studies portfolio choice problems in centralized markets where market prices partially
reveal what others know. In decentralized markets, bilateral transactions produce data. Amador and Weill (2010) and Golosov, Lorenzoni, and Tsyvinski
(2014) study decentralized markets where information diffuses gradually as
counterparties meet and learn from each others' trades.

Quantities can also reveal information. In Chapter 8, a platform learns from
the orders of customers who buy or sell on that platform.

3.3   Active Experimentation

In this section and the next two sections we present the three common active
learning technologies: (i) experimentation, in which actions generate data,
(ii) sticky information, the infrequent acquisition of perfect information, and
(iii) rational inattention, the frequent acquisition of noisy information.

The first type of active learning is experimentation. Active experimentation
means that an agent chooses an action that may generate data. The value of the
data is explicitly incorporated into the agent's choice problem. Such problems
often produce feedback between economic activity and information. Agents
control the information flow (e.g., signal quality) through their actions. These
actions, in turn, depend on the information agents learn.

In a class of models called bandit problems, all actions generate equally precise signals, but the decision is whether to act or not. Bergemann and Valimaki
(2008) survey the use of bandit problems in economics. In another class of
models with experimentation, the signal precision depends on the agent's
action.

3.3.1 A Bandit Problem with N Projects

Consider a firm that chooses how many projects to implement N at two consecutive periods, t and $t+1$. The firm discounts the future at a rate $\beta < 1$. Output $y_{j,t}$ of project j at time t is

$$y_{j,t} = A - (a_t - a_{j,t}^*)^2. \tag{3.12}$$

Implementing a project delivers constant known output A, minus a penalty for not being close to an unobserved project-specific target $a_{j,t}^*$. Each project target is the sum of two elements

$$a_{j,t}^* = a^* + \epsilon_{j,t}, \tag{3.13}$$

where $a^* \sim \mathcal{N}(\mu_a, \sigma_a^2)$ is a fixed common component across projects and $\epsilon_{j,t} \sim \mathcal{N}(0, \sigma_\epsilon^2)$ is an i.i.d. idiosyncratic component uncorrelated across projects and time. Once the number of projects is chosen, the agent chooses an action a_t to maximize output. The cost of implementing projects is increasing and convex in the number of projects. For example, consider a quadratic cost rN^2. Both a^* and $\epsilon_{j,t}$ are unobserved. However, each project's output provides a noisy signal about a^*:

$$s_{j,t} = a_t \pm \sqrt{A - y_{j,t}} = a^* \pm \epsilon_{j,t}. \tag{3.14}$$

Because noise is symmetric, the $\pm$ makes no difference when constructing the signal; thus, we focus on the positive root. The variance of each signal is σ_ϵ^2.

In problems where a quadratic loss generates information, the resulting signal is often not normal. In such a case, usually, the best tractable solution is to approximate the signal. One can approximate a nonnormal signal with a normal signal with the same mean and variance. The quality of the resulting approximate solution will depend on the importance of higher-order moments to the problem. We use the normal approximation here. Implementing N_t projects generates an aggregate unbiased signal s_t about a^*:

$$s_t = N_t^{-1} \sum_{j=1}^{N_t} s_{j,t} = a^* + N_t^{-1} \sum_{j=1}^{N_t} \epsilon_{j,t}.$$

The noise of this aggregate signal decreases with the number of projects N_t:

$$\sigma_s^2 = N_t^{-2} \sum_{j=1}^{N_t} \sigma_\epsilon^2 = N_t^{-1} \sigma_\epsilon^2. \tag{3.15}$$

Define the information set $\mathcal{I}_{t+1} \equiv \mathcal{I}_t \cup \{s_{j,t}\}_{j=1}^{N_t}$. The problem of the firm is to maximize expected total output minus total investment cost:

$$\max_{a_t, a_{t+1}, N_t, N_{t+1}} \mathbb{E}\left[\sum_{j=1}^{N_t} A - (a_t - a^* - \epsilon_{j,t})^2 \Big| \mathcal{I}_t \right] - rN_t^2 \qquad (3.16)$$

$$+ \beta\mathbb{E}\left[\sum_{j=1}^{N_{t+1}} A - (a_{t+1} - a^* - \epsilon_{j,t+1})^2 \Big| \mathcal{I}_{t+1} \right] - \beta rN_{t+1}^2.$$

Optimal Experimentation   To solve for optimal experimentation policies, we work backward. We start by characterizing the optimal choice of actions a_t, a_{t+1} given the number of projects N_t, N_{t+1}. The first-order condition implies that the action in each period equals the expected value of the target:

$$a_t = \mathbb{E}[a^*|\mathcal{I}_t], \qquad a_{t+1} = \mathbb{E}[a^*|\mathcal{I}_{t+1}]. \qquad (3.17)$$

Substituting the solution for a_t in the squared loss term $(a_t - a^* - \epsilon_{j,t})^2$ yields $(\mathbb{E}[a^*|\mathcal{I}_t] - a^* - \epsilon_{j,t})^2$. The expectation of the squared difference $(\mathbb{E}[a^*|\mathcal{I}_t] - a^*)^2$ is the definition of the conditional variance $\mathbb{V}ar[a^*|\mathcal{I}_t]$. The $\epsilon_{j,t}$ term is independent, with expected square σ_ϵ^2. Similarly, expectation of the squared loss term $(a_{t+1} - a^* - \epsilon_{j,t+1})^2$ can be written as the sum $\mathbb{V}ar[a^*|\mathcal{I}_{t+1}] + \sigma_\epsilon^2$. Thus, the firm's choice of the number of projects simplifies to:

$$\max_{N_t, N_{t+1}} N_t\left(A - \hat{\Sigma}_t - \sigma_\epsilon^2\right) - rN_t^2 + \beta N_{t+1}\left(A - \hat{\Sigma}_{t+1} - \sigma_\epsilon^2\right) - \beta rN_{t+1}^2.$$

$$(3.18)$$

We note that the posterior variance in period t equals the prior variance since there is no additional information: $\hat{\Sigma}_t = \sigma_a^2$. In contrast, due to experimentation, the posterior variance in period $t+1$ depends on the number of projects chosen in period t:

$$\hat{\Sigma}_{t+1} = \left(\frac{1}{\sigma_a^2} + \frac{1}{\sigma_s^2}\right)^{-1} = \left(\frac{1}{\sigma_a^2} + \frac{N_t}{\sigma_\epsilon^2}\right)^{-1}, \qquad (3.19)$$

where the variance of the aggregate signal σ_s^2 in (3.15) decreases with N_t. Let us compute its derivative with respect to N_t, which we will use below

$$\frac{\partial \hat{\Sigma}_{t+1}}{\partial N_t} = \frac{\partial \left(\frac{1}{\sigma_a^2} + \frac{N_t}{\sigma_\epsilon^2} \right)^{-1}}{\partial N_t} = -\left(\frac{\sigma_\epsilon^2 + N_t \sigma_a^2}{\sigma_\epsilon \sigma_a^2} \right)^{-2} = -\frac{\hat{\Sigma}_{t+1}^2}{\sigma_\epsilon^2}.$$

$$(3.20)$$

Choice of Number of Projects   In period $t+1$, the posterior variance $\hat{\Sigma}_{t+1}$ is given. Since there are no further periods, the problem is static. The first-order condition with respect to N_{t+1} in (3.18) is $\beta \left(A - \hat{\Sigma}_{t+1} - \sigma_\epsilon^2 \right) - 2\beta r N_{t+1} = 0$. Thus the optimal number of projects N_{t+1} is

$$N_{t+1}^* = \frac{A - \hat{\Sigma}_{t+1} - \sigma_\epsilon^2}{2r}, \qquad (3.21)$$

which is positive for A sufficiently large and decreasing in $\hat{\Sigma}_{t+1}$.

Next, we solve for period-1 choice of projects, considering the effect of N_t on $\hat{\Sigma}_{t+1}$ from experimentation in (3.19). The first-order condition for N_t is

$$N_t^* = \frac{1}{2r} \left[\left(A - \sigma_a^2 - \sigma_\epsilon^2 \right) - \beta N_{t+1} \frac{\partial \hat{\Sigma}_{t+1}}{\partial N_t} \right]. \qquad (3.22)$$

Substituting the derivative in (3.20) and tomorrow's optimal choice N_{t+1}^* in (3.21) yields

$$N_t^* = \underbrace{\frac{A - \sigma_a^2 - \sigma_\epsilon^2}{2r}}_{\text{static}} + \underbrace{\beta \left(\frac{A - \hat{\Sigma}_{t+1} - \sigma_\epsilon^2}{4r^2} \right) \frac{\hat{\Sigma}_{t+1}^2}{\sigma_\epsilon^2}}_{\text{dynamic}}. \qquad (3.23)$$

The previous expression implicitly determines the choice of N_t, as $\hat{\Sigma}_{t+1}$ is also a function of N_t. The first component resembles the static choice obtained for $t+1$ but uses the prior variance σ_a^2 instead of the posterior variance. The second component captures the dynamic aspect of the experimentation, which is the future reduction in uncertainty.

Optimal choices are obtained by solving a nonlinear system of three equations (3.19), (3.21) and (3.23) for three unknowns $\{N_t^*, N_{t+1}^*, \hat{\Sigma}_{t+1}^*\}$. Figure III illustrates how the current and future number of projects vary with uncertainty and how uncertainty varies with the current number of projects. It considers the following parameterization: $A = 1, r = 0.1, \beta = 0.9, \sigma_a^2 = 0.5$, and $\sigma_\epsilon^2 = 0.3$. The solution is given by the crossing of the solid line $N_t(\hat{\Sigma}_{t+1})$ and the dashed-dotted line $\hat{\Sigma}_{t+1}(N_t)$, which yields $N_t^* = 1.7$ and $\hat{\Sigma}_{t+1}^* = 0.13$. Then $N_{t+1}^* = 2.8$ is obtained by crossing the optimal level of uncertainty with the dashed line.

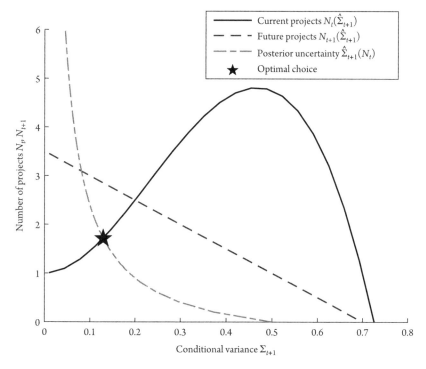

FIGURE III. Optimal Experimentation Policy in a Bandit Problem. *Notes*: This figure plots (i) the optimal choice of current projects N_t (solid black line); (ii) the future number of projects N_{t+1} (dashed dark gray line) as a function of posterior uncertainty $\hat{\Sigma}_{t+1}$; and (iii) the posterior variance $\hat{\Sigma}_{t+1}$ (dashed-dotted light gray line) as a function of the current number of projects N_t. The parameters used are $A = 1, r = 0.1, \beta = 0.9, \sigma_a^2 = 0.5$, and $\sigma_\epsilon^2 = 0.3$. The optimal choices (star) are: $N_t^* = 1.7, N_{t+1}^* = 2.8$ and $\hat{\Sigma}_{t+1}^* = 0.13$.

To understand how experimentation works, let us analyze how the number of current projects varies for exogenous changes in posterior uncertainty (conditional variance). For tiny levels of posterior uncertainty ($\hat{\Sigma}_{t+1} \approx 0$), which would happen if the signal is very precise, only one project is conducted because there are no additional learning gains. As uncertainty increases, more projects are added to reduce it. But this happens up to a point ($\hat{\Sigma}_{t+1} \approx 0.5$), after which the quadratic cost of adding another project rN^2 begins to dominate the benefits of uncertainty reduction, and the number of projects falls. Future projects decline linearly with uncertainty, while uncertainty falls convexly with current projects.

Discrete Number of Projects In this model, we assumed that the number of projects was continuous. But in reality, the number of projects is likely to be discrete. One way to deal with discreteness is as follows. Consider a continuous variable z such that zN is the number of projects, the output in each project is $(a_t - a^* - \epsilon_{j,t})^2/z$, and the precision in each project is $\tau = N_t \tau_\epsilon/z$. Then the problem is invariant to z: higher z gets more projects, but each is less precise. Taking $z \to \infty$ makes the problem quasi-continuous in the number of projects.

3.3.2   Applications of Experimentation

Active learning through experimentation in optimal control problems in macroeconomics arises in Prescott (1972). Since Rothschild (1974), experimentation has been widely applied to price-setting models in which a monopolist learns about uncertain demand. Firms use their prices to learn about demand's slope or intercept (Balvers and Cosimano, 1990; Mirman, Samuelson, and Urbano, 1993; Keller and Rady, 1999; Willems, 2017). In these models, firms are willing to produce output at negative revenue to obtain better information. Bachmann and Moscarini (2011) and Argente and Yeh (2022) build general equilibrium versions of this framework. Other applications of experimentation include investment and growth (Bertocchi and Spagat, 1998); optimal monetary policy (Wieland, 2000; Svensson and Williams, 2007); occupational choice (Antonovics and Golan, 2012); and wage and job mobility within firms (Pastorino, 2023).

3.4   Inattentiveness: Choosing When to See Data

Sticky information, also known as *inattentiveness*, is a learning technology in which agents usually get no information flow; occasionally, however, they observe the entire history of events. It is a lumpy informational flow, with periods of inaction and bursts of information processing. In settings where an agent has to exert some effort to observe information, but that information is relatively easy to process, this technology makes sense. Examples include checking one's bank balance, looking up a sports score, or checking the current temperature. Dynamic models with information choice are notoriously hard to solve. Inattentiveness simplifies these problems by rendering the history of learning choices irrelevant each time an agent decides to learn.

A binary information cost of acquiring data nests two specifications in the literature:

$$\kappa_t = \begin{cases} \bar{\kappa} & \text{with prob.} \quad 1-\lambda \\ 0 & \text{with prob.} \quad \lambda \end{cases} \quad \text{with} \quad \lambda \in [0,1]. \qquad (3.24)$$

Setting $\overline{\kappa} = \infty$ and $\lambda > 0$, this cost structure generates the (passive learning) sticky information model in Mankiw and Reis (2002), in which information arrives freely at an exogenous constant rate λ as in section 3.2.1. Setting $0 < \overline{\kappa} < \infty$ and $\lambda = 0$, this cost structure generates the costly information model in Reis (2006a,b), in which agents face a fixed and constant observation cost $\overline{\kappa}$. Section 5.4 explores the implications of inattentiveness in setups with strategic complementarities.

3.5   Rational Inattention as a Data-Processing Theory

The idea that economic agents have limited ability to process information or to pay attention is often referred to as *rational inattention*. Following Sims (2003), rational inattention has taken on a more specific meaning. Models that use rational inattention either bound the amount of information or charge agents a utility cost for information.

A large subset of the literature simplifies the problem by allowing agents to directly choose the precision with which they observe an exogenously specified set of normal signals. Normal signals are optimal with quadratic payoffs and normal priors (Sims, 2010). We lay out a quadratic-normal model to convey the main ideas from the rational inattention literature in section 4.5.

The standard measure of the quantity of information in information theory is *entropy* (Cover and Thomas, 1991). It is frequently used in econometrics and statistics and has been used in economics to model limited information processing by individuals and to measure model uncertainty (Radner and Van Zandt, 2001; Sims, 2003). Entropy measures the amount of uncertainty in a random variable. It is also used to measure the complexity of information transmitted. Following Sims (2003), in this section, we model the amount of information transmitted as the reduction in entropy achieved by conditioning on that additional information (mutual information).

3.5.1   Entropy

Entropy $H(\theta)$ measures the uncertainty of a random variable. It answers the question: How much information is required, on average, to describe θ with probability density function $p(\cdot)$?

$$H(\theta) \equiv -\mathbb{E}[\log(p(\theta))] = -\sum_{\theta}[p(\theta)\log(p(\theta))] \qquad \text{if } p \text{ discrete.}$$

$$(3.25)$$

For a multivariate continuous distribution f

$$H(\theta) \equiv - \int f(\theta_1, \ldots, \theta_n) \log(f(\theta_1, \ldots, \theta_n)) \, d\theta_1, \ldots, d\theta_n. \qquad (3.26)$$

Entropy is also referred to as a Shannon measure of information (Shannon, 1948). In econometrics, it is a log-likelihood ratio. In statistics, it is a difference between the prior and posterior distributions' Kullback-Leibler distance from the truth. In robust control, it is the distance between two models (Cagetti et al., 2002). It has been previously used in economics to model limited mental processing ability.

To make the idea of entropy more concrete, here are some examples.

Example: Constant If θ is a constant, then $p(\theta) = 1$ at θ. At θ, $p(\theta)$ $\log(p(\theta)) = 1 \cdot 0$, and $p(\theta) = 0$ everywhere else. Thus $H(\theta) = 0$. This is a zero entropy variable because if the variable is known to be a constant, no information needs to be transmitted to know the variable's value. We need a zero-length code to tell us that $2 = 2$.

Example: Binomial Two points each with equal probability.

$$H(\theta) = - \left[\frac{1}{2} \log \left(\frac{1}{2} \right) + \frac{1}{2} \log \left(\frac{1}{2} \right) \right] = - \log \left(\frac{1}{2} \right) = \log(2). \quad (3.27)$$

Suppose we had a code that said if zero is observed, the variable takes on its first value; if one is observed, it takes on its second value. Then, a zero or a one must be transmitted to reveal exactly the value of the variable. This is called one *bit* of information. Bits are information flows measured in base 2. Here, using the natural logarithm, we express information units in *nats*.

Example: Uniform If $\theta \sim \mathcal{U}[0, a]$,

$$H(\theta) = - \int_0^a 1/a \, \log(1/a) \, d\theta = - \log(1/a) = \log(a). \qquad (3.28)$$

Example: Normal If $\theta \sim \mathcal{N}(\mu, \sigma^2)$,

$$H(\theta) = \frac{1}{2} \log(2\pi e \sigma^2). \qquad (3.29)$$

If θ is an $n \times 1$ vector of normal variables, $\theta \sim \mathcal{N}(\mu, \Sigma)$, then it has entropy

$$H(\theta) = \frac{1}{2} \log \left((2\pi e)^n |\Sigma| \right) = \frac{n}{2} \left(1 + \log(2\pi) \right) + \frac{1}{2} \log(|\Sigma|), \quad (3.30)$$

where $|\Sigma|$ denotes the matrix determinant of Σ. A useful property of normal variables is that the normal distribution maximizes entropy over all distributions with a given variance.

3.5.2 Mutual Information

Mutual information is a measure that tells us how much two random variables reveal about each other. Formally, it tells us how much knowing one variable reduces the entropy of the other.

Consider an unknown state θ and a signal s. Conditional entropy tells us how much information is required to describe θ if s is already known:

$$H(\theta|s) = H(\theta, s) - H(s). \tag{3.31}$$

Mutual information $\mathcal{M}(\theta, s)$ is defined as the difference between the state's entropy and its conditional entropy given the signal:

$$\mathcal{M}(\theta, s) = H(\theta) - H(\theta|s). \tag{3.32}$$

A useful property of mutual information is that it is symmetric, that is, what θ tells you about s, s tells you about θ:

$$\mathcal{M}(\theta, s) = \mathcal{M}(s, \theta).$$

Here are two examples.

Example: Univariate Normals   With a normal state $\theta \sim \mathcal{N}(\mu_\theta, \tau_\theta^{-1})$ and a normal signal $s \sim \mathcal{N}(\theta, \tau_s^{-1})$, mutual information takes a simple form:

$$\mathcal{M}(\theta, s) = \frac{1}{2} \log\left(1 + \frac{\tau_s}{\tau_\theta}\right). \tag{3.33}$$

Mutual information increases with signal precision since precise signals reduce entropy by more.

Example: Multivariate Normals   Consider the mutual information between a multivariate normal state $\theta \sim \mathcal{N}(\mu, \Sigma)$ and a vector of signals $s = \theta + \epsilon$, where $\epsilon \sim N(0, \Sigma_s)$. Conditional on a set of normal signals s, the conditional entropy of θ is the same as in (3.30), replacing the higher variance Σ with the lower conditional variance $\hat{\Sigma}$. The mutual information of θ and s is

$$\mathcal{M}(\theta, s) = \frac{1}{2} \log\left(\frac{|\Sigma|}{|\hat{\Sigma}|}\right), \tag{3.34}$$

where $|\cdot|$ denotes the determinant. In the case of diagonal matrices, the determinant is simply the product of the diagonal entries. What determines mutual information is the ratio of the determinants of $\hat{\Sigma} = (\Sigma^{-1} + \Sigma_s^{-1})^{-1}$, the posterior variance-covariance matrix and Σ, the prior variance-covariance matrix. If no data is observed, then $\hat{\Sigma} = \Sigma$ and mutual information is zero. The more precise the data is, the lower the conditional variance $\hat{\Sigma}$ and the higher the mutual information.

Costly Mutual Information   If mutual information is costly, then the objective function should have a cost $\chi(\cdot)$ that is a function of mutual information $\mathcal{M}(\theta, s)$, and the precision of the signals Σ_s^{-1} should show up as choice variables. We will return to this type of problem in Chapter 6 when we consider data choice and investment choice.

3.5.3   Capacity Constraints

Many models that use rational inattention in economics allow an agent to choose a set of signals that can provide information about the true state, subject to a constraint on mutual information, as defined in (3.32):

$$\mathcal{M}(\theta, s) \leq \kappa. \tag{3.35}$$

Capacity κ measures the total available mutual information, often called information capacity. This problem is related (in a duality sense) to the costly mutual information problem posed above.

Example: Univariate Normals   With a normal state $\theta \sim \mathcal{N}(\mu_\theta, \tau_\theta^{-1})$ and a normal signal $s \sim \mathcal{N}(0, \tau_s^{-1})$, the capacity constraint on mutual information takes a simple form:

$$\frac{1}{2} \log\left(1 + \frac{\tau_s}{\tau_\theta}\right) \leq \kappa \quad \text{or} \quad \left(\frac{\tau_\theta + \tau_s}{\tau_\theta}\right) \leq e^{2\kappa}. \tag{3.36}$$

Example: Multivariate Normals   With multidimensional, normally distributed random variables, such a constraint takes the form

$$\frac{|\hat{\Sigma}|}{|\Sigma|} \leq e^{-2\kappa}, \tag{3.37}$$

where $\hat{\Sigma}$ is the posterior variance-covariance matrix and Σ is the prior variance-covariance matrix. The minus sign in the exponent appears here because we write the constraint in terms of variances and not precisions, as in (3.36).

3.5.4   Economic Interpretation of Rational Inattention

This technology represents learning as a process of more and more refined searching. A capacity κ is approximately the number of binary signals that partition states of the world.[2] A simple example is where a first signal tells the agent whether a random variable's realization is above or below the median outcome. The second signal tells the agent, conditional on being in the top

---

2. See Chapter 9.3 of Cover and Thomas (1991) for proof that the entropy of a random variable approximates the number of binary signals needed to convey the same information.

or bottom half, what quartile of the state-space the outcome is in. In conjunction with the first two signals, the third reveals what eighth of the sample space the outcome is in, and so forth. Notice that the interpretation of each signal depends on its predecessors. The second signal alone does not reveal the quartile an outcome is in. Since each signal refines the information conveyed by previous signals, this learning technology has the characteristics of a more and more directed or refined search for an answer. This technology does not imply that agents can dynamically reoptimize their learning choices based on signal realizations. Rather, imagine that in period 1, an agent tells the computer what information to download. In period 2, computer output written in binary code is read. When reading the binary code, the meaning of each 0 or 1 depends on the sequence of 0s and 1s that precede it.

3.6 Linear Cost of Precision

Another popular data cost is linear in signal precision. In the case of two states and two signals, this constraint takes the form

$$\hat{\Sigma}_1^{-1} + \hat{\Sigma}_2^{-1} \leq \kappa, \tag{3.38}$$

where $\hat{\Sigma}_i^{-1}$ is the posterior precision of signal i and κ is a constant. Comparing (3.38) with (3.37), we see that entropy constrains the product of precisions, whereas the linear constraint bounds the sum of precisions.

While the entropy technology represents a process of increasingly refined search, linear costs model search as a sequence of independent explorations. To see the relationship between this technology and entropy, consider a case where all the risks are independent and the signal about each risk has normally distributed errors that are uncorrelated with the other signals. In that case, the prior and posterior variances, Σ and $\hat{\Sigma}$, are diagonal matrices. Since the entropy of a normal variable depends on the determinant of its variance (equation 3.30) and the determinant of a diagonal matrix is the product of its diagonals, the entropy constraint takes the form

$$\prod_{i=1}^{N} \hat{\Sigma}_{ii}^{-1} \leq \tilde{\kappa}, \tag{3.39}$$

while the linear precision constraint would be

$$\sum_{i=1}^{N} \hat{\Sigma}_{ii}^{-1} \leq \tilde{\kappa}' \tag{3.40}$$

for some constants $\tilde{\kappa}$ and $\tilde{\kappa}'$.

With entropy, it is easier to add a fixed amount of signal precision when the agent already has more precise information. If $\hat{\Sigma}_{ii}^{-1}$ is small, then adding one unit of precision to get $\hat{\Sigma}_{ii}^{-1} + 1$ is a large proportional increase and thus requires a large increase in $\tilde{\kappa}$. But if $\hat{\Sigma}_{ii}^{-1}$ is already large, adding one unit of precision is a small proportional increase and requires only a small proportional increase in $\tilde{\kappa}$. In this sense, it is less costly to add precision to risks for which precision is already high. This lower cost represents a form of increasing returns to learning built into an entropy constraint. At the same time, one might argue that precision is not the right metric. Maybe we should be thinking about how difficult it is to reduce variance. As variance falls ($\hat{\Sigma}_{ii} \to 0$), further reducing variance by one unit results in larger and larger increases in precision and requires more and more capacity under either learning technology. Thus, with variance reduction, decreasing returns are built into both measures.

One of the drawbacks to using the additive precision measure of information is that it is not scale-neutral. For example, defining what constitutes one asset share will change the feasible set of signals. Take a share of an asset with payoff $f \sim \mathcal{N}(\mu, \sigma)$ and split it into two shares of a new asset, each with payoff $f/2$. The new asset has payoffs with $1/2$ the standard deviation and $1/4$ the variance. Therefore, the prior precision of information about its payoff is $4\sigma^{-1}$.

The additive learning technology allows agents to add K precision units to their information. If they add K units of precision to their information about the new asset, the new precision is $4\sigma^{-1} + K$. Since the new asset always has four times the payoff precision of the old asset, this implies that the old asset has payoff precision $\sigma^{-1} + K/4$, after they learn. If they added K units of precision to their information about the old asset, the posterior precision would be $\sigma^{-1} + K$. The two posterior precisions are different. Thus, changing what constitutes a share of an asset changes the precision of the information agents can acquire.

In contrast, the entropy learning technology allows agents to multiply the precision of that information by K. Increasing the precision of information about the new asset by a factor of K will result in the precision of information about the old asset also being K times higher. This is the scale neutrality of entropy. The entropy technology in (3.37) is not the only scale-neutral learning technology. The diminishing returns technology in section 3.8 is scale neutral. Similarly, inattentiveness, which is based on fixed costs, is not sensitive to an asset's size.

Van Nieuwerburgh and Veldkamp (2010) and Myatt and Wallace (2012) use linear constraints to jointly study information acquisition and investment decisions in financial markets. Hébert and Woodford (2021) show that the linear constraint (3.38) can be obtained by assuming neighborhood-based information costs that capture notions of perceptual distance. Departures of mutual information in this direction have important welfare implications in general equilibrium, as examined by Angeletos and Sastry (2019) and Hébert and La'O (2023).

3.7 Hybrid Data Costs

Agents' data costs could involve a combination of both sticky information (inattentiveness) and noisy information acquisition (rational inattention). Agents may pay a fixed cost on discrete dates to observe data that perfectly reveals the current and past states of the economy. In between these updates, however, they may observe a flow of data that conveys noisy information about the state. For example, Bonomo et al. (2023) develop a hybrid price-setting model with features from both learning technologies, and Coibion and Gorodnichenko (2012) consider both learning technologies and show that survey data favor models of noisy information.

A cost function developed by Woodford (2009), Stevens (2020) and Khaw, Stevens, and Woodford (2017) is a two-stage form of rational inattention: a decision whether to adjust and then how much to adjust. Although their two-stage adjustment is infrequent, like sticky information, the decision to adjust is nonetheless based on a continuous flow of information. The experimental data in Khaw, Stevens, and Woodford (2017) support this two-stage technology.

3.8 Unlearnable Risk and Diminishing Returns

While data can predict many outcomes well, in most cases, even an infinite amount of data could not predict future outcomes with absolute certainty. Data cannot resolve all uncertainty when there is unlearnable risk. One source of unlearnable risk is fundamental randomness. Fundamental randomness is future outcomes that are not a deterministic function of any outcome that might be observed today. If such fundamental randomness exists, it is a source of unlearnable risk. If it does not exist, that implies that all future outcomes are deterministic, at least one period in advance. When all risk is learnable, and capacity approaches infinity, the posterior variance of the random variables approaches zero. In many settings, achieving zero-variance outcomes is implausible. For example, in a portfolio investment problem, zero variances mean investors have access to an infinitely profitable arbitrage trade.

Adding unlearnable risk is also a way of generating diminishing returns to learning. Incorporating unlearnable risk in a data cost function can make learning more and more about a single risk an increasingly costly activity. To reduce an asset's learnable payoff variance to near zero costs an unbounded amount of information capacity and typically yields only a finite benefit. One way to build unlearnable risk into a model of rational inattention is as follows:

$$\frac{|\hat{\Sigma} - \alpha\Sigma|}{|\Sigma - \alpha\Sigma|} \le e^{-2\kappa}. \tag{3.41}$$

With this data constraint (or the equivalent cost function), eliminating all learnable risks means reducing $\hat{\Sigma}$ to $\alpha\Sigma$, which requires infinite capacity. When $\hat{\Sigma} = \Sigma$, the investor is not learning anything, and no capacity is required. In Chapter 9, unlearnable risk will reappear in a quadratic loss problem. It will be a source of diminishing returns that bounds the productivity gains from data.

Key Ideas

- Data often comes from observing friends, neighbors, or market outcomes.
- Active experimentation is when agents take actions for the purpose of learning about the outcome.
- Entropy, linear precision, and inattentiveness are ways to quantify data that can be used as bounds or costs in a data choice problem.

Practice Questions

3.1. Suppose $\theta \sim \mathcal{N}(\mu_\theta, \sigma_\theta^2)$. What is the entropy of θ?

3.2. Suppose $\theta \sim \mathcal{N}(\mu_\theta, \tau_\theta^{-1})$. What is the entropy of $4\theta + 5$?

3.3. Suppose a variable θ takes on four possible values: 0 with probability 0.25, 1 with probability 0.3, 2 with probability 0.25, and 3 with probability 0.2. What is the entropy of θ? What is the entropy of $2\theta^2$?

3.4. Suppose there is an $n \times 1$ variable $\theta \sim \mathcal{N}(\mu, \Sigma)$ and an $n \times 1$ signal $\eta \sim \mathcal{N}(\theta, \Sigma_\eta)$, where Σ and Σ_η share common eigenvectors: $\Sigma = \Gamma\Lambda\Gamma'$ and $\Sigma_\eta = \Gamma\Lambda_\eta\Gamma'$. Express the mutual information of θ and η, $\mathcal{M}(\theta, \eta)$ as a function of the eigenvalues in Λ and Λ_η. (Hint: Recall that the determinant of a square matrix is the product of its eigenvalues.)

3.5. For the bandit problem with N projects, write a code that solves the system for the optimal choice of projects N_t and N_{t+1} and the posterior variance $\hat{\Sigma}_{t+1}$. Then conduct comparative statics on the four main parameters of the problem $\{A, r, \sigma_a^2, \sigma_\epsilon^2\}$ around the baseline parameterization described in Figure III. Explain the role of each parameter in shaping the optimal choices.

3.6. Show that discrete random variables have nonnegative entropy, among which the point mass has the lowest entropy.

3.7. Show that the entropy for continuous random variables is not bounded from below.

3.8. Show the uniform distribution has maximum entropy among all distributions with the same support.

3.9. Show the univariate normal distribution has maximum entropy among all distributions with the same variance.

3.10. This question concerns unlearnable risk. Consider a partially identified Bayesian system with states $\theta = (\theta_1, \theta_2)' \sim \mathcal{N}(\mu, \Sigma)$. A sequence of noisy signals $s_{1t} = \theta_1 + \epsilon_{1t}$ with $\epsilon_{1t} \sim_{iid} \mathcal{N}(0, \sigma_{\epsilon_1}^2)$ is observed at each t, while no signal about θ_2 is observable. Derive the asymptotic posterior variance of θ, $\lim_{t \to \infty} \hat{\Sigma}_t$ and explain why it is nonzero.

4

Data-Driven Predictions and Aggregate Outcomes

For millennia, humans have used data to keep track of economic transactions. The reason that data has become a current topic of interest is that scientists have discovered and refined new data technologies that allow us to use data on a larger scale than ever before. These technologies, like artificial intelligence and machine learning, are prediction technologies. They assign a probability to an event: Is this image a cat? Was this music composed by Bach? Is demand for blue shirts rising? Answering these questions, or assigning a probability to the outcome that the answer is yes, requires distinguishing information (signal) from noise.

This chapter describes simple models that capture the essence of these types of prediction problems. It does not describe a machine learning algorithm. Instead, it describes how to caricature the types of problems that machine learning and other big data technologies solve in economic settings. Instead of a complex real-world system with thousands or millions of predictive variables, we will consider a model with one random variable or a vector of variables and a small number of signals or data points. These are not tools for making the most accurate predictions possible. Such tools are left for data science textbooks (James et al., 2023). Instead, these are simplified tools for building theories that are transparent enough to communicate ideas about how the economy is evolving.

In the problems described below, firms try to disentangle signals from noise, permanent shocks from transitory ones, or aggregate effects from idiosyncratic or firm-specific effects. The focus is on how firms' information affects economic activity. In this chapter, we take the firms' information sets—the data at their disposal—as given. In other words, learning here is passive. Furthermore, this chapter focuses on settings where firms predict their own outcomes, not those of other firms. Later, in Chapter 5, we explore strategic settings in which firms or agents also use data to forecast others' choices.

4.1 A Tracking Problem

Consider an environment where a firm's payoff depends on the distance from its action to an unknown stochastic target. For example, a firm might profit more if its price increases align with the inflation rate, which is unknown. Prices that are too high or too low will compromise the firm's profit. Similarly, a firm that keeps its stock of capital or inventories close to its optimal level generates more profits. We start with a quadratic tracking problem because it is tractable. One can map many payoffs into a quadratic loss with a second-order approximation to the objective.

The economy is populated by a continuum of firms indexed by $i \in [0, 1]$. Every firm chooses a continuous action $a_{i,t} \in \mathbb{R}$ to minimize the expected distance between its action and an unknown exogenous target $a_{i,t}^*$ drawn by nature. Each firm solves the following problem:

$$\mathcal{L} = \min_{\{a_{i,t}\}_{t=0}^{\infty}} \mathbb{E}\left[\sum_{t=0}^{\infty} \beta^t (a_{i,t} - a_{i,t}^*)^2 \middle| \mathcal{I}_{i,0}\right], \tag{4.1}$$

where $\beta < 1$ is the discount factor and $\mathcal{I}_{i,t}$ denotes firm i's information set at date t. Add and subtract the posterior belief $\hat{a}_{i,t}^* \equiv \mathbb{E}[a_{i,t}^* | \mathcal{I}_{i,t}]$ inside the payoff. Then, use the orthogonality of expectational errors, $\mathbb{E}[(a_{i,t} - \hat{a}_{i,t}^*)(a_{i,t}^* - \hat{a}_{i,t}^*) | \mathcal{I}_{i,t}] = 0$, and the law of iterated expectations, to rewrite the problem in terms of the posterior belief, $\hat{a}_{i,t}^*$ about the target action:

$$\mathcal{L} = \min_{\{a_{i,t}\}_{t=0}^{\infty}} \sum_{t=0}^{\infty} \beta^t (a_{i,t} - \hat{a}_{i,t}^*)^2 + \sum_{t=0}^{\infty} \beta^t \hat{\Sigma}_{i,t}. \tag{4.2}$$

Define the posterior variance to be the expected squared error in the target action forecast:

$$\hat{\Sigma}_{i,t} \equiv \mathbb{E}[(\hat{a}_{i,t}^* - a_{i,t}^*)^2 | \mathcal{I}_{i,t}]. \tag{4.3}$$

The problem is equivalent to minimizing the distance between actions and beliefs. The additional term involving the series of conditional variances $\{\hat{\Sigma}_{i,t}\}_{t=0}^{\infty}$ is a cost that decreases utility but cannot be controlled by the firm because data is exogenous. The first-order condition implies that the optimal action is the expected value of the target action:

$$a_{i,t} = \hat{a}_{i,t}^*. \tag{4.4}$$

This problem is static because previous choices do not affect current choices. Thus, the optimization is done period by period. Later, when we introduce adjustment costs to actions (section 4.4) or infrequent data collection (section 5.4), previous choices will be taken into account when making current choices—the problem becomes *dynamic*.

Next, we discuss two variants of this problem that differ in the sources of uncertainty and the implied stochastic process of the target action $a_{i,t}^*$.

4.2 Persistent versus Transitory Shocks

Firms can be uncertain about the persistence of the shocks they face. For example, when an ice cream parlor observes an increase in the sales of its chocolate flavor, it would like to know if it is coming from a temporary craze or a permanent shift in the demand for chocolate. If the sales increase is purely transitory, the firm might not change its current strategy. In contrast, if the sales increase is persistent, it may decide to devote more resources to chocolate production or raise the chocolate price.

We formalize this idea considering a signal extraction problem in which the target action $a_{i,t}^*$ is idiosyncratic—specific to an individual firm—and experiences both permanent and transitory shocks. Firms cannot distinguish between these permanent and transitory shocks. Their confusion is what generates interesting learning dynamics and aggregate economic fluctuations. To simplify the analysis, suppose the target is an unknown, idiosyncratic, and fixed trait, such as the long-run demand for chocolate ice cream, a worker's innate abilities, or a firm's long-term profitability.[1] In this case, the optimal action $a_{i,t}^*$ from the previous section is the parameter θ_i. Firms use data—unbiased private signals centered at the truth—to learn about their own permanent trait:

$$s_{i,t} = \theta_i + \eta_{i,t}, \quad \text{with} \quad \eta_{i,t} \sim \mathcal{N}(0, \tau_s^{-1}). \tag{4.5}$$

In our examples, the source of the data $s_{i,t}$ may be revenues, costs, or a combination of both. These outcomes provide information about the permanent trait but are contaminated by noise η. Agents learn about the parameter as in section 2.5.1. Given initial values $(\hat{\theta}_{i,0}, \hat{\Sigma}_{i,0})$, the target forecast and its uncertainty evolve according to the Kalman formulas in (2.46), (2.47), and (2.48), which evaluated at $\rho = 1$ and $\tau_\theta^{-1} = 0$, yield:

$$\hat{\theta}_{i,t+1} = \hat{\theta}_{i,t} + \frac{\tau_s}{\hat{\Sigma}_{i,t}^{-1} + \tau_s}(s_{i,t} - \hat{\theta}_{i,t}); \qquad \hat{\Sigma}_{i,t+1}^{-1} = \hat{\Sigma}_{i,t}^{-1} + \tau_s. \tag{4.6}$$

By tracking the expected target, the chosen action $\hat{\theta}_{i,t}$ is stochastic, with volatility that drops over time.

---

1. More generally, the target may follow a persistent process as in section 2.4.1.

4.2.1 Application: Data-Driven Labor Markets

Confusion between permanent and transitory shocks featured prominently in matching theories of labor markets. When recently formed, worker-firm matches may be uncertain about their relationship quality—a permanent trait θ_i. Data generated by productive relationships provides noisy signals $s_{i,t}$ about the quality of the relationship. Therefore, match quality is an "experience good" that is gradually revealed and eventually learned (Jovanovic, 1979, 1984). A key prediction of this type of model is that learning generates a selection effect: over time, poor matches get dissolved, whereas good matches survive. Job tenure—how long the worker has been on the job—becomes a sufficient statistic for match quality and uncertainty.

Work that studies data-driven labor market dynamics includes learning about match-specific productivity (Pries and Rogerson, 2005; Nagypál, 2007; Menzio and Shi, 2011), learning about fixed worker abilities in different types of occupations (Miller, 1984; Neal, 1999; Moscarini, 2001; Groes, Kircher, and Manovskii, 2014; Papageorgiou, 2014; Wee, 2016; Baley, Figueiredo, and Ulbricht, 2022) or learning about fixed firm characteristics (Borovičková, 2016). In these papers, data is generated by production activities. In other papers, observing inactivity is informative data. For example, in Gonzalez and Shi (2010) and Doppelt (2016), the posterior probability of worker quality—her résumé—worsens with the length of an unemployment spell and alters the job-finding rate.

4.2.2 Application: Firm and Government Choices

Besides labor market dynamics, learning about fixed characteristics through noisy data has also been used to examine technology choice (Jovanovic and Nyarko, 1996); entrepreneurship (Minniti and Bygrave, 2001); firm profitability (Pástor, Taylor, and Veronesi, 2009); exporters' demand (Timoshenko, 2015; Berman, Rebeyrol, and Vicard, 2019); durable consumption (Luo, Nie, and Young, 2015); firms' life-cycle (Arkolakis, Papageorgiou, and Timoshenko, 2018; Chen et al., 2023); and the impact of government policy (Pastor and Veronesi, 2012). Policymakers may also behave as Bayesian firms when learning about climate change parameters (Kelly and Kolstad, 1999) or the trade-off between inflation and unemployment (Cogley and Sargent, 2005; Sargent, Williams, and Zha, 2006; Primiceri, 2006).

4.3 Aggregate versus Idiosyncratic Shocks

Lots of data that firms use conflate aggregate trends that affect the entire industry or economy with idiosyncratic factors that are firm-specific. For example, is an observed increase in the cost of supplies a widespread phenomenon, or is it specific to their supplier? Is an increase in demand because a firm produced a hot product, or is demand strong everywhere? To formalize this idea, suppose that the target action $a_{i,t}^*$ is now a linear combination of an aggregate factor common across firms θ_t and an individual factor $\omega_{i,t}$ specific to firm i:

$$a_{i,t}^* = (1-r)\theta_t + r(\omega_{i,t} - \theta_t), \quad \text{with} \quad r \in [0,1]. \tag{4.7}$$

If $r = 0$, firms only track the aggregate state; if $r = 1/2$, firms only track the individual state; and if $r = 1$, they track the difference between the individual and the aggregate state (e.g., their individual costs or demand relative to the rest of the economy).

For simplicity, let us assume that the aggregate factor is i.i.d. across time $\theta_t \sim \mathcal{N}(0, \tau_\theta^{-1})$, and the individual factor is i.i.d. across time and firms $\omega_{i,t} \sim \mathcal{N}(0, \tau_\omega^{-1})$. Firms would like to disentangle the two factors. However, they have access to a unique data source that provides information about their *sum*

$$s_{i,t} = \theta_t + \omega_{i,t}. \tag{4.8}$$

As before, the solution to the tracking problem in (4.4) sets the optimal action equal to the expected target $a_{i,t} = \hat{a}_{i,t}^*$. In this case, the expected target equals

$$\hat{a}_{i,t}^* = (1-2r)\mathbb{E}[\theta_t|\mathcal{I}_{i,t}] + r\mathbb{E}[\omega_{i,t}|\mathcal{I}_{i,t}] = (1-2r)\hat{\theta}_t + r\hat{\omega}_{i,t}. \tag{4.9}$$

Using Bayes' Law to derive the belief about the aggregate and individual states, we obtain:

$$\hat{a}_{i,t}^* = \frac{(1-2r)\tau_\omega + r\tau_\theta}{\tau_\theta + \tau_\omega} s_{i,t}. \tag{4.10}$$

With one signal s and two shocks, firms cannot disentangle the factors and mistakenly attribute part of the aggregate shock θ to the idiosyncratic shock ω and vice versa.

4.3.1 Application: Monetary Nonneutrality

Confusion between firm-specific and aggregate shocks is the centerpiece of the Nobel prize–winning work of Lucas (1972) and Phelps (1970). Lucas's question was about why changes in monetary policy seemed to have a real effect on economic activity. Standard models at the time predicted that money should be neutral: If there is twice as much money, all prices should be twice as high. But nothing else should change. Lucas's explanation for why output changed was that firms did not know that monetary policy had changed. They learned about the change by seeing its effect on their prices. When they see that consumers are willing to pay more for their product, they produce more of it, stimulating aggregate output.

The following is a simplified version of the original model. It abstracts from some economic foundations to deliver a clearer picture of the original "island" model problem agents face.

Setup   There is a continuum of goods in the economy, each produced by a single representative producer i. Each producer can transform labor L_i, one-for-one into good i output Y_i

$$Y_i = L_i. \tag{4.11}$$

Utility is defined over the consumption of a composite good C_i and labor

$$U_i = C_i - \frac{1}{\gamma}L_i^\gamma, \quad \gamma > 1. \tag{4.12}$$

The composite good C_i is constructed to deliver an aggregate demand for good i that depends on aggregate income Y, good i's price P_i relative to the price of the consumption aggregate P, and z_i, a random, mean-zero shock to the preference for good i:

$$Y_i^d = Y\left(\frac{P_i}{P}\right)^{-\eta} \exp(z_i). \tag{4.13}$$

Aggregate income is defined such that $\ln(Y) \equiv \int_i \ln(Y_i) \, di$. Aggregate demand for goods depends on the real money supply M and the aggregate price level P

$$Y = \frac{M}{P}, \tag{4.14}$$

where the price level is defined such that $\ln(P) = \int_i \ln(P_i) \, di$.[2] Finally, an individual's budget constraint is

$$PC_i = P_iY_i. \tag{4.15}$$

Equilibrium   An equilibrium is a set of utility-maximizing labor L_i and consumption C_i choices that respect the budget constraint and prices that equate demand and supply. Substituting the budget constraint (4.15) and the production function (4.11) into the individual's utility (4.12) delivers $U_i = \mathbb{E}[P_iL_i/P] - (1/\gamma)L_i^\gamma$. The first-order condition with respect to L_i reveals that the optimal choice of labor is

$$L_i = \mathbb{E}\left[\frac{P_i}{P}\right]^{1/(\gamma-1)}. \tag{4.16}$$

2. Specifying demand directly like this is obviously a shortcut. See Lorenzoni (2009) for a microfounded model that delivers this form of aggregate demand.

To simplify the following analysis, we transform the problem into logarithms and let lowercase variables denote logs (for example, $\ell_i \equiv \ln(L_i)$).

Data Abundance Undermines Monetary Policy   With full information, we can drop the expectation operator in (4.16). The log of supply (4.16) is $1/(\gamma - 1)$ $(p_i - p)$. The log of demand (4.13) is $y - \eta(p_i - p) + z_i$. Equating these two expressions and rearranging delivers the individual equilibrium price, $p_i = p + \frac{\gamma-1}{1+\eta(\gamma-1)}(y + z_i)$. Since the log aggregate price is defined to be an average of the log individual prices,

$$p = \int p_i \, di = p + \frac{\gamma - 1}{1 + \eta(\gamma - 1)}(y + 0). \qquad (4.17)$$

Subtracting p on both sides leaves log output $y = 0$, meaning that aggregate output Y is always $e^0 = 1$. Using the aggregate demand equation (4.14), it also tells us that $M = P$. Money is neutral and there is no role for monetary policy. When abundant data allows producers to disentangle aggregate from idiosyncratic shocks, changes in the supply of money only affect prices, not output.

Data Scarcity and Monetary Nonneutrality   The critical assumption that causes money to have real effects is that agents do not know the aggregate price level.[3] When choosing how much to produce or work, individuals can see the price of their good p_i, but the aggregate price level p, the money supply m, and the good-specific demand shock z_i are all unobserved. They believe these shocks to be normally distributed:

$$m \sim (\mathbb{E}[m], \mathbb{V}ar[m]), \quad \text{and} \quad z_i \sim \mathcal{N}(0, \mathbb{V}ar[z]). \qquad (4.18)$$

We guess and then verify that p is a linear function of m and z_i. If that is the case, then p will have an unconditional (not conditioning on observing p_i) normal distribution, $p \sim \mathcal{N}(\mathbb{E}[p], \mathbb{V}ar[p])$, for some values $\mathbb{E}[p]$ and $\mathbb{V}ar[p]$. After production takes place, the aggregate price level and money supply are revealed so that consumers' demand can depend on p and m.

Lucas makes a simplifying assumption—certainty equivalence. He assumes that, when choosing their optimal labor supply, agents treat their expectations as if they were the truth. Since the log optimal labor supply (log of equation 4.16) with full information is $1/(\gamma - 1)(p_i - p)$, the certainty equivalent of

---

3. While this is true in this version of Lucas (1972), it is not always the case. In particular, Amador and Weill (2010) write a version of this model in which all agents know the aggregate price level, yet monetary shocks have real effects.

optimal labor is

$$\ell_i = \frac{1}{\gamma - 1} \mathbb{E}[p_i - p].$$ (4.19)

The interpretation is that agents work harder when they believe their goods' relative price $(p_i - p)$ is high. Money has real effects because when money is abundant, most agents observe a high price for their goods. However, each firm cannot tell whether their price is high because their good's relative price is high or the aggregate price level is high. So, they place some probability on each cause. If they think their relative price might have risen, they work harder, which increases output.

The equilibrium price is determined by equating supply (4.19) with demand (the log of equation 4.13). Using (4.14) to substitute out y,

$$\frac{1}{\gamma - 1}(p_i - \mathbb{E}[p|p_i]) = m - p - \eta(p_i - p) + z_i.$$ (4.20)

This is a linear relationship between p and p_i, with normally distributed noise $m + z_i$. Thus, p_i must be equal to a linear function of p, plus noise: $p_i = a + bp + \epsilon_i$ where $\epsilon_i \sim \mathcal{N}(0, \sigma_\epsilon^2)$. Since we know that p is always the average log price, $p = \int p_i \, di = a + bp + 0$. This can only hold for every aggregate price if $a = 0$ and $b = 1$. Thus,

$$p_i = p + \epsilon_i \qquad \epsilon_i \sim \mathcal{N}(0, \sigma_\epsilon^2).$$ (4.21)

Thus the price of an individual good is an unbiased signal about the aggregate price level.

Next, use Bayes' Law to combine this information in the individual good price with the aggregate price to get a conditional expectation $\mathbb{E}[p|p_i]$: a sum of the prior and signal, each weighted by their relative precisions. Thus,

$$\mathbb{E}[p|p_i] = \frac{\sigma_\epsilon^2}{\mathbb{V}ar[p] + \sigma_\epsilon^2} \mathbb{E}[p] + \frac{\mathbb{V}ar[p]}{\mathbb{V}ar[p] + \sigma_\epsilon^2} p_i.$$ (4.22)

Next, substitute for $\mathbb{E}[p|p_i]$ in the labor supply equation (4.19). Define $\alpha \equiv \sigma_\epsilon^2/(\mathbb{V}ar[p] + \sigma_\epsilon^2) \cdot 1/(\gamma - 1)$ and collect terms to get

$$\ell_i = \alpha \left(p_i - \mathbb{E}[p] \right).$$ (4.23)

Averaging over i delivers aggregate production $(\int_i \ell_i \, di = y)$ and using the aggregate demand relationship $y = m - p$ yields

$$m - p = \alpha \left(p - \mathbb{E}[p] \right).$$ (4.24)

Taking the unconditional expectation of both sides of (4.24) tells us that $\mathbb{E}[m] - \mathbb{E}[p] = 0$ or $\mathbb{E}[p] = \mathbb{E}[m]$. The unconditional expected price level is the expected money supply.

Substituting in $\mathbb{E}[m]$ for $\mathbb{E}[p]$ in (4.24) and rearranging, we can express the aggregate price level as a function of the expected and actual money supply

$$p = \frac{\alpha}{1+\alpha}\mathbb{E}[m] + \frac{1}{1+\alpha}m. \tag{4.25}$$

This captures the idea that inflation can be driven by changes in monetary policy m or changes in expectations $\mathbb{E}[m]$.

Output depends on the difference between actual and expected money supply. Using the aggregate demand relationship $y = m - p$ again reveals that

$$y = \frac{\alpha}{1+\alpha}(m - \mathbb{E}[m]). \tag{4.26}$$

The main result of the Lucas-Phelps model is that money supply surprises cause output to rise when data is scarce. The inability to distinguish aggregate from idiosyncratic changes in prices creates a role for monetary policy to have real effects on economic activity.

Related Applications   Hellwig and Venkateswaran (2009) investigate the implications of signals combining aggregate and idiosyncratic shocks in a nominal price-setting context. When an aggregate shock occurs, firms mistakenly attribute it to a firm-specific shock but adjust prices nevertheless. This increases the responsiveness to aggregate nominal shocks and reduces monetary nonneutrality. Venkateswaran (2014) introduces confusion between idiosyncratic and aggregate productivity in a frictional labor market. See section 5.5.1.

4.4   Signal Extraction with Fixed Adjustment Costs

In many settings, firms' data use interacts with fixed adjustment costs for changing actions.[4] Price-setting problems, in which firms estimate marginal costs and face menu costs to change their prices, or investment problems, in which firms estimate profits and face capital adjustment costs, are two leading examples. Managing portfolios, controlling inventories, and consuming durables may also involve a signal extraction problem while incurring adjustment costs.

---

4. In contrast to the costly information acquisition in section 3.4, here we consider situations where firms can freely update their beliefs but face costs to change their actions.

These problems are dynamic by nature, as past choices affect whether or not to adjust today. Moreover, fixed adjustment costs typically make objectives nondifferentiable, and thus, standard tools cannot be applied to characterize the solution. The optimal policy typically consists of an inaction region delimited by two thresholds [S, s], also known as an Ss band. Firms pay the fixed adjustment cost and take action whenever their state falls outside this region; otherwise, agents remain inactive.

When combined with signal extraction, the inaction region depends on beliefs, not the true state. A firm keeps its current course of action if beliefs about the state lie inside the inaction region; it resets its action to a new optimal level if beliefs fall outside the inaction region. Thus, mistakes happen—adjustments that would not have occurred with perfect information.

4.4.1 Application: Data-Driven Price-Setting

Setting prices is one of the most essential things firms do. But setting prices really involves two costs: the information cost of figuring out what price should be set and the cost of implementing the change. While the idea that firms need to incur a cost to stick new price stickers on products seems outdated in a modern economy, such costs are necessary to explain why so many prices do not move for long periods. Perhaps the cost arises from surprising customers with new prices. Whatever its nature, such a cost explains price inaction—the failure of most firms to adjust prices continuously. This is why the combination of action cost and information frictions is most commonly explored in the context of firm price-setting. Continuous time tools are helpful to obtain closed-form expressions for inaction regions.

A Menu-Cost Model   Consider an infinitely lived, profit-maximizing firm that discounts the future at a constant rate r. It chooses the price P_t at which to sell its product and commits to selling any quantity demanded at such price. It faces a downward sloping demand curve given by $P_t^{-\eta}$, where $\eta > 1$ is the demand elasticity. Output is produced with a linear technology, where one unit of labor produces one unit of output. The labor cost C_t is subject to idiosyncratic shocks. Profits equal $\Pi(P_t) = P_t^{-\eta}(P_t - C_t)$. We consider small and continuous disturbances to marginal costs assuming a Brownian motion in logs with volatility σ:

$$\mathrm{dlog}C_t = \sigma\,\mathrm{d}W_t, \quad W_t \sim Wiener. \tag{4.27}$$

Every price change entails paying a fixed menu cost $\varphi > 0$. Without pricing frictions, the price that maximizes per-period profits equals a constant markup over marginal costs: $P_t^* = \mu C_t$ with $\mu = \eta/(\eta - 1)$. Prices would perfectly track marginal costs to keep the price at its desired level. However, with the menu cost, the firm is willing to tolerate costly deviations from P_t^* and its desired markup. Let $\theta_t \equiv \log(P_t/P_t^*)$ denote the price gap, defined as the log difference between the current and the frictionless price. During inaction periods, in which the price is kept constant, price gaps inherit the stochastic process of log marginal costs (because Brownian motions are symmetric): $d\theta_t = \sigma\, dW_t$.

A second-order Taylor expansion to the log of profits around the frictionless price yields per-period quadratic losses around a zero price gap[5]

$$\log \Pi(\theta_t) \approx A - B\theta_t^2, \tag{4.28}$$

where $A \equiv \log \Pi(P_t^*) > 0$ reflects frictionless log profits and $B \equiv \eta(\eta - 1)/2 > 0$ reflects the curvature of the profit function. Next, we characterize the firm's price-setting under different scenarios that vary in the quality of data.

Abundant Data   We assume that data is sufficiently abundant to infer marginal costs and thus know price gaps precisely. Let $V(\theta_0)$ be the value of a firm with an initial price gap θ_0 and information set $\mathcal{I}_0$. Given the price gap, the firm keeps or changes its prices by solving the following stopping-time problem (we ignore the constant A because it does not affect pricing choices):

$$V(\theta_0) = \max_\tau \mathbb{E}\Big[\underbrace{\int_0^\tau -e^{-rs}B\theta_s^2\, ds}_{\text{losses during inaction}} + e^{-r\tau}\underbrace{\Big(-\varphi + \max_{\theta^*} V(\theta^*) \Big)}_{\substack{\text{pay menu cost and} \\ \text{reoptimize}}} \Big| \mathcal{I}_0 \Big].$$

$$\tag{4.29}$$

The random variable τ is the stopping time—the date on which the firm decides to "stop" using its current price and pay the menu cost to set a new price (and a new price gap). The first term with an integral in (4.29) reflects the losses accumulated during periods of inaction. The second term reflects the menu cost and the value of choosing an optimal price gap.

---

5. Take a second-order Taylor expansion to the log of profits around the frictionless price:

$$\log \Pi(P_t) \approx \log \Pi(P_t^*) + \big(\log \Pi(P_t^*)\big)'\, (P_t - P_t^*) + \frac{1}{2}(\log \Pi(P_t^*))''(P_t - P_t^*)^2.$$

The first derivative equals zero because the P_t^* satisfies the first-order condition. The second derivative equals

$$(\log \Pi(P_t^*))'' = \frac{\eta}{(P_t^*)^2} - \frac{1}{(P_t^* - C_t)^2} = \frac{1}{(P_t^*)^2}\left[\eta - \frac{1}{(1 - 1/\mu)^2} \right] = -\frac{\eta(\eta-1)}{(P_t^*)^2}.$$

Substituting the derivatives and approximating $(P_t - P_t^*)/P_t^*$ with $\log(P_t/P_t^*)$, yields the expression for log profits in (4.28).

The optimal pricing policy consists of three numbers: the reset price gap and the two borders of the inaction region. Because the profit function and the stochastic process are symmetric, the reset gap equals zero $\theta^* = 0$ and the inaction region is symmetric $\mathcal{R} = [-\bar{\theta}, \bar{\theta}]$. If the state lies inside the inaction region $\theta \in \mathcal{R}$, the price remains fixed. If the state lies outside the inaction region $\theta \notin \mathcal{R}$, the price is reset so that the gap with the frictionless price is closed.

For small r and small φ, Barro (1972) and Dixit (1991) characterize, up to first order, the borders of the inaction region as follows:

$$\bar{\theta} = \pm \left(\frac{6\varphi}{B} \sigma^2 \right)^{1/4}. \tag{4.30}$$

The inaction region increases with the normalized adjustment cost φ/B (with an elasticity of $1/4$) and the volatility of shocks σ (with an elasticity of $1/2$). The surprising result is that a tiny menu cost φ generates large inaction: menu costs that are fourth-order small generate a first-order effect in the inaction region.

The relationship between volatility and the frequency of price adjustment is complex. On the one hand, more volatile price gaps hit the Ss bands more often, increasing the adjustment frequency ("volatility effect"). On the other hand, higher volatility widens the inaction region to save on menu costs, reducing the adjustment frequency ("option effect"). It can be shown analytically that the first effect dominates, and the adjustment frequency increases with volatility. The expected time between adjustments—the inverse of the frequency—is inversely related to volatility σ:

$$\mathbb{E}[\tau] = \left(\frac{\bar{\theta}}{\sigma} \right)^2 = \left(\frac{6\varphi}{B} \right)^{1/2} \frac{1}{\sigma}. \tag{4.31}$$

Scarce Data   Alvarez, Lippi, and Paciello (2016) introduce noisy information to the firms' pricing problem, assuming that marginal costs are not perfectly observed. Instead, the firm receives noisy data s about its marginal costs (which translates into data about the price gap). Data signals follow a Brownian motion with a drift equal to the true price gap and signal noise volatility γ

$$ds_t = \theta_t \, dt + \gamma \, dZ_t. \tag{4.32}$$

With imperfect information, the pricing problem combines stopping time and filtering theory. The firm forms beliefs $\hat{\theta}_t \equiv \mathbb{E}[\theta_t | \mathcal{I}_t]$ with uncertainty $\hat{\Sigma}_t \equiv \mathbb{E}[(\hat{\theta}_t - \theta_t)^2 | \mathcal{I}_t]$ using the Kalman-Bucy Filter as in section 2.4.2. The inaction region has the same shape as (4.30), but substituting σ for $\hat{\Sigma}_t/\gamma$:

$$\bar{\theta}_t = \pm \left(\frac{6\varphi}{B} \frac{\hat{\Sigma}_t^2}{\gamma^2} \right)^{1/4} \quad \text{with} \quad d\hat{\Sigma}_t = \left(\sigma^2 - \frac{\hat{\Sigma}_t^2}{\gamma^2} \right) dt. \quad (4.33)$$

Because uncertainty evolves, the inaction region is time-varying. As firms accumulate data, their estimates become more and more precise until uncertainty reaches a minimum constant level of $\hat{\Sigma}_\infty = \gamma\sigma$. In the limit, the inaction region and the adjustment frequency become identical to those with perfect information. In other words, a large data set allows firms to set their prices as in the case with perfect information.

Inaction with Fat-Tailed Risk   When fresh technologies are developed, new competitors appear, unfamiliar markets are targeted, or supply chains are disrupted, firms use data to learn about large and persistent changes. Baley and Blanco (2019) introduce noisy data about fat-tailed risk.[6] They assume a jump-diffusion process for the price gap:

$$d\theta_t = \sigma \, dW_t + \nu u_t \, dQ_t, \quad (4.34)$$

where Q_t is a Poisson process with arrival rate $\lambda > 0$ and $u_t \sim \mathcal{N}(0,1)$ are normal infrequent innovations. Crucially, the firm observes the arrival of a regime change but not its size u_t. For example, a firm knows its management has been replaced but does not know how the new regime change will affect its marginal cost and needs to estimate it with data. As before, the firm observes noisy signals as in (4.32). With noisy signals about a state with jumps, firm-level uncertainty cycles appear as in section 2.4.3 (panel A in Figure IV). Time-varying uncertainty generates a time-varying inaction region that never stabilizes (panel B in Figure IV). The inaction region with uncertainty cycles takes the following form:

$$\bar{\theta}_t = \pm \left(\frac{6\varphi}{B} \frac{\hat{\Sigma}_t^2}{\gamma^2} \frac{1}{1+\Lambda_t} \right)^{1/4} \quad \text{with} \quad d\hat{\Sigma}_t = \left(\sigma^2 - \frac{\hat{\Sigma}_t^2}{\gamma^2} \right) dt + \nu^2 \, dQ_t. \quad (4.35)$$

As before, uncertainty directly affects the inaction region in the numerator, reflecting the *option-value effect*. Uncertainty cycles introduce a second indirect effect, measured through the time-varying factor Λ_t that is proportional to $\left(\hat{\Sigma}_t/\hat{\Sigma}^* - 1 \right)$, where $\hat{\Sigma}^* \equiv \gamma(\sigma^2 + \lambda\nu^2)^{1/2}$ is the average level of uncertainty. When uncertainty is above its average $\left(\hat{\Sigma}_t/\hat{\Sigma}^* > 1 \right)$, it is expected

---

6. Gertler and Leahy (2008) and Midrigan (2011) consider fat-tailed risk processes with perfect information.

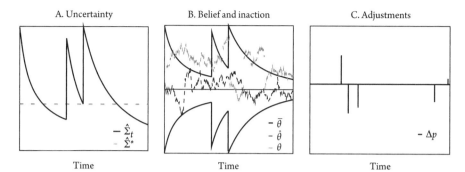

FIGURE IV. Price-Setting with Uncertainty Cycles. *Notes*: This figure illustrates the time evolution of uncertainty, beliefs, inaction regions, and adjustments. Panel A plots the path of uncertainty $\hat{\Sigma}_t$ (solid line) and average uncertainty $\hat{\Sigma}^*$ (dotted line). Panel B plots the inaction region $\bar{\theta}_t(\hat{\Sigma}_t)$ (black thick line), together with the price gap estimate $\hat{\theta}$ (black line) and the true price gap θ (gray line). Panel C plots the size of price adjustments occurring when the price gap estimate hits either border of the inaction region (the adjustment equals the negative of the gap).

to decrease, shrinking the inaction region. Conversely, when uncertainty is below its average $\left(\hat{\Sigma}_t/\hat{\Sigma}^* < 1\right)$, it is expected to increase, widening the inaction region. The total effect of uncertainty on the inaction region depends on parameters. With small menu costs φ and large signal noise γ, the inaction region widens with higher uncertainty, with an elasticity of the inaction region to uncertainty close to $1/2$. Under this assumption, the "volatility effect" dominates the "option effect." Therefore, more uncertain firms change prices more often and by larger amounts than less uncertain firms (panel C in Figure IV).

4.4.2 Cross-Sectional and Aggregate Implications

To examine the cross-sectional and aggregate implications of data-driven price-setting, consider a continuum of ex ante firms solving the price-setting problem with menu costs with uncorrelated shocks across firms. The case with small shocks and abundant data is a simplified version of the model in Golosov and Lucas (2007). All firms have the same inaction region, and there is no dispersion in adjustment frequency. This model generates negligible effects of monetary policy shocks (unanticipated aggregate shocks to firms' marginal costs) because of a "selection effect": price changes occur in the firms with the most significant need to adjust, and money shocks are incorporated rapidly into prices. Scarce data does not alter this conclusion because uncertainty eventually collapses to a constant in the steady state, and the economy resembles that with abundant data.

In contrast, learning about fat-tailed risk generates fluctuations in uncertainty and the frequency and size of price changes at the individual level. In the cross section, firms churn between high and low uncertainty states. Persistent heterogeneity in the frequency of price adjustment amplifies the real effects of monetary shocks because it weakens the selection effect: high uncertainty firms adjust prices frequently, and their prices immediately react to the monetary shock, whereas low-uncertainty firms rarely adjust, and their response to the monetary shock is delayed.

4.5   A Tracking Problem with Data Choice

So far, we've discussed how data can be used to solve simple prediction problems and choose economic actions. But in many cases, firms or consumers can choose what data to acquire, consider, or process. The choice of data and the choice of actions interact. To choose data, we need a way to measure data. We'll use the entropy and mutual information metrics from section 3.5.

Tracking One State   The first example illustrates key trade-offs of rational inattention models in a setting with one random variable to track. The agent chooses signal precision by trading the costs of acquiring data with the benefits of better-informed actions.

The agent chooses the action a that minimizes the expected distance to an i.i.d. state $\theta \sim \mathcal{N}(0, \tau_\theta^{-1})$. They receive noisy data $s = \theta + \eta$, with precision τ_s. Two constraints govern how the agent can choose data. The first is the capacity constraint, which takes the form of an upper bound $\kappa > 0$ on the mutual information of priors and prior plus data: $\mathcal{M}(\theta, s) \leq \kappa$. The second is a "no forgetting" constraint that requires mutual information to be nonnegative: $\mathcal{M}(\theta, s) \geq 0$. The agent can increase capacity κ by paying a proportional utility cost $c\kappa$. The agent solves the following problem:

$$\mathcal{L} = \min_{\{a, \kappa\}} \frac{1}{2} \mathbb{E}\left[(a - \theta)^2 \, |s\right] + c\kappa \tag{4.36}$$

$$\text{s.t.} \quad 0 \leq \mathcal{M}(\theta, s) \leq \kappa,$$

where $\mathcal{M}(\theta, s) = (1/2) \log((\tau_\theta + \tau_s)/\tau_\theta)$ is the mutual information for normal state and signal in (3.34), expressed in terms of prior and posterior precisions.

The solution to the problem takes place in two stages. In the first stage, the agent chooses how much attention to allocate to θ by choosing the total processing capacity κ. This choice determines the optimal signal precision τ_s. In the second stage, the agent receives a noisy signal s with the precision proportional to the attention allocated in the first stage and chooses the action.

To solve the model, we work backward. Suppose the agent receives signal s with precision τ_s. Conditional on this signal, the agent chooses the optimal action

$$a^* = \mathbb{E}\left[\theta|s\right] = \frac{\tau_s}{\tau_\theta + \tau_s} s. \tag{4.37}$$

The expected loss implied by the optimal action is $\mathbb{E}\left[(a^* - \theta)^2\right] = (\tau_\theta + \tau_s)^{-1}$. Since the expected loss decreases with signal precision, the capacity constraint will always bind, and we set $\tau_\theta + \tau_s = \tau_\theta e^{2\kappa}$. Plugging the optimal action and binding capacity constraint into (4.36), and taking the first-order condition with respect to κ, we find the optimal attention capacity and the implied optimal signal precision. And conditional on these choices, we find the optimal action.

There are two solutions depending on the parameters. If the marginal cost of increasing capacity is high $\tau_\theta c \geq 1$, then all choices are zero: $k^* = \tau_s^* = a^* = 0$ (the action equals the prior, zero in this example, $\mathbb{E}[\theta] = 0$). Otherwise, if the marginal cost is low $\tau_\theta c < 1$, then the optimal choices are:

$$\kappa^* = \frac{1}{2}\ln\left(\frac{1}{\tau_\theta c}\right); \qquad (\tau_s^* + \tau_\theta)^{-1} = c; \qquad a^* = (1 - \tau_\theta c)\, s. \tag{4.38}$$

Optimal attention κ^* falls with the state's precision τ_θ and the marginal cost c.

Tracking Multiple States   Assume the agent tracks two i.i.d. states

$$(\theta_1, \theta_2) \sim \mathcal{N}(0, \Sigma), \tag{4.39}$$

where Σ denotes the prior variance-covariance matrix. The agent chooses an action a to minimize the distance to both states subject to a bound on mutual information:

$$\mathcal{L} = \min_{\{a,\kappa\}} \frac{1}{2}\mathbb{E}\left[(a - \theta_1 - \theta_2)^2\right] + c\kappa, \tag{4.40}$$

$$s.t. \quad 0 \leq \frac{1}{2}\ln\left(\frac{|\Sigma|}{|\hat{\Sigma}|}\right) \leq \kappa, \tag{4.41}$$

where $\hat{\Sigma}$ denotes the posterior covariance matrix. Mutual information with multivariate normal variables reflects the ratio of the determinants of the prior and the posterior variances.

The problem of tracking two states has a simple solution when the agent can choose the signals' variance-covariance structure. To see this, define the target

$$\theta^* \equiv \theta_1 + \theta_2, \tag{4.42}$$

and assume the agent receives a single noisy signal of this target. The problem can be restated as a single-state problem, with the optimal allocation of attention taking the same form as (4.38). This one signal allows the agent to achieve the same expected loss as two independent signals while requiring lower mutual information.

Rationally inattentive agents generally prefer signals about a linear combination of the payoff-relevant states. However, restricting the set of signals to be independent and associated with a specific state is a plausible economic constraint in many settings. Following Maćkowiak and Wiederholt (2009), suppose the states are independent of each other, and the agent receives two independent and unbiased signals,

$$s_1 = \theta_1 + \eta_1, \qquad s_2 = \theta_2 + \eta_2, \tag{4.43}$$

with respective precisions τ_{s1}, τ_{s2}. The prior Σ and posterior $\hat{\Sigma}$ variances are diagonal matrices, and the entropy constraint simplifies to

$$\frac{\hat{\Sigma}_{11}^{-1} \hat{\Sigma}_{22}^{-1}}{\tau_{\theta 1} \tau_{\theta 2}} \le e^{2\kappa}, \qquad \text{where} \quad \hat{\Sigma}_{ii}^{-1} = \tau_{\theta_i} + \tau_{si} \quad \text{for} \quad i = 1, 2. \tag{4.44}$$

The expected loss associated with the action is equal to

$$\mathbb{E}\left[\left(a^* - \theta\right)^2\right] = \hat{\Sigma}_{11} + \hat{\Sigma}_{22}. \tag{4.45}$$

In the case $c \ne 0$, total capacity κ can be chosen and the problem reduces to two independent single-state problems like (4.36). The optimal allocation of attention for each state is given by expression (4.38), replacing τ_θ with the corresponding precision of each state $(\tau_{\theta 1}$ or $\tau_{\theta 2})$. In the dual problem in which total capacity is fixed, the capacity constraint always binds. In this case, more attention to one state reduces the attention allocated to the other. The ratios of posterior to prior precisions are increasing in the other state's precision:

$$\frac{\tau_{s1}^* + \tau_{\theta 1}}{\tau_{\theta_1}} = e^\kappa \sqrt{\frac{\tau_{\theta 2}}{\tau_{\theta 1}}}; \qquad \frac{\tau_{s2}^* + \tau_{\theta 2}}{\tau_{\theta_2}} = e^\kappa \sqrt{\frac{\tau_{\theta 1}}{\tau_{\theta 2}}}. \tag{4.46}$$

These expressions highlight a crucial lesson from multivariate rational inattention models: agents optimally pay more attention to the more volatile state, as it generates more significant welfare losses. That can make actions appear unresponsive to the more subtle changes in the economic environment.

A crucial assumption is that the payoff depends on the sum of the two shocks. Firms cannot take action to reduce their exposure to one shock or another. We will see different data choices in later chapters, largely because agents can take actions to avoid volatile shocks and then can safely ignore them.

4.5.1   Application: Rational Inattention Models of Price-Setting

If firms can choose to acquire data about aggregate or firm-specific shocks, they might end up choosing firm-specific data. In that case, knowing little or nothing about aggregate shocks would make prices unresponsive to those shocks. Prices that do not respond to aggregate monetary policy shocks are sticky prices that cause monetary policy to have real economic effects.

The monetary economics question of how much inertia in price-setting this mechanism generates is ultimately an empirical one. Maćkowiak and Wiederholt (2009) calibrate the stochastic processes to measures of the volatility of nominal aggregate demand shocks and the volatility of firm-level shocks as measured by the average size of a firm's price change. They calibrate the preference parameters to values for price sensitivities used in the monetary literature. They find that firms optimally allocate 94% of their attention to firm-specific conditions. Little attention is paid to aggregate shocks because firm-specific shocks are about ten times more volatile in the United States. Because price-setters devote little attention to aggregate shocks, prices do not covary highly with these shocks. As a result, monetary policy has a minimal contemporaneous effect on prices and a real effect on economic activity.

4.5.2   Application: Data Choice in Production Economies

Using rational inattention tools to model data choice in a production economy raises new challenges: If output is unknown, then the agent cannot choose both consumption and savings. If they choose consumption, savings must be whatever is left—the residual. If they choose savings, consumption is the residual. Choosing consumption and choosing savings are two different problems. To further complicate model-building, one must decide how information revealed by equilibrium prices should be incorporated into the data constraint.

Maćkowiak and Wiederholt (2015) resolve these tensions by reformulating the mutual information constraint on data choice. They constrain the mutual information between actions and the optimal, full-information action. There is a choice of data that would deliver the same solution. But they never model or solve for the chosen data directly.

For example, suppose a firm chooses price p and labor input ℓ. Given full information about the state of the economy, the firm would choose p^*, ℓ^*. Then, this constraint would bound the mutual information $\mathcal{M}(\{p, \ell\}, \{p^*, \ell^*\})$. This constraint represents the same physical learning process as the constraint on signal precisions. If actions are conditioned on any kind of signal that contains information about the true state, mutual information $\mathcal{M}$ rises. Thus, the constraint incorporates the effect of all information from both exogenous signals and endogenous sources, such as market prices. Because learning from market prices requires capacity, this model does not need to introduce shocks that make market prices noisy to keep information heterogeneous. The data flow restriction ensures that all firms extract noisy heterogeneous information, even from public signals like prices.

The main result is that changes in monetary policy produce delayed, hump-shaped consumption and output responses, just as they do in the data. In a similar setting, Paciello and Wiederholt (2014) study optimal monetary policy and Maćkowiak and Wiederholt (2015) introduce rationally inattentive households.

4.5.3   Further Applications of Data Choice

Unlike the simple static problems we presented, many applications feature dynamic settings in which states evolve persistently over time. This is technically challenging. Steiner, Stewart and Matějka (2017); Maćkowiak, Matějka, and Wiederholt (2018); Miao, Wu, and Young (2019); Afrouzi and Yang (2021a); and Jurado (2023) study dynamic inattention problems and propose algorithms to solve them.

Applications of rational inattention on the firm side include hiring decisions (Acharya and Wee, 2020); price-setting (Woodford, 2009; Stevens, 2020; Turen, 2023; Yang, 2020; Afrouzi and Yang, 2021a,b); portfolio allocation (Mondria, 2010); and startups (Melcangi and Turen, 2023). On the household side, applications include insurance choice (Brown and Jeon, 2019); marriage markets (Cheremukhin, Restrepo-Echavarria, and Tutino, 2020); labor markets (Wu, 2020); migration (Porcher, 2020; Bertoli, Moraga, and Guichard, 2020); and consumption (Luo, 2008; Matějka and McKay, 2012; Kőszegi and Matějka, 2020). There are also DSGE models with rational inattention on both the firm and household sides, in baseline New Keynesian (Maćkowiak and Wiederholt, 2015) and RBC (Maćkowiak and Wiederholt, 2023) models.

Other applications include electoral competition (Matějka and Tabellini, 2021); discrimination against minorities (Bartoš et al., 2016); international trade (Dasgupta and Mondria, 2018); mutual fund management (Kacperczyk, Van Nieuwerburgh, and Veldkamp, 2016); and expectation formation (Fuster et al., 2022; Gutiérrez-Daza, 2022).

Maćkowiak, Matějka, and Wiederholt (2023) comprehensively reviews the rational inattention literature.

Key Ideas

- Data is used for prediction. Imperfect prediction affects aggregate outcomes differently depending on whether the prediction is used to disentangle a permanent from a transitory effect or separate an aggregate shock from a location or firm-specific shock.
- When there are fixed costs of taking an action, we need to use a separate class of models, so-called Ss models to determine the effect of data.
- Combining a data friction with measures of data from Chapter 3 allows us to formulate simple models of data choice.

Practice Questions

4.1. Derive the optimal action in (4.10) step by step.

4.2. In the tracking problem described in section 4.3, assume that the aggregate factor follows a random walk $\theta_t = \theta_{t-1} + \varepsilon_t$ with $\varepsilon_t \sim \mathcal{N}(0, \tau_\theta^{-1})$, while the individual factor remains i.i.d. across time and firms $\omega_{it} \sim \mathcal{N}(0, \tau_\omega^{-1})$. Derive the optimal action.

4.3. In the tracking problem described in section 4.3, assume that agents observe a noisy individual signal about the sum of the aggregate and the idiosyncratic factors $s_{it} = \theta_t + \omega_{it} + \eta_{it}$ with $\eta_{it} \sim \mathcal{N}(0, \tau_s^{-1})$, where the signal noise distribution is the same across agents. Additionally, assume prior means different from zero μ_θ and μ_ω. Derive the optimal action.

4.4. Derive an expression for the firm value (4.29) with imperfect information as a function of the price gap belief $\hat{\theta}_t \equiv \mathbb{E}[\theta_t | \mathcal{I}_t]$ and its variance $\hat{\Sigma}_t \equiv \mathbb{E}[(\theta_t - \hat{\theta}_t)^2 | \mathcal{I}_t]$. (*Hint: Use the law of iterated expectations.*)

4.5. For the menu cost model with uncertainty cycles, show that the elasticity of the inaction region $\bar{\theta}(\hat{\Sigma}_t)$ to uncertainty $\hat{\Sigma}_t$ in (4.35) is less than one. What does this imply for the joint dynamics of uncertainty and inaction regions?

5

Using Data in Strategic Settings

Strategic settings are those in which one firm or agent's optimal choice depends on what others will do. A firm whose price depends on its competitor's price or an investor who wants to buy assets that another investor does not buy wants to forecast what another agent will do. This gives rise to a new use for data—forecasting the actions of others.

The end of the chapter sketches models of specific economic settings with strategic motives. But before we lay out the economic specifics, we consider an abstract game used to approximate how information is used in many settings. In this game, agents care about how far their chosen action is from a target action—just like they did in the frameworks in the previous chapter. However, there is an additional, new ingredient: agents also consider the distance between their action and the average action of others. The fact that only the average of others' actions matters simplifies the problem. Agents do not need to forecast what every other agent believes and what every other agent will do. They just need to forecast the average action, a considerably simpler task. This feature of the model that no other individual's action matters by itself places this model in a class of problems called "mean-field games."[1] Such games include a class of problems called "global games," popularized by Morris and Shin (1998).

Strategic Complementarity and Substitutability An action a_i by firm i is a strategic complement if the optimal choice of a_i increases in the average action of others $a \equiv \int a_j \, dj$. In other words, actions are strategic complements when agents prefer to take actions that are similar to each other. Examples of strategic complementarity include speculative attacks in financial markets, bank

---

1. Lasry and Lions (2007) coined the term "mean-field games" for situations that involve a huge number of rational players with limited information on the game. Each player chooses their optimal strategy given the global information available, which results from all players' actions.

runs, price setting in models of monopolistic competition, and investment in the presence of increasing returns.

An action a_i by firm i is a strategic substitute if the optimal choice of a_i decreases in the average action of other agents a. In other words, when actions are strategic substitutes, agents prefer actions that differ from others' actions. In standard portfolio choice models, investment is usually a strategic substitute because when other investors buy more of an asset, its price rises. The more expensive the asset is, the less of it investor i chooses to buy. Likewise, hiring labor is a strategic substitute in a standard production economy. When other firms hire, the wage rate rises, making hiring less attractive to other firms.

We introduce coordination motives through the target action a_{it}^*, which is a linear combination of an exogenous stochastic state θ_t and the average action in the economy a_t:

$$a_{it}^* = (1 - r)\theta_t + ra_t, \quad \text{where} \quad a_t \equiv \int_0^1 a_{jt}\, dj, \quad \text{and} \quad r \in [-1, 1]. \quad (5.1)$$

The parameter r governs the type of strategic interaction. If $r = 0$, the optimal action is independent of the actions of others, as in the models in section 4.2. When $r \neq 0$, actions become strategic. If $r > 0$, there is strategic complementarity, as the optimal action is increasing in the actions of others. If $r < 0$, there is strategic substitutability, as the optimal action is decreasing in the actions of others.

This chapter examines how strategic motives in actions generate the same kind of strategic motives in using or acquiring information. We make this point in a passive learning model in which information is exogenous. Section 5.6 revisits these models, adding information choice.

5.1 Forecasting the Forecasts of Others

Strategic settings are those where agents' choices depend on the choices of others. When we pair such a strategic motive with heterogeneous information, we arrive at a problem called "forecasting the forecasts of others." The models we present below offer a solution to make such forecasts tractable. But it is crucial to understand this problem to appreciate why these models are crafted the way they are and what their limitations are. Higher-order beliefs are also helpful for creating more uncertainty, more inertia, or, in some cases, economic fluctuations.

An agent's first-order belief is their belief about an unknown state. This is the type of belief or conditional expectation we have been constructing and using since Chapter 2. A second-order belief is an expectation about another agent's first-order beliefs.

For example, suppose two agents i, j are predicting an unknown state θ, each using a private signal s_i or s_j, which is informative about θ. Agent i's first-order belief is

$$\mathbb{E}[\theta | s_i]. \tag{5.2}$$

Agent i's second-order belief about agent j is what i thinks that j thinks about the state:

$$\mathbb{E}\left[\mathbb{E}[\theta | s_j] | s_i\right]. \tag{5.3}$$

Agent i's third-order belief is what i thinks that j thinks that i thinks about the state:

$$\mathbb{E}\left[\mathbb{E}\left[\mathbb{E}[\theta | s_i] | s_j\right] | s_i\right]. \tag{5.4}$$

Similarly, we can define an infinite hierarchy of beliefs, from first-order to infinite-order beliefs. The assumption of common knowledge means that everyone knows something, and everyone knows that others know it, and everyone knows that . . . up to the infinite-order belief.

Higher-Order Beliefs and Uncertainty   Higher-order beliefs are typically more uncertain. While one is unsure of the state, there is even more uncertainty about what someone else thinks the state is. This higher uncertainty plays a key role in some models we explore later.

To understand why uncertainty rises with the order of beliefs, consider the following example. Two agents $k = i, j$ have a diffuse prior on a parameter $\theta \sim \mathcal{U}(-\infty, \infty)$. Each observes a signal with independent signal noise, $s_k = \theta + \eta_k$, where $\eta_k \sim \mathcal{U}[-\varepsilon, \varepsilon]$ and $\eta_i \perp \eta_j$.

Agent i's first-order belief is $\theta | s_i \sim \mathcal{U}[s_i - \varepsilon, s_i + \varepsilon]$. After observing the signal s_i, the agent knows that the state must lie between ε below and ε above the signal. But every outcome in this interval is equally likely. One can prove this with Bayes' Law by using the probability density of the uniform signal. The steps would be roughly

$$p(\theta | s_i) \propto p(s_i | \theta) p(\theta) \propto \mathbb{1}_{\{s_i \in [\theta - \varepsilon, \theta + \varepsilon]\}} = \mathbb{1}_{\{\theta \in [s_i - \varepsilon, s_i + \varepsilon]\}}. \tag{5.5}$$

The conditional expectation of the state becomes the signal: $\mathbb{E}_i[\theta | s_i] = s_i$.

Agent i's second-order belief is noisier. To understand why, consider what the lowest possible belief that i thinks j might hold is. Recall that the conditional expectation is the signal, $\mathbb{E}_j[\theta | s_j] = s_j$. So the lowest possible belief j can hold is the lowest possible signal j might observe. Given i's signal, s_i, the lowest possible state that i believes is possible is $s_i - \varepsilon$. But j's signal is the state, plus or minus noise, that is, at most ε. So if the state were $s_i - \varepsilon$, j could have a signal as low as $s_i - 2\varepsilon$. Similarly, the highest state i believes is possible is $s_i + \varepsilon$.

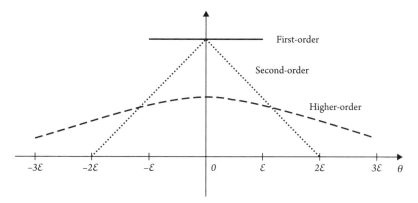

FIGURE V. Higher-Order Beliefs and Uncertainty. *Notes:* This figure illustrates how higher-order beliefs about the state θ place probability mass on a more dispersed set of outcomes, increasing uncertainty. For an agent i with signal $s_i = 0$, the first-order beliefs (solid line) place mass over $[-\varepsilon, \varepsilon]$; second-order beliefs (dotted line) place mass over $[-2\varepsilon, 2\varepsilon]$; third-order beliefs (dashed line) place mass over $[-3\varepsilon, 3\varepsilon]$, and so on and so forth.

But this implies that the highest possible signal j might observe, and thus the highest possible belief j might hold is $s_i + 2\varepsilon$.

Thus, while i's first-order belief has the support $[s_i - \varepsilon, s_i + \varepsilon]$, i's second-order belief about j places positive probability on a wider range of outcomes, $[s_i - 2\varepsilon, s_i + 2\varepsilon]$. Similarly, if i forms third-order beliefs, they will consider that if j has a belief that is at the lower bound $s_i - 2\varepsilon$, then j could conceivably believe that i's signal and i's belief is as low as $s_i - 3\varepsilon$. Figure V illustrates how the support of possible outcomes grows as the order of beliefs rises. This is the higher uncertainty that accompanies higher-order beliefs.

5.2 A Mean-Field Game with Exogenous Data

We simplify the tracking problem in (4.1) to a static model. The economy is populated by a continuum of firms indexed by $i \in [0, 1]$. They all play a one-shot game. Each firm chooses its action a_i to minimize the expected distance to the common target $a^* = (1 - r)\theta + ra$, where $a \equiv \int_0^1 a_j \, dj$ is the average action and θ is an unknown, exogenous state. Each firm solves the following problem:

$$\mathcal{L}_i = \min_{a_i} \ \mathbb{E}\left[(a_i - (1 - r)\theta - ra)^2 \big| \mathcal{I}_i \right]. \tag{5.6}$$

The order of events is as follows. Nature draws the state θ from a normal distribution $\mathcal{N}(\mu_\theta, \tau_\theta^{-1})$ with mean μ_θ and precision τ_θ. These parameters are common knowledge and summarize all prior public information. Second, each firm receives additional information about the state that is revealed by two data sources, a public signal z and a private signal s_i:

$$z = \theta + \eta_z, \quad \text{with} \quad \eta_z \sim \mathcal{N}(0, \tau_z^{-1}) \tag{5.7}$$

$$s_i = \theta + \eta_{s,i} \quad \text{with} \quad \eta_{s,i} \sim_{iid} \mathcal{N}(0, \tau_s^{-1}). \tag{5.8}$$

Private data of firm i, s_i, is independent from the private data of firm j, s_j, and from public data z. The signals' precisions τ_z and τ_s are equal across firms. Finally, given their information set $\mathcal{I}_i = \{z, s_i\}$, each firm forms beliefs about θ and a, chooses an action a_i, and payoffs are realized. We look for a symmetric Nash equilibrium to solve the game. Morris and Shin (2002) prove this symmetric equilibrium is the unique Nash equilibrium.

Beliefs and Equilibrium   The first-order condition of (5.6) with respect to action a_i equals $2(a_i - (1-r)\mathbb{E}[\theta|\mathcal{I}_i] - r\mathbb{E}[a|\mathcal{I}_i]) = 0$, implying that the optimal action is a convex combination of the belief about the state and the belief about the average action

$$a_i = (1-r)\mathbb{E}[\theta|\mathcal{I}_i] + r\mathbb{E}[a|\mathcal{I}_i]. \tag{5.9}$$

Averaging across agents, we get the average action as a function of the average beliefs

$$a = (1-r)\overline{\mathbb{E}}[\theta] + r\overline{\mathbb{E}}[a], \quad \text{where} \quad \overline{\mathbb{E}}[\cdot] = \int_i \mathbb{E}[\cdot|\mathcal{I}_i]\, di. \tag{5.10}$$

The aggregate action a can be described as an infinite sum of higher-order expectations. To see this, recursively substitute for a on the right side of (5.10) to get

$$a = (1-r)\sum_{k=1}^{\infty} r^{(k-1)}\overline{\mathbb{E}}^k[\theta], \tag{5.11}$$

where the superscript k represents the kth-order average expectation. For example, $\overline{\mathbb{E}}^1[\theta] = \overline{\mathbb{E}}[\theta]$ is the average belief about θ, while $\overline{\mathbb{E}}^2[\theta] = \overline{\mathbb{E}}[\overline{\mathbb{E}}^1[\theta]]$ is the average belief about the average belief of θ, and so forth. Working with this infinite sum is complex. To avoid this, we follow Morris and Shin (2002) by conjecturing and verifying a symmetric strategy.

Full Information   Before we continue, we solve the full information problem in which the realization of θ is known. The optimal action is $a_i = (1-r)\theta + ra$. Integrating across agents yields $a = (1-r)\theta + ra$, or simply $a = \theta$, which implies that $a_i = \theta$ for all i. This is the unique Nash equilibrium.

Heterogeneous Imperfect Information   To compute the optimal action in (5.9) requires forming beliefs about the state θ and the average action a. To form beliefs about θ we use Bayes' Law:

$$\mathbb{E}[\theta|\mathcal{I}_i] = \frac{\tau_\theta\mu_\theta + \tau_z z + \tau_s s_i}{\tau_\theta + \tau_z + \tau_s}, \qquad \mathbb{V}ar[\theta|\mathcal{I}_i]^{-1} = \tau_\theta + \tau_z + \tau_s. \quad (5.12)$$

The best estimate is a convex combination of the prior mean μ_θ, the public data z, and the private data s_i, with weights equal to their relative precisions. The posterior precision equals the sum of the precisions. Since precision is equal across agents, we denote it by $\hat{\Sigma}^{-1} \equiv \mathbb{V}ar[\theta|\mathcal{I}_i]^{-1}$. Defining relative precisions as

$$\alpha_\theta \equiv \hat{\Sigma}\tau_\theta, \qquad \alpha_s \equiv \hat{\Sigma}\tau_s, \qquad \alpha_z \equiv \hat{\Sigma}\tau_z, \qquad (5.13)$$

where $\alpha_\theta + \alpha_z + \alpha_s = 1$, we write the expected state as $\mathbb{E}[\theta|\mathcal{I}_i] = \alpha_\theta\mu_\theta + \alpha_z z + \alpha_s s_i$. To form beliefs about the average action $\mathbb{E}[a|\mathcal{I}_i]$, we guess and later verify that the individual action is linear in the data signals

$$a_i = \mu_\theta + \gamma_z(z - \mu_\theta) + \gamma_s(s_i - \mu_\theta), \qquad (5.14)$$

where the coefficients γ_z and γ_s are to be determined. Integrating the guess across agents, using the fact that the mean of the private signals s_i equals the true state θ, and taking expectations:

$$\mathbb{E}[a|\mathcal{I}_i] = \mu_\theta + \gamma_z(z - \mu_\theta) + \gamma_s(\mathbb{E}[\theta|\mathcal{I}_i] - \mu_\theta). \qquad (5.15)$$

Substituting the beliefs about the state (5.12) and the average action (5.15) in the first-order condition (5.9), rearranging terms, and matching coefficients, we obtain the optimal weights on public and private data

$$\gamma_z = \frac{\alpha_z}{1 - \alpha_s r}, \qquad \gamma_s = \frac{\alpha_s(1 - r)}{1 - \alpha_s r}. \qquad (5.16)$$

We verify the conjecture that the action is linear in data signals by checking that the weights on the prior μ_θ is $\gamma_\theta = 1 - \gamma_z - \gamma_s = \frac{\alpha_\theta}{1-\alpha_s r}$. Finally, by substituting the optimal action and the average equilibrium action into the loss function (5.6), we obtain (the proof is left as an exercise):

$$\mathcal{L}_i = (1 - r)^2 \left(\frac{\gamma_\theta^2}{\tau_\theta} + \frac{\gamma_z^2}{\tau_z}\right) + \frac{\gamma_s^2}{\tau_s}. \qquad (5.17)$$

The expected loss (which is identical across agents) decreases in the precision of both data sources and the prior belief. Without additional externalities in payoffs, more data is always welfare-improving. With additional externalities, however, more data can be welfare-reducing, as we examine in section 11.6.

Optimal Data Use   The solution has two key features. First, due to Bayesian updating, optimal actions a_i weigh data $\{z, s\}$ according to their precision. If data is too noisy relative to the prior, the weight on the prior γ_θ dominates. If public data is very noisy relative to private data $\alpha_z < \alpha_s$, then the weight on the public data is smaller $\gamma_z < \gamma_s$, and actions will not move much with z. As private heterogeneous data becomes more important, dispersion in actions increases. The opposite happens if public data is relatively more precise than private data. Second, the weight γ_z agents put on the public data when forming their action increases with the value of coordination r. Agents who want to do what others do make their actions more sensitive to the information others know. Whenever there is strategic complementarity in actions $(r > 0)$, we have $\gamma_z > \alpha_z$, which means that agents' actions react more to changes in public data than their beliefs do. Conversely, when there is substitutability in actions $(r < 0)$, agents weigh private data more in their actions than in their beliefs.

Responsiveness to Shocks   To describe the effects of information and coordination motives on aggregate outcomes, we define the *responsiveness to shocks* as the covariance of the average action with the state, normalized by fundamental volatility:

$$\frac{\mathbb{Cov}[a, \theta]}{\mathbb{Var}[\theta]} = \gamma_z + \gamma_s = \frac{\alpha_z + \alpha_s(1 - r)}{(1 - \alpha_s r)}. \tag{5.18}$$

It is equal to the sum of the weights on signals and thus depends on relative precisions. Also, this covariance measures the informativeness of actions and could, in principle, be used to measure how much information the average firm has.

In the extreme case with perfect information, all agents set their action equal to the known state $a = \theta$ (there is no cross-sectional dispersion); responsiveness is highest at a value of 1, and expected welfare losses are zero $\mathcal{L} = 0$. At the other extreme, with complete ignorance (private and public signals have zero precision), actions equal the prior $a = \mu_\theta$ and do not correlate with the state (but are equal to each other). Responsiveness is lowest at a value of 0. Even if everyone takes the same action, utility losses arise because actions are far from the state.

Between these two informational extremes, the strength of strategic motives r matters for the optimal use of information and the implied responsiveness to shocks. In particular, the responsiveness measure in (5.18) decreases with r. We use this fact in the discussion that follows.

5.3   Strategic Complementarity and Aggregate Inertia

With strategic complementarity $(r > 0)$, agents want to do what others do, making their actions more sensitive to the information others know. To achieve this goal, agents' actions strongly comove with public information. For $r > 0$, the optimal weighting in (5.16) sets $\gamma_z > \alpha_z$ so that actions react more to public signals z than beliefs. Moreover, γ_z increases with the value of coordination r. With extreme complementarity $(r = 1)$, all agents take the same action since welfare only depends on the closeness to others; agents completely ignore their private information $(\gamma_s = 0)$ because it would only cause their choices to diverge. The dependence on public information generates *aggregate inertia* or delays in adjusting aggregate variables to shocks. Even if agents' private information tells them to adjust to changing economic conditions, they wait for others to do so. Thus responsiveness to shocks is low.

Strategic complementarity arises naturally in Bertrand (price) competition since firms have incentives to coordinate price-setting. They set a higher price if the competitor's price is higher, and vice versa. Woodford (2003) introduces price complementary in the island model of Lucas (1972) discussed in section 4.3.1. Optimal prices not only depend on the state of nominal demand θ_t but also on the average level of prices charged by others a_t. Other strategic complementarity settings include increasing returns to aggregate investment, technology spillovers, or speculative attacks.

5.3.1   Application: Inertia in Price-Setting and Real Exchange Rates

The Lucas island model's results, discussed in section 4.3.1, are important because they describe how monetary policy can be used to manage the real economy. They embody an expectations-augmented Phillips curve—the idea that when inflation (or money growth) is higher than expected, the economy's output will be above trend. It is the inability to distinguish between aggregate and idiosyncratic changes in prices that creates a role for monetary policy to have real effects on economic activity. The problem with Lucas's explanation is that once producers produce and turn into consumers, they observe all posted prices. If the aggregate price level from period t is known in period $t + 1$, then the real effects of monetary policy should be only one-period lived. Yet, in the data, monetary policy has its greatest effect on output six quarters after the monetary shock, and after ten quarters, this effect is still one-third the size of the peak effect (Woodford, 2003; Christiano, Eichenbaum, and Evans, 2005).

Of course, one could argue about the length of periods in the Lucas model. But with all the statistics released daily through the prices in financial markets and published quarterly by government bureaus, it is difficult to defend the idea that aggregate price information is not available more than two years after the fact.

Woodford (2003) argues that public information about the aggregate price level is readily available. The friction is that firms cannot process all the data they observe. They can observe it freely, but figuring out what it means and how to use it to set their good's price requires capacity, in limited supply. This limited capacity is modeled as a noisy exogenous signal that each firm gets about the state of the economy, whose signal noise is independent of other firms' signals. That noisy signal informs firms about the current and past periods' states so that beliefs converge slowly to the truth.

Woodford makes a second important change to the Lucas model: he introduces complementarity into the payoff structure. It gives firms an incentive to coordinate price-setting. To coordinate effectively, they want to forecast other firms' beliefs. When data is private, learning about what others know is much slower than learning the value of an exogenous state variable. This is because higher-order beliefs are much more uncertain than first-order beliefs. This slow updating helps monetary policy shocks have long-lived effects. We can see this effect in (5.16) where the weight on private information is less than public information and decreases in the coordination motive r. More desire for coordination produces less weight or less prompt and vigorous response to private data.

Real Exchange Rate Dynamics   Candian (2019) applies the recipe for inertia—strategic complementarity and heterogenous information—in international trade to explain why real exchange rates are highly volatile and persistent. When producers face strategic complementarities in price-setting, uncertainty about competitors' beliefs generates sluggish price adjustments that can generate large and long-lived real exchange rate movements. The estimated model with US and Euro Area data shows that 50% of the persistence is due to the inertial dynamics of higher-order beliefs.

5.4   Infrequent Data Collection

While the previous model featured agents with noisy data, this model considers agents who either learn nothing or get perfectly accurate data. This type of model is better for explaining choices that stay fixed for a while. While noisy signals might explain why a choice does not react as much to a variable observed with noise, it rarely predicts no change. This model describes a learning process where information has a fixed cost, like the cost of looking something up. If you look up the answer, you get the correct answer. If you do not look it up, you get no information. This type of data cost is different because the resulting strategies are state-dependent. State-dependent rules are data choices that depend on what is currently happening—the state of the economy.

The following model introduces infrequent data collection and information updating to the tracking problem in (4.1).

Setup   Time is discrete and infinite. There is a continuum of agents $i \in [0, 1]$. Each agent chooses an action a_{it} to minimize its distance from an unknown stochastic target a_t^* that an agent with full information would set:

$$\mathcal{L} = \min_{\{a_{it},\, U_{it}\}} \mathbb{E}_0 \left[\sum_{t=0}^{\infty} \beta^t \left(\left(a_{it} - a_t^*\right)^2 + U_{it}\kappa_{it} \right) \Big| \mathcal{I}_{it} \right], \qquad (5.19)$$

where $U_{it} \in \{0, 1\}$ is the decision to update the information set $\mathcal{I}_{it}$ which requires paying an idiosyncratic cost $\kappa_{it} > 0$. The updating cost is realized at the beginning of period t. The target is a convex combination of an unobserved exogenous state θ_t and the average action a_t. The average action is defined as:

$$a_t^* = (1 - r)\theta_t + ra_t, \quad \text{with} \quad a_t = \int_i a_{it} \, di. \qquad (5.20)$$

The state follows a random walk $\theta_t = \theta_{t-1} + \varepsilon_t$ with i.i.d. innovations $\varepsilon_t \sim \mathcal{N}(0, \sigma^2)$.

Information Dynamics   We assume the binary updating cost from section 3.4:

$$\kappa_{it} = \begin{cases} \overline{\kappa} & \text{with prob.} \quad 1 - \lambda \\ 0 & \text{with prob.} \quad \lambda \end{cases} \quad \text{with} \quad \lambda \in [0, 1]. \qquad (5.21)$$

An agent who last updated in period $\hat{\tau}$ enters period t with an information set that contains state realizations from every period up to and including $\hat{\tau}$: $\mathcal{I}_{\hat{\tau}} = \{\theta_\tau\}_{\tau=0}^{\hat{\tau}}$. If an agent chooses to update in the current period ($U_{it} = 1$), their new information set will contain all state realizations up to and including the current state: $\mathcal{I}_{it} = \mathcal{I}_t = \{\theta_\tau\}_{\tau=0}^{t}$. If the agent does not update in the current period ($U_{it} = 0$), they will not observe any new information, even endogenous information such as the average action ($\mathcal{I}_{it} = \mathcal{I}_{i(t-1)}$). Individual information sets $\mathcal{I}_{it}$ evolve according to

$$\mathcal{I}_{it} = \begin{cases} \mathcal{I}_{\hat{\tau}} = \{\theta_\tau\}_{\tau=0}^{\hat{\tau}} & \text{if} \quad U_{it} = 0 \\ \mathcal{I}_t = \{\theta_\tau\}_{\tau=0}^{t} & \text{if} \quad U_{it} = 1. \end{cases} \qquad (5.22)$$

Equilibrium and Optimal Choices   The equilibrium consists of sequences of information choices $\{U_{it}\}$ and actions $\{a_{it}\}$ of every agent that are measurable with respect to their information set $\mathcal{I}_{it}$ and minimize (5.19), taking as given the choices of all other agents. The first-order condition dictates that agent i, who last updated at date $\hat{\tau}$, sets an action equal to the expected target at time t:

$$a_{it} = \mathbb{E}\left[a_t^*|\mathcal{I}_{\hat{\tau}}\right] = (1-r)\mathbb{E}\left[\theta_t|\mathcal{I}_{\hat{\tau}}\right] + r\mathbb{E}\left[a_t|\mathcal{I}_{\hat{\tau}}\right]. \tag{5.23}$$

Since the state is a random walk, $\mathbb{E}\left[\theta_t|\mathcal{I}_{\hat{\tau}}\right] = \theta_{\hat{\tau}}$. We guess and verify that the average action is also a random walk, $\mathbb{E}\left[a_t|\mathcal{I}_{\hat{\tau}}\right] = a_{\hat{\tau}}$. Let $\lambda_{t,\hat{\tau}}$ denote the measure of agents who last updated in period $\hat{\tau} \leq t$. Then the average action a_t is a weighted sum of the expected target of all agents:

$$a_t = \sum_{\tau=0}^{t} \lambda_{t,\tau}\mathbb{E}\left[a_t^*|\mathcal{I}_\tau\right] = \sum_{\tau=0}^{t} \lambda_{t,\tau}\left((1-r)\theta_\tau + ra_\tau\right). \tag{5.24}$$

Recursively substituting for a_τ reveals that the average action is a weighted sum of all past innovations:

$$a_t = \sum_{\tau=0}^{t} \frac{\Lambda_{t,\tau}(1-r)}{1-r\Lambda_{t,\tau}}\varepsilon_\tau, \tag{5.25}$$

where $\Lambda_{t,\hat{\tau}} \equiv \sum_{\tau=\hat{\tau}}^{t} \lambda_{t,\tau}$ denotes the measure of agents who last updated between dates $\hat{\tau}$ and t. Substituting (5.25) in (5.20) tells us that the target action is

$$a_t^* = \sum_{\tau=0}^{t} \frac{1-r}{1-r\Lambda_{t,\tau}}\varepsilon_\tau. \tag{5.26}$$

Agents who last updated at date $\hat{\tau}$ set their action to

$$a_{it} = \mathbb{E}\left[a_t^*|\mathcal{I}_{\hat{\tau}}\right] = \sum_{\tau=0}^{\hat{\tau}} \frac{1-r}{1-r\Lambda_{t,\tau}}\varepsilon_\tau. \tag{5.27}$$

Their expected one-period loss (which agents compare to the information-processing cost) depends on all the innovations since the last update:

$$\mathcal{L}_{t,\hat{\tau}} \equiv \mathbb{E}\left[(\mathbb{E}\left[a_t^*|\mathcal{I}_{\hat{\tau}}\right] - a_t^*|\mathcal{I}_{\hat{\tau}})^2\right] = \sum_{\tau=\hat{\tau}+1}^{t} \left(\frac{1-r}{1-r\Lambda_{t,\tau}}\right)^2 \sigma^2. \tag{5.28}$$

The longer since an agent updated their information, the higher the incentives to update in the current period. If data arrives exogenously, firms have no choice but to update at rate λ. In contrast, when data is actively chosen by paying the fixed cost κ_{it}, the updating policy consists of threshold dates such that agents who last updated at date $\hat{\tau} < \tau_t^*$ update at date t. In contrast, those who last updated at $\hat{\tau} > \tau_t^*$ find not updating to be strictly optimal.

Complementarity in Information Choice Expression (5.28) highlights the updating complementarity. For any $\tau = \hat{\tau} + 1, \ldots, t$, the one-period loss increases with the strategic motive parameter:

$$\frac{\partial \mathcal{L}_{t,\hat{\tau}}}{\partial \Lambda_{t,t-\tau}} > 0 \quad \Longleftrightarrow \quad r > 0. \tag{5.29}$$

When actions are complements $(r > 0)$, there is complementarity in information acquisition: the more agents are aware of a shock that has occurred since the agent last updated, the higher the per-period loss of not being aware of this shock. The complementarity in updating information delays adjusting to changing economic conditions, or *inertia*. The converse is true when actions are strategic substitutes $(r < 0)$. This general principle, discussed in the static games of section 5.2, reappears in dynamic settings.

5.4.1 Application: Price-Setting with Inattentiveness

Sticky information has been extensively used to explain observed inflation inertia because price-setting firms slowly update their information about money supply and demand. In Mankiw and Reis (2002) and Ball, Mankiw, and Reis (2005), firms passively update information on random dates. In Reis (2006b), the adjustment dates are actively chosen by paying an observation cost.

A simple version of these models builds on the quadratic-loss model from (5.19), reinterpreting actions as log prices.[2] There is a continuum of firms with measure one indexed by $i \in [0, 1]$. Each firm's objective is to minimize their loss function

$$\mathcal{L} = \min_{\{p_{it}, U_{it}\}} \mathbb{E}\left[\sum_{t=0}^{\infty} \beta^t \left((p_{it} - p_t^*)^2 + U_{it}\kappa \right) \Big| \mathcal{I}_{it} \right], \tag{5.30}$$

where p_{it} denotes firm i's (log-)price in period t; $U_{it} \in \{0, 1\}$ is its decision to acquire information (update); p_t^* is an unknown, stochastic target price that a

---

2. The quadratic objective function comes from a second-order approximation to a micro-founded model. Ball and Romer (1990) derive this price-setting model from first principles. A technical appendix to Hellwig and Veldkamp (2009) shows that their foundations produce the same objective in a setting with costly information.

firm with full information would set and $\beta \in (0, 1)$ is the firm's discount rate. For simplicity, $\kappa > 0$ is a constant updating cost.

As in New Keynesian models of monopolistic competition, the target price is

$$p_t^* = (1-r)m_t + rp_t, \tag{5.31}$$

where m_t is the log of nominal demand in period t; $m_t - p_t$ is the log of real demand, and $p_t = \int_0^1 p_{it}\, di$ is the average log price. The parameter $r > 0$ measures strategic complementarity or real rigidity in price setting. For simplicity, we assume that demand follows a random walk

$$m_t = m_{t-1} + \varepsilon_t, \qquad \varepsilon_t \sim \mathcal{N}(0, \sigma^2). \tag{5.32}$$

Coordination motives in actions (here, price-setting) imply coordination motives in information acquisition. This generates additional inertia, beyond that in Woodford (2003). The additional effect is that, as firms move away from perfect information, the value of any single firm becoming informed diminishes. As firms acquire information less frequently, prices become more sticky. Information complementarity is important because it delays price adjustment, which price-setting models are designed to explain.

The complementarity in updating delays price adjustment. To illustrate this, we next consider one particular equilibrium of this updating game which has been the focus of previous work (Reis, 2006b). In this equilibrium, updating decisions are *staggered*, meaning that all firms update after a fixed number of periods T, and each period a fraction $1/T$ of firms updates. This means that if $\tau < t - T$, then $\lambda_{t,\tau} = 0$ and $\Lambda_{t,\tau} = 1$, but if $t - T < \tau \le t$, then $\lambda_{t,\tau} = 1/T$ and $\Lambda_{t,\tau} = (t - \tau + 1)/T$. Therefore, a firm who last updated at date $\hat{\tau}$ has a one-period loss at date t

$$\mathcal{L}_{t,\hat{\tau}} = \begin{cases} \sigma^2 \sum_{v=1}^{t-\hat{\tau}} \left(\dfrac{1-r}{1-rv/T} \right)^2 & \text{if } \hat{\tau} > t - T \\[2mm] \mathcal{L}_{t,\hat{\tau}+1} + \sigma^2 & \text{if } \hat{\tau} \le t - T. \end{cases} \tag{5.33}$$

Complementarity $(r > 0)$ generates delays in price adjustment through two channels: First, because many other firms have prices based on old information, firms that update temper their reactions to recent information. This is the effect Woodford (2003) identified and it shows up here in equation (5.25). Second, complementarity reduces the frequency of information acquisition. This effect shows up as $\mathcal{L}_{t,\hat{\tau}}$ decreasing in r in equation (5.33). When pricing complementarity causes firms to temper their reactions to new information, the loss incurred from having old information is smaller. As other firms delay updating, this loss falls even more. Firms that update information less frequently have more inertia in their prices.

More generally, complementarity and covariance are mutually reinforcing. With more incomplete information, the covariance of average prices and demand falls. As that covariance decreases, demand innovations contain less information about changes in average price. If demand innovations are less helpful in coordinating price-setting, the incentive for a firm to update its information about demand diminishes. If firms update less, the covariance of prices and demand falls even further. This feedback is a crucial feature of the incomplete-information price-setting models that allows them to match the degree of price inertia in the data.

Alvarez, Lippi, and Paciello (2016) generalize this price-setting setup to allow for additional heterogeneity in observation costs, introducing κ_{it} instead of κ. This explains why we observe different distributions of the time between price changes across firms.

5.4.2 Further Applications of Infrequent Data Collection

Sticky information or infrequent data collection has been put forward as an explanation for the equity premium puzzle (Gabaix and Laibson, 2001) and the excess sensitivity and excess-smoothness puzzles of aggregate consumption (Reis, 2006a; Carroll et al., 2020). Auclert, Rognlie, and Straub (2020) show that embedding sticky expectations in a heterogeneous-agent New Keynesian model reconciles the micro and macro responses to monetary policy shocks.

On the empirical side, Klenow and Willis (2007) test inattentiveness models of price-setting by asking whether data revealed in past periods act as a shock to prices in the current period. In a similar exercise with asset prices, Hong, Torous, and Valkanov (2007) and Cohen and Frazzini (2008) find that industry information affects the market index value with a lag. Andrade and Le Bihan (2013) document that professional forecasters fail to systematically update their forecasts and disagree when updating, suggesting inattention.

Inattentiveness is often mixed with adjustment costs for actions by combining information updating with ideas and tools from the Ss literature. Bonomo and Carvalho (2004) and Alvarez, Lippi, and Paciello (2011, 2017) study price-setting problems in which firms pay an observation cost to discover their target price and a menu cost to change their price. Similarly, Álvarez, Guiso and Lippi (2012) and Abel, Eberly, and Panageas (2013) study portfolio choice in which investors pay an observation cost to reveal the value of a risky asset and a transaction cost to adjust their portfolio. In these papers, small information and adjustment costs generate infrequent adjustments, yielding long periods of inertia. (See section 4.4 for models that combine noisy signals with Ss models).

5.5 Strategic Substitutability and Aggregate Volatility

With strategic substitutability ($r < 0$), agents want to do the opposite of what others do. They weigh private signals more in their actions than in their beliefs $\gamma_s > \alpha_s$, and their actions strongly move with private information. Information substitutability generates overreaction in the adjustment of aggregate variables to shocks, or *aggregate volatility*. That is, responsiveness is high.

In which environments is it natural to observe strategic substitutability? Market clearing is one mechanism that generates strategic substitutability through the equilibrium movement of prices. For instance, when firms compete by choosing quantities through Cournot competition, if a firm increases its production, its good becomes more abundant, and their price decreases. Therefore, others want to produce less when one firm produces more. Similarly, consumers want to buy goods others do not want because the goods others demand will be more expensive. The same logic applies to financial investment since investors want to buy assets with low demand, low price, and high return. Lastly, models with returns to specialization are also situations in which agents want to behave differently from other agents.

5.5.1 Application: Hiring Decisions and Labor Market Volatility

Hiring decisions in frictional labor markets also feature strategic substitutability. The greater the aggregate number of job vacancies posted in the economy, the lower the incentive for an individual firm to post vacancies to hire workers. Venkateswaran (2014) examines this mechanism to explain the volatility in labor market outcomes. We present a simplified version highlighting the basic economic mechanism at work.

Setup The economy is populated by a unit measure of risk-neutral firms and workers. There are 2 periods $t = 1, 2$ and the future is discounted at the risk-free gross rate $R > 1$. Let N_{it} denote the mass of employed workers at a firm i in period t. At the beginning of period 1, workers and firms are uniformly matched, that is, $N_{i1} = 1$ for all firms i.

Each period, the firm's i output is produced according to decreasing returns-to-scale technology using labor as its only input:

$$Y_{it} = \exp(\theta_t + \omega_{it})N_{it}^{\alpha}. \tag{5.34}$$

Productivity has an aggregate θ_t and an idiosyncratic ω_{it} component. In period 1, both components are mean-zero, normally distributed random variables

$$\theta_1 \sim \mathcal{N}(0, \sigma_\theta^2) \quad \text{and} \quad \omega_{i1} \sim \mathcal{N}(0, \sigma_\omega^2). \tag{5.35}$$

Both productivity components are persistent and equal to

$$\theta_2 = \rho_\theta \theta_1 \quad \text{and} \quad \omega_{i2} = \rho_\omega \omega_{i1} \qquad (5.36)$$

where $\rho_\theta, \rho_\omega \in [0, 1]$ reflect the respective persistence of aggregate and idiosyncratic shocks. Assuming the law of large numbers applies to the cross-sectional distribution of ω_{i1}, then $\int \omega_{i1}\, di = 0$, that is, the idiosyncratic shocks wash out in the aggregate. Therefore, the only source of aggregate uncertainty in this economy is θ_1.

Hiring Decisions as Strategic Substitutes   After period-1 production, all worker-firm matches are destroyed. Firms must engage in a frictional hiring process characterized by random matching in a single labor market. Firms post vacancies V_i at unit marginal cost. The matching process between vacancies and potential employees is described by a constant returns-to-scale aggregate matching function $M(U, V)$, which inputs the mass of unemployed U and the total number of vacancies posted in the economy $V = \int V_i\, di$. The mass of successful matches is

$$M(U, V) = \zeta U^\gamma V^{1-\gamma} = \zeta V^{1-\gamma}, \qquad (5.37)$$

where ζ is the matching efficiency and $\gamma \in [0, 1]$ is the elasticity of the matching function to unemployment. The last equality follows from the assumption that all matches are destroyed in period 1, which leads to $U = 1$. The vacancy filling rate of all firms equals $M/V = \zeta V^{-\gamma}$. Thus, if firm i posts V_i vacancies, its employment in period 2 equals

$$N_{i2} = \zeta V_i V^{-\gamma}. \qquad (5.38)$$

The number of new hires each vacancy generates decreases with economy-wide hiring, reflecting congestion and rendering hiring decisions strategic substitutes. The strength of the strategic substitutability is embedded in the parameter γ. If $\gamma = 0$, then a firm's vacancy yield (how much it hires) is independent of what other firms do; if $\gamma = 1$, then the vacancy yield is proportional to the ratio V_i/V.

In both periods, wages are determined by a simple bargaining game. In the first period, the firm holds all the bargaining power and appropriates the entire output. In period 2, with probability χ, the firm gets to make a take-it-or-leave-it zero-wage offer to the workers, and with probability $1 - \chi$, the workers make a zero-profit offer to the firm. Given this wage protocol, expected profits in the two periods are

$$\pi_{i1} = \mathbb{E}_i[Y_{i1}] - V_i = \mathbb{E}_i[\exp(\theta_1 + \omega_{i1})] - V_i \qquad (5.39)$$

$$\pi_{i2} = \chi \mathbb{E}_i[Y_{i2}] + (1 - \chi)0 = \chi \mathbb{E}_i\left[\exp(\theta_2 + \omega_{i2})\left(\zeta V_i V^{-\gamma}\right)^\alpha\right] \quad (5.40)$$

where $\mathbb{E}_i$ denotes expectations of firm i. The problem of each firm consists of choosing the number of vacancies to post V_i to maximize its expected discounted stream of profits

$$\max_{V_i} \quad \pi_{i1} + \frac{1}{R}\pi_{i2}, \tag{5.41}$$

subject to (5.39) and (5.40). The first-order condition for optimality equalizes the marginal cost of a vacancy, on the left side, with the expected marginal value of vacancy posting, on the right side:

$$1 = \frac{\chi\alpha\zeta^\alpha}{R} V_i^{\alpha-1} \mathbb{E}\left[\exp(\theta_2 + \omega_{i2})V^{-\alpha\gamma}\right]. \tag{5.42}$$

Denote log vacancies as $v_i \equiv \log V_i$ and aggregate log vacancies as $v \equiv \int v_i \, di$.[3] Take logs of (5.42) and rewrite as

$$(1-\alpha)v_i = \log(\chi\alpha\zeta^\alpha/R) + \log\mathbb{E}_i\left[\exp(\theta_2 + \omega_{i2} - \alpha\gamma v)\right]. \tag{5.43}$$

Next, we need to compute the expectation. To do it, we conjecture firms' beliefs about aggregate vacancies v. We use the method of undetermined coefficients and guess and verify an affine relationship between aggregate log vacancies with the aggregate shock $v = \bar{\phi} + \phi\theta_1$. Under this guess, and noting that total productivity is a normal random variable, we compute the expectation using properties of the lognormal distribution in expression (A.16) as follows:

$$\mathbb{E}_i\left[\exp\left(\theta_2 + \omega_{i2} - \alpha\gamma v\right)\right]$$

$$= \exp\left(\mathbb{E}_i\left[\theta_2 + \omega_{i2} - \alpha\gamma v\right] + \frac{1}{2}\text{Var}_i\left[\theta_2 + \omega_{i2} - \alpha\gamma v\right]\right)$$

$$= \exp\left(-\alpha\gamma\bar{\phi} + (\rho_\theta - \alpha\gamma\phi)\mathbb{E}_i[\theta_1] + \rho_\omega\mathbb{E}_i[\omega_{i1}]\right)$$

$$\times \exp\left(\frac{1}{2}\left((\rho_\theta^2 + \alpha^2\gamma^2\phi^2)\sigma_\theta^2 + \rho_\omega^2\sigma_\omega^2\right)\right),$$

where we have substituted (5.36) and the guess for total vacancies. Substituting the expectations back into (5.43) yields the optimal vacancy choice as a function of beliefs about aggregate and idiosyncratic productivity:

$$v_i = \frac{\rho_\theta - \alpha\gamma\phi}{1-\alpha}\mathbb{E}_i[\theta_1] + \frac{\rho_\omega}{1-\alpha}\mathbb{E}_i[\omega_{i1}] - \frac{\alpha\gamma\bar{\phi}}{1-\alpha} + \Omega, \tag{5.44}$$

3. Note that $v = \int \log V_i \, di \neq \log \int V_i \, di = \log V$ because of Jensen's inequality applied to a concave function, see appendix A.2.

where $\Omega \equiv \frac{1}{1-\alpha} \log(\chi \alpha \zeta^{\alpha}/R) + \frac{1}{2(1-\alpha)} \left((\rho_{\theta}^2 + \alpha^2 \gamma^2 \phi^2)\sigma_{\theta}^2 + \rho_{\omega}^2 \sigma_{\omega}^2 \right)$ is a constant term. Optimal vacancy posting increases with the beliefs about aggregate and idiosyncratic productivity at a rate proportional to the persistence of the shocks ρ_{θ} and ρ_{ω}. However, because of strategic substitutability arising from labor market congestion, the responsiveness to the perceived aggregate productivity is dampened by the term $-\alpha \gamma \phi$. The dampening effect is stronger the larger the elasticity of the individual hiring to aggregate vacancies (γ) and the response of aggregate vacancies to aggregate productivity (ϕ). Depending on the strength of this congestion effect relative to the persistence of aggregate productivity, hiring increases or decreases with the perceived aggregate shock.

Abundant Data   As a useful benchmark, we first characterize the solution under abundant data, in which firms observe the components of their productivity separately. This means that $\mathbb{E}_i[\theta_1] = \theta_1$ and $\mathbb{E}_i[\omega_{i1}] = \omega_{i1}$. Substituting these values into (5.44), integrating across all firms, and using $\int \omega_{i1} \, di = 0$, we obtain:

$$v = \frac{\rho_{\theta} - \alpha \gamma \phi}{1 - \alpha} \theta_1 - \frac{\alpha \gamma \overline{\phi}}{1 - \alpha} + \Omega. \qquad (5.45)$$

The affine conjecture $v = \overline{\phi} + \phi \theta_1$ is verified by matching coefficients:

$$\phi = \frac{\rho_{\theta} - \alpha \gamma \phi}{1 - \alpha}, \quad \text{and} \quad \overline{\phi} = -\frac{\alpha \gamma \overline{\phi}}{1 - \alpha} + \Omega. \qquad (5.46)$$

Therefore, optimal vacancy posting expressed in terms of fundamental parameters is

$$v = \frac{\rho_{\theta}}{1 - \alpha + \alpha \gamma} \theta_1 + \frac{1 - \alpha}{1 - \alpha + \alpha \gamma} \Omega. \qquad (5.47)$$

The responsiveness of aggregate log vacancies—their covariance with aggregate shocks relative to aggregate volatility—equals

$$\frac{\mathbb{C}ov[v, \theta_1]}{\mathbb{V}ar[\theta_1]} = \frac{\rho_{\theta}}{1 - \alpha + \alpha \gamma}. \qquad (5.48)$$

Thus vacancies' responsiveness to the (known) aggregate shock increases with its persistence ρ_{θ} and decreases with the strength of congestion effects reflected in the vacancy yield elasticity γ.

Scarce Data   Next, we assume that, before making hiring decisions, firms only observe data about the total period-1 productivity $\theta_1 + \omega_{i1}$. Thus firms face a signal extraction problem to disentangle aggregate from transitory

shocks, as discussed in section 4.3. To construct beliefs about each component, we use Bayesian updating formulas

$$\mathbb{E}_i[\theta_1] = K(\theta_1 + \omega_{i1}) \quad \text{and} \quad \mathbb{E}_i[\omega_{i1}] = (1 - K)(\theta_1 + \omega_{i1})$$

$$\text{with} \quad K \equiv \frac{\sigma_\theta^2}{\sigma_\theta^2 + \sigma_\omega^2}, \tag{5.49}$$

where the weights K reflect the relative volatility of the shocks. Thus firms
mistakenly attribute their observations to both components, exactly as in the
Lucas (1972) island model discussed in section 4.3.1. With similar steps as
before, we substitute the beliefs, integrate across firms, and match coefficients,
to obtain

$$v = \frac{K\rho_\theta + (1 - K)\rho_\omega}{1 - \alpha + \alpha\gamma K}\theta_1 + \frac{1 - \alpha}{1 - \alpha + \alpha\gamma}\Omega. \tag{5.50}$$

The solution nests the case with abundant data for $K = 1$. Responsiveness of
vacancies to aggregate productivity is now

$$\frac{\mathbb{C}ov[v, \theta_1]}{\mathbb{V}ar[\theta_1]} = \frac{K\rho_\theta + (1 - K)\rho_\omega}{1 - \alpha + \alpha\gamma K}. \tag{5.51}$$

Key Result: Labor Market Volatility Comparing the responsiveness with
abundant data in (5.48) and scarce data in (5.51) reveals two important results. First, because shocks cannot be observed separately, vacancies'
responsiveness depends on the convex combination of the persistence of both
shocks (in the numerator). This implies that if idiosyncratic shocks are more
persistent than aggregate shocks, $\rho_\omega > \rho_\theta$, vacancies move more with productivity than in the perfect information case. Second, since scarce data affects the
expectations about aggregate labor market conditions, firms underestimate
the strength of congestion effects. This is reflected in a smaller denominator as the congestion term $\alpha\gamma$ is now multiplied by $K < 1$, which dampens it.
Because of strategic substitutability in hiring decisions, underestimating congestion increases the response of individual vacancy postings. In the aggregate,
both effects increase the volatility of aggregate vacancies.

Venkateswaran (2014) shows that the basic mechanism extends to considering different matching protocols between workers and firms (random
versus directed search) and additional features that allow the model to match
various empirical patterns. In particular, it can explain the significant volatility of vacancies observed in the data, which is hard to explain within the
standard search and matching framework (also known as the Shimer (2005)
puzzle).

5.6   Data Choice in Strategic Settings

In settings with strategic behavior in actions, an agent's choice to acquire data depends on others' data acquisition. Hellwig and Veldkamp (2009) introduce data choice in the mean-field game in (5.6) from section 5.2. Agents can choose private or public data precision. Choosing public data precision requires wrestling with some conceptual issues discussed below.

Setup   Agents choose their actions a_i to match an unknown target that depends on the exogenous state θ and the average action in the economy $a = \int_i a_i \, di$. But before playing the action game, agents choose how much to pay to acquire a common signal $z \sim \mathcal{N}\left(\theta, \tau_z^{-1}\right)$ and/or a private signal $s \sim \mathcal{N}\left(\theta, \tau_s^{-1}\right)$. The cost of information acquisition $\kappa(\tau_z, \tau_s)$ is increasing, convex, and twice differentiable in signal precisions.

Each agent solves the following problem:

$$\mathcal{L} = \min_{a_i, \tau_z, \tau_s} \; \mathbb{E}\left[(1-r)(a_i - \theta)^2 + r(a_i - a)^2 \middle| z, s_i\right] + \kappa(\tau_z, \tau_s). \quad (5.52)$$

The interpretation of the private signal choice s is straightforward. For example, the agent might choose how much independent research to do about the state θ. The common signal requires some explanation because common information is only truly common if all agents know it, meaning they must choose to observe it. Suppose that every agent gets an identical newspaper delivered to their door. Each agent begins at the start of page 1 and decides how far to read. Each additional word provides additional information, so the choice of the number of words is a choice of signal precision. Of course, the number of words is an integer. So, imagine a limiting version of this environment where words become less informative and less costly to read at the same rate. This limit economy approximates the continuous choice of signal precision examined below.

Solving the Model   We solve for a symmetric equilibrium: a precision τ_s^* or τ_z^*, common to all agents. Using backward induction, we solve the action game and compute the expected utility as a function of an individual's information precision. That expected utility is the objective in the first-stage information choice game.

Solving the second-stage action game requires distinguishing between an individual agent's data precision and the precision of all other agents' data. This distinction is important. An agent can only choose their own data precision, not others'. The optimal choice of data may differ greatly from the true solution if one does not respect this distinction. This is similar to big-K, little-k problems in macroeconomic models of capital investment choice.[4]

Let τ_s^*, τ_z^* be the data choice of all other agents and τ_s, τ_z be agent i's data choice. Since one agent has zero mass, the other agents are playing a game where the average agent has the same precision data as they do. Their optimal actions are given by the weights γ_s^* and γ_z^* on private and public information, as given in (5.16). In contrast, the agent choosing their own data precision takes the form of the average action as given and chooses their own optimal action given information precision τ_s and τ_z. Call the weights that solve this problem $\tilde{\gamma}_s$ and $\tilde{\gamma}_z$, so that $a_i = (1 - \tilde{\gamma}_s - \tilde{\gamma}_z)\mu_\theta + \tilde{\gamma}_s s_i + \tilde{\gamma}_z z$.

The next step is to compute the expected utility. When agents choose the amount of public data to acquire, the solution must treat the case where the agent is considering acquiring more public data than others separately from the case where they consider acquiring less. With some algebra, we can express the first term in expected utility (5.52) as

$$\mathbb{E}[(a_i - \theta)^2] = (1 - \tilde{\gamma}_s - \tilde{\gamma}_z)^2 \tau_\theta^{-1} + \tilde{\gamma}_s^2 \tau_s^{-1} + \tilde{\gamma}_z^2 \tau_z^{-1}. \qquad (5.53)$$

The second term in utility is the distance of one's action from the average action $\mathbb{E}[(a_i - a)^2]$. This is the term that depends on whether the agent observes more public signals than others do or not. If $\tau_z \leq \tau_z^*$, then others observe more public signals than what i knows. Let z^* be the public signal others see. The additional data that others observe and i does not, $(z^* - z)$, has signal noise that is uncorrelated with the noise in z, $(z - \theta)$. Thus,

$$\mathbb{E}[(a_i - a)^2] = \tilde{\gamma}_s^2 \tau_s^{-1} + (-\tilde{\gamma}_s + \gamma_s^* - \tilde{\gamma}_z + \gamma_z^*)^2 \tau_\theta^{-1} + (\tilde{\gamma}_z - \gamma_z^*)^2 \tau_z^{-1}$$
$$+ (\gamma_z^*)^2 (\tau_z^* - \tau_z)^{-1}. \qquad (5.54)$$

However, if $\tau_z \geq \tau_z^*$, then the additional public information that i learns, beyond what others know, is effectively private. Thus $z - z^*$ is treated like private information in agents' actions and expected utility. Let $\dot{\gamma}_s$ be the optimal weight on $s_i + z - z^*$, which is a private signal with precision $(\tau_s + \tau_z - \tau_z^*)$. Likewise, let $\dot{\gamma}_z$ be i's optimal weight on the information that is common knowledge, z^*.

$$\mathbb{E}[(a_i - a)^2] = \dot{\gamma}_s^2 (\tau_s + \tau_z - \tau_z^*)^{-1} + (-\dot{\gamma}_s + \gamma_s^* - \dot{\gamma}_z + \gamma_z^*)^2 \tau_\theta^{-1}$$
$$+ (\dot{\gamma}_z - \gamma_z^*)^2 (\tau_z^*)^{-1} \qquad (5.55)$$

The negative sum of $\mathbb{E}[(a_i - \theta)^2]$ and either (5.55) or (5.54) is the objective function when an agent chooses data.

---

4. See Ljungqvist and Sargent (2018), Chapter 12.

The solution has a useful feature: Expected utility does not depend on signal realizations. It only depends on the precision of each signal and the equilibrium weights of each signal in the action game. Even with heterogeneous prior beliefs (means differed), there would be no uncertainty about anyone's expected utility from additional information.[5]

Data Choice Mirrors Strategic Motives in Actions   The main result is that the strategic motives in data choice mirror the strategic motives in actions. If actions are strategic complements $(r > 0)$, then data acquisition is also complementary. Conversely, if actions are strategic substitutes $(r < 0)$, then data is a strategic substitute as well.

Let the marginal value of private data τ_s and public data τ_z be

$$B\left(\tau_s\right) = -\frac{\partial}{\partial \tau_s}\mathcal{L}\left(\tau_s, \tau_z; \tau_s^*, \tau_z^*\right) \tag{5.56}$$

$$B\left(\tau_z\right) = -\frac{\partial}{\partial \tau_z}\mathcal{L}\left(\tau_s, \tau_z; \tau_s^*, \tau_z^*\right). \tag{5.57}$$

Hellwig and Veldkamp (2009) prove the following results hold:

$$r > 0 \iff \frac{\partial}{\partial \tau_s^*}B(\tau_s),\ \frac{\partial}{\partial \tau_z^*}B(\tau_z) > 0$$

$$r = 0 \iff \frac{\partial}{\partial \tau_s^*}B(\tau_s),\ \frac{\partial}{\partial \tau_z^*}B(\tau_z) = 0$$

$$r < 0 \iff \frac{\partial}{\partial \tau_s^*}B(\tau_s),\ \frac{\partial}{\partial \tau_z^*}B(\tau_z) < 0.$$

The result says that strategic motives in actions generate strategic motives in data choice. Data changes the economy's *responsiveness to shocks*, defined in (5.18) as the covariance of the average action with the state, normalized by fundamental volatility: $\mathbb{C}ov[a, \theta]/\mathbb{V}ar[\theta]$. Intuitively, what is going on is that data changes the covariance between the average action and the state. That is what makes information more or less valuable.

When actions exhibit complementarity $(r > 0)$ and other agents have precise data (high $\tau_z + \tau_s$), responsiveness $\mathbb{C}ov(a, s)$ is high. When the average action and the state covary, the agent faces more payoff uncertainty because if the chosen action turns out to be far from θ, it will also be far from a, and the agent will be penalized twice. This added utility risk raises the value of accurate data. Data acquisition is complementary. Correlation in information

5. This feature of the problem is similar to the model of the data feedback economy in Chapter 9 and will help to keep that recursive problem tractable.

choice induces further correlation in actions, such as financial investment (Veldkamp, 2006a), production (Veldkamp and Wolfers, 2007), and price-setting (Gorodnichenko, 2008).

Conversely, when actions are substitutes ($r < 0$) and other agents have precise data (high $\tau_z + \tau_s$), responsiveness $\mathbb{C}ov(a, s)$ is again high, meaning that if the agent chooses an action that turns out to be far from θ, it will also be far from a. But in this case, that covariance reduces payoff uncertainty: Taking an action far from a confers a utility benefit while being far from the state θ incurs a utility cost. The cost and benefit partially cancel each other. The risk of being far from the state θ hedges the risk of taking action close to a. This hedging reduces the variability of overall utility. When others know more, the state and average action are more aligned and offset each other more effectively. The offset dampens utility fluctuations, and less utility risk lowers the data value. Thus, information is a strategic substitute because its value is less when others acquire more. Exploring strategic substitutability in information has a long tradition in the portfolio choice literature, starting with Grossman and Stiglitz (1980).

5.6.1   Application: Data in First-Price Auctions

Another setting where agents have strategic complementarity is in first-price auctions. First-price auctions are also called *pay-what-you-bid* auctions. If a bidder's bid is among the highest, they get the units they bid for at the price they bid. Low bids get few or no units. The logic of complementarity is as follows: If other bidders bid low, then you can bid low, still win an allocation at the auction, and pay less. If other bidders bid high, you should raise your bid if it is below your willingness to pay to improve your chances of winning. This is complementarity in bidding.

Cole, Neuhann, and Ordoñez (2022) explore the role of asymmetric information—or private data—in first-price auctions. They argue that data acquisition can trigger cross-border contagion in financial crises. The key mechanism for this contagion is the complementarity in information acquisition. When other bidders acquire information about an asset's value, that makes those bids less predictable to an uninformed bidder. The additional uncertainty about others' bids motivates the bidder also to acquire information. In other words, others' purchases of information generate strategic uncertainty and risk, which in turn creates a complementarity in the desire to acquire data.

The last twist in this theory is that contagion may happen even if the value of assets in different countries is uncorrelated. When bidders start acquiring information about Italy, other bidders have two choices. Either they become informed themselves (the complementarity described above) or move funds to another country with less informed bidders, say Spain. But since now some bidders are more exposed to Spanish bonds, the value of getting informed in Spain increases, and then Spain can move into a regime of intensive information acquisition. The information moves this way across countries, following capital flows, causing a cascade of price changes.

5.7 Games with Correlated Data

Hellwig, Kohls, and Veldkamp (2012) consider data signals that can be purely private, purely public, or correlated. Before playing a mean-field game like the one described above, agents can choose how much and what type of data to acquire. Introducing correlated data creates a new complication in the problem. Agents need to form expectations both about the state and about the public component of their signal. When a purely public signal is observed, everyone knows what that public signal is. When signals are purely private, there is no public signal, creating a common shock to the average action. But when signals are correlated, there is a public component to the signal that matters for the average action but is not separately observed. Correlated signals about the state contain information about the state and the common shock that makes the signal correlated.

Correlated signals can be described as a vector that is a weighted sum of the state, some signal noise that is common to all agents, plus some private signal noise. Varying the weights of the private and public noise regulates the degree of correlation:

$$s_i = \theta + A_i \eta_z + B_i \eta_{si} \tag{5.58}$$

where $\eta_z \sim \mathcal{N}(0, I_N)$, $\eta_{si} \sim_{iid} \mathcal{N}(0, I_N)$ are $N \times 1$ vectors, and A_i and B_i are $N \times N$ matrices that agents might choose. Or, one can think of A and B being exogenous matrices common to all agents, but where agents choose which elements of the vector s_i to observe. This would be like choosing which newspaper or website to read. The term η_z is often called sender noise because it is transmitted to all observers of this signal, while η_{si} is receiver noise because each signal recipient adds different noise.

The key to forming beliefs about the pair $[\theta, \eta_z]$ is to use the state-space methods from Chapter 2.2.2. It is simple to describe signals as weights on the exogenous shocks $[\theta, \eta_z, \eta_{s1}, \ldots, \eta_{sN}]$. Applying the formulas for state-space updating allows one to easily form beliefs about the state and the common shock z, to include in the optimal strategy of the games described above.

Key Ideas

- When agents have heterogeneous information and interact strategically, they care about what others believe and what others believe that they believe. This infinite-order of beliefs problem is called "forecasting the forecasts of others."
- Beliefs about the aggregate state can serve as a sufficient statistic for others' forecasts.
- Data choices in strategic settings typically inherit the strategic motives in actions: If actions are complements, agents want to learn what others know. If actions are substitutes, agents prefer private information or learning at times when others learn less.

Practice Questions

5.1 In the mean-field game in section 5.2, suppose there is only a public signal: $z = \theta + \eta_z$, where $\eta_z \sim \mathcal{N}(0, \tau_z^{-1})$ and $\theta \sim \mathcal{N}(\mu_\theta, \tau_\theta^{-1})$. Solve for the firm's optimal action a_i^*.

5.2 In the case of heterogeneous incomplete information, express the optimal action in equation (5.14) in terms of r, μ_θ, s_i, and z. Show that the coefficients on μ_θ add up to $1 - \gamma_z - \gamma_s$. (*Hint: Use* $\alpha_s + \alpha_\theta + \alpha_z = 1$.) Interpret this fact. What does it tell us about the relationship between signals and actions?

5.3 Show that the loss function under the optimal actions takes the form in (5.17).

5.4 In the model of data choice of section 5.6, show that when actions are complements $r > 0$, it is not optimal for one agent to deviate from a symmetric equilibrium by acquiring more or less public information than other agents do.

5.5 Suppose an agent has a choice over the precision of a correlated signal that takes the form $v_i = s_i + z$, where s_i and z are signals about θ with equal precision, and where s_i is private and z is public in the sense of section 5.6. The utility is given by equation (5.52), and actions are strategic substitutes $(r < 0)$. What level of signal precision constitutes an equilibrium?

5.6 Construct an example where higher-order beliefs have more cross-sectional dispersion than first-order beliefs.

6
Using Data to Guide Investment

This chapter explores settings where there is at least one risky investment, and possibly many, and an agent needs to choose how much to invest. Of course, a common application is financial investing, where an investor chooses how much equity or debt of various firms to hold and how much to keep in cash. But it can also represent the problem of a firm choosing how much of each good to produce when the demand or cost of that good is unknown. We will explore the equivalence between some portfolio choice problems and auction models with common or correlated values. Since new data technologies are forecasting technologies, it is natural to study the use and choice of data in a class of models where uncertain outcomes are central. This framework will provide us with one way of valuing a data set.

In this chapter, we begin with a classic portfolio choice problem for an investor that already has some data and is deciding how to use it to guide their investment. Next, we ask what such an investor's expected utility is and how happy they would expect to be if they had a particular data set. That expected utility is the expected payoff, or value, to obtaining that particular data set. Once we know the value of data, we can add a cost function for data and explore data choice. Along the way, we will explore the assumptions of the noisy rational expectations equilibrium (often referred to as NREE) framework we are building on. Subsequent chapters will add market power and data intermediation to this model to explore the relationship between data and market power.

Following Van Nieuwerburgh and Veldkamp (2010), we introduce a general framework of the NREE model for multiple assets in the market. The framework consists of two chronological stages: in the first stage, data is priced and investors choose what information to gather; in the second stage, the information is treated as exogenous and imperfectly aggregated as the market prices of the assets. In the following, we derive the second-stage equilibrium price at time-1 based on exogenous information and then solve for the first-stage game by valuing the data at time-0.

6.1   Modeling Investment Choice with Data

This model is a modified version of Admati (1985), with a different prior information structure. Agents' data set is taken as given. We are solving for the optimal choice of risky assets for each agent to hold and the equilibrium price of those assets.

Setup   There are N risky assets with payoffs given by the $N \times 1$ random vector $f \sim \mathcal{N}(\mu, \Sigma)$, which is exogenous but unknown, serving as the common prior beliefs in the economy. There is a riskless asset with a return $r \geq 1$.

This is a perfectly competitive market. There is a continuum of agents indexed by $i \in [0, 1]$, each with zero mass. The agent i has an initial wealth W_{0i}. Consider the mean-variance preferences[1]

$$\mathbb{E}[U_i | \mathcal{I}_i] = \mathbb{E}[W_i | \mathcal{I}_i] - \frac{\rho}{2} \mathbb{V}ar[W_i | \mathcal{I}_i], \qquad (6.1)$$

where ρ is the absolute risk aversion and W_i is the final wealth of individual i. Their budget constraint is

$$W_i = (W_{0i} - q_i'p)r + q_i'f, \qquad (6.2)$$

where q_i is the $N \times 1$ vector of asset shares agent i chooses to hold and p is the $N \times 1$ vector of risky asset prices. In the static model, the agents are endowed with data that takes the form of private signals about asset payoffs. As we discuss later, we can combine this data into one composite signal that takes the form

$$s_i = f + \varepsilon_i, \quad \varepsilon_i \sim_{iid} \mathcal{N}(0, \Sigma_{\varepsilon_i}). \qquad (6.3)$$

Note that asset payoffs may be correlated with other asset payoffs. Signals have noise that is correlated with other signals' noise. In other words, neither Σ nor Σ_{ε_i} need to be diagonal.

The supply $\bar{x} + x$ of risky assets is random, where $\bar{x}$ is known and $x \sim \mathcal{N}(0, \sigma_x^2 I)$.

Equilibrium   An equilibrium is a set of optimal portfolios q_i for each investor i and a vector of asset prices p such that

  (i) Investors choose q_i to maximize $\mathbb{E}[U_i | \mathcal{I}_i]$ subject to (6.2);
  (ii) Investors form beliefs according to Bayes' Law after observing their data and the prices $\mathcal{I}_i = \{s_i, p\}$;

---

1. Exponential utility, $U_i = -e^{-\rho W_i}$, would deliver the same optimal portfolio choice (6.5) and the same equilibrium price solution as mean-variance preferences. This version simplifies data choices later in the chapter.

(iii) The market price p equates the total demand $\int_0^1 q_i \, di$ with the supply $\bar{x} + x$.

To solve for the equilibrium, we follow six steps.

Step 1: Compute Expected Utility, Given the Portfolio   Substitute the budget constraint (6.2) into (6.1) to rewrite utility as

$$\mathbb{E}[U_i|\mathcal{I}_i] = (W_{0i} - q_i'p)r + q_i'\mathbb{E}[f|\mathcal{I}_i] - \frac{\rho}{2}q_i'\mathbb{V}ar[f|\mathcal{I}_i]q_i. \qquad (6.4)$$

Step 2: Optimal Portfolio Choice   Since the mean-variance objective is concave in q_i, the first-order condition, $\partial\mathbb{E}[U_i|\mathcal{I}_i]/\partial q_i = 0$, delivers investor i's optimal portfolio. Differentiating (6.4) with respect to q_i and setting it to zero yields $-pr + \mathbb{E}[f|\mathcal{I}_i] - \rho\mathbb{V}ar[f|\mathcal{I}_i]q_i = 0$. Rearranging to solve for q_i reveals that the optimal portfolio choice is

$$q_i = \frac{1}{\rho}\mathbb{V}ar[f|\mathcal{I}_i]^{-1}\left(\mathbb{E}[f|\mathcal{I}_i] - pr\right). \qquad (6.5)$$

Step 3: Extract Information from Asset Prices   A characteristic feature of noisy rational expectations models is that agents learn from the equilibrium price. We discuss the realism of this assumption in the next subsection. As a practical matter, the assumption that agents can extract an informative signal from prices creates a dilemma: How do we figure out what prices convey without first solving for equilibrium prices? But how can we solve for equilibrium prices without knowing agents' beliefs, which determine their demands? Agents' beliefs depend on the price information they see. This is referred to as a fixed-point problem, where each part of the problem depends on the solution to the other part. The way around this dilemma is to guess a solution to one part of the problem, use the guess to solve the other part, and then go back and solve that guess.

Therefore, we guess (and later verify) that the price is a linear function of the asset payoffs f and the supply shocks x:

$$p = A + Bf + Cx. \qquad (6.6)$$

This price is an $N \times 1$ vector that reports the price per share of each of the N assets. The $N \times 1$ vector A and the $N \times N$ matrices B and C are unknown coefficients that we will have to solve for. When we solve for the coefficients, we will verify that the linear conjecture (6.6) is indeed an equilibrium.

Since the prices depend, in part, on the realized payoffs f, these prices contain information about f. But because the prices depend on the unknown supply shock x, prices are noisy signals about payoffs. In order to extract the information about f, we need to transform the price to make it an unbiased signal about f. To do this, we divide the price by any term that multiplies f and subtract additive terms that are not mean-zero random variables (see section 2.1.3). Thus, the unbiased price signal that investors learn from is

$$s_p = B^{-1}(p - A) = f + B^{-1}Cx. \tag{6.7}$$

This signal is a linear transformation of the price. It is also equal to the true payoff, plus the signal noise, which is $B^{-1}Cx$. Since the supply shock x was distributed $\mathcal{N}(0, \sigma_x^2 I)$ and is pre-multiplied by the coefficients $B^{-1}C$, the signal noise is still mean zero, but with a variance that is the coefficients squared, times the variance of the shock x. In other words, $B^{-1}Cx \sim \mathcal{N}(0, \Sigma_p)$, where

$$\Sigma_p \equiv B^{-1}C(B^{-1}C)'\sigma_x^2 \tag{6.8}$$

denotes the variance-covariance matrix of the noise in the signals extracted from the N prices.

Step 4: Update Beliefs with Bayes' Law   We use Bayes' Law to combine the prior beliefs of f and the information $\mathcal{I}_i$ to form the posterior beliefs, or conditional mean and variance. Recall that the conditional expectation for normal variables is the weighted average of the prior and each signal, where each is weighted by their relative precision. In this case, the prior mean of f is the mean μ. There are two signals: one comes from the data, s_i in (6.3), and the other is the signal extracted from the price level, s_p in (6.7). Posterior beliefs are:

$$\mathbb{E}[f|\mathcal{I}_i] = \mathbb{V}ar[f|\mathcal{I}_i](\Sigma^{-1}\mu + \Sigma_{\varepsilon_i}^{-1}s_i + \Sigma_p^{-1}s_p), \tag{6.9}$$

$$\mathbb{V}ar[f|\mathcal{I}_i]^{-1} = \Sigma^{-1} + \Sigma_{\varepsilon_i}^{-1} + \Sigma_p^{-1}. \tag{6.10}$$

The second equation also follows from Bayes' Law for normal variables (see section 2.1.1). It reflects the rule that the conditional precision—the inverse of the variance—is the sum of the prior precision and the precision of each signal observed. Next, we substitute the conditional mean and variance into the optimal portfolio choice (6.5):

$$q_i = \frac{1}{\rho}\mathbb{V}ar[f|\mathcal{I}_i]^{-1}\left(\mathbb{V}ar[f|\mathcal{I}_i](\Sigma^{-1}\mu + \Sigma_{\varepsilon_i}^{-1}s_i + \Sigma_p^{-1}s_p) - pr\right)$$

$$= \frac{1}{\rho}\left(\Sigma^{-1}\mu + \Sigma_{\varepsilon_i}^{-1}s_i + \Sigma_p^{-1}B^{-1}(p - A) - \mathbb{V}ar[f|\mathcal{I}_i]^{-1}pr\right). \tag{6.11}$$

Step 5: Equate Supply and Demand   To solve for the asset price, we impose the market clearing condition

$$\int_0^1 q_i \, di = \bar{x} + x.$$

Substituting (6.11) for the asset demand q_i yields

$$\frac{1}{\rho} \int_0^1 \left(\Sigma^{-1}\mu + \Sigma_{\varepsilon_i}^{-1}s_i + \Sigma_p^{-1}B^{-1}(p-A) - \mathbb{V}ar[f|\mathcal{I}_i]^{-1}pr \right) di = \bar{x} + x.$$
(6.12)

To integrate this over the continuum of investors i, notice the signal from i data times its precision, $\Sigma_{\varepsilon_i}^{-1}s_i$. The data, s_i, is a signal about the asset payoff vector f, with mean-zero, independent noise. Thus, the average signal is the true value of payoffs: $\int s_i \, di = f$.

Define the average data precision to be $\bar{\Sigma}_\varepsilon^{-1} \equiv \int \Sigma_{\varepsilon_i}^{-1} \, di$. Note that this makes $\bar{\Sigma}_\varepsilon$ the harmonic mean of the data variance across agents.

In principle, there would be some covariance between the signal and its precision that we would need to account for. But because normal variables have the property that the mean and variance are uncorrelated, the integral of the product is the product of the integrals. Equating average demand to supply yields,

$$\Sigma^{-1}\mu + \bar{\Sigma}_\varepsilon^{-1}f + \Sigma_p^{-1}B^{-1}(p-A) - \int \mathbb{V}ar[f|\mathcal{I}_i]^{-1} \, di \, pr = \rho(\bar{x}+x).$$
(6.13)

Define $\Psi \equiv \Sigma_p^{-1}B^{-1} - r \int \mathbb{V}ar[f|\mathcal{I}_i]^{-1} \, di$. Then we can rearrange the market clearing condition (6.13) to see that the price is

$$p = \Psi^{-1}[\rho(\bar{x}+x) - \Sigma^{-1}\mu - \bar{\Sigma}_\varepsilon^{-1}f + \Sigma_p^{-1}B^{-1}A].$$
(6.14)

This verifies our conjecture in (6.6) that the price is linear in f and x.

Step 6: Solve for Price Coefficients   Recall that the coefficients A, B, and C were guesses that are unknown. To solve them, we use the method of undetermined coefficients. To do this, we take all terms in (6.14) that multiply the payoff f and equate those to the coefficient B. That delivers $B = -\Psi^{-1}\bar{\Sigma}_\varepsilon^{-1}$. Next, equate all terms multiplying the asset supply shock x to C. That produces the expression $C = \Psi^{-1}\rho$. Finally, the rest of the terms that multiply neither f nor x, equate those to the constant A, to get $A = \Psi^{-1}(\rho\bar{x} - \Sigma^{-1}\mu + \Sigma_p^{-1}B^{-1}A)$.

Then, rearrange and substitute these equations into each other to derive the equilibrium asset prices. Define $\bar{V} \equiv \left(\int \mathbb{V}ar[f|\mathcal{I}_i]^{-1} \, di \right)^{-1}$ to be the harmonic mean of the posterior variances of all agents about the asset payoffs. Then, the solution to the equilibrium price is described by the three coefficients,

$$A = \frac{1}{r}\bar{V}(\Sigma^{-1}\mu - \rho\bar{x}),$$
(6.15)

$$B = \frac{1}{r}\left(I - \bar{V}\Sigma^{-1}\right), \tag{6.16}$$

$$C = -\frac{\rho}{r}\left(I - \bar{V}\Sigma^{-1}\right)\bar{\Sigma}_\varepsilon. \tag{6.17}$$

Finally, solve explicitly for the coefficients in terms of parameters by noting that $B^{-1}C = -\rho\bar{\Sigma}_\varepsilon$. Thus, the noise in the price signal is $\rho^2\sigma_x^2\bar{\Sigma}_\varepsilon'\bar{\Sigma}_\varepsilon$ and the harmonic mean of posterior variances is $\bar{V} = [\Sigma^{-1} + \bar{\Sigma}_\varepsilon^{-1} + 1/(\rho^2\sigma_x^2)(\bar{\Sigma}_\varepsilon'\bar{\Sigma}_\varepsilon)^{-1}]^{-1}$. Substituting $\bar{V}$ in the coefficient equations above delivers a solution that depends only on parameters.

Interpreting the Coefficients A is related to the risk premium. The first term of A, along with the expected value $B\mathbb{E}[f]$, just represents the expected present value of each asset μ/r. The second term of A pushes the price below that expected value to compensate the investors for the risk they must bear. The price discount, or risk premium, depends on the risk aversion ρ, the posterior variance or amount of risk $\bar{V}$ the (harmonic) average investor faces from a share of each asset, and the size of the risk $\bar{x}$ that that average investor must bear.

When the second coefficient B is high, the price is very responsive to changes in asset payoffs. This is true when the average agent is well-informed about payoffs. Price is also more responsive to payoffs when agents have prior information that is not too precise. Recall that signals get weighted more when priors are less informative. When the price is highly responsive to payoffs, the price is an informative signal. Thus, the coefficient B is also closely related to the empirical measure of price informativeness in Bai, Philippon, and Savov (2016). Price informativeness is often used as a metric of financial market efficiency. It is thought to have real economic benefits because informative prices would direct resources efficiently to firms that will deliver high future payoffs.

Finally, C represents the sensitivity of the price to asset supply shocks. If a noninformational trade does not have much of an impact on prices, this is what we might call a liquid market. Thus, a high C represents a high price impact of trades and an illiquid asset market.

6.2 Understanding the NREE Assumptions

Next, we discuss the main assumptions behind the NREE investment model regarding information sets, preferences, and risks.

Price in the Information Set   The idea that investors should know what price level will prevail when deciding how much to buy sounds like theory fiction, divorced from reality. However, investors do not need to actually know what the price level will be in order to act this way.

Suppose an investor does not know what price will prevail when executing his order. However, the order can submit some price-contingent quantities. They can submit a demand curve, $q(p)$, where q is the number of shares demanded if the price at the time of trade execution is p. This type of price-contingent trade is known as a limit order. When constructing the demand curve $q(p)$, an investor should rationally ask: If the price turns out to be p, what information should I infer from that? If, for each price p, in the domain of $q(p)$, the investor asks and answers this what-if question, then for any realized price p, the demand q will be as if the investor knew the price. Being able to condition one's action on an outcome is functionally the same as knowing which outcome will arise.

This idea arises in auction theory as well. In a common-value auction, it is common for the winning bidder to overbid. This is called the "winner's curse." The way bidders are taught to avoid the winner's curse is to ask themselves the following question: If I win the auction, it will mean that everyone else bid less than I did. If that were true, what would I infer about what others know about the value of this good? Conditioning on equilibrium outcomes like winning or the price is a way of avoiding overpaying for a common-value asset. Putting a price in investors' information sets simply means they do not systematically fall victim to the winner's curse.

Constant Absolute Risk Aversion (CARA)   Mean-variance preferences are derived from an exponential utility exhibiting constant absolute risk aversion. Of course, people do not typically exhibit risk aversion that is constant in their wealth. Risk aversion is typically decreasing—wealthier individuals are typically open to taking larger gambles. For some applications, the relationship between risk aversion and wealth is not central to the point. In those cases, mean-variance poses no problem. However, when studying inequality, heterogeneity, or the role of large investors or funds, it is important to model a richer relationship between risk aversion and wealth.

A simple way to incorporate diminishing absolute risk aversion is to make an agent i's risk aversion a function of their initial wealth $\rho(W_{0i})$. Using absolute risk aversion is not a problem. Every utility function has a level of absolute risk aversion at each level of consumption or wealth. The model described above does require that absolute risk aversion be constant within a period. However, a dynamic model version does not require constant risk aversion between periods. While the model solved above assumed that all agents have the same risk aversion, this was only for simplicity. The model is still tractable if agents have different risk aversions ρ_i. The only difference is that when aggregating demand to solve for the equilibrium price that clears the market, one needs to integrate these risk aversions. Instead of ρ in the price coefficients, one needs to use the harmonic mean $\bar{\rho}$, defined as

$$\bar{\rho} \equiv \left(\int 1/\rho_i \, di \right)^{-1}. \tag{6.18}$$

In some cases, where risk aversion and information precision are correlated, one needs to keep track of the harmonic mean of the product of these

$$\left(\int 1/\rho_i \, \mathbb{V}ar[f|\mathcal{I}_i]^{-1} \, di \right)^{-1}. \tag{6.19}$$

But after using this average value in the pricing formula, the rest of the model solution is unchanged. In short, heterogeneous preferences and wealth effects are easy to incorporate.

Normal Distributions Another strong assumption of the noisy rational expectations framework is that payoffs and information noise are normally distributed. There are certainly instances where normality is a poor approximation to the truth. The problem with relaxing the distributional assumption is that Bayesian updating quickly becomes intractable. Even if one can choose a prior belief and a signal such that the posterior is a tractable analytical expression, the information from prices is usually not compatible with this updating scheme.

However, there is a way to approximate this model with nonnormal distributions. It draws from an idea that arises in risk-neutral asset pricing. Risk-neutral asset pricing is a technique to value an asset without modeling an agent's preferences. For any preferences within a broad class, there exists a probability measure such that the asset value for an agent that prices the asset under such probability measure and linear (risk-neutral) preferences is the same as the asset value for an agent with the true preferences and the true probability measure.

Expected utility or expected value is an integral of a random variable x, with a utility function u and a probability function π operating on it, multiplied together: $EV = \int u(x)\pi(x)dx$. Risk-neutral pricing recognizes that we can form a new probability measure $\tilde{\pi}(x)$ and a new utility function $\tilde{u}(x)$ such that their product is the same as $u(x)\pi(x)$ for each x. In our case, we can choose $\tilde{\pi}$ to be a normal probability function and then find the $\tilde{u}(x)$ that makes the product the same.

When the true probability π is a concave transformation of the normal distribution $\tilde{\pi}$, then the distribution π is negatively skewed. The transformed utility $\tilde{u}$ will, therefore, be a concave transformation of the true utility u. In other words, it will exhibit more risk aversion. See appendix A.4.2.

Noise Traders   Noise traders are an important yet controversial part of the framework. See section 6.7 for a detailed discussion of their role and modeling alternatives.

Relationship to Grossman and Stiglitz (1980)   Perhaps the most well-known model in the noisy rational expectations literature is the one by Grossman and Stiglitz (1980). Since many readers might already be familiar with it, it could be useful to describe how it relates to the model here. What is similar is the structure and the logic. Exponential or mean-variance utility, normal variables, linear prices, and noise in the price are features of both. Also, the main idea that information is a strategic substitute will also appear in this setting.

What differs is the richness of the asset market and the types of information choices that will be possible. Grossman and Stiglitz (1980) has only one risky asset. That limitation makes it difficult to use for measurement. More importantly, agents can only choose to acquire a signal or not. There is no possibility of acquiring more information or different information from what others choose. This framework will allow us to consider a data economy where exactly what kind of data one has makes a big difference.

Finally, agents in Grossman and Stiglitz (1980) who acquire a signal observe exactly the same signal as every other agent that acquired information. In other words, the information is not private. It is not exactly public unless every agent chooses to acquire it. But it is potentially public. That may not be such a bad assumption for some data economy applications. If you acquire some satellite images, they will be the same images that everyone else who acquires that data set will see. The data in the model here is private information. It is as if everyone can potentially see the images but will process that information differently, adding their own idiosyncratic noise in the processing. One can add potentially public or correlated signals to this model. Those are just signals with noise that have no i subscript. This will show up in aggregate demand as signals that do not average to the true payoff. Instead, on average, signals will be the true payoff plus the public component of signal noise. The public signal noise will appear as an extra term in the equilibrium price, with its own coefficient. But such a model is solvable.

Representing Data as a Noisy Signal   Three types of questions arise when choosing to model data as a noisy signal: Why is it only one signal? Why is it a signal about an unknown state? And why is that signal noisy?

The idea that data can be represented as one signal comes from Bayes' Law. For normal variables, updating with multiple signals is exactly the same as forming a precision-weighted average of those signals and then updating with the average signal. One could write this model as one where agents have different numbers of data points about each asset, and the solution would be exactly the same. For nonnormal data points, there is still some equivalent representation of multiple data points as a composite signal. However, the form of that composite signal will depend on the distribution of the payoff and the data noise.

The idea that data is used to forecast an unknown state, like the payoff of an asset, is very natural in finance. Many financial sector employees are engaged in trying to predict asset returns. However, even in finance, data could also be used to estimate risk. Data could improve variance of covariance estimates, as in section 2.5.2. It could also be used to estimate the shape of the distribution, as in section 2.5.3 or 2.5.4. The problem is that we do not have tractable frameworks to solve for the equilibrium when agents are engaged in this type of learning and have asymmetric information. Without allowing some agents to know information that others do not, we cannot meaningfully model the data economy. That would be a fruitful area for future theory research.

6.3   The Value of Investment Data

This model gives us a tool to value data or choose data. The value of data, or the objective when choosing data, is the expected utility of an agent who has the data minus the expected utility of an agent that does not. There are two types of expected utility one can compute. One is the expected utility after observing the data and knowing what the data says. That is what we call *conditional expected utility* because it is conditioned on knowing the data. The other is an expected utility, knowing what the precision or quality of the data will be but not knowing what precise message the data will deliver. The second is what we call *unconditional expected utility*. We first compute the conditional expected utility and then use the law of iterated expectations to compute the unconditional expectation.

In computing both expectations, we assume that equilibrium objects that an agent could infer from knowing the model and second moments—variances and covariances—are known. Furthermore, if an agent is valuing a data set or choosing data, the precision of the data is known. While the contents of the price signal are not known when agents value information (s_p is a random variable), the precision of the price information can be inferred from equilibrium. So Σ_p is known. That implies that the conditional variance $\mathbb{V}ar[f|\mathcal{I}_i]$ in (6.10) is also known. On the other hand, the conditional expectation $\mathbb{E}[f|\mathcal{I}_i]$ in (6.9) is unknown. It depends on the signals s_i and s_p, whose distributions we must solve for.

Conditional Expected Utility   Substituting the optimal portfolio (6.5) into the budget constraint (6.2) yields agents' final wealth (at the end of the model):

$$W_i = W_{0i}r + \frac{1}{\rho}\left(\mathbb{E}[f|\mathcal{I}_i] - pr\right)' \mathbb{V}ar[f|\mathcal{I}_i]^{-1}(f - pr). \qquad (6.20)$$

Since utility (6.1) depends on the conditional mean and variance of this wealth W_i, we need to compute those moments.

$$\mathbb{E}[W_i|\mathcal{I}_i] = W_{0i}r + \frac{1}{\rho}\left(\mathbb{E}[f|\mathcal{I}_i] - pr\right)' \mathbb{V}ar[f|\mathcal{I}_i]^{-1}\left(\mathbb{E}[f|\mathcal{I}_i] - pr\right);$$

$$\mathbb{V}ar[W_i|\mathcal{I}_i] = \frac{1}{\rho^2}\left(\mathbb{E}[f|\mathcal{I}_i] - pr\right)' \mathbb{V}ar[f|\mathcal{I}_i]^{-1}\left(\mathbb{E}[f|\mathcal{I}_i] - pr\right).$$

Substitute $\mathbb{E}[W_i|\mathcal{I}_i]$ and $\mathbb{V}ar[W_i|\mathcal{I}_i]$ into the expected utility in (6.1) and simplify:

$$\mathbb{E}[U_i|\mathcal{I}_i] = W_{0i}r + \frac{1}{\rho}\left(\mathbb{E}[f|\mathcal{I}_i] - pr\right)' \mathbb{V}ar[f|\mathcal{I}_i]^{-1}\left(\mathbb{E}[f|\mathcal{I}_i] - pr\right)$$

$$- \frac{\rho}{2}\cdot\frac{1}{\rho^2}\left(\mathbb{E}[f|\mathcal{I}_i] - pr\right)' \mathbb{V}ar[f|\mathcal{I}_i]^{-1}\left(\mathbb{E}[f|\mathcal{I}_i] - pr\right)$$

$$= W_{0i}r + \frac{1}{2\rho}\left(\mathbb{E}[f|\mathcal{I}_i] - pr\right)' \mathbb{V}ar[f|\mathcal{I}_i]^{-1}\left(\mathbb{E}[f|\mathcal{I}_i] - pr\right). \quad (6.21)$$

It is useful to define the risk-adjusted expected excess return, known as the Sharpe ratio:

$$z \equiv \mathbb{V}ar[f|\mathcal{I}_i]^{-\frac{1}{2}}\left(\mathbb{E}[f|\mathcal{I}_i] - pr\right). \qquad (6.22)$$

Using z, conditional expected utility becomes

$$\mathbb{E}[U_i|\mathcal{I}_i] = W_{0i}r + \frac{1}{2\rho}z'z. \qquad (6.23)$$

Unconditional Expected Utility   The conditional expected utility in (6.23) is the utility of an agent who has already observed the data in the information set $\mathcal{I}_i$. But when someone chooses data or values a data set, they typically do not yet know what information that data will convey. They might know the precision and covariance but not what the signal actually says. Therefore, the next step is to take a prior expectation of this conditional expectation. This answers the question: How happy do I expect to be after seeing the additional information in my data set (including the asset prices)? We need to compute $\mathbb{E}[\mathbb{E}[U_i|\mathcal{I}_i]]$.

To form this unconditional or prior expectation, separating the part of $\mathbb{E}[U_i|\mathcal{I}_i]$ that is random before data is observed is helpful. Before observing data, z is random because the price p and the payoff forecast $\mathbb{E}[f|\mathcal{I}_i]$ are unknown. The conditional expectation is ex ante random because before observing their data, agents do not know what they will believe. They are uncertain about what they will learn.

Once we know the mean and variance of z, we can easily compute the unconditional expected utility. As explained in the discussion of the price coefficient, the prior mean of $(f - pr)$ is $\rho \bar{V} x$. Thus, the mean of z' is $\rho \bar{x}' \bar{V}' \mathbb{V}ar[f|\mathcal{I}_i]^{-1/2}$. To compute the variance of z, it is helpful to apply the law of total variance (recall it from section 2.1.4, and note that for normal variables, the conditional variance is not stochastic, and thus we drop the expectation in the second term):

$$\mathbb{V}ar[\mathbb{E}[f - pr|\mathcal{I}_i]] = \mathbb{V}ar[f - pr] - \mathbb{V}ar[f - pr|\mathcal{I}_i]. \qquad (6.24)$$

Since the price is in the information set $\mathcal{I}_i$, then $\mathbb{E}[f - pr|\mathcal{I}_i] = \mathbb{E}[f|\mathcal{I}_i] - pr$. Likewise, the conditional variance $\mathbb{V}ar[f - pr|\mathcal{I}_i] = \mathbb{V}ar[f|\mathcal{I}_i]$. These are conditional expectations and variances that we have already solved for. The remaining piece is the unconditional variance $\mathbb{V}ar[f - pr]$. This is not straightforward because the payoff f and the price p are correlated. To account for this, substitute in the price formula from (6.6) and combine terms in f to get $\mathbb{V}ar[f - pr] = \mathbb{V}ar[(I - Br)f - rCx] = (I - Br)\Sigma(I - B'r) + r^2 \sigma_x^2 CC'$. Substituting in the solution for B from (6.16) and multiply by $\mathbb{V}ar[f|\mathcal{I}_i]^{-1}$ to obtain the distribution for the variable $z' \sim \mathcal{N}(\mathbb{E}[z], \mathbb{V}ar[z])$, where:

$$\mathbb{E}[z'] = \rho \bar{x}' \bar{V}' \mathbb{V}ar[f|\mathcal{I}_i]^{-1/2} \qquad (6.25)$$

$$\mathbb{V}ar[z] = \mathbb{V}ar[f|\mathcal{I}_i]^{-\frac{1}{2}}(\bar{V}\Sigma^{-1}\bar{V} + r^2 CC' \sigma_x^2)\mathbb{V}ar[f|\mathcal{I}_i]^{-\frac{1}{2}} - I. \qquad (6.26)$$

The derivations of this mean and variance are left as exercises.

If z is a multivariate normal variable, then $z'z$ is a noncentral χ^2 variable (see appendix A.4.1). Applying the χ^2-square mean formula, the unconditional expectation of expected utility in (6.23) becomes[2]

$$\mathbb{E}[U_i] = W_{0i}r + \frac{1}{2\rho}\left(\mathbb{E}[z]'\mathbb{E}[z] + \text{Tr}(\mathbb{V}ar[z])\right), \qquad (6.27)$$

where Tr is the trace operator and equals the sum of its diagonal elements. Since the trace is a linear operator, utility is linear in the precision of an agent's posterior belief precision, $\mathbb{V}ar[f|\mathcal{I}_i]^{-1}$. If an agent chooses data, that choice

---

2. Because variance matrices are symmetric, we can drop transposes and reorder them in multiplication.

does not affect asset supply, the average agent's variance, or pricing coefficients. The choices of all other agents collectively affect averages and prices. But the only way that i's data choice matters for agent i's utility is through the precision $\mathbb{V}ar[f|\mathcal{I}_i]^{-1}$.

Transforming Expected Utility to a Data Value   The expected utility we just worked out can be the objective function in a data choice problem. We simply need to reexpress the objective in terms of data, make an assumption about the cost of data, and then maximize it.

The expected utility in (6.27) reveals a linear relationship between expected utility and the precision of beliefs. Recall that Bayes' Law for normal variables says that the posterior precision is the sum of the prior precision and the signal precisions: $\mathbb{V}ar[f|\mathcal{I}_i]^{-1} = \Sigma^{-1} + \Sigma_p^{-1} + \Sigma_{\varepsilon_i}^{-1}$, where Σ_{ε_i} is the precision of agent i's data. So, if the expected utility is linear in posterior precision, it is also linear in data precision.

Recall also that the precision of a normally distributed composite signal is simply the precision of each data point times the number of data points. If we normalize the precision of a data point to 1, then $\Sigma_{\varepsilon_i}^{-1}$ represents the number of data points an agent observes or chooses to observe.

Substituting the formula above for $\mathbb{V}ar[f|\mathcal{I}_i]^{-1}$ into (6.27) and gathering all the constant terms in utility that are not affected by agent i's data choice into the term α_0, we can reexpress prior expected utility as

$$\mathbb{E}[U_i] = \alpha_0 + \frac{1}{2\rho}\text{Tr}\left(\Sigma_{\varepsilon_i}^{-1/2}\left(\bar{V}\Sigma^{-1}\bar{V}\right)\Sigma_{\varepsilon_i}^{-1/2}\right) + \frac{\rho}{2}\bar{x}'\bar{V}\Sigma_{\varepsilon_i}^{-1}\bar{V}\bar{x}.$$

$$(6.28)$$

6.3.1   Independent Investment Risks and Independent Data

Until now, we have allowed arbitrary asset covariance and arbitrary signal covariance. However, allowing an agent to choose every entry of the matrix $\Sigma_{\varepsilon_i}^{-1}$, but requiring it to be a well-behaved precision matrix (positive, semidefinite, symmetric) is a messy problem. If, instead, we assume that assets are independent and signals have independent signal noise, this objective collapses to a simple weighted sum of precisions:

$$\mathbb{E}[U_i] = \alpha_0 + \frac{1}{2\rho}\sum_{j=1}^{N}\Sigma_{\varepsilon_i,jj}^{-1}\underbrace{\bar{V}_{jj}^2(\Sigma_{jj}^{-1} + \rho^2\bar{x}_j^2)}_{\text{marginal utility of data (MUD}_j)} \,, \qquad (6.29)$$

where the subindex (jj) indicates the jth diagonal entry of the matrix and the subindex (j) denotes the jth entry of a vector. Notice that the variance-covariance matrix of the price signal, Σ_p, will also be diagonal now.

We learn that the marginal value of a private signal ε_j of precision 1 about any asset j is

$$\text{MUD}_j \equiv \bar{V}_{jj}^2(\Sigma_{jj}^{-1} + \rho^2\bar{x}_j^2). \tag{6.30}$$

The marginal value of data is increasing in the uncertainty of others $\bar{V}_{jj}^2$. That is the strategic substitutability in information acquisition that is described by Grossman and Stiglitz (1980). The value of data is increasing in one's prior knowledge about the asset Σ_{jj}^{-1}. This is the increasing returns to learning or the benefit of specialization. Finally, it is useful to learn about assets that are in abundant supply $\bar{x}_j^2$. This is the returns to scale in data. The absolute risk aversion ρ is the market-wide risk aversion. If agents are not symmetric, ρ should be a harmonic mean of risk aversions, not the risk aversion of the individual whose data value is being computed.

6.3.2 Valuing Data with Correlated Risks

Another case in which computing the value of data is relatively simple is when data is collected principal component by principal component. If the market is the first principal component, then we can learn about the market. If the next component is an industry-specific risk, we can learn about that. But if some industry-specific risk is statistically unrelated to the global economy, we cannot obtain data directly on the sum of the two risks. We can learn about each risk and construct the sum, the difference, or any other linear combination. However, there is no technology for generating correlated information about independent risks. If that assumption holds, then it implies that signal noise has the same factor structure as the noise in assets. Section 2.2.1 introduced correlated risks and updating methods using principal components, for exactly this type of data structure.

If data has this structure, we can simply redefine assets and redefine signals to express the real problem, with correlated assets and correlated signals, as if it were a problem with independent assets and independent signals. To implement this approach, use an eigendecomposition to form linear combinations of assets that are independent of each other. If the vector of asset payoffs is distributed $f \sim \mathcal{N}(\mu, \Sigma)$, then for any well-defined variance-covariance matrix Σ, there is an eigendecomposition $\Gamma\Lambda\Gamma' = \Sigma$ such that Λ is a diagonal matrix and $\Gamma'\Gamma = I$. The $N \times N$ matrix Γ contains weights such that $\Gamma'f$ is a set of N linear combinations of the N original assets.

Once we have those new, synthetic, independent assets, we can transform the data s_i to be about the synthetic asset payoffs: $\tilde{s}_i = \Gamma's_i = \Gamma'f + \tilde{\varepsilon}_i$, where the rotated signal noise $\tilde{\varepsilon}_i$ has a diagonal variance-covariance matrix.

Solve the portfolio problem and the equilibrium price problem for the synthetic assets to value data about these synthetic assets. In other words, value data as if all assets and data were independent, as in the last section. Finally, take the synthetic-asset solutions, undo the linear transformation, and back out the data values for the original assets.

We learn that the marginal value of a private signal of precision 1 about any risk factor j is

$$\text{MUD}_j \equiv \bar{\Lambda}_{jj}^2 (\Lambda_{jj}^{-1} + \rho^2 \bar{x}_j^2). \tag{6.31}$$

where $\bar{\Lambda}_{jj}$ is the harmonic mean of others' posterior uncertainty about risk j, Λ_{jj}^{-1} is the precision of the priors about risk j, and $\bar{x}_j = \Gamma_j' \bar{x}$ is the average supply of risk j, which is a linear combination of the supplies of all the assets that load on risk j.

The synthetic assets used here are also referred to as *Arrow-Debreu securities*. Principal component analysis is frequently used in the portfolio literature (Ross, 1976). Principal components could represent business-cycle, industry-specific, or firm-specific risks. As long as the market is complete (the asset payoff variance-covariance matrix is full-rank), one can rewrite the problem in terms of the independent synthetic assets with data about each synthetic asset.

6.4   Data Choice

Using the value or utility of data as an objective, the next step is to let agents choose data to maximize that objective, subject to a cost for data. There are many cost functions one might use. We will consider two: costs that are linear in precision (section 3.6) and entropy-based information costs (section 3.5). Another natural choice would be to use the constraint with unlearnable risk (section 3.8) to capture the idea of diminishing returns to data.

Now that we know that a world with correlated assets and signals can be reexpressed as though there were independent assets and independent signals, we will proceed with the simpler model with independence. Regardless of the cost function, agents are choosing the signal precisions $\Sigma_{\varepsilon_i,jj}^{-1}$ to maximize unconditional expected utility (6.29), minus a cost that is an increasing function of the precisions, or subject to a constraint on signal precisions. To simplify the exposition, define data quality or information precision as $\tau_{ij} \equiv \Sigma_{\varepsilon_i,jj}^{-1}$. This is the choice variable. It represents how much data to acquire.

Data Choices with Linear Precision Costs   Suppose that the cost of data was linear in the precision of each signal discovered. This cost could be a monetary cost or represent the effort cost of learning. If we let the marginal cost of signal precision about risk j be denoted χ_j, then the data choice problem is

$$\max_{\{\tau_{ij}\}_{j=1}^N} \sum_{j=1}^N \tau_{ij}\bar{V}_{jj}^2(\Sigma_{jj}^{-1} + \rho^2\bar{x}_j^2) - \sum_{j=1}^N \chi_j\tau_{ij} \quad \text{s.t.} \quad \tau_{ij} \geq 0, \forall i,j. \quad (6.32)$$

The marginal value of data is increasing in others' uncertainty $(\bar{V})$, risk aversion (ρ), the amount of this risk in the market $(\bar{x})$, and one's own prior information (Σ^{-1}). It is important to impose the nonnegativity constraint on signal precision. Otherwise, an agent may choose to learn a negative amount about some risks. That negative choice of τ_{ij} would be a mathematical solution that is not economically meaningful.

If this is a data choice with a linear cost of data, then the solution to this model is simple: learn an infinite amount about all assets for which the marginal benefit $\bar{V}_{jj}^2(\Sigma_{jj}^{-1} + \rho^2\bar{x}_j^2)$ exceeds the marginal cost χ_j. Acquire no data about all other risks. Since the solution is not finite, imposing a linear cost is probably not the right modeling choice for most purposes.

If this is a data choice subject to a linear constraint on the amount of data, the solution is still a corner solution. Suppose the investor maximizes expected utility, subject to the constraint that $\sum_{j=1}^N \tau_{ij} \leq \kappa$. The solution is to devote all κ units of data precision to acquiring data about one risk, the risk with the highest marginal utility of data, $\bar{V}_{jj}^2(\Sigma_{jj}^{-1} + \rho^2\bar{x}_j^2)$. Acquire no data about all other risks. In this case, the solution is bounded by the constraint and thus finite.

Data Choices with Entropy Data Costs   Suppose that the cost of data or the constraint on data was related to the mutual information of signals and asset payoffs. Recall from section 3.5.2 that the mutual information of a normal signal about a normal state is

$$\mathcal{M}(f,\mathcal{I}_i) = \frac{1}{2}\ln\left(\frac{|\mathbb{V}ar[f]|}{|\mathbb{V}ar[f|\mathcal{I}_i]|}\right) \quad (6.33)$$

where $|\cdot|$ denotes the determinant. For diagonal matrices, like $\mathbb{V}ar[f]$ and $\mathbb{V}ar[f|\mathcal{I}_i]$, the determinant is simply the product of the diagonal entries.

A capacity constraint on mutual information $\mathcal{M}(f,\mathcal{I}_i) \leq \kappa$ can be rewritten as an upper bound on the posterior precision

$$|\mathbb{V}ar[f|\mathcal{I}_i]|^{-1} \leq |\mathbb{V}ar[f]|^{-1}e^{-2\kappa} \equiv \tilde{\kappa} \quad (6.34)$$

where $|\mathbb{V}ar[f|\mathcal{I}_i]|^{-1} = \Sigma_{jj}^{-1} + \Sigma_{p,jj}^{-1} + \tau_{ij}$. The data choice problem involves a Lagrange multiplier $\chi \geq 0$ on the data constraint (6.34):

$$\max_{\{\tau_{ij}\}_{j=1}^{N}} \sum_{j=1}^{N} \tau_{ij} \bar{V}_{jj}^2 (\Sigma_{jj}^{-1} + \rho^2 \bar{x}_j^2) - \chi \prod_{j=1}^{N} (\Sigma_{jj}^{-1} + \Sigma_{p,jj}^{-1} + \tau_{ij} - \bar{\kappa}),$$

$$\text{s.t.} \quad \tau_{ij} \geq 0, \ \forall i, j. \tag{6.35}$$

Alternatively, we can define an increasing and convex cost function of mutual information $\chi(\mathcal{M})$, for example:

$$\chi(\mathcal{M}) \equiv \chi |\mathbb{V}ar[f]|^{-1} e^{2\mathcal{M}(f,\mathcal{I}_i)} = \chi |\mathbb{V}ar[f|\mathcal{I}_i]|^{-1} \tag{6.36}$$

for some parameter $\chi > 0$. The data choice problem is identical to (6.35).

Maximizing a sum, subject to a product constraint or a product cost function yields corner solutions. Again, an investor should specialize, putting all their data purchasing power into one asset. In the case of correlated assets, they should specialize in learning about one risk factor, a single linear combination of risks. Whether χ is an actual cost of purchasing data as in (6.36) or is a shadow cost or Lagrange multiplier on a data constraint such as (6.34), the solution involves specialization in both cases.

Which risk should an investor learn about? If we take the partial derivative of the objective in (6.35) with respect to τ_{ij}, we find that the marginal value of acquiring a marginal unit of data about risk j is

$$\bar{V}_{jj}^2 (\Sigma_{jj}^{-1} + \rho^2 \bar{x}_j^2) - \chi \prod_{l \neq j}^{N} (\Sigma_{ll}^{-1} + \Sigma_{p,ll}^{-1} + \tau_{il}). \tag{6.37}$$

The three forces that make data valuable—others are uncertain $(\bar{V})$, own prior is precise (Σ^{-1}), and the market risk is large $(\bar{x})$—are the same as in the linear cost problem. However, there is one new force that arises because of the multiplicative form of data costs: the marginal cost of data is lower for a risk that you already know more about. The marginal cost of data is $\chi \prod_{l \neq j}^{N}(\Sigma_{ll}^{-1} + \Sigma_{p,ll}^{-1} + \tau_{il})$. If agents acquire data about a risk j they know little about, then posterior precision $(\Sigma_{ll}^{-1} + \Sigma_{p,ll}^{-1} + \tau_{il})$ is high for all other assets l, because those are assets they know more about. But when agents acquire data about the risk j that they are best informed about, the marginal cost, which is the product of precisions for all other assets $l \neq j$ is minimized. Learning about what one already knows well is specialization in data acquisition.

"Water-filling" Data Equilibrium   While each investor wants to specialize in acquiring data about one asset or one risk, equilibrium forces work to make investors indifferent regarding what data to acquire. Notice that part of the marginal value of data is $\bar{V}_{jj}^2$, the average uncertainty of others. If a type of data

is valuable, many agents will acquire that data. More data will make them less uncertain, which will drive down the value of that data. If investors are identical, this process should make them indifferent regarding a number of data sets. The cheaper or more abundant data gets, the larger the indifference set grows, and the more different types of data are acquired. In information theory, this type of result is called "water-filling."

For intuition's sake, consider constructing the Nash equilibrium by letting investors choose how to allocate their capacity sequentially. The first investor learns about the risk factor that is most valuable when no other learning takes place. This is risk 1, with the highest learning index. Subsequent investors will continue to allocate their capacity to risk 1 until the value of learning about it has dropped sufficiently that it equals the value of learning about the next most valuable risk factor, risk 2. Then, some investors will find it beneficial to learn about risk 2. The proportion of investors learning about risk 1 and about risk 2 is such that all investors remain indifferent. Subsequent investors will continue to allocate capacity to these two risks until all investors become indifferent between learning about risk 1, risk 2, and some third risk 3. This process continues until all capacity is allocated. Because of strategic substitutability, the equilibrium aggregate information allocation is unique.

Figure VI illustrates the "water-filling" equilibrium for three economies that differ in data usage levels, parametrized by the capacity constraint on mutual information κ. In the low-data economy (low κ), there is complete data specialization in risk $j \in \{1\}$. The capacity constraint is so tight that even if all investors specialize in learning about this risk, the marginal utility of data remains above that of other risks. In the medium-data economy, others' data choices lower the marginal utility of data for risk 1 (MUD_1) and increase the marginal utility of data for risk 2 (MUD_2); in equilibrium, marginal utilities are equalized within the subset of risks $j \in \{1, 2\}$, and data about both risks is equally valuable in the margin ($MUD_1 = MUD_2$). Lastly, in a high-data economy (high κ), investors are indifferent between specializing in the subset risks $j \in \{1, 2, 3\}$, equalizing marginal utilities of learning about any of the three risks ($MUD_1 = MUD_2 = MUD_3$). See Veldkamp (2011) for more discussion of this equilibrium allocation.

6.4.1   Application: Financial Income Inequality

Since richer investors have lower absolute risk aversion, they value data more and acquire more data. With better data, rich investors get richer. Kacperczyk, Nosal, and Stevens (2019) explore this mechanism. They trace out the quantitative predictions for financial income inequality. Mihet (2021) considers the idea that an investment management sector might overcome this problem. Funds can pool the resources of poorer investors and then process data on

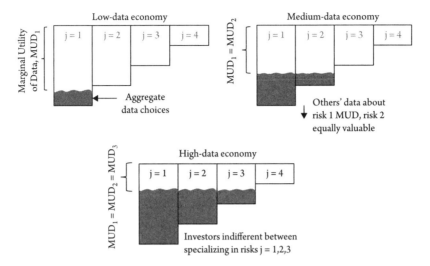

FIGURE VI. Water-Filling Equilibrium. *Notes*: This figure illustrates how the water-filling data equilibrium works in three economies that vary in their amount of data. In the low-data economy, all investors specialize in learning about risk $j \in \{1\}$, and its marginal utility MUD_1 is the largest. In the medium-data economy, other's data about risk 1 lower its marginal utility, and investors learn about the subset $j \in \{1, 2\}$, equating their marginal utilities $MUD_1 = MUD_2$. In the high-data economy, investors are indifferent between learning about three risks and $j \in \{1, 2, 3\}$, equating their marginal utilities $MUD_1 = MUD_2 = MUD_3$.

their behalf, offering them the returns that a richer investor can achieve. However, funds have fixed costs that deter the poorest. Also, when funds grow, the return to uninformed investing falls. The rise of managed funds changes the nature of inequality and helps some investors but does not resolve income inequality.

6.5   Sentiment Data

The data agents choose to observe does not need to be about the fundamental value of an asset. Nonfundamental data that creates noise in prices can also be valuable to learn about. We'll call such data "sentiment" data. Sentiment could be an irrational component to demand, like a feel-good factor from buying an asset. Sentiment could result from noise in public news. If a famous equity analyst is featured on television, recommending that viewers buy Tesla, the price of Tesla is likely to surge, regardless of whether the analyst was correct. Finally, sentiment could be a change in the price of risk or the need to hedge risk.

Since such nonfundamental data is typically assumed to be independent of the asset payoff f, one might think that it is useless in forecasting asset payoffs.

However, sentiment data can be useful to remove noise from the price signal. Recall that the information extracted from the vector of asset prices p was $B^{-1}(p - A) = f + B^{-1}Cx$. The left side is how an investor should transform prices to make them an unbiased signal about payoffs. The right side tells us that such a signal conveys information about payoffs f, with noise $B^{-1}Cx$.

If an agent gets a signal about the noise x, they can use that information to remove some of the noise from the price signal. Specifically, if a sentiment signal leads an agent to forecast that x takes the value $\mathbb{E}[x|\mathcal{I}_i]$, then they should form a new price signal that is

$$B^{-1}(p - A - C\,\mathbb{E}[x|\mathcal{I}_i]) = f + B^{-1}C(x - \mathbb{E}[x|\mathcal{I}_i]). \tag{6.38}$$

If the old price signal has precision Σ_p^{-1}, the new price signal has precision

$$\Sigma_p^{-1} + (C^{-1}B)' V_x^{-1} C^{-1}B, \tag{6.39}$$

where V_x is the variance matrix of the sentiment signals.

Farboodi and Veldkamp (2020) use this idea to study the choices of investors to acquire fundamental data (about f) or sentiment data (about x). They find that when data is scarce, fundamental data is more valuable. But as data technologies improve and data becomes more abundant, the demand for sentiment data should rise. This is because when data becomes more abundant, prices become more informative. This shows up as a higher pricing coefficient B. When B is higher, a given precision sentiment signal increases the informativeness of the price signal $(\Sigma_p^{-1} + (C^{-1}B)' V_x^{-1} C^{-1}B)$ by more. The idea is that if investors trade on more data, prices contain more information and mining that information from prices is more fruitful.

6.6   Data About Long-Lived Assets

So far, we've described a static model where assets pay off after one period, and then the model ends. In reality, lots of data are about equities that are long-lived assets. This feature subtly changes the data choice. When assets are long-lived, the choice of data today depends on what agents believe others will learn tomorrow. The following model is a version of Wang (1993), with the richer information structure of Farboodi et al. (2022b).

Setup   Consider a model with the same N assets and the same continuum of investors with mean-variance utility. An asset is a claim to an infinite stream of dividend payoffs, which follow an AR(1) process:

$$d_{t+1} = \bar{d} + \gamma d_t + y_{t+1}, \qquad y_{t+1} \sim_{iid} \mathcal{N}(0, \Sigma_y), \tag{6.40}$$

where the innovation y_{t+1} is i.i.d. across time. The dividend is an $N \times 1$ vector of dividends for N assets. Data will be informative about dividend innovations.

There is a continuum of investors with overlapping generations. In each period t, a generation is born, observes data, and makes portfolio choices. In the following period $t + 1$, these investors sell their assets, consume the dividends and the proceeds of their asset sale, and exit the model. Each investor i born at date t has initial endowment $W_{i,t}$. They maximize utility over total end-of-life consumption $c_{i,t+1}$. At date t, investors choose their portfolio of risky assets, a vector $q_{i,t}$ of the number of shares held of each asset. They also choose holdings of one riskless asset with return r, subject to the budget constraint

$$c_{i,t+1} = r \left(W_{i,t} - q'_{i,t} p_t \right) + q'_{i,t} \left(p_{t+1} + d_{t+1} \right). \tag{6.41}$$

Each investor has access to H distinct data sources. Signals from each of these data sources (indexed by h) provide information about dividend innovations y_{t+1}, possibly from a linear combination ψ_h of assets:

$$s_{i,h,t} = \psi_h y_{t+1} + \Gamma_h \varepsilon_{i,t}, \quad \varepsilon_{i,t} \sim \mathcal{N}(0, I). \tag{6.42}$$

Here, $\varepsilon_{i,t}$ is i.i.d. across time but not necessarily independent across investors or across assets. In other words, data can have public and private signal noise. Public signal noise captures the idea that many data sources are available to, observed by, and used by many investors. In addition, all investors know the variance and covariance of prices, dividends, and the data they observe.

A representative noise trader buys x_t shares of the asset, where $x_t \sim \mathcal{N}(0, \sigma_x^2 I)$ is independent of other shocks in the model and independent over time. The equilibrium is the same as the one defined in (6.1), except with the budget constraint defined in (6.41) and beliefs updated about the dividend innovation y_{t+1}, instead of f.

Solution: Choosing Long-Lived Data   If the data noise $\varepsilon_{i,t}$ has a common component, call that component the public component of data ν_t. Then, one can guess and verify that there exists an equilibrium price that is linear in current dividend d_t, future dividend innovations y_{t+1}, demand shocks x_t, and the noise in the public component of data ν_t:

$$p_t = A_t + B d_t + C_t y_{t+1} + D_t x_t + F_t \nu_t. \tag{6.43}$$

Given this guess, form the unbiased signal about the dividend innovation y_{t+1}, conveyed by prices:

$$s_{pt} = C_t^{-1} (p_t - A_t - B d_t - F_t \mathbb{E}[\nu_t | \mathcal{I}_{i,t}]). \tag{6.44}$$

Agents use this price signal, along with any other signals, to update beliefs using Bayes' Law. Similar to the case of games with correlated data in section 5.7, when signals have a public noise component, agents also need to form beliefs about the common component of signal noise, $\mathbb{E}[\nu_t|\mathcal{I}_{i,t}]$, to interpret the price correctly.

Since the price rule in (6.43) should hold in every period, we can write the payoff of a share of each asset purchased at date t as

$$d_{t+1} + p_{t+1} = A_{t+1} + (B+I)d_{t+1} + C_{t+1}y_{t+2} + D_{t+1}x_{t+1} + F_{t+1}\nu_{t+1}. \tag{6.45}$$

The investor has no relevant data about the future shocks y_{t+2}, x_{t+1} or ν_{t+1}. In the expected payoff, all get set to their mean, which is zero. Forming an expectation about this payoff is simply forming an expectation about the random variable d_{t+1}, which has known components, plus y_{t+1}. So, forecasting payoffs in this setting is not much more complicated than solving the static model. Using the price signal and the data to form beliefs about y_{t+1} and then add and multiply the expectation by known numbers to get the expected payoff.

However, the additional mean-zero terms in the payoff (6.45) do increase the conditional variance of the asset payoff. This variance reduces the size of the optimal portfolio. These new terms also create a form of unlearnable risk in asset returns. The presence of unlearnable risk reduces the data value. If most risks that one faces cannot be learned about, data about the learnable risk is less valuable. Notice also that the variance of this unlearnable risk depends on future price coefficients like C_{t+1} and F_{t+1}. These coefficients, in turn, depend on what future investors learn. When future investors learn more, C_{t+1} and F_{t+1} are higher, creating more risk for investors today. This is called *future information risk*.

After forming the conditional mean and variance of the payoff, the rest of the model solution, including the information choice, is the same as in the static model. The conditional mean and variance tell us optimal portfolios. Summing optimal portfolios yields aggregate demand, which delivers an equilibrium price when equated to supply. Substituting the portfolio and price back in expected utility and taking an ex ante expectation yields a utility as a function of data. This can be the objective function in a data choice problem.

6.7 Rationalizing Noise Traders

Many researchers object to the use of noisy rational expectations models because of the noise. In order for the price to not fully reveal the true payoff f, it is essential to have a source of noise in prices. In this model, that source of noise is supply risk x (Diamond and Verrecchia, 1981). Of course, the supplies of assets do not randomly fluctuate. Instead of random supply, many prefer to call this same shock random demand (with the opposing sign). Sometimes, this random demand is referred to as the demand of noise traders. The problem is that these noise traders are not rational. They do not maximize any objectives. This is problematic both because it does not explain their trading behavior but also because it makes it impossible to make welfare statements about the model. If there is a group of traders with no specified preferences, we cannot say how their welfare is affected when there is more or less information in the market.

Fortunately, there are many possible solutions to this problem.

(i) *Noise from Hedging Nonfinancial Income*   Medrano and Vives (2004) developed a noisy rational expectations framework that is particularly useful for welfare analysis. Their price noise comes from trading by agents with well-defined utility. To do this, they developed a clever, rational foundation for the price noise. They developed a model with nonfinancial income risk that investors want to hedge.

Assume that investor i is endowed with a set of nonfinancial and non-tradable assets whose payoffs are correlated with the asset sold by the issuer. For simplicity, consider the case where there are N nonfinancial assets, each perfectly correlated with a financial asset. (This extreme correlation is not necessary.) The number of units of each asset that an investor is endowed with is $e_i = \omega + \varepsilon_i$, where $\omega \sim \mathcal{N}(0, h_\omega^{-1})$ is an aggregate component of this endowment, while $\varepsilon_i \sim \mathcal{N}(0, h_\varepsilon^{-1})$ is independent and identically distributed across investors. This assumption will allow rational traders with well-specified utility functions to create price noise. It captures the idea that other motives for trade can arise to create noise in prices. The nonfinancial endowment could be a labor income risk.

The reason that this assumption works to create noise in prices is that investors will now want to trade the asset, in part, to hedge this endowment risk. Having endowment risk that is correlated with the payoff of an asset is like already owning some of the asset. The optimal portfolio will, therefore, be the solution in (6.5), minus the endowment exposure to the risk, in this case, e_i, for each investor i. Since the investor-specific endowment shock ε_i integrates out to zero on average, the effect on the average investor's demand for the asset is ω. This aggregate demand shock, working through the rational hedging motive, plays the same role as asset supply noise x in the previous model.

The one complication of this noise microfoundation is that each investor's endowment, e_i, is now an informative signal about the noise in prices, ω. To solve for the information extracted from prices, one now needs to de-bias the price, as in (6.7), but then also subtract $B^{-1}C\mathbb{E}[\omega|e_i]$, the expectation of the price shocks from the endowment. That conditional expectation $\mathbb{E}[\omega|e_i]$ combines the prior that $\omega = 0$, with the signal $e_i = \omega + \varepsilon_i$. This is an unbiased signal of ω because the mean of the investor-specific shock ε_i is zero. After adjusting the price signal, the model can be solved following the same steps as above.

(ii) Public Signal Noise   If investors get signals that are public or are just correlated, there will be a common component to the signal noise that will show up as noise in prices. Suppose that instead of the information structure from section 6.1, we assume that data has both sender noise that is common to all and receiver noise that is observer-specific. We can summarize the information in such a data set as a signal with the structure

$$s_i = f + \nu + \varepsilon_i, \quad \text{where } \nu \sim_{iid} \mathcal{N}(0, \Sigma_\nu), \ \varepsilon_i \sim_{iid} \mathcal{N}(0, \Sigma_{\varepsilon_i}).$$

This is just an orthogonal decomposition of signal noise into a common component and an individual-specific component defined as a signal noise orthogonal to the common component. The common signal noise ν represents the sender noise. If the sender of a signal introduces noise, it is incorporated into the information of every receiver. This could be an error in data sets, government statistic mismeasurement, or simply news that is correct but portrays the situation as more positive or negative than it really is.

The precision of this signal is $(\Sigma_\nu + \Sigma_{\varepsilon_i})^{-1}$. Given this signal, agents update their beliefs about the asset payoff, as usual, using Bayes' Law. Their asset demand first-order condition is still (6.5). However, when we integrate over all demands to clear the market, the term $\int q_i \, di$ has inside it a term that is the average signal. Whereas, before the average signal was the true payoff f, now it is $\int s_i \, di = f + \nu$. The price is still linear. But now, it is linear in f and ν. In other words, even without noisy supply or noise traders, there is noise in prices from the common signal noise ν.

However, there is one additional complication. Each agent's signal s_i is also informative about the noise ν. That additional information can be used to remove some, but not all, of the price noise. To form this expectation $\mathbb{E}[\nu|s_i]$, agents combine the prior that ν is zero, with the signal $s_i - \mu$, which is $\nu + (f - \mu) + \varepsilon_i$. The precision of this signal, about the noise ν is $(\Sigma + \Sigma_{\varepsilon_i})^{-1}$. The price signal becomes $s_p = B^{-1}(p - A - C\mathbb{E}[\nu|s_i])$. Since the covariances here can quickly become difficult, one might consider using the state-space updating method to jointly form expectations about f and ν, as described in section 2.2.2.

(iii) Expectation Errors   Hassan and Mertens (2017) consider investors who make small, correlated errors when forming expectations. Instead of adding

public noise ν to signals, they add a shock ν directly to beliefs. This is easier to model because agents are behavioral and do not try to infer their own irrationality rationally. There is no need to deal with the $\mathbb{E}[\nu|s_i]$ term. Because the expectations are correlated, they create noise in prices.

The authors embed this idea in a macroeconomic model in which information is about future productivity. When prices reflect less information, uncertainty rises and distorts consumption, capital accumulation, and labor supply.

(iv) Making Prices Costly to Process　A different solution is to allow prices to be perfectly revealing but simply assume that uncovering price information is costly. One could include the signal precision Σ_p^{-1} in a data cost function or constraint. In reality, inverting a variance-covariance matrix of thousands of assets is very costly and usually returns garbage for estimates. This is why asset pricing embraced factor models as a way of making such estimation more efficient and reliable. Surely, extracting the true value of firms from their prices is not free.

The advantage of this approach is that it is simple. Instead of adding extra complications like the methods above, it simplifies the problem, potentially eliminating the need to determine the precision of price information if investors choose not to observe all price information.

The main drawback of this approach is that financial asset prices are typically much more volatile than any measure of fundamental firm value can explain. Without price noise, the price is fully determined by fundamentals. If this missing price volatility is not important for the research application at hand, then this solution is appropriate. But if one is building a model that needs to speak to variances quantitatively, then having no source of noise in prices will pose a challenge.

(v) Market Power and Finite Traders　When a finite number of market participants affects market prices, each investor's signal noise matters. Without a continuum, the signal noises do not wash out. While the integral of an infinite number of signals about the payoff f will be the payoff f, by the central limit theorem, this does not happen with a small number of investors and a small number of signals. When we introduce a finite number of investors in section 7.10, we will see individual private signal noises show up in prices to create noise. In such a setting, prices do not fully reveal payoffs. That makes noise traders or a random supply unnecessary.

6.8　Financial Data and Increasing Returns

How do agents choose what to learn about? Should they increasingly learn about a random variable, or would they prefer to learn about many variables?

The solution depends on the objective function. If the objective is convex on signal precision (has a positive definite matrix of second derivatives), agents choose to specialize their learning. And what delivers a convex objective that delivers specialized learning? The literature proposes at least four mechanisms: preference for early resolution of uncertainty, home bias, scale economies, and constraints in information acquisition, such as rational inattention.

Learning specialization can explain the home bias puzzle in mutual fund investment: the higher proportion of mutual funds investing domestically and the higher market value of mutual funds investing domestically. In Dziuda and Mondria (2012), delegated fund managers choose whether to specialize in domestic or foreign assets. Individual investors are uncertain about managers' abilities, and they are more informed about domestic markets. This makes domestic investments less risky and generates home bias. In Van Nieuwerburgh and Veldkamp (2010), scale economies in information acquisition make investors specialize in learning about a set of highly correlated assets, and resulting asset portfolios appear under-diversified from the perspective of standard theory.

Big data in finance and firm dynamics may also interact. Begenau, Farboodi, and Veldkamp (2018) argue that using big data in financial markets can significantly lower the cost of capital for large firms relative to small ones; thus, big data disproportionately benefits big firms. Because they have more economic activity and a longer firm history, large firms have produced more data. As processor speed rises, abundant data attracts more financial analysis. Data analysis improves investors' forecasts and reduces equity uncertainty, reducing the firm's cost of capital. When investors can process more data, large firm investment costs fall more, enabling large firms to grow larger.

Information has increasing returns in portfolio problems because it can be used to evaluate one share of an asset or many shares of an asset. When a decision-maker has lots of an asset, information about the asset's payoff is more valuable. Investors who are initially wealthier acquire more information because they have more asset value to apply that information to, and they will also earn higher returns on their investments. Poor individuals may stay poor while the rich get richer. This mechanism has been shown to account for inequality in portfolio holdings of risky assets (Peress, 2004) and the increase in capital income inequality due to investor sophistication (Kacperczyk, Nosal, and Stevens, 2019) and financial innovation (Gambacorta, Gambacorta, and Mihet, 2023).

Key Ideas

- A noisy rational expectations model applies in settings where agents choose how much to engage in multiple risk activities, and they have different data sets to forecast the payoffs of those activities.
- Agents prefer data about actions with expected high profits and prefer data that others do not have.
- When assets are long-lived, the fact that future agents will learn information that will move future prices is a new source of payoff risk today. That unlearnable risk creates diminishing returns to learning.

Practice Questions

6.1 Starting from equation (6.13), derive the price coefficients A, B, and C step by step.

6.2 How would the coefficients in the previous question change if the signal had a public and private noise? Write out the form of the new price equation. Point out and interpret the difference.

6.3 Derive the ex ante variance of $\mathbb{E}[f|\mathcal{I}_i] - pr$ in the portfolio choice model.

6.4 Suppose there are N risky assets whose payoffs are independent. If the asset payoffs are independent (Σ is diagonal), is this sufficient for the pricing coefficient matrix B to be diagonal? If not, what other assumptions are needed to ensure a diagonal B matrix?

6.5 Suppose the risky asset has a private value component: The asset's payoff to each agent i is $f + \xi_i$, where $\xi_i \sim \mathcal{N}(0, \Sigma_\xi)$ is independent across agents. Each agent is presumed to know their private value ξ_i, but uses data to learn about the common-value component of the payoff f, as in the chapter.

   (a) Derive agent i's first-order condition. Describe the vector of optimal quantities of each asset to hold in terms of the mean and conditional variance of f.

   (b) Derive the equilibrium prices. How do they differ from the model without private values? Are there conditions under which the prices in the model with and without private values are the same?

6.6 In equation (6.22), we defined $z \equiv \mathbb{V}ar[f|\mathcal{I}_i]^{-\frac{1}{2}}(\mathbb{E}[f|\mathcal{I}_i] - pr)$. Derive its distribution.

6.7 Suppose that processing or extracting the information in prices is costly. Consider an agent who can choose between getting a marginal increase in their private data precision or getting a marginal increase in the precision of the information in prices. Both options are equally costly.

  (a) Which type of information precision yields the higher increase in marginal utility?

  (b) Will agents ever choose to learn from prices if private data collection or processing has the same cost? If so, under what conditions?

6.8 Sentiment data: Suppose agents now have a fundamental signal about the value of f and a nonfundamental signal about the noise x, as in section 6.5. Write down the equilibrium market clearing condition for this model. What form does price p take? What shocks does it depend on?

6.9 Hedging nonfinancial income: Consider a noisy rational expectation equilibrium. Investors are endowed with a set of nonfinancial and nontradable assets whose payoffs correlate with the asset the issuer sells. Solve for the equilibrium pricing coefficients in the model described in section 6.7 that rationalizes noise traders as noise from hedging nonfinancial income. Preferences are mean-variance as in equation (6.1) .

6.10 In the dynamic model of section 6.6, derive each of the time-t price coefficients and show how it is related to the coefficients at time $t + 1$.

6.11 Solve for optimal data choice with N independent assets and standard noise traders but when signals are about the noise. Assume the marginal cost or marginal shadow cost of one unit of precision is constant and the same for both signals.

6.12 What is the expected value of data when utility is exponential? (*Hint: Look up the formula for the mean of a Wishart distribution*). What would happen if an agent chose data subject to a constraint on the mutual information of all signals and payoffs?

7

Data and Market Power

This chapter explores strategic settings where there are a finite number of firms or financial investors. In this setting, data can be a source of market power; it can benefit consumer welfare; and it can change how market power is used. We start by exploring a Cournot-style model, where firms compete by choosing quantities to produce, with a twist: we adopt the assumption from corporate finance that firms price risk. This is an important twist to include in a tool to understand the data economy. Recall that data is information, which is a tool to resolve uncertainty. Starting from the premise that uncertainty is irrelevant to firms misses much of the importance of data.

We start from a single-good model where firms use data to forecast firm-specific demand shocks. We can interpret this as data used to choose quantities of production. One by one, the chapter adds features to this model. Next, we add a multidimensional product space. Not only are there multiple products, but the demand for these products covaries. That is important because it means that data about one product's demand is also informative about the demand for other products. The existence of multiple products also informs the discussion that follows about markups. The interpretation of this model is that firms use data to select what goods to produce.

When firms can choose the attributes of a product, the mechanics of the model are nearly identical, but the new interpretation is that firms use data for product design or innovation.

A markup is a price divided by a marginal cost. Data affects risk, firm size, and the composition of the goods firms produce, all of which affect markups. The trade-off between these forces depends on the level of aggregation at which markups are measured. This framework speaks to empirical facts about markups. These aggregation effects also form the basis for a data measurement strategy discussed in Chapter 10.

Next, the chapter shows how to generalize the model to correlated or aggregate shocks across firms. In this setting, data helps to forecast a firm's own demand and also helps forecast the production of the firm's competitors. In other words, data now resolves strategic uncertainty. The interpretation in this model is that firms use data to understand their competition.

Then, we adapt and reinterpret the framework as a noisy rational expectations financial market, similar to that explored in Chapter 6, but now with market power. The new model ingredient required to turn a Cournot model into an NREE model is learning from prices. This model can then be used to explore topics such as the price impact of financial trades and the price elasticity of financial markets.

Finally, we review papers that use other frameworks to explore the relationship between data and market power.

7.1   A Single-Good Production Economy: How Much to Produce?

The following model, adapted from Eeckhout and Veldkamp (2022), starts with firms endowed with a given number of data points. It is a Cournot economy, where producers choose quantities to produce, considering that more output lowers prices. This model has a feature that is not typical of Cournot models but is typical in corporate finance and has lots of empirical support: firms price risk. One can merge this theory with one of the ideas about where data comes from in Chapter 3. But first, we explore what effects more data has on a firm that is competing imperfectly, with some market power.

Setup   Consider n_F firms, indexed by $i \in \{1, 2, \ldots, n_F\}$. Each firm chooses the number of units, q_i, of a single good they want to produce to maximize risk-adjusted profit U_i, where the price of risk is ρ_i.

$$U_i = \mathbb{E}\left[\pi_i | \mathcal{I}_i\right] - \frac{\rho_i}{2}\mathbb{V}ar\left[\pi_i | \mathcal{I}_i\right] - \chi(c_i). \tag{7.1}$$

Firm production profit π_i depends on quantities chosen q_i, the firm's price of the good p_i, and the marginal cost of production of that good c_i:

$$\pi_i = q_i\left(p_i - c_i\right). \tag{7.2}$$

Before observing their data, each firm chooses an up-front investment. The up-front investment choice is modeled as a choice of marginal production cost c_i, at an investment cost $\chi(c_i)$, to maximize $\mathbb{E}[U_i]$. The function χ is strictly decreasing and convex in c_i and $\lim_{c_i \to 0} \chi(c_i) = +\infty$. Since lower choices of c_i involve greater costs, this is like choosing a larger firm.

The price of the good depends on the amount every firm produces of that good. More production lowers the price. There is an average market price for the good that takes the form

$$p^M = \bar{p} - \frac{1}{\phi} \sum_{i=1}^{n_F} q_i. \tag{7.3}$$

This expression is an inverse demand curve. It implies that aggregate demand for each good takes the form $\phi(\bar{p} - p^M)$. The sensitivity of aggregate demand to a change in the average market price is $\partial Q / \partial p^M = -\phi$. Thus, the price elasticity of demand, defined as the percentage change in demand from a percentage change in price is $-\phi p^M / Q$, where $Q = \sum_{i=1}^{n_F} q_i$ is aggregate supply, which must equal aggregate demand.

Each firm does not receive the average market price for its good. Rather, each firm i has a firm-specific price p_i, that depends on a firm-specific demand shock b_i. This vector is random and unknown to the firm: $b_i \sim \mathcal{N}(0, 1)$. For simplicity, b_i is i.i.d. across firms. But this is not essential. The price firm i receives per unit is

$$p_i = p^M + b_i. \tag{7.4}$$

Each firm has n_{di} data points. Each data point is a signal about the firm's demand shock

$$s_{i,z} = b_i + \varepsilon_{i,z}, \quad \varepsilon_{i,z} \sim \mathcal{N}(0, \Sigma_\varepsilon). \tag{7.5}$$

Signal noises Σ_ε are uncorrelated across signals and across firms.

Assume data is public information. All firms can observe all the data generated by each firm. Of course, other firms' data is irrelevant for inferring b_i. But this allows firms to know what other firms will do. This assumption is not realistic. It simply eliminates strategic uncertainty about what other firms will do, which simplifies the model. Section 7.7 relaxes this assumption, assumes data is private and solves the model with strategic uncertainty.

Equilibrium   An equilibrium consists of the following elements:

(i) Each firm chooses marginal cost c_i, taking as given other firms' cost choices. Since the data realizations are unknown in this ex ante investment stage, the objective is $\mathbb{E}[U_i]$, the unconditional expectation of the utility in (7.1).

(ii) After observing the realized data, each firm's information set is $\mathcal{I}_i = \{\{s_{i,z}\}_{z=1}^{n_{di}}\}_{i=1}^{n_F}$. They update beliefs with Bayes' Law and then choose the quantity to produce, q_i, to maximize conditional expected utility in (7.1)–(7.4), taking as given other firms' choices.

(iii) Prices clear the market for the good, by following (7.3).

7.2   Cournot Model Solution

Bayesian Updating   According to Bayes' Law for normal variables, observing n_{di} signals, each with signal noise variance Σ_ε is the same as observing the average signal

$$s_i = \frac{1}{n_{di}} \sum_{z=1}^{n_{di}} s_{iz} = b_i + \epsilon_i, \tag{7.6}$$

where the variance of ϵ_i is $\Sigma_{\epsilon_i} = \Sigma_\varepsilon / n_{di}$. Therefore, do a change of variable, replacing the set of data points in the information set, with the composite signal s_i. In this representation, more data points (higher n_{di}) show up as a lower composite signal noise Σ_{ϵ_i}.

Define K_i as the sensitivity of beliefs about demand b_i to the signal. In a dynamic model, this K_i would be called the Kalman gain. According to Bayes' Law: $K_i \equiv (1 + \Sigma_{\epsilon_i})^{-1}$. Then firm i's expected value of the shock b_i can be expressed simply as $\mathbb{E}[b_i | \mathcal{I}_i] = K_i s_i$. Firm i's expected value of other firms' production $\sum_{i'=1}^{n_F} q_{i'}$ is the realized production of the other firms. This is what the assumption that data is public achieves. Since a firm knows what other firms observe, it knows what other firms will do. Notice that the amount of data about firm i is still relevant to firm i because only data about firm i is informative about that firm's demand shock b_i. The expectation and variance of the pricing function (7.3) are

$$\mathbb{E}\left[p_i | \mathcal{I}_i\right] = \bar{p} + \mathbb{E}\left[b_i | \mathcal{I}_i\right] - \frac{1}{\phi} \sum_{i'=1}^{n_F} q_{i'} = \bar{p} + K_i s_i - \frac{1}{\phi} \sum_{i'=1}^{n_F} q_{i'} \tag{7.7}$$

$$\mathbb{V}ar\left[p_i | \mathcal{I}_i\right] = \mathbb{V}ar\left[b_i | \mathcal{I}_i\right] = \left(1 + \Sigma_{\epsilon_i}^{-1}\right)^{-1}. \tag{7.8}$$

Optimal Production Decisions   The first-order condition with respect to goods production q_i yields $\mathbb{E}\left[p_i | \mathcal{I}_i\right] - c_i + \frac{\partial \mathbb{E}[p_i | \mathcal{I}_i]}{\partial q_i} q_i - \rho_i \mathbb{V}ar\left[p_i | \mathcal{I}_i\right] q_i = 0$. Rearranging delivers optimal production:

$$q_i = \left(\rho_i \mathbb{V}ar\left[p_i | \mathcal{I}_i\right] - \frac{\partial \mathbb{E}\left[p_i | \mathcal{I}_i\right]}{\partial q_i}\right)^{-1} \left(\mathbb{E}\left[p_i | \mathcal{I}_i\right] - c_i\right). \tag{7.9}$$

Define the object

$$\hat{H}_i \equiv \left(\rho_i \mathbb{V}ar\left[p_i | \mathcal{I}_i\right] - \partial \mathbb{E}\left[p_i | \mathcal{I}_i\right] / \partial q_i\right)^{-1}. \tag{7.10}$$

From differentiating the pricing function (7.3), we find that the price impact of one additional unit of output is

$$\frac{\partial \mathbb{E}\left[p_i | \mathcal{I}_i\right]}{\partial q_i} = -\frac{1}{\phi}. \tag{7.11}$$

Substitute in the price impact (7.11) and conditional expectation (7.7) in the optimal quantity choice (7.9) to get $q_i = \hat{H}_i \left(\bar{p} + K_i s_i - \frac{1}{\phi} \sum_{i'} q_{i'} - c_i \right)$.

Equilibrium Price   Next, sum production over all firms i to get total production $\sum_{i'} q_{i'}$. This sum has a $\sum_{i'} q_{i'}$ on both the left and right hand sides. Collect these terms and rearrange to get $\sum_{i'} q_{i'} = \left(I + \frac{1}{\phi} \sum_{i'} \hat{H}_{i'} \right)^{-1} \left[\sum_{i'} \hat{H}_{i'} \left(\bar{p} + K_{i'} s_{i'} - c_{i'} \right) \right]$.

Substituting this total production expression for $\sum_{i'=1}^{n_F} q_{i'}$ in firm i's optimal production (7.9) yields the optimal production of each firm i, in terms of signals s_i, costs c_i, and data, which is captured in the term $\hat{H}_i$:[1]

$$q_i = \hat{H}_i \left(\bar{p} + K_i s_i - c_i - \frac{1}{\phi} \left(I + \frac{1}{\phi} \sum_{i'} \hat{H}_{i'} \right)^{-1} \left[\sum_{i'} \hat{H}_{i'} \left(\bar{p} + K_{i'} s_{i'} - c_{i'} \right) \right] \right). \tag{7.12}$$

Substituting the total production expression for $\sum_{i'=1}^{n_F} q_{i'}$ in the pricing function (7.3) yields an equilibrium average price of the good:

$$p^M = \bar{p} - \frac{1}{\phi} \left(1 + \frac{1}{\phi} \sum_i \hat{H}_i \right)^{-1} \left[\sum_i \hat{H}_i \left(\bar{p} + K_i s_i - c_i \right) \right]. \tag{7.13}$$

Expected Utility   To solve for the firms' cost choices, we need to solve for the expected utility of each firm. We start with the expected profits, conditional on data. A firm's profit is its quantity times its profit per unit:

$$q_i' \left(\mathbb{E}\left[p_i | \mathcal{I}_i \right] - c_i \right) = q_i' \hat{H}_i^{-1} q_i,$$

where the equality follows from rearranging the firm's production first-order condition, $q_i = \hat{H}_i \left(\mathbb{E}\left[p_i | \mathcal{I}_i \right] - c_i \right)$, and substituting in $\hat{H}_i^{-1} q_i$ for $\left(\mathbb{E}\left[p_i | \mathcal{I}_i \right] - c_i \right)$. Next, we need to know the conditional variance of the firm's profit. Since the firm knows its own output choice q_i and its chosen marginal cost c_i, the only source of variance is the price:

$$\mathbb{V}ar\left[q_i' \left(p_i - c_i \right) | \mathcal{I}_i \right] = q_i' \mathbb{V}ar\left[p_i | \mathcal{I}_i \right] q_i.$$

---

1. Since all signals are normally distributed, this formula does tell us that production can potentially be negative. We could bound choices to be nonnegative, but this would make analytical solutions for covariances impossible. If parameters are such that firms want negative production, then the solution is to redefine the product as its opposite. Simply choose parameters that make negative production extremely unlikely.

Then, we substitute the mean and variance into the mean-variance utility function in (7.1):

$$U_i = q_i' \left(\hat{H}_i^{-1} - \frac{\rho_i}{2} \mathbb{V}ar\left[p_i|\mathcal{I}_i\right] \right) q_i - \chi(c_i).$$

For convenience, let's define $H_i \equiv \hat{H}_i^{-1} - \frac{\rho_i}{2} \mathbb{V}ar\left[p_i|\mathcal{I}_i\right]$. Then, the expected objective of a firm, at the time when they have observed their data and are choosing output q_i, can be expressed as $q_i' H_i q_i$, minus the initial investment cost $\chi(c_i)$.

When the firm needs to choose its up-front investment of how big a factory to build, it does not know what its data will tell it. The firm knows how much data will come in. But it does not know whether that data will reveal good or bad news. We call this period of time before the firm knows its data the ex ante stage. In the ex ante period, q_i is unknown to the firm. Before learning from its data, the firm does not know what it will choose in the future. Thus, to choose the size of the investment, the firm needs to maximize $\mathbb{E}[U_i]$, the unconditional expectation of its future utility. Since q_i is a linear function of normally distributed signals, q_i is a normally distributed random variable. However, q_i enters in utility U_i twice, multiplicatively. Thus, U_i is a multivariate squared normal variable known as a chi-square variable. Using the formula for the mean of a noncentral, chi-square N (see appendix A.4.1) we can express ex ante expected utility as

$$\mathbb{E}[U_i] = \mathbb{E}\left[q_i' H_i q_i\right] - \chi(c_i) = \left(\mathbb{E}[q_i]' H_i \mathbb{E}[q_i]\right.$$
$$\left. + \mathrm{Tr}\left(H_i \mathbb{V}ar[q_i]\right)\right) - \chi(c_i). \tag{7.14}$$

In the one-good economy, $\mathrm{Tr}\left(H_i \mathbb{V}ar[q_i]\right)$ is simply $H_i \mathbb{V}ar[q_i]$. In the multi-good economy, it will be the matrix trace. Using the first-order condition (7.9), $\mathbb{V}ar[q_i] = \hat{H}_i \mathbb{V}ar[\mathbb{E}[p_i|\mathcal{I}_i]]\hat{H}_i$. By the law of total variance (section 2.1.4), this is $\hat{H}_i(\mathbb{V}ar[p_i] - \mathbb{V}ar[p_i|\mathcal{I}_i])\hat{H}_i$. This variance term depends on the precision of the firm's data and parameters, but not on the firm's cost choice.

Optimal Investment Choices   Firm i chooses cost c_i to maximize its unconditional expected utility $\mathbb{E}[U_i]$, taking others' costs as given. The optimal cost c_i for an interior solution satisfies

$$\frac{\partial \mathbb{E}[U_i]}{\partial c_i} = \frac{\partial \mathbb{E}[q_i]' H_i \mathbb{E}[q_i]}{\partial c_i} - \frac{\partial \chi(c_i)}{\partial c_i} = 0. \tag{7.15}$$

The second term is the marginal cost of the up-front investment. The first term is the marginal benefit of that investment. Lower production costs enable production at a greater scale and higher profit per unit. Notice that the marginal benefit of a lower c_i (a larger, more efficient factory) is increasing in H_i, which itself is decreasing in the conditional variance of demand, $\mathbb{V}ar[q_i]$. When a firm has more data, they use this data to make their demand forecast more precise, decreasing the conditional variance, raising H_i, and making a larger firm investment optimal. Firms with more data know they can use their production infrastructure more profitably, producing the right amount at the right time. The greater profitability makes investing more in the larger, lower-cost factory worthwhile. This is data-investment complementarity.

7.3   The Substitutability of Market Power and Risk

One of the ideas this framework makes clear is that market power and risk affect prices and quantities in similar ways. Recall that data reduces uncertainty or risk. This means that a firm with market power is similar to a firm with less data. Market power and risk are not observationally equivalent. The difference will be apparent when we discuss aggregation effects in a few pages. But they have many effects that are similar. A risk-averse firm will scale back its production plans and respond less sensitively to changes in expected profit. A firm that has market power does the same.

We can see this similarity mathematically by examining the firm's optimal production choice in (7.9). The denominator of optimal production is

$$\rho_i \mathbb{V}ar\left[p_i|\mathcal{I}_i\right] - \frac{\partial \mathbb{E}\left[p_i|\mathcal{I}_i\right]}{\partial q_i}. \tag{7.16}$$

The first term is the price of risk, times risk. The second term is how much the firm expects an extra production unit to reduce the price. The partial derivative $\partial p_i/\partial q_i$ is negative because more supply lowers the price. Since the second term enters with a minus sign, we effectively add these two positive forces together. Adding means that more of one substitutes for the other. A firm facing more risk (less data) or a higher price of risk acts like a firm with more market power, and vice-versa.

One reason this substitutability matters is that when data is scarce and risk is high, small changes in market power will have little effect. Suppose the risk term is 100. The market power term, $\partial p_i/\partial q_i$, rises from 2 to 3. This is an enormous, 50% increase in the firm's ability to manipulate prices. The sum of these two terms enters the denominator of the firm's supply choice. In other words, the firm will produce an amount equal to expected profit times $1/102$ in one case and expected profit times $1/103$ in the other. That is a tiny difference. When the risk is high, it drowns out the effect of market power. More data reduces risk. This makes firms' use of market power more apparent. This adds a new twist to the discussion of the rise of market power in the modern economy.

The converse is also true. When market power is large relative to risk, changes in the firm's data set have little effect on the firm's decision. High market power can also drown out the effect of data.

7.4 Data, Product Markups, and Market Power

Using the solution to the Cournot model, we can now explore what effect data has on markups and market power. In what follows, we highlight how markups differ with aggregation—at the product, firm, or industry level.

Product-Level Markup   We define the product-level markup of a product produced by firm i as

$$M_i^p \equiv \frac{\mathbb{E}[p_i]}{c_i}. \tag{7.17}$$

To derive an expression for the product markup, we divide the expected product price (7.13) by the marginal cost, c_i:

$$M_i^p \equiv \frac{\mathbb{E}[p_i]}{c_i} = \frac{1}{c_i}\left(\bar{p} - (\phi + \bar{H})^{-1}\left(\sum_i \hat{H}_i\left(\bar{p} + K_i s_i - c_i\right)\right)\right) \tag{7.18}$$

where $\bar{H} \equiv \sum_{i=1}^{n_F} \hat{H}_i$.

What Makes a Markup Large?   Most causes of high markups in equation (7.18) are unsurprising. For example, having high expected demand $\bar{p}$ relative to the cost c raises the markup. Also, having fewer firms raises markups: low n_F lowers $\bar{H}$, which makes the negative term on the right smaller. This is the classic concern with concentrated markets.

Markups are also compensation for risk. When firms are more sensitive to risk, or the price of risk in capital markets is high (high ρ), this raises markups. This force works through $\bar{H}$, making it low. When firms are very sensitive to risk, they are less sensitive to prices and costs (lower H's). They won't produce much more when there are small changes in profits because they are too sensitive to the additional risk that additional production will entail.

How Does This Relate to Data?   Two forces show up in the markup formula that are affected by how much data a firm has. Those forces are risk and the choice of marginal cost. Data is a tool to reduce uncertainty or lower risk, reducing the risk premium and markups. However, a firm with more data has a larger benefit from investing more to reduce their marginal cost. A lower cost c_i, raises the markup. The net effect depends on the price of risk ρ and the investment cost function χ.

7.5   Multiple Products: What to Produce?

A useful feature of the Cournot-with-risk framework is that it can be extended to consider competition with multiple products with correlated demand. Pellegrino (2023) pioneered this approach, while Ederer and Pellegrino (2022) show that its linear hedonic pricing structure empirically outperforms other demand systems. Multiple products and correlated demand are useful because they make the framework more appropriate for measurement. With multiple products, there is another dimension of competition: firms can compete by choosing a location in the product space. Introducing multiple products also allows us to see how data creates composition effects in our measures of market competition. These composition effects are the subject of debate in the empirical literature. They also turn out to be useful for measuring data, a topic we return to in Chapter 10.

Products and Attributes   The product space has N attributes, indexed by $j \in \{1, 2, \dots, N\}$. Attributes could be the color, material, size, or function of a product. Goods, indexed by k, are linear combinations of attributes. Each good k can be represented as an $N \times 1$ vector a_k of weights that the good places on each attribute. The jth entry of vector a_k describes how much of attribute j the kth good requires. This collection of weights describes a good's location in the product space. Let the collection of a_k's for each good k, be a matrix A.[2]

One can allow firms to choose how to position their product in the product space by choosing A's. For ease of exposition, we will take A to be given and identical for each firm.

The quantity of attributes that a firm i produces is a vector $\tilde{q}_i$, with jth element $\tilde{q}_{ij}$. The attribute vector is the vector of firm i's product quantities, q_i, times the attribute matrix A:

$$\tilde{q}_i = A q_i. \tag{7.19}$$

The entries of A describe how much of each attribute each product contains. For example, a blue, cotton sweater might have a loading of 1 on each of the attributes blue, cotton, and sweater. A blue phone might have a large weight on phone and a small weight on blue, if color is not such an important characteristic of a phone.

---

2. For a reader who is at ease with the portfolio choice model of Chapter 6, it might be helpful to see an analogy between attributes, which are like risk factors or Arrow-Debreu securities. Then, products become like assets, which can always be expressed as a portfolio, or linear combination, of Arrow securities. Firms will then choose portfolios of products to produce, which is like choosing a portfolio of risky assets to invest in. Both offer uncertain returns.

The marginal cost of producing a good depends on the up-front investment the firm makes and on the good's attributes. The firm's up-front investment of $\chi(\widetilde{c}_i)$ allows it to produce each attribute j at a unit cost of $\widetilde{c}_{ij}$. The vector $\widetilde{c}_i$ is the $N \times 1$ vector of all marginal production costs of firm i, for each attribute. The vector $c_i = A' \widetilde{c}_i$ is the vector of firm i's marginal cost for each product. The cost of producing a unit of good k for firm i is therefore $c_{ik} = a_k' \widetilde{c}_i$. To keep the investment problem bounded, the investment cost function χ is convex in each element $\widetilde{c}_{ij}$.

The price a firm receives for a unit of good k is therefore $p_k + \sum_{j=1}^{N} a_{jk} b_{ij}$. The demand shocks are still firm-specific. Now they are also attribute-specific. The vector b_i is a vector with jth entry b_{ij} that represents all the demand shocks that affect firm i. The vector b_i is multivariate normal $b_i \sim \mathcal{N}(0, \Sigma_b)$, where Σ_b is a diagonal $N \times N$ matrix. This structure allows demand shocks to be correlated across goods. The correlation depends on how much the goods load on similar attributes. This correlation structure is important to consider because it implies that data about the demand for one good will also be informative about another. Firms with abundant data in one area of the product space may choose to produce a set of related products for which they have demand-forecasting expertise.

We can solve this model, just as before, if we first change the choice of how many goods to produce, into a choice of how many units of each attribute to produce, the vector $\widetilde{q}_i$. Once we do that, the choice problem becomes additively separable in attributes. In other words, one can solve for optimal choices of each attribute as if only one attribute or one good existed in the market. Similarly, the choice of the marginal cost of an attribute $\widetilde{c}_i$ is also additively separable. One can solve as if each attribute were the only good in a market. Once the optimal attribute choices are solved, simply map them back into optimal product production and cost choices by premultiplying by the matrix A^{-1}.

7.6 Data and Composition Effects in Aggregation

The following discussion about exactly how markups are measured gets a bit into the weeds of the empirical literature on market competition. The reason to take this detour is because understanding how to construct such measures points us to new ways of measuring data.

We begin by defining firm markups to explore their relationship to the product markups defined previously.

Firm Markup   Firm i's markup equals its revenue divided by its total variable costs:

$$M_i^f \equiv \frac{\mathbb{E}[q_i' p_i]}{\mathbb{E}[q_i' c_i]}. \tag{7.20}$$

To understand the relationship between firm markups and product markups, we can rewrite the expectation of the product of price and quantity as the product of expectations, plus a covariance term:

$$M_i^f = \frac{\mathbb{E}[q_i]'\mathbb{E}[p_i] + \text{Tr}\,[\mathbb{C}ov(p_i, q_i)]}{\mathbb{E}[q_i'c_i]} = \underbrace{\frac{\sum_{j=1}^{N} M_{ij}^p c_i(j)\mathbb{E}[q_i(j)]}{\sum_{j=1}^{N} c_i(j)\mathbb{E}[q_i(j)]}}_{\text{Cost-weighted product markups}}$$

$$+ \frac{\text{Tr}[\mathbb{C}ov\,(p_i, q_i)]}{\sum_{j=1}^{N} c_i(j)\mathbb{E}[q_i(j)]}. \tag{7.21}$$

The second equality takes the definition of the product markup and substitutes: $\mathbb{E}[p_i(j)] = M_{ij}^p c_i(j)$. Then, rewrite the resulting vector products as a sum. We learn that the firm markup is a cost-weighted sum of product markups plus a term that depends on the covariance of prices and quantities. Firm data acts on this last term. It allows firms to produce more of the goods that turn out to have high demand and thus a high price.

Data Accumulation Widens the Wedge between Product and Firm Markups   For reasonable parameters, an increase in firm i's data about any attribute increases $M_i^f - \overline{M}_i^p$ where $\overline{M}_i^p = \frac{1}{N}\sum_j M_{ij}^p$. (Eeckhout and Veldkamp, 2022).

Firm markups rise when data increases the covariance of the firm's production decision q_i with the price p_i in (7.21). Without any data to predict demand, this covariance is low: firms cannot know which markups would be high and when (or which goods in a multiproduct setting) to produce more of. The positive effect of data on the price-quantity covariance shows up in the production first-order condition (7.9), where a reduction in the conditional variance of demand makes production decisions q_i more sensitive to expected changes in price p_i. That higher sensitivity is a higher covariance.

Not only is data one possible explanation for covariance, but data also makes covariance between actions and states possible. Data makes it possible for the firm to skew the composition of their products in the direction of high-markup goods. Every firm would like to produce more high-profit goods. But such a strategy is not feasible in measure-theory parlance. Such a strategy is not a measurable strategy without predictive data. This idea that data governs action-outcome covariances is a theme that recurs across models.

Industry Markups   Typically, researchers are interested in the markup for an industry because the regulatory question of interest is whether that industry is a competitive one or not. However, there are multiple ways to aggregate the markups for each firm into a single industry measure. Eeckhout and Veldkamp (2022) construct four of the most common measures to understand how they differ. Then, they compare their theoretical predictions to empirical evidence. The model lends an interpretation to the different trends and different cyclical behaviors found by empirical researchers who measure industry markups. The different behaviors of each markup measure come from composition effects. The firms that use abundant data to produce many goods with higher product markups have high firm markups. These same firms choose significant investments to lower their marginal cost and produce more. Thus, weighting large firms more weights high-data, high-markup firms more. Furthermore, the large firms that chose to have low marginal costs have higher sales weights relative to their total cost weights. Their cost weights are relatively lower because of the low choice of cost. The point is that data changes the covariance between the firms' choices and outcomes. These covariances often show up in empirical work as composition effects. Thus, composition changes can signal that firms are using data.

7.7   Adding Strategic Uncertainty

In the versions of the imperfect competition model presented so far, firms knew what other firms' data said. Therefore, they knew what output decisions other firms would make. That assumption is not realistic. But it simplified the model. In reality, others' actions are uncertain. We call the uncertainty about what others will do *strategic uncertainty*. Data can help to resolve such strategic uncertainty. Data can be used to forecast the forecasts of others. We have seen data used in this way already: in the Morris and Shin (2002) model of Chapter 5, agents used data to forecast the state and the average action. Here, we explore how to insert such strategic uncertainty into our model of a production economy with market power.

The key new assumptions are that data is private and demand shocks are correlated across firms. Private data means that firms here do not know what other firms know. Thus, there is a "forecasting the forecasts of others" problem, similar to that in section 5.2. That is the strategic uncertainty. The fact that demand shocks are correlated means that one firm's data is relevant for forecasting other firms' data and another firm's forecast. We will solve the single-good version of the model. However, this solution method can easily be extended with vectors of goods, as in section 7.5.

Each firm sees a private signal: s_i is standard normal and $s_i = b + \varepsilon_i$ where the variance of b and ε_i are Σ_b and $\Sigma_{\epsilon_i} = \Sigma_\varepsilon / n_{di}$ respectively.

Each firm has the same mean-variance objective and chooses the number of units q_i of a product to produce, at per-unit cost c_i. The market price depends linearly on the demand shock b, now an aggregate, rather than firm-specific shock, a constant term $\bar{p}$ and the total production of all firms:

$$p = \bar{p} + b - \frac{1}{\phi} \sum_{i=1}^{n_F} q_i. \tag{7.22}$$

Solution From the firm's first-order condition with respect to q_i (7.9) and the price impact equation (7.11), we can express optimal production as $q_i = \hat{H}_i \left(\mathbb{E}\left[p_i | \mathcal{I}_i \right] - c_i \right)$. This first-order condition looks the same as with public data and no strategic uncertainty. The difference is in how the price expectation $\mathbb{E}\left[p_i | \mathcal{I}_i \right]$ is formed.

Let $\varepsilon_{i'}$ be the noise in the signal of firm i'. We guess and verify a linear price function with coefficients D, F, and $\{h_i\}_{i=1}^{n_F}$,

$$p = D + Fb + \sum_{i'=1}^{n_F} h_{i'} \varepsilon_{i'}. \tag{7.23}$$

Notice that each firm's signal and the market price are imperfectly correlated. The signal can forecast the aggregate demand shock Fb. But it is also relevant to form a belief about what each firm's own signal noise ε_i is. This falls squarely in the category of messy signal structures that call for using state-space methods. Using the Bayesian updating tools in section 2.2, we can write the conditional expectation and variance as:

$$\mathbb{E}[p|s_i] = D + \beta_i s_i \tag{7.24}$$

$$\mathbb{V}ar[p|s_i] = \mathbb{V}ar(p) - \beta_i \mathbb{C}ov(p, s_i)' \tag{7.25}$$

$$\beta_i = \mathbb{C}ov(p, s_i) \mathbb{V}ar(s_i)^{-1}. \tag{7.26}$$

The optimal production is

$$q_i = \hat{H}_i (D - c_i + \beta_i s_i). \tag{7.27}$$

Since signals are all about the same demand shock, b, with independent noise, we can write one firm's expectation of another firm's signal as $\mathbb{E}[s_j|s_i] = \mathbb{E}[b|s_i]$. Note that this collapses the problem of forecasting the forecasts of others to a problem of forecasting the state, which is substantially simpler. Using this insight and the optimal production in (7.27), we can now write firm i's expectation of firm l's output as $\mathbb{E}[q_l|s_i] = \hat{H}_l(D - c_l + \beta_l \mathbb{E}[b|s_i])$. Adding up firm i's expectations of all firms output yields firm i's expectation of aggregate output: $\mathbb{E}[\sum_{l=1}^{n_F} q_l|s_i] = q_i + \sum_{l \neq i} \hat{H}_l(D - c_l + \beta_l \mathbb{E}[b|s_i])$. The conditional variance of aggregate output is $\sum_{l \neq i} \hat{H}_l \beta_l \mathbb{V}ar[b|s_i]\beta_l' \hat{H}_l'$.

Once we know each firm's belief and conditional variance of aggregate output, we can substitute these back into the price rule and determine firm i's expectation and uncertainty about the price. With the mean and variance of the price, we can use the first-order condition for each firm (7.9) to re-solve each firm's production decision in terms of that firm's signal.

Finally, we add up the production choices of all the firms. If we substitute this aggregate output into the equilibrium price rule (7.22), and then equate that equilibrium price to the linear price guess in (7.23), we can solve for the price coefficients:

$$F = I_N - \frac{1}{\phi} \sum_{i=1}^{n_F} \hat{H}_i \beta_i \tag{7.28}$$

$$h_i = -\frac{1}{\phi} \hat{H}_i \beta_i, \quad \forall\, i = 1, \ldots, n_F \tag{7.29}$$

$$D = \left(I_N + \frac{1}{\phi} \sum_{i=1}^{n_F} \hat{H}_i \right)^{-1} \left(\bar{p} + \frac{1}{\phi} \sum_{i=1}^{n_F} \hat{H}_i c_i \right), \tag{7.30}$$

where the Bayesian updating weight, β_i, and the sensitivity of demand to expected price changes, $\hat{H}_i$, are

$$\beta_i = \left(F \Sigma_b + h_i \Sigma_{\epsilon_i} \right) \left(\Sigma_b + \Sigma_{\epsilon_i} \right)^{-1}$$

$$\hat{H}_i = \left[\rho_i \left(F \Sigma_b F' + \sum_{i=1}^{n_F} h_i \Sigma_{\epsilon_i} h_i' - \left(F \Sigma_b + h_i \Sigma_{\epsilon_i} \right) \left(\Sigma_b + \Sigma_{\epsilon_i} \right)^{-1} \right. \right.$$

$$\left. \left. \left(F \Sigma_b + h_i \Sigma_{\epsilon_i} \right)' \right) + \frac{I_N}{\phi} \right]^{-1}.$$

Notice that there is a fixed-point problem. The price coefficient F on the aggregate demand shock depends on each firm's output sensitivity to expected profit $\hat{H}_i$. But each firm's output sensitivity, in turn, depends on F. The lack of an explicit solution makes this model more difficult to work with than the version without strategic uncertainty. However, the implicit function theorem can still deliver comparative statics.

7.8   Using Data for Product Innovation

We have explored firms' use of data to choose how much to produce and then which goods to produce. But in many cases, firms use data to design new goods. A simple rotation of the multiproduct problem allows this framework to describe how data enables product innovation.

In section 7.5, we introduced the idea of product attributes. Attributes created demand covariance so that a single piece of data might be informative about the demand for multiple products. Previously, we held the attributes of each product fixed. In reality, firms choose attributes.

Suppose each firm produces a single product. The firm chooses how many units of the product to produce and what weight the product should place on each attribute. Formally, firm $i \in \{1, 2, \ldots, n_F\}$ chooses an $N \times 1$ vector a_i that describes their location in the product space, such that $\sum_j a_{ij} = 1$. As before, the jth entry of vector a_i describes how much of attribute j firm i's good contains.

The rest of the model assumptions, including consumer demand and the nature of data, are the same as in the previous sections. We denote the firm-specific price of the attributes as $\tilde{p}_i$ and the firm's marginal cost of each attribute as $\tilde{c}_i$. The firm's production problem is

$$\max_{a_i, q_i} \mathbb{E}\left[q_i a_i' \left(\tilde{p}_i - \tilde{c}_i\right) | \mathcal{I}_i\right] - \frac{\rho_i}{2} \mathbb{V}ar\left[q_i a_i' \left(\tilde{p}_i - \tilde{c}_i\right) | \mathcal{I}_i\right] - \chi(\tilde{c}_i), \quad (7.31)$$

subject to the constraint $\sum_j a_{ij} = 1$.

Like the previous problem, each firm chooses its attribute cost vector $\tilde{c}_i$ before observing its data. Since the data realizations are unknown in this ex ante investment stage, the objective is the unconditional expectation of the utility in (7.1)

$$\max_{c_i} \mathbb{E}\left[\mathbb{E}\left[q_i a_i' \left(\tilde{p}_i - \tilde{c}_i\right) | \mathcal{I}_i\right] - \frac{\rho_i}{2} \mathbb{V}ar\left[q_i a_i' \left(\tilde{p}_i - \tilde{c}_i\right) | \mathcal{I}_i\right]\right] - \chi(\tilde{c}_i).$$
$$(7.32)$$

Optimal Production Firm i's optimal production from the first-order condition looks identical to the one before, except that now it is the product of quantity and attributes that achieve this solution.

$$q_i a_i = \left(\rho_i \mathbb{V}ar\left[\tilde{p}_i | \mathcal{I}_i\right] + \frac{\partial \mathbb{E}\left[\tilde{p}_i | \mathcal{I}_j\right]}{\partial (q_i \tilde{a}_i)}\right)^{-1} \left(\mathbb{E}\left[\tilde{p}_i | \mathcal{I}_i\right] - \tilde{c}_i\right). \quad (7.33)$$

This tells us that the solution to the problem is essentially unchanged. It replaces the quantity vector times attribute matrix $A q_i$ with the scalar quantity times attribute vector $q_i a_i$ of the newly designed good.

The only thing that changes in this formulation of the problem is the interpretation of what constitutes a product. In the previous problem, a product had a fixed set of attributes. In this problem, a product is a fraction of the firm's total output. Therefore the product markup here is more like what the firm markup was before. In other words, data affects the composition of a product now. Firms with data choose to produce products with higher-value attributes.

7.9 Customer Capital

In the modern data economy, firms spend substantial resources on marketing, advertising, branding, and selling. In 2021, companies spent $1 trillion on marketing globally. Advertising comprises around 40% of marketing, or 2.5% of US GDP.[3] The rise of digital advertising, which is tightly linked to the use of big data, is staggering. According to Cavenaile et al. (2023), online advertising revenue in the United States grew from $8 billion in 2000 to $190 billion in 2021, outgrowing any other advertising method. In 2022, digital advertising accounted for 67% of total advertising revenue worldwide and is expected to surpass 70% by 2025.

These enormous expenditures reveal frictions in product markets, which require firms to spend time and resources to attract, retain, and learn about their customers. Customer capital is a form of intangible capital based on knowledge and data records of customer demographics and preferences. Traditionally, advertising has allowed consumers to get to know new products. The data economy has further allowed them to select the best products among those they know.

Customer capital may be a source of firms' market power. Since search is costly and time-consuming, producers and customers pursue long-term relationships to split the implied rents. Firms may exert market power as customers get locked in to their products.[4]

In what follows, we focus on the role of data for customer capital and market power in the context of firms and consumers. Still, the same ideas apply to firm-to-firm relationships in production networks (Bernard et al., 2022).

7.9.1 Customer Capital Dynamics

To organize ideas, consider the law of motion for a firm's customer capital. Let c_t be the customer base (the number of incumbent customers) and n_t be the number of new customers acquired at date t. The customer base evolves

3. Douglas Galbi, "US Advertising Expenditure Data," purple motes (website), September 14, 2008, https://www.purplemotes.net/2008/09/14/us-advertising-expenditure-data/.

4. There is an active debate about whether markups increase in the firm's life cycle due to customer concerns. Some disagree with the view that firms with more extensive customer bases charge higher markups and instead argue that markups are flat, and any demand accumulation dynamics are nonpecuniary (i.e., not through prices, price discounts, markups, etc.) but through active investments, such as advertising (Argente et al., 2021).

according to

$$c_t = \underbrace{\rho_t}_{\text{retention}} c_{t-1} + \underbrace{n_t}_{\text{acquisition}} . \tag{7.34}$$

The retention rate $\rho_t \in (0, 1)$ is the share of incumbent customers at $t-1$ that remain loyal to the firm at t; alternatively, the depreciation rate $1 - \rho_t$ is the share of customers that leave the firm. Higher ρ_t implies a more inertial customer base in the sense that customers tend to choose the same products and firms over time.

Customer capital relates to data in two ways. First, data in the form of customer lists is digital intangible capital. However, part of this capital is also a customer relationship. Second, lists with information may be used as predictive data. Accurate predictions can help firms attract and retain customers. In this way, the retention ρ_t and acquisition n_t components are a function of data, which is derived from customer capital accumulated in the past.

The law of motion in (7.34) reflects customers' extensive-margin demand. It presumes that firms only care about how many customers it has and not how much each of them purchases. Alternatively, we can interpret c_t as intensive-margin demand, reflecting how demand changes for the already matched customers. Afrouzi, Drenik, and Kim (2023) present empirical evidence on the extensive and intensive margins of customer accumulation.

Customer Acquisition   A first factor limiting customer acquisition n_t is search frictions—impediments to meeting, matching, and agreeing on the terms of a partnership between firms and customers (Hall, 2008). The literature on frictional product markets borrows and expands the ideas from the labor search literature. Like unemployed workers meeting job vacancies, Burdett and Judd (1983) and Gourio and Rudanko (2014) model meetings between idle firms and potential customers through a frictional matching process. More and better data ameliorates search frictions and accelerates the matching process.

Customer acquisition may also be hampered when markets are segmented, for instance, across customer groups with shared demographic characteristics or geographic proximity (Kaplan and Menzio, 2015). Market segmentation allows firms to tailor their marketing and sales strategies to the needs of specific groups. It may give rise to pricing-to-market strategies, where producers choose markups that vary across segmented markets for the same good. Data plays a crucial role in identifying potential consumer segments, for example, through targeted advertising as discussed below.

Customer Retention   Customer retention for firms is inertia for customers. Factors explaining inertia include deep habits (Ravn, Schmitt-Grohé, and Uribe, 2006; Gilchrist et al., 2017), brand preferences (Bronnenberg, Dubé, and Gentzkow, 2012), and switching costs (Klemperer, 1987). A firm may also provide incentives that deter its incumbent customers from changing to a competitor. Data processing helps design retention incentives by tracking and extracting clients' preferences from their purchases. Bornstein (2020) suggests population aging as a different source of consumer inertia: older adults are substantially less likely to switch products than the young. Aging economies with higher retention rates have lower firm entry and higher profit shares. In this context, consumer age and habits data are particularly useful for marketing strategists.

Firms use diverse strategies to accumulate customer capital. Next, we discuss pricing, segmentation, and advertising strategies.

7.9.2   Pricing Strategies

One way to attract new customers is to charge low prices for some time and offer entry discounts. For example, internet providers offer lower monthly rates to first-time users, and credit card companies waive fees during the first year.

Lambrecht et al. (2014) explore the trade-off between various income sources, such as delivering premium content or offering free content to attract customers and maximize advertising revenues.

Pricing under customer capital involves a trade-off between increasing market share in the future by lowering price today and exploiting existing customers by raising price today (Phelps and Winter, 1970; Rotemberg and Woodford, 1991). Therefore, the optimal current markup depends on current sales and the present value of future sales. If the present value of future profits is high, the firm gains by reducing its markup to build its customer base. By contrast, high current demand relative to the present value of future profits raises the incentive to exploit current customers by raising the markup. These effects are characterized by Burdett and Coles (1997) in an equilibrium model of price dispersion: Smaller (younger) firms announce lower prices and grow faster than larger (established) firms. Furthermore, the youngest firms set prices below marginal cost to build the business up quickly, anticipating extracting customer switching rents. More recently, Roldan-Blanco and Gilbukh (2021) examine dynamic pricing contracts that balance attracting new customers and exploiting preexisting ones, showing that these contracts provide a quantitatively good fit to retail establishments' life cycle and cross-sectional properties. Chiavari (2023) extends this search framework to consider customers that switch directly from firm to firm (an analogy for on-the-job search).

Temporary sales are another type of incentive and an equilibrium outcome in frictional product markets with long-term relationships (Rudanko, 2022). Price stickiness is another strategy in which firms reduce the pass-through of costs to prices (Bils, 1989; Paciello, Pozzi, and Trachter, 2019). Both temporary sales and lower pass-through may coexist. For instance, Nakamura and Steinsson (2011) and Gourio and Rudanko (2014) show that if consumers form habits in individual goods, firms face a time-inconsistency problem: firms are incentivized to promise low prices in the future to attract customers in the present but overcharge when the future arrives. Firms commit to a sticky price with frequent sales to circumvent this incentive problem. Microdata from the retail industry provides empirical support for these predictions.

7.9.3 Product Segmentation and New Varieties

Product segmentation helps attract and retain customers. As search frictions in the market for a consumer product decline due to targeted advertising, buyers can locate and access more and more sellers. In response, sellers choose to design varieties of products that are more and more specialized to take advantage of the heterogeneity in buyers' preferences. Menzio (2023) characterizes conditions under which the increase in specialization exactly offsets the decline in search frictions. Under these conditions, the extent of competition and price dispersion remain constant over time, even though search frictions are vanishing. Buyers' surplus and sellers' profit, however, grow over time at a constant endogenous rate, as the increase in specialization allows sellers to cater better and better to the preferences of individual buyers.

Baslandze et al. (2023) study how the advent of digital advertising stimulated more product variety and provide micro-level evidence of a positive correlation between the growth in digital ads and the growth in product varieties.

7.9.4 Traditional and Targeted Advertising

Advertising is a collection of firm strategies with the objective of making consumers aware of a new product. It also aims to sustain consumers' awareness stock, which depreciates over time as individuals forget or lose interest in products or services they know about. Within advertising, we can distinguish between traditional, "untargeted" advertising and "targeted" advertising. Traditional, undirected advertising aims to make all consumers aware of a product and then hope that a significant fraction of them make a purchase. For example, a beer ad during the Super Bowl is worth millions because it reaches millions of consumers. However, these consumers may or may not be interested in that particular beer brand or not even drink alcohol. In contrast, targeted advertising aims to increase the likelihood that new consumers will have a high preference for their product. It involves personalized advertising experiences and ads tailored to consumers' interests, preferences, and behaviors. Data increases the effectiveness of both traditional and targeted advertising, as consumers are more likely to engage with ads relevant to their interests.[5]

Since advertising shifts customers' demand away from competitors, it is also a source of market power. Moreover, advertising may exacerbate differences across firms and promote market concentration and market power. For instance, in Cavenaile et al. (2023), the best firms advertise more to raise their markups. However, in general equilibrium, advertising partly remedies the misallocation from market power. In Dinlersoz and Yorukoglu (2012), firms are heterogeneous in their ability to process data and advertise to consumers. Similarly, customer accumulation exacerbates differences in firm-level returns to scale in Chiavari (2023). In both papers, reducing the cost of advertising results in higher industry concentration, higher firm turnover and growth, and higher dispersion in firm size and value. Morlacco and Zeke (2021) argue that large firms increase their advertising spending significantly more than small firms following an interest rate decline, increasing their market share. The model provides a rationale for the rise in market concentration and market power in recent decades while interest rates fell.

7.9.5   A Model of Targeted Advertising

Using data for advertising involves a prediction problem. Serving costly ads to specific consumers is an investment with an uncertain return. Allocating the resources in an advertising budget is a portfolio problem informed by data. The tools we have developed for portfolio choice under uncertainty can be applied to advertising. What follows is one example.

Customers   There is a continuum of customers with different demands for firms' goods. A customer's demand determines the expected value of their relationship with the firm. Customer characteristics determine both. There are N_c such characteristics. The firm's present discounted value of acquiring a customer associated with each characteristic is an unknown $N_c \times 1$ vector $\chi \sim \mathcal{N}(\bar{\chi}, \Sigma)$. Customer i's preferences and thus value to the firm are

---

5. See Goldfarb and Tucker (2019b) for a survey on how big data and digital technologies have reshaped, and continue to reshape, advertising and marketing strategies.

summarized by a loading vector on each characteristic, m_i. This means that if a firm acquires customer i, it will earn a profit of $\chi' m_i$.

Firms   There are n_F firms, indexed by $\in \{1, 2, \ldots, n_F\}$, producing a homogeneous product. Firm j chooses the amount of advertising a_{ijt} to each customer i to maximize its expected profit. Each advertising unit is normalized to have a cost of 1. The value of advertising depends on the customers it targets and their characteristics. The probability of acquiring a customer, with an amount of advertising a_{ijt} is $\Psi(a_{ijt})$. Assume $\Psi(a_{ijt})$ is a concave function.

Firm j's expected profit $\mathbb{E}[\Pi_{jt}]$ at time t is the probability of acquiring each customer times the value of each customer, minus the cost of advertising to them:

$$\mathbb{E}[\Pi_{jt}] = \mathbb{E}\left[\sum_i \Psi(a_{ijt}) \chi' m_i - a_{ijt} \bigg| \mathcal{I}_{jt} \right]. \tag{7.35}$$

Since customers are linear combinations of characteristics, if the characteristics span the customer space, one could instead model a choice of characteristics to target instead of specific customers to advertise to. That model would be a linear rotation of this one.

One could also incorporate a price of risk. Notice that there are two sources of risk here: the risk in Π of acquiring the customer or not and the uncertain χ, which maps characteristics into values.

Information   Firms learn about the value of a customer by advertising to them. Let $\tilde{\psi}_{ij} = 1$ if customer i buys from firm j and $= 0$ otherwise. Then, assume the amount of data firms learn about each characteristic is the number of customers who buy from them, times the characteristic weight for each of those customers: $n_{jt}^d = \sum_i \tilde{\psi}_{ij} m_i$. Let τ_{jt} be a diagonal matrix with the vector n_{jt}^d on its diagonal. Collectively, this data conveys the information described by the signal $s_{jt} = \chi + e_{jt}$ where $e_{jt} \sim N(0, \tau_{jt}^{-1})$. These assumptions embody the idea that firms learn about segments of the market they sell to. But if they do not advertise to and do not sell to a type of customer, they do not learn about their preferences. Firm j's time-t information set is the information they have at the start of period t: $\mathcal{I}_{jt} = \{s_{j,z}\}_{z=0}^{t-1}$.

Equilibrium   Firms choose the advertising $\{a_{ijt}\}_i$ to maximize the expected present value of the future flow of customer values, $\sum_t \mathbb{E}[\Pi_{jt}]$. Each period, they observe the information in s_{jt} and update their beliefs with Bayes' Law.

This problem is where firms learn about a fixed object χ. Because χ does not change, data does not depreciate. One could introduce data depreciation by making χ a stochastic process. We will see an example in Chapter 9.

In this model, firms combine their prior belief about customer value, $\mathbb{E}[\chi|\mathcal{I}_{jt}]$ with their new time-t information s_{jt}, weighting each by their relative precision, as dictated by Bayes' Law:

$$\mathbb{E}[\chi|\mathcal{I}_{jt+1}] = (\mathbb{V}ar[\chi|\mathcal{I}_{jt}]^{-1} + \tau_{jt})^{-1}(\mathbb{V}ar[\chi|\mathcal{I}_{jt}]^{-1}\mathbb{E}[\chi|\mathcal{I}_{jt}] + \tau_{jt}s_{jt}).$$
(7.36)

Conditional variance is updated by summing the prior precision and signal precision and inverting the sum: $\mathbb{V}ar[\chi|\mathcal{I}_{jt+1}] = (\mathbb{V}ar[\chi|\mathcal{I}_{jt}]^{-1} + \tau_{jt})^{-1}$.

The optimal advertising strategy a_{jt} is the vector with entries $[a_{1jt}, a_{2jt}, \ldots]$ that describe the choice of resources firm j allocates to every customer i. This choice will balance the marginal value of additional current profits $\Psi'(a_{jt})(\mathbb{E}[\chi'm] - a_{jt})$, with the benefits of experimentation. To characterize the solution, write the firm's objective as a recursive function with $\mathbb{E}[\chi|\mathcal{I}_{jt}]$ and $\mathbb{V}ar[\chi|\mathcal{I}_{jt}]$ as state variables of the value function. Then, the value of experimentation with advertising to customer i could be represented as $\partial V(\cdot)/\partial \mathbb{V}ar[\chi|\mathcal{I}_{jt+1}] \cdot \partial \mathbb{V}ar[\chi|\mathcal{I}_{jt+1}]/\partial a_{ijt}$. Of course, ads also affect conditional expectations $\mathbb{E}[\chi|\mathcal{I}_{jt+1}]$. However, the martingale property of expectations means that, in expectation, this effect is zero.

This is a nonstrategic problem where one firm's decision does not interact with another. It allows the model user to explore the trade-off between the benefits of advertising to high-value customers and the future payoffs of experimentation in new market segments. However, the model does not capture the essence of competition. A simple way to incorporate competition would be to let the probability of customer acquisition Ψ depend on firm j's advertising a_{ijt}, as well as the advertising of all other firms $\bar{a}_{it}$. If firm j's acquisition probability is decreasing in other firms' ads $\bar{a}_{it}$, then there is a strategic and competitive aspect to firms' decisions. For other sorts of questions, it might be necessary to fully specify consumer preferences and solve for equilibrium prices that clear markets. That is a fruitful future direction for research.

7.9.6 Firm, Industry, and Aggregate Dynamics of Customer Capital

Foster, Haltiwanger, and Syverson (2008) argue that the demand side is critical to explaining heterogeneity in firm-level outcomes and provide key evidence supporting demand-driven firm dynamic theories, such as customer capital. The evolution of customer capital matters for firm-level dynamics (Klemperer, 1995; Fishman and Rob, 2003; Luttmer, 2006) as well as industry dynamics (Kleshchelski and Vincent, 2009). Einav et al. (2021) documents the importance of customers in accounting for sales variation across merchants, stores within retail chains, and over time for individual merchants and stores. In the same spirit, Afrouzi, Drenik, and Kim (2023) show that the endogenous nature of customer acquisition increases markup dispersion, suggesting significant efficiency losses due to customer misallocation. Shen (2023) studies how a decline in marketing costs has boosted advertising's role in mitigating informational frictions in a search environment. Shen emphasizes a positive feedback loop of customer base accumulation to explain increasing market concentration and declines in productivity growth.

Customer capital also has implications for business cycle dynamics, particularly markup cyclicality. On the one hand, models in which firms initially offer low markups to attract new customers but later exploit customer lock-in to increase the markups give rise to countercyclical markups. On the other hand, models in which firms instead use nonprice actions such as marketing and advertising to build market share give rise to procyclical markups. Retail microdata can be used to test these different models (Argente et al., 2021). Lastly, customer capital has been widely studied in international trade to explain exporting dynamics and the effects of trade policy (Atkeson and Burstein, 2007; Arkolakis, 2010; Drozd and Nosal, 2012; Fitzgerald, Haller, and Yedid-Levi, 2016; Kozeniauskas and Lyon, 2023; Lenoir, Martin, and Mejean, 2023).

7.10   Market Power in Financial Markets

We can use the model of risky asset portfolio choice from section 6.1 and ideas from this chapter to study market power in financial markets. There are N assets with normally distributed payoffs. Some n_I investors, indexed by i, have mean-variance preferences (exponential utility) with risk aversion ρ_i and private information about the asset payoffs. In this version of the model, we change one assumption—the assumption that investors take prices as given. Instead, we consider a market with a finite number of investors n_I, who consider that when they buy, they push the market clearing price up. When they sell, it puts downward pressure on the price. This is a multiasset version of Kyle (1989).

When the price depends on the investor's demand, it changes the first-order condition for purchasing the optimal number of shares. For an investor who maximizes (6.4), subject to a market clearing condition that total demand equals total supply, $\sum_i q_i(p) = \bar{x} + x$, the new first-order condition is $\mathbb{E}[f|\mathcal{I}_i] - pr - (\mathrm{d}p/\,\mathrm{d}q_i)q_i - \rho_i \mathbb{V}ar[f|\mathcal{I}_i]q_i = 0$. Assuming that neither risk aversion ρ_i nor utility u_i is zero, we can rearrange this condition to reveal the optimal demand for the vector of risky assets:

$$q_i = \left(\rho_i \mathbb{V}ar\,[f|\mathcal{I}_i] + \frac{\mathrm{d}p}{\mathrm{d}q_i} \right)^{-1} (\mathbb{E}\,[f|\mathcal{I}_i] - pr). \qquad (7.37)$$

Notice that this optimal asset demand looks nearly identical to the optimal production decisions (7.9) of firms in the noisy-price Cournot economy. If we replace asset payoffs f with production prices p_i and asset prices p with marginal production costs c_i, this is the same expression. However, there is an important difference between the models: the information contained in the information set $\mathcal{I}_i$. In the portfolio problem, that information set includes the information in the realized asset price. In the production economy, there is no learning from prices because firms cannot condition their production on realized demand. Price is not in the information set.

This difference in information sets between the oligopoly production economy and the portfolio choice problem also changes the nature of the price impact dp/dq_i. In both problems, agents can affect the prices they face by changing their purchase or production decisions. They buy less or produce less to make the price more favorable. In an auction version of this model, that would be called "bid shading." However, when there is learning from prices, a second component of market power arises. When others learn from prices and one firm's actions affect prices, a firm can affect what others learn. This second term is called "signal jamming" (Boyarchenko, Lucca, and Veldkamp, 2021).

Investors combine their private information and the information gleaned from prices with prior beliefs. Using Bayes' Law, each investor i forms a posterior mean $\hat{\mu}_i$ and posterior variance $\hat{\Sigma}_i$, given by (6.9) and (6.10).

Determinants of Financial Market Power   To solve this model, follow the steps in section 6.1: Update beliefs with Bayes' Law, clear the market, and match coefficients in the pricing rule to determine the equilibrium price. However, there is one extra step. One must also solve for the price impact, or market power term dp/dq_i. To do that, construct a residual demand curve. To solve for the effect on the price of a change in investor i's asset demand, take the demand q_i of only investor i to be exogenous. For all other investors, their optimal equilibrium asset demand is given by (7.37). Equate this expression of total demand to asset supply to get a residual demand curve:

$$q_i + \sum_{l \neq i} \left(\rho_l \mathbb{V}ar\left[f | \mathcal{I}_l\right] + \frac{dp}{dq_l} \right)^{-1} \left(\mathbb{E}\left[f | \mathcal{I}_l\right] - p_l \right) = \bar{x} + x. \qquad (7.38)$$

Finally, apply the implicit function theorem to this equation to obtain the term dp/dq_i. Notice that this price impact term will depend on the equilibrium price coefficients, which, in turn, depend on price impact. There is typically no explicit solution to the model. Instead, the solution to the asset market equilibrium is a set of three equations in three unknowns.

Market Power and Data Choice Kacperczyk, Nosal, and Sundaresan (2023) explore the impact of market power on price informativeness. Market power is characterized by asset ownership of large investors (oligopolists), who have a price impact and learn from private signals. Price informativeness is proportional to B in the pricing equation (6.6). It reflects how clear the price is as a signal about firm value.

Using a model like the one described here, they find that (i) price informativeness is hump-shaped in the size of the oligopolistic sector; (ii) price informativeness decreases when investor concentration rises; and (iii) price informativeness decreases with the growth of passive investors who fail to acquire data. These results work through two channels: a learning channel and an information pass-through channel. The learning channel depends on the quality of an investor's private signals. The information pass-through channel depends on the sensitivity of an investor's demand to their beliefs. The pass-through channel is judged to be the major driving force of variation in price informativeness.

Market power also diminishes the value of data. When investors who try to trade on their data move the price, they extract less value from the data. We will explore this more when we discuss valuing data in Chapter 10.

7.11 Data, Market Power, and Financial Price Elasticity

When investors' trades move market prices, there is a price elasticity that measures how sensitive the price is to changes in demand. There is also a demand elasticity that measures how sensitive demand is to price. These elasticities have been the focus of a new, growing literature in asset pricing. Here, we connect empirical measures used to quantify asset market price elasticity with theoretical counterparts in our financial model with data and market power.

Koijen and Yogo (2019) set up an asset characteristic–based demand system that they use to explore how investor demand matters for asset prices. To do this, they first estimate how price affects investor demand and then map this into how demand affects price. They estimate this log demand function:

$$
\underbrace{\log\left(\frac{w_{ik}}{w_{i0}}\right) - p_k}_{\text{quantity demanded}} = \underbrace{\underline{d}_{0i} + \underline{d}'_{1i}X_k^{(d)}}_{\text{asset characteristics}} - E_{ik}p_k + \underbrace{\varepsilon_{ik}}_{\text{unobserved characteristics}}
$$

$$(7.39)$$

where w_{ik} is the weight investor i places on asset k, and w_{i0} is the weight on the outside asset, which is a stand-in for all investor i wealth, beyond the assets included in the study. Note that this portfolio weight is a price times a quantity. Even when it is normalized by other weights, it still confounds prices and quantities. Therefore, Koijen and Yogo (2019) divide this portfolio weight by prices. In logs, this requires subtracting the log price to create a quantity measure on the left side of (7.39). On the right side are a constant, asset characteristics $X_k^{(d)}$, and loadings of prices on those characteristics $\underline{d}_{1i}$. The last term is called unobserved characteristics and serves as a noise source. The middle term on the right is the term of interest: $-E_{ik}p_k$ describes the effect of a change in the log price p_k of asset k on the log quantity demanded of asset k, on the left side. The demand elasticity E_{ik} describes the sensitivity of log demand to changes in log price.

In the terminology of the model from section 7.10, the Koijen and Yogo (2019) empirical measure of demand elasticity is

$$E_i \equiv -\frac{\partial \log q_i}{\partial \log p} \approx -\frac{\% \Delta q_i}{\% \Delta p}. \tag{7.40}$$

What we have called demand elasticity in the product markets and financial markets is

$$\mathcal{E}_i \equiv -\frac{\partial q_i}{\partial p} = \frac{1}{\rho \mathbb{V}ar[f|\mathcal{I}_i] + \mathrm{d}p/\mathrm{d}q_i}. \tag{7.41}$$

Clearly, the model and data elasticity are not the same. But they are related. Log (percentage) changes are larger for low levels: $E_i = \mathcal{E}_i * (p/q_i)$.

Data affects demand elasticity because it lowers the conditional variance $\mathbb{V}ar[f|\mathcal{I}_i]$. Lower variance makes the asset effectively less risky to the investor. Low risk encourages the investor to take big positions on small expected profits. That inclination to take large positions makes demand very sensitive to price. Thus, data raises demand elasticity.

Market power lowers demand elasticity because it makes demand less sensitive to price. An investor who knows that their purchases of an asset will push up its prices will buy less. Conversely, if their sales reduce prices, they sell less. The higher the price impact (market power) $\mathrm{d}p/\mathrm{d}q_i$, the lower the demand elasticity $\partial q_i/\partial p$.

Note that while price impact and demand elasticity have a qualitative inverse relationship, when there is heterogeneity in investors' data, we cannot easily obtain the effect of demand on asset prices from demand elasticity. Despite the notation that suggests one can invert demand elasticity to obtain price impact, this is not true. The inverse of (7.41) is not $\mathrm{d}p/\mathrm{d}q_i$. When measuring, it is useful to keep in mind that data (conditional variance) confounds the relationship between elasticity and price impact.

The idea that information matters for demand elasticity led Haddad, Huebner, and Loualiche (2021) to explore how the rise of passive investing, or investing without information, might have changed elasticity. Using data from the Center for Research in Security Prices (CRSP), Compustat, and the Securities and Exchange Commission (SEC), they estimate demand elasticities for each quarter from the second quarter of 2000 to the fourth quarter of 2016. They find that while active investing decreased by 30% over the last 20 years, demand became less elastic by 15%. They use a combination of model and data to argue that the decline in data-informed trading is the cause.

7.12 Cournot, Kyle, Multiunit Auctions, and Learning from Prices

When firms choose a portfolio of products to produce, given uncertain prices, this is similar to an investor choosing a portfolio of risky assets to purchase. In both cases, there is a budget to invest, or the budget constraint, which is a shadow cost of capital. That capital or production cost must be allocated across options with unknown payoffs. In most portfolio choice models with uncertainty, asset markets are assumed to be competitive (as in Chapter 6). However, there is a version of a noisy rational expectations equilibrium model where investors have price impact (Kyle, 1989).

Even after introducing price impact into the portfolio choice problem, there is still an important difference between that model and the Cournot economy described above. The difference between the models is learning from prices. In the noisy rational expectations model, investors are assumed to have the information contained in the market clearing price in their information set. As discussed in section 6.2, an interpretation of the learning from price assumption is that investors can condition on the realized price p when they submit asset demand orders, $q(p)$. In finance parlance, these are limit orders.

In the Cournot model of oligopolistic production, why don't firms also condition on the market clearing price? Firms must produce, transport and distribute before they sell. While an investor can place a limit order that says how many shares of an asset they want to buy or sell at each price, a firm cannot decide how many units of a good to produce instantaneously, depending on the price. Most goods are not produced on demand. Since firms cannot condition their production on current prices, firms should not put current prices in their information set when they maximize expected profit. Firms can learn from past prices. We simply incorporate that information in the prior beliefs. Thus, while investors can use information from current prices to choose quantities, most firms cannot.

The idea that demand should incorporate price information also arises in auction theory. The failure to account for such information is called the "winner's curse." (See section 6.2 for more discussion of the winner's curse.) Not only is the logic the same, but the mathematics of a multiunit, common-value auction, where bidders can submit price-quantity pairs, is the same as the formulation of a market for risky assets. Submitting demand functions to a market clearing mechanism is the same as submitting bid functions to an auctioneer. With a finite number of bidders, the price impact of a bid on the auction price is an important consideration, just as it is in the Kyle (1989) model. Thus, in formulating the financial investment problem in section 7.10, a reader might simply change the vocabulary to describe the problem and interpret this as an auction model.

7.13   Using Market Power to Protect Data

We have explored how data affects market power. The reverse could also be true. Firms may use market power to protect their data. Gan and Riddiough (2008) provide a model to explain the incumbent lender's incentives to protect their data advantages in a supplier-dominated home mortgage market when data is a source of market power, such as loan credit quality. The incumbent will deter new entrants when faced with potential competitive entry by signaling poor credit quality. By charging high prices to higher-quality borrowers, incumbent lenders choose not to price all of their data into prime market mortgage loan rates.

Key Ideas

- A large stock of data is a strategic advantage for a firm and, therefore, a potential source of market power. Data may be about demand, firm operations, customers, or anything that is uncertain and profit-relevant.
- Firms charge markups, both because they have market power and because they require compensation for risk. Producing goods is risky. By improving revenue forecasts, data reduces this risk.
- Price elasticity measures in finance capture both market power of large investors and uncertainty.

Practice Questions

7.1. Would an additional piece of data affect a firm's markup more when the firm's market power (dp/dq) is high or low? Why?

7.2. In equation (7.21), the trace of the covariance matrix $\mathbb{C}ov[p_i, q_i]$ is an essential ingredient in the firm's markup.

    (a) What is the maximum possible covariance achieved by a firm with no informative data about demand shocks? (*Hint: Exclude the possibility of lucky guesses. The covariance is an expectation.*)

    (b) How does this trace of the covariance matrix relate to the precision of a firm's data on a demand shock of one product (i.e., calculate the derivative of trace to each diagonal element of the precision matrix)?

7.3. For a firm with informative data, will the firm markup always be higher than the unweighted average product markup? Justify your answer.

7.4. Assume there is no up-front investment to produce, just marginal production costs. Suppose the firm chooses data before choosing production, with a constant linear cost of signal precision. Characterize the optimal data choices.

7.5. In the model of section 7.1, what if the firm chooses an up-front investment in lowering the marginal cost of production at the same time as it chooses data? How does that change what sort of data the firm might choose?

8

Data Markets and
Data Platforms

The literature on platforms is active and exploding. This chapter will only scratch the surface, focusing on models that build on the previous ideas about data as information. After showing how the previous models can be extended to incorporate a platform, we touch on a few key ideas about platforms from the industrial organization literature.

A key function of platforms is to collect and share information. Platforms observe the trades that they intermediate between buyers and sellers. This knowledge enables them to understand consumer types, aggregate demand, production trends, pricing patterns, and other market trends. Platforms often share some of this information with their users. They might recommend other products to buyers (matching them) based on their knowledge of similar customers' demands. Platforms also provide statistics to sellers on their sales relative to others. This data sharing is not charity. The shared data provides value to customers and sellers, which gives them an incentive to continue using the platform.

Of course, platforms also provide other services. They often sell advertisements that monetize customers' attention. Platforms may provide payment services or, in some cases, credit and enforcement services as well. We start with a platform that is a pure information mechanism and then discuss the other potential platform functions. The end of the chapter explores how data is traded in markets and used as a form of payment.

The Cournot model of firm competition is a foundation for exploring platforms. When all players' information is known (as in section 7.1), information sharing has no effect. Therefore, to model a production economy with a data platform, we will build on the model version with asymmetric information and strategic uncertainty from section 7.7. Instead of uncertain customer demand, we introduce customers' uncertainty about the quality of the goods

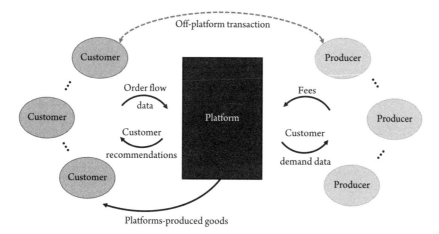

FIGURE VII. Data Platforms. *Notes:* This figure represents the interactions between data platforms, customers, and producers. Customers on the left send order flow data to platforms in exchange for customer recommendations and platform-produced goods. Producers on the right pay fees to the platforms in exchange for the customer demand data. The arrow at the top represents direct off-platform transactions between customers and producers.

they purchase. While the interpretation is different, the mechanics of this model are largely the same.

Data platforms intermediate exchanges between customers and sellers, as in Figure VII. Customers submit orders to the platform, which observes those orders and can use the order data. Sellers deliver goods or services through the platform and may also pay a fee. Many platforms provide data to customers, in the form of a recommendation, star ratings, or user reviews. Sometimes, platforms also provide data to sellers about the characteristics of their customers, high-value market segments, or other popular products. Finally, Figure VII illustrates the possibility that customers might choose to transact directly with firms, off the platform and that platforms sometimes produce goods, under their own brand name, to sell directly to consumers.

8.1 A Data Platform Model

The model economy lasts for one period. Customers submit demand curves for goods with uncertain quality. Quality might reflect materials, durability, customer service, or any dimension of the retail experience that affects customer utility. The true quality of the good is unknown and is distributed $f \sim \mathcal{N}(\mu_f, \tau_f^{-1})$. The nonplatform supply of such goods is normalized to

1. Platforms also choose how many units to produce of the good that is a perfect substitute. The price of the good is determined in the equilibrium and equates demand and supply. Platforms do not choose prices directly and cannot conduct price discrimination.[1]

Customers   We consider four types of market participants: platforms, direct and indirect customers, and "noisy buyers," who demand quantities that do not depend on prices. Each customer/platform can submit a continuous function that specifies a quantity demanded for every possible clearing price p. All platforms and direct customers place orders directly in the market. Indirect customers order through a platform instead of buying directly. For simplicity, the number of each type of customer is fixed. One can add a choice of whether to bid on the platform or to bid directly. There are N_I platform customers, which we index by $i = \{1, \ldots, N_I\}$ and N_J direct (off-platform) buyers, which we index by $j = \{1, \ldots, N_J\}$.

Each customer has initial wealth $W_{0,i}$, and chooses the quantity of the good to buy, as a function of the price, $q_i(p)$, to maximize expected utility, which exhibits constant absolute risk aversion over a sum of wealth and the private utility of the good consumption:

$$\mathbb{E}[-\exp(-\rho(W_i + q_i(f + v_i))|\mathcal{I}_i], \qquad (8.1)$$

where ρ denotes absolute risk aversion, and $f + v_i$ represents a utility value that customer i gets from the good. This utility value has a common component f that we refer to as the good's quality. There is also an individual-specific (private) value v. For direct and indirect customers, $v_j \sim_{iid} \mathcal{N}(0, \tau_{vJ}^{-1})$ and $v_i \sim_{iid} \mathcal{N}(0, \tau_{vI}^{-1})$ per unit. There are many reasons why customers may value goods differently.

Final wealth is initial wealth minus the amount paid at the market price p

$$W_i = W_{0,i} - q_i p. \qquad (8.2)$$

Both on- and off-platform customers internalize the effect they have on market prices. Because they strategically consider their price impact, they are not perfectly competitive. They maximize their utility subject to the market clearing condition. This assumption is not essential. It allows one to study two-sided market power. But it is easy to remove price impact later. The two-sided market power assumption puts the customers on the same strategic footing as the platforms themselves.

1. There is a lot of concern about price discrimination. In practice, we do not see platforms charging personalized prices. They could. Doing so would raise profits. Perhaps they do not because of fear of regulatory intervention.

Platforms   There are N_D platforms, which we index by $d = \{1, \ldots, N_D\}$. Then the total number of market participants, excluding the random noise buyers, is

$$N = N_I + N_J + N_D. \tag{8.3}$$

Platforms intermediate the purchases of buyers. They can use this information to produce their own goods for sale on the platform. For example, if Amazon sees that the margins on crackers are high, they produce Happy Belly (their house brand) crackers for sale on the platform. While this practice has been controversial, we allow platforms to do this in the model, to better understand its effect.

Platforms have a constant marginal cost of production v_d. Firms' marginal costs could be private information. But to keep things simple, we will allow all market participants to know this cost function.

Platforms choose good production functions q_d to maximize

$$\mathbb{E}[-\exp(-\rho q_d(p - v_d)) | \mathcal{I}_d]. \tag{8.4}$$

Platforms do not know what the price p will be when they choose their output. They use their prior beliefs and data to form price expectations.[2] Platforms are large players who internalize the impact their production decisions have on the price.

Describing Data Sets and Updating Beliefs with Correlated Signals   Before trading, each customer and platform gets a signal about the quality of a good. This signal could be their own experience with the good, or could be a visual inspection, or could have almost no information content at all. Signals are unbiased, normally distributed, and have private noise:

$$s_i = f + \epsilon_i, \quad \epsilon_i \sim \mathcal{N}(0, \tau_s^{-1}). \tag{8.5}$$

Customers can observe data from multiple sources: their own private signal, signals from others who may share data with them, and their private value v_i. The customers' values v_i are also private data. In addition, customers can avoid the winners' curse by conditioning their bids on the data that would be revealed if each price were realized (see sections 6.2 and 7.12). This price information just keeps agents rational but is not essential.

By placing orders through platforms, customers reveal their order flow $q_i(p)$ to their platform, which in the model is equivalent to sharing their expected value of the good $\mathbb{E}_i[f] + v_i$. Each platform d receives orders

---

2. One might also give platforms a price of risk by replacing the exponential operator with mean-variance utility. That would yield the same solution. The variance discount is like a Capital Asset Pricing Model's price of risk correction for a firm valuation. One could also simply make platforms expected profit-maximizers.

from N_I/N_D customers.[3] Each customer's order reveals their conditional expectation of quality plus private valuation: $\mathbb{E}[f|\mathcal{I}_i] + v_i$. Orders do not fully reveal what the customer knows because neither component is known. Since $\mathbb{E}[f|\mathcal{I}_i]$ is an unbiased signal about f and v_i is mean zero, $\mathbb{E}[f|\mathcal{I}_i] + v_i$ is an unbiased signal about product quality.

The platform constructs $\bar{s}_d$, which is an average of its customers' expected quality plus private valuations:

$$\bar{s}_d = \frac{N_D}{N_I} \left(\sum_{i \in \Upsilon_d} \mathbb{E}[f|\mathcal{I}_i] + v_i \right), \tag{8.6}$$

where Υ_d is the set of customers buying through platform d. The sum of signals is multiplied by N_D/N_I because that is the same as dividing by N_I/N_D, which is the number of orders each dealer observes. So, this is just a simple average of the information conveyed by the order flow of each of the clients of dealer d.

Platforms, in turn, can share some of this order flow data with their customers. In reality, data sharing typically takes the form of recommendations. Telling a customer that others similar to them liked another product, or sharing user reviews, uses data from some customers' orders to inform others. In the model, platform-customer data sharing takes the form of a noisy signal about $\bar{s}_d$, the summary statistic for everything the platform learned from customer order flow. That noisy signal from dealers to customer i is

$$s_{\xi i} = \bar{s}_d + \xi_i, \quad \xi_i \sim \mathcal{N}(0, \tau_\xi^{-1}). \tag{8.7}$$

The noise ξ_i varies by platform and by customer.

This signal structure captures two extreme cases—perfect data sharing between platforms and customers ($\tau_\xi = \infty$) and no data sharing ($\tau_\xi = 0$)— as well as the cases in between.[4]

In addition, platforms may share data with third parties, which are other platforms. Let ψ be the size of the group of platforms who share their data

---

3. It is quite plausible that a platform might also include its own private signal in the data it transmits to customers. However, the policy debate focuses on the effect of platforms' sharing of customer data. We therefore exclude platforms' private data from $\bar{s}$, to isolate effects from the sharing of customer order data. Note also that platforms' signals to customers covary with customers' private and public data. Our solution method accounts for this covariance.

4. If one endogenized the choice of a customer to buy on- or off-platform, then this signal given to the customer is essential to induce customers to buy through the platform. The cost is that they forfeit some of their data. The benefit is that they get information to help them select better products.

with each other. In other words, each platform reveals all of its signals to $\psi - 1$ other platforms. No sharing between platforms is the case where $\psi = 1$. All data sharing is mutual. One might want to allow for this form of data sharing because this third-party data sharing is what much of the data privacy regulations target.

The final piece of data that customers condition on is the market clearing price p. Notice that this price signal is correlated with other signals that customers observe. We guess and verify later a linear function of price p:

$$p = A + B_I \bar{s}_I + B_J \bar{s}_J + B_D \bar{s}_D + C_I \bar{v}_I + C_J \bar{v}_J + G \bar{\xi}_I + Hx \quad (8.8)$$

where $\bar{s}_I \equiv N_I^{-1} \sum_{i=1}^{N_I} s_i$, $\bar{s}_J \equiv N_J^{-1} \sum_{j=1}^{N_J} s_j$, and $\bar{s}_D \equiv N_D^{-1} \sum_{d=1}^{N_D} s_d$ are the average signals of indirect customers (I), direct customers (J), and platforms (D); $\bar{v}_I \equiv N_I^{-1} \sum_{i=1}^{N_I} v_i$ and $\bar{v}_J \equiv N_J^{-1} \sum_{j=1}^{N_J} v_j$ are the average private values of indirect customers (I) and direct customers (J); $\bar{\xi}_I \equiv N_I^{-1} \sum_{i=1}^{N_I} \xi_i$ is the average noise across indirect customers; and x represents noise traders.

Signal vectors for the three types of agents are as follows: A customer who bids directly observes a vector of signals $S_j = [s_j, p]$. Customers who bid through platforms observe the larger signal vector $S_i = [s_i, p, s_{\xi i}]$. While these customers observe an extra signal, they also will end up making bids that covary more with price data. While customers can buy more or less, depending on the price, platforms must commit to a production amount in advance. That means that a platform observes the exact order flows of its customers but does not get to learn from the price when they choose output. Thus, platforms take orders but cannot observe the market clearing price. For platform d, $S_d = [s_d, \bar{s}_d]$. Since platform cost functions v_d are common knowledge, we don't include them in S. But every customer accounts for them.

For every agent, we use Bayes' Law to update beliefs about f. The correlation in the signal errors complicates Bayesian updating. Price information and platforms' recommendations are correlated with private signals and with each other. Therefore, we use the state-space filtering method introduced in section 2.2. The vector of state variables is

$$z \equiv \left[f, \quad \underbrace{\{\xi_i\}_{i=1}^{N_I}}_{\text{dealer} \to \text{customer noise}} , \underbrace{\{\varepsilon_i\}_{i=1}^{N_I}, \{\varepsilon_j\}_{j=1}^{N_J}, \{\varepsilon_d\}_{d=1}^{N_D}}_{\text{private signal noises}}, \underbrace{\{v_i\}_{i=1}^{N_I}, \{v_j\}_{j=1}^{N_J}}_{\text{consumer values}}, x, 1 \right]$$

$$(8.9)$$

The matrix Γ_i that maps the state variables to the indirect buyers' signal vector S_i is

$$
\Gamma_i = \begin{pmatrix}
1 & 0 & 1 & \cdots & \cdots & 0 & 0 & 0 & 0 \\
B_I + B_J + B_D & \frac{G}{N_I} & \frac{B_I}{N_I} & \frac{B_J}{N_J} & \frac{B_D}{N_D} & \frac{C_I}{N_I} & \frac{C_J}{N_J} & H & A \\
\frac{N_D}{N_I} \sum_{i \in \Upsilon_d} \left(\beta_i' \Gamma_i + e_{vi}' \right) + e_{\xi_i}' + \left(\mu_f - \beta_j' \bar{S}_j \right) \cdot e_m'
\end{pmatrix} \quad (8.10)
$$

where we define basis vectors e with length equal to the number columns in Γ_i that have all zeros, except for a single entry of 1: e_{vi} puts weight 1 on the entry corresponding to v_i, e_{ξ_i} weights ξ_i, and e_m weights the constant, which is the last element in the state variable vector z. The first row of Γ describes the buyer's private signal. It has 1s in the position corresponding to f, the true value, and the private signal noise ϵ_i. The sum of these two elements represents the private signal. The second row of Γ corresponds to the price signal. It weighs on the true value f, but also all agents' signal noises, including direct, indirect, and platforms' signal noises. Lastly, the price has a weight of H on the noise shock x and a weight of A on the constant 1. The last row of Γ represents the information from the platform. It depends on the true value and the noise of the platform's customers.

For the direct buyer, the matrix is the same, excluding the third row, which corresponds to the signal from the platform. For the platform, the matrix is the same, except that the second row representing the price signal is missing and in the third row of (8.10), and we exclude the noise e_{ξ_i}' in the signal they send to customers since they can see the pre-noise version of that information.

The following are the optimal linear projection formulas in the context of this model:

$$
\mathbb{E}\left[f|S_j\right] = \mu_f + \beta_j'(S_j - \bar{S}_j) \quad (8.11)
$$

$$
\mathbb{V}ar\left[f|S_j\right] = \mathbb{V}ar\left(f\right) - \mathbb{C}ov\left(f, S_j\right)' \mathbb{V}ar\left(S_j\right)^{-1} \mathbb{C}ov\left(f, S_j\right) \equiv \hat{\tau}_j^{-1}, \quad (8.12)
$$

$$
\beta_j \equiv \mathbb{V}ar\left(S_j\right)^{-1} \mathbb{C}ov\left(f, S_j\right) \quad (8.13)
$$

where m is the number of signals in the vector S_j, the covariance vector is $\mathbb{C}ov\left(f, S_j\right) = 1_m \tau_f^{-1}$, and the signal variance-covariance $\mathbb{V}ar\left(S_j\right)$ is $\Gamma_i' \mathbb{V}ar[z] \Gamma_i$. The vector $\beta_j = [\beta_{sj}, \beta_{\xi j}, \beta_{pj}]$ dictates how much weight an agent puts on signals $[s_j, s_{\xi j}, p]$ in the posterior expectation. $\bar{S}_j$ is the unconditional mean of the signals. For the price signal, that mean is $(B_I + B_J + B_D)\mu_f + A$. For the other signals, the mean is the prior value μ_f. In a Kalman filtering problem, β is like the Kalman gain.

Equilibrium   A Bayesian Nash equilibrium, for a given data-sharing arrangement (τ_ξ, ψ) is

(i) A direct or indirect customer bid function $q_i(p)$ that maximizes (8.1), subject to the budget constraint (8.2), accounting for price impact through (8.14).

(ii) A platform bid function that maximizes (8.4), accounting for price impact through (8.14).

(iii) A market clearing price equates demand and supply:

$$\sum_{i=1}^{N_I} q_i + \sum_{j=1}^{N_J} q_j - \sum_{d=1}^{N_D} q_d = 1. \tag{8.14}$$

Solving the Model   We work out the market equilibrium with various data-sharing arrangements. One could compare payoffs from a set of structures and allow the platform operator to choose the one that maximizes their objective. In this version, each one of these information structures is exogenously imposed.

Since all customers' posterior beliefs about f turn out to be normally distributed, we will use the properties of a lognormal random variable to evaluate the expectation of each agent's objective function. We then substitute the budget constraint in the objective function, evaluate the expectation, and take the log. The customer maximization problem simplifies to

$$\max_{q_j(p)} \; q_j(\mathbb{E}[f|S_j] + v_j - p) - \frac{1}{2}\rho q_j^2 \mathbb{V}ar[f|S_j] \tag{8.15}$$

subject to the market clearing condition (8.14), where the price is not taken as given. The first-order condition with respect to q_j reveals that customers demand

$$q_j(p) = \frac{\mathbb{E}[f|S_j] + v_j - p}{\rho \mathbb{V}ar[f|S_j] + dp/\,dq_j}. \tag{8.16}$$

For platforms, the expression is similar but in reverse. As producers, platforms earn the price per unit p as revenue but pay v_d as a marginal cost. The platform's payoff does not depend directly on quality. But the platform is uncertain about the market clearing price. The first-order condition for the optimal platform production decision is

$$q_d = \frac{\mathbb{E}[p|S_d] - v_d}{\rho \mathbb{V}ar[p|S_d] + dp/\,dq_d}. \tag{8.17}$$

Between (8.16) and (8.17), the sign on the market power term $dp/\,dq_d$ flips. This is because consumer demand raises prices, while platform supply reduces prices. Thus, for platforms, $dp/\,dq_d$ is negative.

Equilibrium Market Clearing Price   The price of goods depends on the information-sharing arrangement. We explore various cases here. Others are also possible.

The no-data-sharing world is one with "data privacy regulation," where platforms cannot use customer data to inform their own or their customers' purchases. Each agent sees only their own private signal s_i, and customers see the price information p, which they can condition their bid on, but not any signal from the platform: $S_i = [s_i, p]$.

In the data-sharing cases, customers observe the larger signal vector $S_i = [s_i, s_{\xi i}, p]$. The signal $s_{\xi i}$ includes data from customers and/or data shared across platforms.

The equilibrium market price is obtained by adding up all customers' and platforms' good demands and the volume of market orders x and equating them with the total supply. As in most models with exponential utility, the price turns out to be a linear function of each signal. Data sharing changes the linear price weights, which affects utility. To the extent that signals are shared with more customers, that signal will influence the demand of more customers, and the weight of those signals in the price function will be greater.

There are three data-sharing regimes:

(i) Platforms share data imperfectly with customers, but not with other platforms.
(ii) Platforms share data with customers (and potentially other platforms as well).
(iii) There is no data sharing at all. Platforms cannot use customer trades as data on which to condition their own bid (data privacy regulation).

For all three regimes, market revenues are always a linear function of signals s_i and of customers' average private values $\bar{v}$:

$$p = A + B_I \bar{s}_I + B_J \bar{s}_J + B_D \bar{s}_D + C_I \bar{v}_I + C_J \bar{v}_J + G \bar{\xi}_I + Hx \quad (8.18)$$

The equilibrium pricing coefficients A, B_I, B_J, B_D, C_I, C_J, G, and H differ by model. Solve for them by equating supply and demand, forming expectations, and matching coefficients.

Price coefficients are a solution to a complex system of nonlinear equations. The complication is two-fold: (i) there are strategic agents whose demands are not linear in the coefficients of the price function, and (ii) shared signals are correlated with price data. Both sources of complexity are essential to understand how data sharing affects market revenue. Boyarchenko, Lucca, and

Veldkamp (2021) prove that an equilibrium exists and is unique in four classes of models: low market power, little data sharing, widespread data sharing, and sufficiently symmetric customers. Outside these classes, one should establish existence numerically.

Market Revenues   Data sharing results in more data for the average customer. By its nature, data reduces uncertainty or conditional variance. Goods with less uncertain payoffs are less risky. One of the most robust findings in finance and economics is that less risky goods consistently command higher prices. Because the supply of the good is normalized to one, the price and market revenue are the same. Since private values and noisy demands are both mean zero, from (8.18), an average market's revenue is: $A + (B_I + B_J + B_D)f$, where f is the good's quality. The term $A < 0$ incorporates both the risk premium needed to induce risk-averse buyers to purchase the good, as well as market power. The term $(B_I + B_J + B_D)$ is the sensitivity of the price to changes in quality. The next result shows that, in many cases, both A and B rise when data improves.

Data Sharing Raises Revenue   For a range of parameters, $\{\tau_{vI}, \tau_{vJ}, \tau_f, \tau_s, \tau_\xi\}$, when customers and platforms all have more data from others (lower or equal $\mathbb{V}ar[f|S]$ for all), then market revenue p rises, on average.

The reason that data sharing raises revenues is that it reduces risk. It lets customers forecast better their utility for products. With less uncertainty, they buy more. Prices rise. We can see this in (8.16). Data might increase or decrease the conditional expectation of quality. But a normally distributed signal always decreases the conditional variance. In other words, forecasts conditioned on more data are more accurate. When $\mathbb{V}ar[f|S_j]$ falls because customers have more data, on average, demand q_d rises.

However, remember that nonplatform production of the good was fixed at 1. If we let nonplatform suppliers choose production, they would produce more at higher prices p. When data is more abundant, the negative effect of high price p on consumer surplus would compete with the positive effect of lower uncertainty and higher production. The net effect would be ambiguous. Future work might quantify each force to assess the net effect of these trade-offs.

Prohibiting Data Sharing   If one were to introduce data privacy regulation that prohibits platforms from using the data in their customers' orders, the functional difference between customers and platforms disappears. Of course, platforms can produce goods while consumers demand the goods. But this is not a meaningful distinction. This is just the same quantity choice with an opposite sign. Both choices enter the same way in the equilibrium outcomes. In other words, eliminating all data sharing effectively eliminates data intermediation as well. We discuss data-sharing prohibitions and their welfare consequences in Chapter 11.

8.2   Financial Intermediaries as Data Platforms

With some minor modifications, the platform model just explored can also speak to financial trading platforms. This version merges the platform model with the financial portfolio problem with market power from Chapter 6. Adding a financial information intermediary who observes trades and potentially advises clients changes the information variance-covariance matrix. The main differences between this model and the goods market platform model are that financial assets have a common value, and financial dealers (platforms) can condition on price information when they trade. It is a simplified version of Boyarchenko, Lucca, and Veldkamp (2021), where we interpret their primary dealer as a data platform.

Setup   Consider a single risky asset that is one-period lived and has a terminal payoff $f \sim \mathcal{N}(\mu_f, \tau_f^{-1})$. There is also a single riskless asset with price 1 and payoff r. There are three types of market participants: platforms, direct investors, and indirect investors. Direct investors are those who buy the asset without using the services of the platform. Indirect investors place their orders on the platform, which, in turn, enters those orders into the market. In doing so, the platform observes the investor's order and may transmit information back to the investor. There are N_I indirect bidders, which we index by $i = \{1, \ldots, N_I\}$, N_J direct investors, which we index by $j = \{1, \ldots, N_J\}$ and N_D dealers, which we index by $d = \{1, \ldots, N_D\}$. Then $N = N_I + N_J + N_D$ is the total number of investors, indexed generically by l.

Each investor has initial wealth W_l. An investor who buys q_l shares of the risky asset at a price p has $(W_l - q_l p)$ units of initial wealth left to buy riskless assets, which return r per unit and earns $q_l f$ on their risky assets. Therefore, their ending wealth is $(W_l - q_l p)r + q_l f$.

Each type of investor can submit a continuous function that specifies a quantity demanded for every possible clearing price p. The platform also trades assets on its own account. We model this as if each investor observes the price p and then chooses a quantity q of shares to buy. Short-selling is allowed and is represented by $q < 0$. All investors choose q_l to maximize the expected exponential utility of their ending wealth:

$$\max_{q_l} \mathbb{E}[-\exp(-\rho((W_l - q_l p)r + q_l f)) | \mathcal{I}_l]. \tag{8.19}$$

The supply of the asset is $\bar{x} + x$, where $\bar{x}$ is a constant that is common knowledge and $x \sim \mathcal{N}(0, \sigma_x^2)$ is unknown to all. This is the source of noise in prices that prevents prices from revealing all private information.

Each investor, including the dealer (the platform), receives a noisy private signal s_l about the asset payoff f. Since all investors can condition trades on the price, they all have price in their information set. Thus, the information set of direct, off-platform investors is $\mathcal{I}_j = \{s_j, p\}$. The signal takes the same form as in the previous platform model, as defined in (8.5). The dealer/ platform observes all of their customers' trades and can therefore form the signal $\bar{s}_d$, defined in (8.6). Dealers' information set is therefore $\mathcal{I}_d = \{s_d, p, \bar{s}_d\}$. Finally, the customers who buy through the platform observe their private signal, condition on the price information, and get a recommendation from the platform $s_{\xi i}$, as defined in (8.7). Therefore, the information set of the platform customers is $\mathcal{I}_i = \{s_i, p, s_{\xi i}\}$.

The equilibrium is each investor's choice of q_l that maximizes their expected utility and a price p that clears the asset market. Note that the investors do not take prices as given. Each internalizes its price impact.

Solving the Financial Platform Model   Given conditional means and variances, the first-order conditions of this problem are the same as the ones in section 7.10. What the platform changes is the information sets. On average, getting different signals does not systematically make the conditional expectations higher or lower. But it does change the conditional variance: more data makes investors less uncertain. Importantly, it also changes the covariance. Having one's private information observed by others raises the covariance of beliefs with others' beliefs.

The technique to solve for each type of investor's conditional expectations and variances is exactly the same state-space technique introduced in the last section. The only difference is the dealer's signal vector, which now includes p.

By reinterpreting the consumer good platform model to be about financial markets, one can use the same kind of framework to consider financial market data policy, such as restrictions on data sharing, the consequences of selling customer order flow, or prohibitions on some kinds of proprietary trading.

One can make various assumptions about the signals observed by various parties and what information is shared. As long as these signals are linear combinations of state variables, all of this can be captured by differences in the Γ matrix from (8.10) that maps the states into signals. The fact that the model does not need to be fully re-solved for each information structure facilitates the exploration of various data policies.

8.3   Platforms and Market Power Concerns

Much of the research and writing about digital platforms focuses on market power and its dangers. Digital platforms exhibit strong network effects and economies of scale, shielding dominant firms from competition. As a result, they extract a significant proportion of the market surplus (Crémer et al., 2021).

However, how market power manifests itself in a market where the digital service typically has a zero price may be quite different from a nondigital market. Rosenquist, Morton, and Weinstein (2021) argue that addictive content and user-specific advertising on many platforms diminish their product quality. When the quality of a zero-price service declines, that is equivalent to an increase in quality-adjusted pricing. If imperfect competition allows platforms to lower quality this way, that is antitrust harm. Because of the platform's market power, consumers who desire a higher-quality, less-harmful product have few alternative options.

Morton and Dinielli (2020) study alleged anticompetitive behavior of one particular digital platform, Google. They argue that Google deters entry into digital display advertising by using its market power in the search market. Google created a data set for its ad tech services that used user data from its search engine. This search data allowed Google to target advertising more effectively than its competitors. While Google did achieve greater efficiency, it allegedly did so by using its dominance of the search market.

8.4 Platforms as a Matching Technology

Recent research has explored the costs and benefits of data platforms that provide matching services. They focus on the role that platforms play in bringing buyers and sellers together. One such study by Kirpalani and Philippon (2020) considers buyers and sellers who can match directly offline or use a two-sided platform to match online. Consumers face a trade-off when sharing their data with the platform: sharing data improves the quality of the match, allowing them to purchase goods they value more; it also gives the platform market power to extract more rents from the sellers. This increased market power is a cost borne by all consumers, making it an externality. Since consumers do not internalize this externality, there is excessive consumer reliance on platforms.

Bergemann and Bonatti (2022) explore the trade-off between match quality and price discrimination. This study also considers an online and an offline market, which limits the degree of online price discrimination. As the platform has access to better data, the quality of consumer-advertiser matches increases, but so does the platform's ability to price discriminate. Too much market power hurts customers along both dimensions.

8.5 Two-Sided Platforms: Attention and Payments

Two-sided platforms act as intermediaries between buyers and sellers in an economic transaction. While the platforms described previously had buyers and sellers, the literature on two-sided platforms treats both parties as strategic. Models such as Rochet and Tirole (2003, 2006) exhibit two main externalities: membership and usage.

The membership externality arises when the platform attracts more users. For example, a platform with many buyers might be a more attractive place for a seller to sell goods. Conversely, a platform with more sellers could be a more interesting place for a buyer to shop. The participation of each side affects the utility and strategy of the participants on the other side of the platform. A usage externality arises when the way in which one side uses the platform affects others. The models examined thus far had usage externalities: customers' demand generated information for the platform and potentially for other platforms or other customers. However, these models took the participants as given without considering membership externalities.

Since the focus of these papers is more on market structure and industrial organization, a more detailed treatment of this topic can be found in Rochet and Tirole (2006).

Platforms as Attention Brokers   Attention and data are not identical. One is a resource of a human being that is in limited supply. The other is a tradable asset with no natural limit on its quantity. Yet, the two are linked by the digital economy. This literature is distinct from the data economy but makes contact with it in researchers' thinking about digital platforms. Therefore, we briefly describe a few papers on the frontier of this growing literature.

In digital platforms like Google and Facebook, consumer prices are typically zero and do not determine competitive outcomes. Instead, competition takes place on the producers' side: producers who reach out to users through advertising on platforms. Prat and Valletti (2022) and Chen (2022) model digital platforms as attention brokers with proprietary data about their users' product preference ("attention data"). These platforms sell targeted ad space to retail product industries. When online platforms are concentrated, the number of ads sold by attention brokers decreases, reducing the number of retail firms that have access to consumers and increasing their market power. Consumers would suffer due to the reduced supply since they would have fewer options and pay higher prices. In this sense, customers end up paying with their attention data.

Rachel (2021) embeds such an attention-grabbing platform in a macro model with a labor leisure choice. The platform provides valuable leisure services in return for attention, which can be sold to firms through ads. The model explains the rise of leisure and contributes new approaches to measuring the free digital services economy.

Trading and Payment Platforms   While payment systems and cryptocurrencies fall outside the scope of this book, they occasionally intersect with the economics of data platforms. For instance, Brunnermeier and Payne (2022) consider a platform that matches producers and customers and maintains a digital payment ledger. The ledger is a record of all transactions on the platform. This record enables customers to access uncollateralized credit. The reason customers repay is that if they default on their payments, they forfeit future credit and platform purchases. Despite this risk, the credit history is owned exclusively by the platform. Platform ownership of data creates a cost of switching platforms and a lock-in effect for customers.

The paper explores the potential impact of policies like "interoperability" and "open banking" on the platform's market power and markup. Interoperability would require platforms to share data with one another; open banking would give customers more control over their data sharing. Both policies could decrease the platform's market power and markup, but open banking may also limit consumers' access to credit due to increased costs associated with defaults.

8.6   Incentives of Data Providers

In both traditional markets and online platforms, those who control the flow of information have their motives and interests. To analyze the incentives of digital platform designers, researchers can apply frameworks used in the study of traditional media markets to the digital realm.

News media and data platforms are similar in that they aggregate and disseminate information. One of the primary services media outlets provide is the selection of which events to report, giving them significant influence as purveyors of *curated* information. Media outlets may strategically focus on unusual or extreme events to attract more readers (Nimark and Pitschner, 2019). By selectively emphasizing specific observations, media outlets can create biases even among rational consumers, potentially leading to increased volatility and aggregate fluctuations (Nimark, 2014; Chahrour, Nimark, and Pitschner, 2021). These insights from the traditional media domain could be extended to studying data platforms and their effects on market outcomes.

Key Ideas

- A platform observes customers' orders and delivers some of that data to sellers and some to other customers, to induce them to purchase on the platform.
- Data sharing by platforms creates surplus by resolving uncertainty for all parties.
- Data is a tradable asset. But it is nonrival. One can sell data and still keep a copy.

Practice Questions

8.1. If the data platforms model has no noise traders or random supply, does that mean the price perfectly reveals the good quality? Why or why not?

8.2. Suppose platforms bought goods and valued them at v_d, instead of producing and selling goods. What about the model solution would change?

8.3. If the platform had a quadratic cost of production instead of a linear one, how would that change their first-order condition?

8.4. How does data sharing between platforms affect the covariance of customers' signals?

    (a) What is covariance $\mathbb{C}ov[s_{\xi d}, s_{\xi d'}]$ without data sharing between platforms?

    (b) What is covariance $\mathbb{C}ov[s_{\xi d}, s_{\xi d'}]$ for two platforms d and d' that share information?

    (c) What is covariance $\mathbb{C}ov[s_{\xi d}, s_{\xi d'}]$ for two platforms d and d' in a model where platforms share data with $\psi - 1$ other platforms, but d and d' are not in the same data-sharing group?

8.5. Derive the constant term in the last row of the state-space filtering equation (8.10) and show that it is equal to $(\bar{f} - \beta_j' \bar{S}_j) \cdot e_m'$.

9

Data in Production and the Data Feedback Loop

We have considered data use in tracking and strategic problems, in portfolio choice, and its interactions with market power. Data is also an important input in modern business activity. This chapter considers how data functions in a production economy and how it changes economic dynamics. Introducing dynamics and a long-lived role for data will help us to value data as an asset in Chapter 10.

A central idea in our study of a data production economy is the *data feedback loop*. This loop is a two-way feedback between data and economic activity. Economic activity generates data, and the data affects economic activity. This feedback is important because it can be a source of increasing returns: more data enables a firm to grow larger and produce even more data. Data begets data. This dynamic makes the economy distinct from a traditional economy. It alters aggregate output dynamics and firm competition.

A model of the data feedback loop has three parts, illustrated in Figure VIII. The first part is a relationship between a firm's productivity and its output. This relationship is present in almost every macroeconomic model. More productive firms grow bigger, produce, and sell to more customers. Consider a simple economy with a continuum of firms $i \in [0, 1]$. Each firm i chooses its labor input $\ell_{i,t}$ and produces output $y_{i,t}$, given idiosyncratic productivity $A_{i,t}$:

$$y_{i,t} = A_{i,t}\ell_{i,t}^{\alpha}, \quad \alpha \leq 1. \qquad (9.1)$$

Of course, most production economies have multiple factors of production, often capital and labor. One can enrich this production function in many ways and still maintain the link between productivity and output.

The second part of the feedback loop is that economic transactions generate data. This piece is new to the data economy and is central to the feedback. The third part is that data improves firms' productivity. Since the

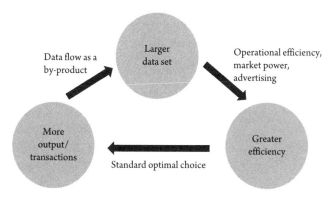

FIGURE VIII. The Data Feedback Loop. *Notes*: This figure represents the data feedback loop. Starting from the bottom left circle, a firm with more output or transactions generates a larger data flow as a by-product of economic activity; the larger data set improves operational efficiency, market power, and advertising strategies, leading to greater efficiency; lastly, more efficiency improves standard optimal choices such as labor hiring and capital purchases.

bottom leg—productive firms producing more—is so standard, the following discussion focuses on the top two legs of the triangle.

Of course, there is an antecedent to the idea that economic production generates a form of knowledge. In models of learning-by-doing (Arrow, 1962; Lucas, 1988; Jovanovic and Nyarko, 1996), firms become more productive as they produce more. However, they do not form predictions, which, as this chapter shows, naturally generate diminishing returns. Also, learned actions do not exhibit higher covariance with payoffs, a key testable prediction of data models explored in Chapter 10. Finally, data is tradable; learning from experience is not. The idea that others can observe data and it can be bought and sold, is central to the discussion of data markets and data platforms.

9.1   Data Is a By-Product of Economic Activity

One of the novel features of a data economy that distinguishes data from other productive assets is the way in which data is produced. Data is generated as a by-product of economic activity. Much of the data that firms use to predict is data about customer behavior. A firm that wants to forecast future demand to manage its inventory, investment, transportation, and hiring will use demand data—data about what customers have purchased in the past. The act of purchasing generates such data. In other words, data is a by-product of economic transactions.

Transactions generate a new data flow that gets added to an existing stock. Recall from section 3.1 that we define firm i's stock of data or knowledge about a random state θ_t at date t as its conditional precision $\Omega_{i,t} \equiv \mathbb{V}ar[\theta_t|\mathcal{I}_{i,t}]^{-1}$. If $\delta_{i,t}$ is the inflows of new data and ζ is the depreciation rate, then the law of motion for the data stock is

$$\Omega_{i,t+1} = (1 - \zeta)\Omega_{i,t} + \delta_{i,t}. \tag{9.2}$$

A simple way of representing data production as a by-product of economic transactions is by making the production of new data points (the flow) proportional to a firm's output:

$$\delta_{i,t} = z_i y_{i,t}, \tag{9.3}$$

where $\delta_{i,t}$ can be interpreted as a number of data points but without any integer constraint. The firm-specific parameter z_i reflects "data-savviness." A data-savvy firm (with high z_i) harvests lots of data per unit of output. Data savviness reflects a firm's ability to process data.

Of course, not all data a firm uses comes from its own production. Plenty of data is purchased. We add data purchases, as explored in Chapter 8, after we solve the simplest version of this model.

Another way to enrich the theory of data accumulation is to consider data storage and processing costs. Many people are employed to be data managers. Data managers maintain equipment like servers, structure data, fix broken links, or make structured data consistent with the searchable database of the firm. This labor input takes raw data, possibly purchased data and/or the by-product of economic activity, and turns it into usable, structured data for a firm. Section 10.8 returns to this idea and shows how to model and measure it.

Finally, one might think about production in a multigood setting. Section 9.6 considers this extension.

9.2 Data Enhances Firms' Productivity

The final leg of the data feedback loop is the connection between data and firm productivity or profitability. We have explored market power already in Chapter 7. This is certainly one channel through which data makes firms more profitable. Here, we focus on the way in which data might also increase firms' productivity.

Microeconomics and management literatures focus on how firms use data and are detail-rich in their descriptions (e.g., Goldfarb and Tucker, 2019a). For macroeconomics, the precise mechanism by which data improves a firm's productivity is typically of less interest. However, whether data adds directly to productivity/knowledge, speeds discovery, or predicts uncertain outcomes, does matter for the aggregate outcomes. We explore each of these three possibilities next.

9.2.1 Data as a Tool for Prediction

The first approach considers data as information that reduces uncertainty and guides decision-making. We follow Farboodi and Veldkamp (2021) and consider data as information for forecasting an optimal production technique.

Firms face a tracking problem, as in section 4.1. They choose a production technique $a_{i,t}$ to match a common optimal technique $a_t^* = \theta_t + \varepsilon_t$, which consists of persistent θ_t and transitory ε_t components. We assume that θ_t follows an AR(1) process, $\theta_{t+1} = \rho\theta_t + \nu_{t+1}$ with $\nu_{t+1} \sim_{iid} \mathcal{N}(0, \sigma_\theta^2)$, and $\varepsilon_t \sim_{iid} \mathcal{N}(0, \sigma_\varepsilon^2)$. Better forecasts of the optimal technique (lower forecast errors) increase product quality $A_{i,t}$:

$$A_{i,t} = \bar{A} - (a_{i,t} - a_t^*)^2 = \bar{A} - (a_{i,t} - \theta_t - \varepsilon_t)^2, \quad \text{for} \quad \bar{A} > 0. \quad (9.4)$$

More information is good. The reason that quality should depend on the *squared* distance between the chosen action $a_{i,t}$ and the optimal action a_t^* is that this structure makes conditional variance (or precision) a sufficient state variable. It is tractable. To maximize quality, an agent should choose an action $a_{i,t}$ that is their best guess of the optimal action. In other words, they should set $a_{i,t} = \mathbb{E}[\theta_t + \varepsilon_t | \mathcal{I}_{i,t}]$. If they take this optimal action, then the squared difference in (9.4) is $(\mathbb{E}[\theta_t + \varepsilon_t | \mathcal{I}_{i,t}] - (\theta_t + \varepsilon_t))^2$. The expected squared difference between the conditional expectation of a random variable and the realization of that random variable is the definition of conditional variance. Thus, expected quality equals

$$\mathbb{E}[A_{i,t} | \mathcal{I}_{i,t}] = \bar{A} - \mathbb{E}[(a_{i,t} - \theta_t - \varepsilon_t)^2 | \mathcal{I}_{i,t}]$$
$$= \bar{A} - \mathbb{V}ar[\theta_t + \varepsilon_t | \mathcal{I}_{i,t}] = \bar{A} - \Omega_{i,t}^{-1} - \sigma_\varepsilon^2. \quad (9.5)$$

This equality simplifies the mathematics enormously because it makes the conditional precision $\Omega_{i,t}^{-1}$ a sufficient statistic for the contents of an agent's data.

Each data point contains information about θ_{t+1}. Following the rules in section 2.1.1, Bayes' Law tells us that we should de-bias each signal and then, assuming each data point has equal precision τ_s, we should average the $\delta_{i,t}$ data points. The result is a noisy signal $s_{i,t}$ about θ_{t+1}, whose precision increases with the number of new data points $\delta_{i,t}$:

$$s_{i,t} = \theta_{t+1} + \eta_{i,t}; \quad \eta_{i,t} \sim \mathcal{N}(0, (\tau_s \delta_{i,t})^{-1}). \quad (9.6)$$

If data points are not equally precise, one should form a weighted average. The precision of the resulting signal is the sum of all the data point precisions.

A General Function of Forecast Errors   Farboodi and Veldkamp (2021) consider a more general relationship between forecast errors and quality:

$$A_{i,t} = g((a_{i,t} - \theta_t - \varepsilon_t)^2); \qquad \varepsilon_t \sim_{iid} \mathcal{N}(0, \sigma_\varepsilon^2), \qquad (9.7)$$

where g is a decreasing function. The function g should be decreasing because that captures the idea that larger forecast errors reduce quality. For a nonlinear g function, if g is not too convex, then quality is still a decreasing function of expected forecast errors.[1] In that case, expression (9.5) would be a good local approximation for small shocks to θ and ε (we leave the proof as an exercise). Put simply, more data precision increases the quality of a firm's good.

9.2.2 Data as Productivity

The second approach treats data as something that contributes directly to productivity. The following is a simplified version of Jones and Tonetti (2020) without fully depreciating data as in (9.2). The stock of data $\Omega_{i,t}$ improves the quality of ideas and directly increases firm productivity $A_{i,t}$. Data relevance for productivity is mediated by the parameter η:

$$A_{i,t} = \Omega_{i,t}^{\eta}. \qquad (9.8)$$

The flow of data from other firms is a by-product of their output. This data can be added to firm i's stock of data at the *nonrivalry* rate $(1 - \iota)$.

$$\Omega_{i,t} = (1 - \zeta)\Omega_{i,t-1} + \int (1 - \iota)y_{j,t}\, dj. \qquad (9.9)$$

If $\iota = 1$, then data are fully rival. This means that data from other firms cannot be used by firm i. When ι is lower, each firm i observes more data from other firms. A firm's own data does not show up here because each firm has zero mass. Being so small, an individual firm is assumed to be uninformative on its own. Integrating the flow term yields $(1 - \iota)y_t$, where $y_t = \int y_{j,t}\, dj$ is aggregate output.

---

1. To compute expected quality for a nonlinear g, take a second-order Taylor approximation of (9.7), expanding around the expected value of its argument: $g(v) \approx g(\mathbb{E}[v]) + g'(\mathbb{E}[v]) \cdot (v - \mathbb{E}[v]) + (1/2)g''(\mathbb{E}[v]) \cdot (v - \mathbb{E}[v])^2$. Next, we take an expectation of this approximate function: $\mathbb{E}[g(v)] \approx g(\mathbb{E}[v]) + g'(\mathbb{E}[v]) \cdot 0 + (1/2)g''(\mathbb{E}[v]) \cdot \mathbb{V}ar[v]$. Recognizing that the argument v is a chi-square variable with mean $\Omega_{i,t}^{-1} + \sigma_\varepsilon^2$ and variance $2(\Omega_{i,t}^{-1} + \sigma_\varepsilon^2)$, the expected quality of firm i's good at time t can be approximated as

$$\mathbb{E}[A_{i,t}|\mathcal{I}_{i,t}] \approx g\left(\Omega_{i,t}^{-1} + \sigma_\varepsilon^2\right) + g''\left(\Omega_{i,t}^{-1} + \sigma_\varepsilon^2\right) \cdot \left(\Omega_{i,t}^{-1} + \sigma_\varepsilon^2\right).$$

Substituting $\Omega_{i,t}$ into $A_{i,t}$ in (9.9) and $A_{i,t}$ into the production function (9.1) yields:

$$y_{i,t} = [(1-\zeta)\Omega_{i,t-1} + (1-\iota)y_t]^\eta \ell_{i,t}^\alpha, \quad \alpha \le 1. \qquad (9.10)$$

If we further assume a symmetric equilibrium $(y_{i,t} = y_t)$ and full data depreciation $\zeta = 1$, then output is expressed as:

$$y_t = (1-\iota)^{\frac{\eta}{1-\eta}} \ell_t^{\frac{\alpha}{1-\eta}}. \qquad (9.11)$$

For $\eta > 1 - \alpha$, data production leads to increasing returns and long-run growth.

Aghion et al. (2019) argue that one of the main drivers of changes in firm dynamics has been a change in the cost of running large organizations. This change in the span of control is another way to envision the mechanism by which data adds to productivity.

9.2.3 Prediction as a Research Input

In the third approach, data is used for prediction, but those predictions enhance research and development. This formulation is a hybrid of the first two approaches. It captures the idea of a data-driven endogenous growth while still formulating data as information in a data feedback loop. This approach of mapping data directly into knowledge is similar to the approach used by Cong, Xie and Zhang (2021), in which data is used for research and development (R&D) in an endogenous growth model. For this formulation to make economic sense, information derived from transactions must be useful to develop productive growth-sustaining technologies. If that is true, then this model, with its prediction for sustained long-run growth, would be more relevant for long-term economic forecasts than the previous two formulations, which predicted diminishing returns and diminishing rates of growth. To what extent each representation is correct is an open empirical question.

Instead of equation (9.4), assume the evolution of quality follows

$$A_{i,t} = A_{i,t-1} + \max\{0, \Delta A_{i,t}\}$$
$$\Delta A_{i,t} = \bar{A} - (a_{i,t} - \theta_t - \varepsilon_{i,t})^2.$$

The solution inherits the same structure as before: $\mathbb{E}[\Delta A_{i,t}] = \bar{A} - \mathbb{E}\left[(\mathbb{E}[\theta_t|\mathcal{I}_{i,t}] - \theta_t - \varepsilon_{i,t})^2\right]$. Using the definition of conditional variance and the fact that $\varepsilon_{i,t}$ is mean zero, the expected change in quality of firm i's good at time t is $\mathbb{E}[\Delta A_{i,t}|\mathcal{I}_{i,t}] = \bar{A} - \mathbb{V}ar[\theta_t + \varepsilon_t|\mathcal{I}_{i,t}]$. Since $\varepsilon_{i,t}$ is independent of θ_t and the information set $\mathcal{I}_{i,t}$,

$$\mathbb{E}[\Delta A_{i,t}|\mathcal{I}_{i,t}] = \bar{A} - \Omega_{i,t}^{-1} - \sigma_\varepsilon^2. \qquad (9.12)$$

The interpretation is that more data allows for more precisely targeted inno-vations, which increase the size of the technology advance. Depending on $\bar{A}$, data might be necessary to make $\Delta A_{i,t}$ positive. According to this formulation, technological progress is not viable without some data to guide it.

While it is tempting to use this structure to argue that data accumulation can sustain growth, in reality, the fraction of data used for innovation may be small. How large that fraction is, is an open question for measurement. But this sort of structure should only be applied to data that is input into an R&D process. Just like accounting distinguishes between capital investment for ordinary capital and capital investment that is for R&D, it would be useful for future data measurement to do the same.

9.3   Solving the Data Feedback Model

For the rest of the chapter, we need to pick one model of the link between data and output to work with. We will use the first approach, where data is used to predict an optimal action in a way that improves process efficiency and product quality.

Finding the State Is an Art   The key to solving a dynamic recursive prob-lem such as this one is to find the right state variable. We use the conditional precision of the posterior beliefs about the persistent state θ_t, the stock of knowledge $\Omega_{i,t} \equiv \mathbb{V}ar[\theta_t|\mathcal{I}_{i,t}]^{-1}$, as the state variable to keep track of the amount of data a firm has. The reason the conditional mean is not also a state variable is because of the quadratic loss form of (9.4). The expected difference between the forecast of the state and the realization of the state depends only on the conditional variance, not on the conditional mean. Therefore, keeping track of the precision and its dynamics in (9.2) is sufficient to solve firm i's problem.

One could instead use conditional variance. The only reason for using the precision instead is that a higher level of precision represents more or better data. So, using precision lends itself to thinking naturally about cumulating a stock of something valuable.

Sequential Problem   When data is used for prediction, the problem of firm i is as follows: taking the price per unit of quality p and the wage rate w as given, choose a sequence of techniques $a_{i,t}$ and labor $\ell_{i,t}$ to solve

$$\max_{a_{i,t}, \ell_{i,t}} \sum_{\tau=t}^{\infty} \left(\frac{1}{1+r}\right)^{\tau-t} \mathbb{E}\left[p\tilde{y}_{i,t} - w\ell_{i,t} \mid \mathcal{I}_{i,t}\right] \qquad (9.13)$$

subject to

$$\tilde{y}_{i,t} = A_{i,t}\ell_{i,t}^{\alpha}, \tag{9.14}$$

$$s_{i,t} = \theta_{t+1} + \eta_{i,t}, \quad \eta_{i,t} \sim \mathcal{N}(0, (\tau_s z_i \ell_{i,t}^{\alpha})^{-1}), \tag{9.15}$$

and the data evolution function (9.2), with $\tilde{y}_{i,t} = \ell_{i,t}^{\alpha}$. Note that $A_{i,t}$ is determined by (9.4), which depends on the chosen technique $a_{i,t}$ and the state θ_t. There is a distinction here between quality-adjusted output $\tilde{y}_{i,t}$ and units of output $y_{i,t}$. The reason to make that distinction is that the number of new units of data depends on output $y_{i,t}$, which is not random because it is only a function of choice variables. If we equated $\tilde{y}_{i,t}$ to output, then future data would be stochastic. That changes little but makes the model harder to solve. The structure used here makes the number of units of data and thus $\Omega_{i,t+1}$ deterministic.

Firms update beliefs about θ_t using Bayes' Law. Information sets are defined recursively as $\mathcal{I}_{i,t} = \{\mathcal{I}_{i,t-1}, s_{i,t-1}\}$.[2]

Firms take price p and wage w as given because they are exogenous. In the full model, the price clears the goods market, and the wage is determined in a non-data sector. We focus here on the data sector.

Optimal Choice of Technique and Expected Quality   Taking a first-order condition with respect to the technique choice $a_{i,t}$, we find that the optimal choice is $a_{i,t}^* = \mathbb{E}[\theta_t | \mathcal{I}_{i,t}]$. Thus, expected quality of firm i's good at time t in (9.4) can be rewritten as $\mathbb{E}[A_{i,t}] = \mathbb{E}[(\mathbb{E}[\theta_t | \mathcal{I}_{i,t}] - \theta_t - \varepsilon_t)^2]$. The squared term is a squared difference between the forecast of $\theta_t + \varepsilon_t$ and its realization. Note that the expected value $\mathbb{E}[\varepsilon_t] = 0$ does not appear because it is zero. This is an expected squared forecast error. That is a conditional variance, of $\theta_t + \varepsilon_t$. Since the two terms are uncorrelated, we can add their conditional variances. That conditional variance sum is $\Omega_{i,t}^{-1} + \sigma_{\varepsilon}^2$.

A Recursive Solution for Labor Choice   The optimal sequence of labor choices $\{\ell_{i,t}\}$ solve the following recursive problem:

2. Firms can also learn about θ_t from observing their quality-adjusted output $\tilde{y}_{i,t}$ at the end of each period. This information is not simply additional units of data because the output reveals information about what the state was (θ_t), while new data reveals information about what the state will be (θ_{t+1}). Thus, if the information learned from observing output is $\tilde{\sigma}_a$, one needs to add this to the prior stock of knowledge before depreciating it: $\Omega_{i,t+1} = (1-\zeta)(\Omega_{i,t} + \tilde{\sigma}_a) + \tau_s \delta_{i,t}$.

$$V(\Omega_{i,t}) = \max_{\ell_{i,t}} p\left(\bar{A} - \Omega_{i,t}^{-1} - \sigma_\varepsilon^2\right)\ell_{i,t}^\alpha - w\ell_{i,t}$$

$$+ \left(\frac{1}{1+r}\right) V\left(\Omega_{i,t+1}\right) \tag{9.16}$$

$$\Omega_{i,t+1} = (1-\zeta)\Omega_{i,t} + \tau_s z_i \ell_{i,t}^\alpha.$$

This result greatly simplifies the problem by collapsing it to a deterministic problem with one choice variable ℓ and one state variable, $\Omega_{i,t}$, the stock of knowledge. In expressing the problem this way, we have already substituted the optimal choice of production technique.

Since $\Omega_{i,t}$ can be interpreted as a discounted stock of data, $V(\Omega_{i,t})$ captures the value of this data stock. $V(\Omega_{i,t}) - V(0)$ is the present discounted value of the net revenue the firm receives because of its data. Therefore, the marginal value of one additional piece of data, of precision 1, is simply $\partial V_t/\partial \Omega_{i,t}$. When we consider markets for buying and selling data, $\partial V_t/\partial \Omega_{i,t}$ represents the firm's demand, its marginal willingness to pay for data.

The necessary first-order condition for the optimal choice of labor input $\ell_{i,t}$ is:

$$\frac{\partial V(\Omega_{i,t})}{\partial l_{i,t}} = p\left(\bar{A} - \Omega_{i,t}^{-1} - \sigma_\varepsilon^2\right)\alpha\ell_{i,t}^{\alpha-1} - w$$

$$+ \left(\frac{1}{1+r}\right)\frac{\partial V(\Omega_{i,t+1})}{\partial \Omega_{i,t+1}}\underbrace{\frac{\partial \Omega_{i,t+1}}{\partial \ell_{i,t}}}_{\tau_s z_i \alpha \ell_{i,t}^{\alpha-1}} = 0. \tag{9.17}$$

According to (9.3), the amount of new data from the additional output that the marginal worker $l_{i,t}$ generates is simply $z_i \tau_s$ times the marginal product of labor. Thus, the amount of new data is $\partial\Omega_{i,t+1}/\partial\ell_{i,t} = \tau_s z_i \alpha \ell_{i,t}^{\alpha-1}$. In this optimality condition, we do not yet have a solution for the $\partial V(\Omega_{i,t+1})/\partial\Omega_{i,t+1}$ term that represents the value of this additional future data. We can, however, solve for a similar marginal value that is time-t dated:

$$\frac{\partial V(\Omega_{i,t})}{\partial \Omega_{i,t}} = p\Omega_{i,t}^{-2}\ell_{i,t}^\alpha + \left(\frac{1}{1+r}\right)\frac{\partial V(\Omega_{i,t+1})}{\partial \Omega_{i,t+1}}\underbrace{\frac{\partial \Omega_{i,t+1}}{\partial \Omega_{i,t}}}_{1-\zeta}. \tag{9.18}$$

The second term equals $\partial\Omega_{i,t+1}/\partial\Omega_{i,t} = 1-\zeta$; this is the fraction of time-t data that is not lost due to depreciation. Next, we forward this equation one period to find the expression for $\partial V(\Omega_{i,t+1})/\partial\Omega_{i,t+1}$. Substituting back into (9.17), we obtain an Euler equation that equalizes the marginal cost of labor (the wage w) to its marginal benefits, given by current productivity and future gains in knowledge. It connects the labor and data choice across any consecutive periods t, $t+1$ and $t+2$:

$$w = p\left(\bar{A} - \Omega_{i,t}^{-1} - \sigma_\varepsilon^2\right)\alpha\ell_{i,t}^{\alpha-1} + \left(\frac{\tau_s z_i \alpha \ell_{i,t}^{\alpha-1}}{1+r}\right)$$

$$\left[p\Omega_{i,t+1}^{-2}\ell_{i,t+1}^{\alpha} + \left(\frac{1-\zeta}{1+r}\right)\frac{\partial V(\Omega_{i,t+2})}{\partial\Omega_{i,t+2}}\right]. \tag{9.19}$$

Steady State   Just like in standard dynamic general equilibrium models with capital accumulation, there is no analytical solution for the entire transition path of data or output. However, there is a special case where the model has analytical solutions—in a steady state. Steady state is the solution the model converges to, in which the value of variables no longer changes from time t to time $t+1$ (and thus we can drop time subscripts). For example, in steady state, $\partial V/\partial\Omega_{i,t} = \partial V/\partial\Omega_{i,t+1}$. If we impose this equality in (9.18), then we can rearrange to solve for $\partial V/\partial\Omega_i = p\Omega_i^{-2}\ell_i^{\alpha}/(1 - (1-\zeta)/(1+r))$. Next, substitute in this value for $\partial V/\partial\Omega_i$ in (9.17) and rearrange to get the steady-state Euler equation:

$$w = p\alpha\ell_i^{\alpha-1}\left[\left(\bar{A} - \Omega_i^{-1} - \sigma_\varepsilon^2\right) + \frac{\tau_s z_i \Omega_i^{-2}\ell_i}{r+\zeta}\right]. \tag{9.20}$$

The level of labor ℓ_i^{ss} that solves this polynomial equation is firm i's steady-state level of labor. The steady-state flow of data is $\tau_s z_i \ell_i^{\alpha}$. In a steady state, for the stock of data to be constant, this data flow must equal data depreciation:

$$\tau_s z_i \ell_i^{\alpha} = \zeta\Omega_i. \tag{9.21}$$

Given the parameters, the two equations for Ω_i and ℓ_i in two unknowns (9.20) and (9.21) characterize the steady-state solution.

Value Function on the Transition Path   Outside of a steady state, solutions are numerical. There are many techniques to compute solutions to recursive problems like this, given specific parameter values. One simple approach to approximate the value function is a grid search: Make a grid of values for Ω (state variable) and ℓ (choice variable). Guess functions $V_0(\Omega)$ and $\ell_0(\Omega)$ on this grid. For example, one could guess a vector of ones for each. For each value of Ω on the grid, use the guesses to determine the values of $\ell(\Omega)$ and $V(\Omega)$ in (9.16) and (9.19). These equations will deliver new values of $V_1(\Omega)$ and $\ell_1(\Omega)$, which serve as the next guess for the function value at each of the grid points. Iterate until the value function approximation converges. Given an approximated V and choice of ℓ, one can then simulate the evolution of the economy. See Judd (2023) for more detail on this approach and many others.

Adjustment Costs   Without a data adjustment cost, transitions are usually short-lived. There will not be rich dynamics from data accumulation if firms can simply produce a large amount at a loss, in order to quickly generate a large amount of data. Such production is costly. But it is not dissimilar to an investment cost. This is problematic because, in reality, new firms always start small and grow gradually.

Just like the investment literature uses capital adjustment costs to create a more realistic path for firm dynamics, data economy models could use a data adjustment cost. Adjustment costs allow that gradual dynamics. To prevent new firms from immediately jumping to their optimal level of data, one can introduce a data adjustment cost function $\Psi(\cdot)$. That adjustment cost could be a function of the change in the stock of data $\Omega_t - \Omega_{t-1}$. For example, a quadratic function $\psi(\Omega_t - \Omega_{t-1})^2$ is one simple form for an adjustment cost that would cause firms to grow slowly, as they do in reality. However, such a cost might not be necessary for questions unrelated to firm size or heterogeneity.

Illustrating Data Dynamics   Figure IX illustrates one possible dynamic path for a firm growing through data accumulation. When the firm is young and data-poor, it grows slowly. This is the flatter portion of the transition path on the left. In this region, because the firm has little data, its product quality is low. With low product quality, the optimal level of production is low. Because production is low, the firm does few transactions, generates little new data, and remains data-poor. Eventually, the firm accumulates more data. As it does so, product quality improves, output rises, and data production speeds up. The midlife firm grows quickly. When data enters its old phase with abundant data, growth slows down again. The flatter section of Figure IX on the right represents the firm approaching its steady-state level of output. Growth slows down when the firm has abundant data because the firm has resolved almost all the uncertainty that data can possibly resolve. With many data points already, the additional data does little to reduce the firm's forecast error. Diminishing returns sets in and slows firm growth to zero. A data-rich firm can still grow. But innovation or ideas are needed. More data alone will not cause that growth.

Unlearnable Risk   One important feature of (9.4) is the presence of unlearnable risk. Notice that the signal in (9.6) is informative about θ_{t+1}, but not about ε_{t+1}. Because of this, even with infinite data, an agent cannot form a perfect forecast of a_t^*. Consider the general function of forecast errors in

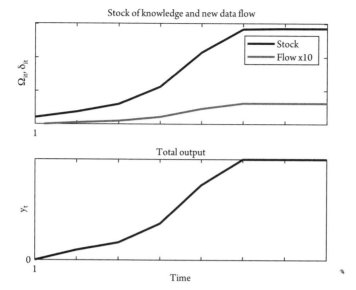

FIGURE IX. Growth of a Firm through Data Acquisition: Increasing Then Decreasing Returns. *Notes*: The figure illustrates one possible dynamic path for the growth of a data firm over time. The top panel illustrates the evolution of the stock of knowledge $\Omega_{i,t}$ and the flow of knowledge $\delta_{i,t} \times 10$. The bottom panel illustrates the evolution of aggregate output y_t.

(9.7). Assuming that the productivity function g is finite for every strictly positive entry, productivity is bounded. The assumption that g is finite for every positive entry means that an economy cannot make forecasting mistakes and be infinitely productive. Maybe an economy cannot be infinitely productive, even with perfect forecasts (perhaps $g(0) \neq \infty$). But it certainly can't be infinitely productive with mistakes. Since unlearnable risks imply that firms always make some mistakes, expected productivity is always finite and bounded. That is important because an economy with bounded productivity cannot grow forever. In short, when there is unlearnable risk, data used for prediction cannot sustain long-run growth. See section 3.8 for more discussion of unlearnable risk.

Endogenizing Prices For simplicity of exposition, this data economy model holds fixed the price of the goods. It is not a general equilibrium model. How might equilibrium price effects change the model's predictions? To answer this question, Farboodi and Veldkamp (2021) endogenize the price of the good and offer a utility-based model of household demand. One key prediction of the model that changes is that, if firms start out collectively data-poor, they grow quickly. The convex, slow-growth region on the left side of Figure IX disappears. The reason this happens is that when all firms have poor data and produce inefficiently, quality goods are scarce. Scarce goods cause prices to rise to clear the goods market. But if goods prices are high, then firms produce more. The incentive for higher production stimulates data production as a by-product. Faster data accumulation stimulates faster growth in the low-data phase. However, this equilibrium price force only works when all firms are data-poor. If data-rich firms are already present in the market and one data-poor firm enters, that one firm faces low goods prices from its productive competitors. This single firm will grow more slowly, as illustrated above.

Endogenizing prices also creates a technical complication: The price will depend on other firms' data stocks. So if firms are asymmetric, endogenizing prices may increase the number of state variables.

Should Firms Learn from Prices?   In the noisy rational expectations models in Chapter 6, an important feature was that agents learned from equilibrium prices. In this real economy model, there were exogenous prices. In the version with endogenous prices, agents still do not form signals from those prices. The reason is that real output and goods prices depend on squared deviations of choices from the optimal choice. Observing high output or low prices tells the observer how close other firms' choices are to the targets. But it says nothing about whether those target actions are higher or lower. Thus, even when endogenized, prices contain no useful information about the mean of the state θ.

9.4   Incorporating Data Trade

Incorporating data sales is important because an increasing amount of economic activity is transactions in data.

Recall from section 1.2 that data is nonrival. Data sold is not lost. However, in a competitive market, selling data needs to have some cost for an equilibrium to exist. If it is costless to sell, then at any positive price, firms will make an infinite profit selling data over and over again. One way to circumvent this problem is to introduce market power. When firms affect prices, they use market power to raise prices by restricting quantities, making data sales finite.

In a perfectly competitive model, we can solve this nonexistence problem by introducing partially rival data. When data is sold, a fraction ι of it is lost. This loss can capture the loss of profits that arise from trading on information that everyone knows versus information that only the data seller knows. Sharing data in a widespread way reduces its value, and this value reduction can be modeled as losing some of that data. If a firm sells another firm 10 bits of data, the data seller effectively loses a few bits of the data. The firm is not actually losing data, but this data loss captures the notion that the data is less valuable once it has been sold.

Stock of Knowledge with Data Trade   Representing this semi-rivalry formally requires using indicator functions because when data is purchased, all the purchased data is acquired. But when data is sold, not all sold data is lost. That is a kink in the effective price of data at zero.

We define a variable representing the trade data choice. Let $\gamma_{i,t}$ be that data purchase/sale variable. If $\gamma_{i,t}$ is positive, that represents a purchase of data. If $\gamma_{i,t}$ is negative, that represents a data sale. This variable $\gamma_{i,t}$ is not the net flow of new data. The net new data $(\delta_{i,t})$ includes both data from a firm's own production $(z_i \ell_{i,t}^\alpha)$ and data purchases or sales $(\gamma_{i,t})$. As in Jones and Tonetti (2020), ι represents data rivalry; $(1 - \iota)$ is the nonrivalry rate.

The stock of knowledge that the firm has tomorrow, $\Omega_{i,t+1}$, still includes the depreciated knowledge that it has today $(1 - \zeta)\Omega_{i,t}$ and new knowledge it collects from its transactions. There are two additional terms for data purchases and the loss from data sales:

$$\Omega_{i,t+1} = (1 - \zeta)\Omega_{i,t} + \tau_s \left[\underbrace{z_i \ell_{i,t}^\alpha}_{\text{transactions}} + \underbrace{\gamma_{i,t} \mathbb{1}_{\gamma_{i,t}>0}}_{\text{data purchases}} - \underbrace{\iota\gamma_{i,t} \mathbb{1}_{\gamma_{i,t}<0}}_{\text{loss from data sales}} \right].$$

$$(9.22)$$

If the firm purchases data, it gets all the data it purchased. If the firm sells data, the firm loses a fraction $(\iota < 1)$ of the data that is sold. Thus, the effective price per data unit is higher when the firm sells than when it buys. If the data price is π, then the effective price of a data purchase is π per unit of data acquired. But the effective price of data sold is π/ι per data unit forfeited. This is a negative bid-ask spread. This is similar to models with transaction costs and bid-ask spreads but in reverse.

The Price of Traded Data   Data trade creates the possibility of new sources of revenue from data sales or new costs from data purchases. To capture these, we define the price of traded data as π_t and add $-\pi_t\gamma_{i,t}$ to the firm's current period profits. If a firm buys data $(\gamma_{i,t} > 0)$, then the cost of the purchase $\gamma_{i,t}\pi_t$ is subtracted from revenue. If data is sold, $\gamma_{i,t}\pi_t$ is negative. But since it enters with a minus sign, this augments current revenue.

The optimal sequence of labor choices $\{\ell_{i,t}\}$ and data sales $\{\gamma_{i,t}\}$ solve the following recursive problem:

$$V(\Omega_{i,t}) = \max_{\ell_{i,t}, \gamma_{i,t}} p\mathbb{E}[A_{i,t}|\mathcal{I}_{i,t}]\ell_{i,t}^{\alpha} - \pi_t \gamma_{i,t} - w\ell_{i,t} + \left(\frac{1}{1+r}\right) V(\Omega_{i,t+1})$$

(9.23)

where the law of motion for $\Omega_{i,t}$ is given by (9.22).

The feedback loop at the start of the chapter describes a force for increasing returns. More data boosts quality and output, which creates more data. Firm growth begets more firm growth. That force is still present with data trade. However, the ability to acquire data without producing goods dampens this feedback force.

9.5 Data as a Means of Payment: Partial Data Barter

When data is valuable and is a by-product of economic activity, firms may give away products "for free." In practice, many modern firms do offer zero-price digital services to customers. Facebook, Google searches, and many phone apps are offered for zero price. But are they really free? These services typically collect customer data. That customer data is a valuable asset. In a way, customers are paying for the search platform or their weather app with their data.

This is a barter trade. The customer is bartering their data, at a monetary price of zero, in return for a digital service that is also valuable. This can happen in any dynamic model where data produced as a by-product of economic transactions has future value.

Not only are there pure barter trades, there are potentially many more goods or services exchanged for a monetary payment and data. Whole Foods offered customers a 5% discount on their groceries if they allowed the cashier to scan a QR code that linked their grocery purchase to their Amazon Prime account. In this instance, customers paid for 95% of their grocery bill with money or credit; they paid 5% of the bill with their data. Explicit discounts for data are still fairly rare. However, consider that Amazon and Uber lost money for years before being profitable. This suggests they were pricing below cost to grow their data. Such less-visible forms of partial data barter could be pervasive.

Because partial barter trades are not very visible, a data economy model might be useful to infer this value. While we leave the details of measurement to Chapter 10, consider the following objects in the model that correspond to aspects of the data barter trade. First there is the value to the firm of a unit of data, which could be represented as $V(\Omega_t) - V(\Omega_t - 1)$ or as $\partial V(\Omega_t)/\partial \Omega_t$

in (9.18). Of course, this value is a value per unit of information precision. This is not the value of data per customer or per transaction. The precision of the information conveyed in a transaction would also need to be estimated or calibrated.

A second approach might be to value the additional output undertaken by a firm, for the purpose of collecting additional data. The additional units of labor input that a firm chooses, because of their desire to augment their data set is $\ell^{data} = \left(\frac{1}{1+r} \right) \frac{\partial V(\Omega_{i,t+1})}{\partial \Omega_{i,t+1}} \frac{\partial \Omega_{i,t+1}}{\partial \ell_{i,t}}$, which is the third term in the labor first-order condition, (9.17). The amount of output associated with this labor, times the price of output, is $p_t A_{it} (\ell^{data})^\alpha$. This is the extra GDP generated by the data barter trade. But it is not exactly the value of the data itself.

A third approach is to consider the value of a representative firm with and without the data it generates in a period. Define a counterfactual firm value function without period-t data:

$$\hat{V}(\Omega_{i,t}) = p \left(\bar{A} - \Omega_{i,t}^{-1} - \sigma_\varepsilon^2 \right) (\ell_{i,t}^*)^\alpha - w\ell_{i,t}$$

$$+ \left(\frac{1}{1+r} \right) V \left((1 - \zeta)\Omega_{i,t} \right). \tag{9.24}$$

Notice that the difference between $\hat{V}(\Omega_{i,t})$ and $V(\Omega_{i,t})$ defined in (9.16) is that in the counterfactual value function $\hat{V}$, the next period's data set is just the depreciated data set from period t. However, the optimal production level, determined by the labor choice $\ell_{i,t}^*$ is the same as the optimal output in the original economy. The difference $V(\Omega_{i,t}) - \hat{V}(\Omega_{i,t})$ corresponds to the aggregate value of the data transferred from consumers to firms in period t. If an economist calibrates or estimates the original model parameters, computing this counterfactual value is straightforward. It could be used to predict the value of the free goods and services exchanged for valuable data in the economy.

In the policy world, claims abound that firms are not paying consumers for their data. It is possible that the value of data barter trades is very small, and this is close to true. But the Whole Foods evidence, the market value of data-intensive firms, and the low revenues of early-stage data platforms all suggest that data's value might not be so small. Firms do not need to be altruistic to compensate consumers for data. Simple dynamic profit maximization suggests that if data is a valuable asset and the market is competitive, customers should be paid for their data in the form of cheaper goods. More measurement is needed to determine whether the data discounts are fair compensation or not.

9.6 Data Feedback and Product Innovation

Empirical research argues that many firms use data for product innovation (Babina et al., 2024). To enable the model to speak to innovation, we can reformulate the model of the data production economy presented before with an N-dimensional state. The reformulation allows firms to learn about different regions of the product space by producing similar goods. This active exploration of the product space generates data that incentivizes firms to do product innovation.

Setup Consider a continuum of products whose profits depend on N attributes. These attributes could be related to cost and optimal operations. They could be related to fads and fashion. These attributes could represent dimensions of worker skills and human resources decisions a firm must make.

For each attribute, there is an optimal action: the best supplier of a material, the hottest color, or the optimal degree of quantitative versus verbal skill needed in a new manager. For attribute k, this optimal choice is the kth entry of the $N \times 1$ vector $\theta_t + \epsilon_{i,t}$. The $N \times 1$ state θ_t follows the AR(1) process

$$\theta_t = \bar{\theta} + \rho(\theta_{t-1} - \bar{\theta}) + \nu_t. \tag{9.25}$$

The $N \times 1$ innovation vector $\nu_t \sim \mathcal{N}(0, \Sigma_\theta)$ is i.i.d. across time. The innovations are independent across attributes. In other words, Σ_θ is a diagonal matrix.[3] Firms have a noisy prior about the realization of θ_0. The transitory $N \times 1$ shock $\varepsilon_t \sim \mathcal{N}(0, \sigma_\varepsilon)$ is i.i.d. across time and firms, with diagonal σ_ε, and is unlearnable.

The quality of attribute j produced by firm i at time t is then the jth entry of the vector

$$A_{i,t} = \bar{A} - (a_{i,t} - \theta_t - \varepsilon_{i,t}) \odot (a_{i,t} - \theta_t - \varepsilon_{i,t}), \tag{9.26}$$

where $\odot$ denotes the Hadamard product (element-by-element multiplication). This quality expression represents the same squared loss function as in the univariate case.

Firms use data for product innovation and design. After observing and analyzing their data, they choose a location in the product space, represented by the $N \times 1$ vector $x_{i,t}$. The jth entry of $x_{i,t}$ reports the weight firm i's product

---

3. This is without loss of generality. If attributes have correlated innovations, we could construct a new linear combination of goods that has independent innovations and call that the attributes. For example, we might think of attributes as the principal components of the variance of goods shocks. Those components are, by construction, independent. See section 2.2.1 for more information on principal components, eigendecompositions, and other orthogonalization procedures.

places on attribute j. The quality of firm i's product is then $x_{i,t} \odot A_{i,t}$. To have a distinct notion of quantity and product location, we normalize the sum of the entries of x to one: $x_{i,t}' \mathbf{1}_N = 1$.

Each firm produces a single product with its chosen attributes and chooses how much to produce. As before, there is one input, which we will call labor $\ell_{i,t}$. Although a product has many dimensions, since each firm produces only one product, $\ell_{i,t}$ is 1×1, a scalar labor input into firm i's single product.

To add richness to the product space and still see the mechanisms clearly, it is useful to simplify the model along other dimensions. From here on, we assume that the production technology for goods is linear, meaning that the production exponent is $\alpha = 1$. To focus on product choice, we shut down data markets by setting $\iota = \infty$. Since data is no longer traded, we do not need an adjustment cost and set $\psi(\cdot) = 0$. Instead, we use a quadratic production cost $w\ell_{i,t}^2$ to keep the problem concave.[4] Finally, equation (9.26) represents a linear $g(\cdot)$ function for quality.

Firms' information sets take a similar form to before. Data is a by-product of economic activity. In this case, firms get data about the optimal attribute choice for every attribute they produce. They get more data about attributes their good loads on more heavily. The effective number of data points a firm sees about each attribute is the vector $z_i \ell_{i,t} x_{i,t}'$. As before, each data point has precision τ_s. Thus, the new data inflow is $\delta_{i,t}' = \tau_s z_i \ell_{i,t} x_{i,t}'$.

Firms update beliefs with Bayes' Law. Following exactly the same steps, one can easily show that the evolution of the stock of knowledge is the same as (9.2) in the univariate problem, but with a vector-matrix representation. In $\Omega_{i,t+1} = (1 - \zeta)\Omega_{i,t} + \mathrm{Diag}(\delta_{i,t})$, where Diag is a function $\mathbb{R}^{n+} \to \mathbb{R}^{n+\times n+}$ that takes in a nonnegative vector and turns it into a diagonal matrix. Note that, in this representation, the depreciation rate ζ becomes a diagonal $n \times n$ nonnegative matrix as well.

Equilibrium The equilibrium price of each attribute P_t depends on the aggregate supply of that attribute. P_t is a vector of prices per quality unit of each attribute:

$$P_t = \bar{P}\tilde{Y}_t^{-\gamma}, \tag{9.27}$$

$$\tilde{Y}_t = \int_i (x_{i,t} \odot A_{i,t})\ell_{i,t}\, di$$

---

4. A quadratic labor cost is unusual. It could represent a quadratic investment cost if the input is capital. This could also capture a combination of a linear labor cost and diminishing returns to firm scale. There are many reasons why firms do not become infinitely large. This is just a placeholder for one of those mechanisms.

where P_t and $\tilde{Y}_t$ are $N \times 1$ vectors of the equilibrium prices and quality-adjusted supplies of each of the N attributes. The price of the good that firm i produces is $x'_{i,t}P_t$, the linear combination of the price of each attribute, P_t, weighted by the intensity of that attribute in i's good, $x_{i,t}$.

If there are two types of firms i and j, the sequential problem of firm i can be expressed recursively as,

$$V(\Omega_{i,t}, \Omega_{j,t}) = \max_{x_{i,t}, \ell_{i,t}} x'_{i,t}(P_t \odot \mathbb{E}[A_{i,t}|\mathcal{I}])\ell_{i,t} - w\ell_{i,t}^2$$

$$+ \left(\frac{1}{1+r}\right) V(\Omega_{i,t+1}, \Omega_{j,t+1}), \qquad (9.28)$$

where Ω_{jt} is the data stock of the firm that is not like firm i. This additional state variable is necessary to determine the equilibrium price of goods P_t. Firms choose both the product design $x_{i,t}$, which is a vector, and the quantity to produce, which corresponds to a scalar choice of $\ell_{i,t}$. More labor scales up the number of units the firm produces of whatever good it chooses to produce.

To solve for the firm's optimal choices, it is useful to define a single choice variable $\tilde{x}_{i,t} \equiv x_{i,t}\ell_{i,t}$. We will first solve for the firm's joint choice of quantity and product location, and second, we will impose the constraint that location weights in x must sum to one to decompose the decisions. In a competitive market, the first-order condition for the optimal choice of $\tilde{x}_{i,t}$ is

$$\tilde{x}_{i,t} = \frac{1}{2r}\left[P_t \odot \mathbb{E}[A_{i,t}|\mathcal{I}] + \left(\frac{1}{1+r}\right)\frac{\partial V(\Omega_{i,t+1}, \Omega_{j,t+1})}{\partial \Omega_{i,t+1}}\sigma_\epsilon^{-2}\right]. \quad (9.29)$$

To recover product design and quantity separately, recognize that if the elements of $x_{i,t}$ must sum to one, then $\ell_{i,t} = \tilde{x}'_{i,t}\mathbf{1}$ is the sum of the entries of $\tilde{x}_{i,t}$ and the product choice is $x_{i,t} = \tilde{x}_{i,t}/\ell_{i,t}$.

The first-order condition tells us that firms like to produce goods that load more on attributes they know lots about (high $\mathbb{E}[A_{i,t}|\mathcal{I}]$), attributes they value learning more about (high $\partial V/\partial\Omega_{i,t+1}$) and, of course, attributes that make the good sell for a higher price (high P_t). The problem is not obvious because the first two criteria point the firm in opposite directions. Current profits will be higher if the firm does what it knows well. Future profits may be higher if the firm experiments with new attributes and learns about more valuable products to produce. This trade-off will not be constant over the life cycle of a firm. The changing tension between expertise and experimentation could be used to explain changes in the nature and scope of firms over their life cycle.

9.7   Data Feedback, Superstar Firms, and Firm Dynamics

In the data feedback loop, big firms generate big data sets. The abundance of data allows those firms to operate more profitably and enables them to grow even bigger. This increasing returns force can rationalize the existence of superstar firms. Superstar firms are a relatively small number of firms that dominate the activities in which they engage (Rosen, 1981). The revenues of such large companies often rival those of national governments (Zingales, 2017). For example, only eight governments in the world generate as much revenue as Walmart does.

One reason to believe that the superstar firm phenomenon is tied to data is that Tambe et al. (2020) find evidence of striking cross-firm heterogeneity in digital capital value, with most of the value concentrated in superstar firms. They define superstars as those with market values in the top decile. The authors document that by 2016, the stock of digital capital accounted for about 25% of the total capital stock for firms in their sample. They conclude that inequality in digital capital among firms is growing. The top firms' digital capital is growing faster than the rest. Similarly, Aghion et al. (2019) argue that innovations in information and communications technologies in the 1990s allowed high-productivity firms to expand profitably and become superstars.

The increasing returns of the data feedback framework described here naturally generate returns to scale and superstar firms. Furthermore, if we extend the model above to allow firms to choose their data processing efficiency z_i, with a higher cost for higher efficiency, the increasing returns force would grow even stronger. Not only would large firms get more data from doing more transactions, they would also invest in data processing capabilities that allow them to extract more knowledge from their data. This would advantage large firms even more.

There are related theories to this. One comes from the rational inattention literature. In Radner and Van Zandt (1995), an entropy-based complexity constraint creates returns to scale and determines the optimal size of a firm. Another related theory arises in finance. Begenau, Farboodi, and Veldkamp (2018) argue that data improves investors' forecasts and reduces equity uncertainty. Lower uncertainty reduces firms' cost of capital, facilitating firm growth. If large firms produce more data, this financial channel simulates more growth for these large firms, breeding superstar firms.

Data Poverty Traps   The flip side of the advantage large firms extract from data is the disadvantage to small firms. The idea that increasing returns keeps resource-poor entities poor comes from growth theory (Easterly, 2002) and is known as a poverty trap. We call the data analog a data poverty trap. It corresponds to the slow-growth phase on the left of Figure IX. This could explain the decline in business dynamism. Lower dynamism refers to the fact that fewer new firms enter, and those firms that enter are less likely to exit. Akcigit and Ates (2021) study the sources of this declining dynamism and find that the primary cause is the decline in knowledge diffusion from the largest to the smallest firms. If data lends itself to less diffusion than traditional technologies, then the growing data economy could be responsible for the decline in firm dynamism. Traditional technologies were more like processes. One might remember a process and take a similar idea to another firm. This is called technological leakage. But data—records of transactions, traffic, or clicks—is not a process. It is a set of statistics that is hard to remember and hard to import into a new firm.

Local Data Leakage   Superstar dynamics and data poverty traps are forms of divergence. One force for convergence is local learning. In many cases, firms, investors, or consumers learn from the actions of those around them. Others' data may be private, but their actions reveal something about what they know. The existing work on data growth and data-driven fluctuations primarily uses either social learning, whereby agents learn from everyone's experience, or private learning, exclusively from one's own experience. However, one could also adopt the intermediate case of local learning from section 3.2.2 and develop a model where some data or informative action is observed from one's neighbors. Local could mean something broader than geographically close and considers agents who are close in some characteristic space or social network. In this case, learning from others' data could produce a rich set of dynamics and fluctuations that could differ by region, socioeconomic group, social network, or industry. For a review of the role of social networks on economic and financial decision-making, see Kuchler and Stroebel (2021).

9.8   Data Feedback and Economic Fluctuations

So far, we have been considering the long-term consequences of data accumulation. The feedback loop between data and economic activity can also amplify or propagate the business cycle. The main idea is that booms are times of both high activity and abundant information production. This also provides a rationale for the finding that recessions are times of high economic uncertainty (Bloom, 2009).

To examine how data affects business cycle dynamics, we do not need firm heterogeneity. So, consider a simple case with a representative firm.

Setup   A representative firm produces output y_t with labor ℓ_t, with decreasing returns to scale $\alpha < 1$. The firm has productivity θ_t, which it does not know. The firm's prior belief is that $\theta_t \sim \mathcal{N}(\mu_\theta, \sigma_\theta^2)$.[5] It also experiences a random idiosyncratic output shock v_t that is i.i.d. over time. The production function is given by

$$y_t = \theta_t \ell_t^\alpha - v_t; \qquad v_t \sim_{iid} \mathcal{N}(0, \sigma_v^2). \qquad (9.30)$$

The term v_t may capture a fixed cost of firm entry (Fajgelbaum, Schaal, and Taschereau-Dumouchel, 2017), idiosyncratic productivity (Van Nieuwerburgh and Veldkamp, 2006) or an investment payoff (Veldkamp, 2005).

Firms use output y_t to form beliefs about the productivity θ_t. The unbiased signal derived from output is

$$s_t = y_t / \ell_t^\alpha = \theta_t + v_t / \ell_t^\alpha. \qquad (9.31)$$

The key property to notice is that the variance of the signal noise is $\sigma_v^2 / \ell_t^{2\alpha}$. The larger the labor input ℓ_t, the less noisy and the more informative the output data is. In other words, more economic activity generates more (or more informative) data. In Fajgelbaum, Schaal, and Taschereau-Dumouchel (2017), the mechanism is that more firms enter when the economy is in a good state, and each firm generates a signal. In Veldkamp (2005), more investment projects are undertaken in good states, and each investment project generates a piece of data. In all of these models, data is a by-product of economic activity.

Data Feedback A firm chooses to produce more (high ℓ_t) if its productivity belief is high. When economic activity is high (large y_t), data is abundant. Abundant data makes firms' beliefs more sensitive to changes in the true state. To see this, define in the information set of the firm to be all past output realizations: $\mathcal{I}_t = \{y_\tau\}_{\tau=1}^t$. Then use Bayes' Law for normal variables to express the posterior belief about productivity $\mathbb{E}[\theta_t | \mathcal{I}_t]$ as the weighted average of the prior belief $\mathbb{E}[\theta_t | \mathcal{I}_{t-1}]$ and the signal s_t: $\mathbb{E}[\theta_t | \mathcal{I}_t] = (1 - \gamma_t)\mathbb{E}[\theta_t | \mathcal{I}_{t-1}] + \gamma_t s_t$. The Bayesian weight γ_t on the new data is the data precision $\ell_t^{2\alpha} / \sigma_v^2$ divided by the sum of the data precision and the prior precision $\mathbb{V}ar[\theta_t | \mathcal{I}_{t-1}]$. Since the signal is the true state plus noise, the sensitivity of posterior beliefs to a change in the true state is simply the Bayesian updating weight on the signal:

$$\frac{\partial \mathbb{E}[\theta_t | \mathcal{I}_t]}{\partial \theta_t} = \gamma_t = \frac{\ell_t^{2\alpha}}{\ell_t^{2\alpha} + \sigma_v^2 \mathbb{V}ar[\theta_t | \mathcal{I}_{t-1}]}. \qquad (9.32)$$

Beliefs are more sensitive to changes in the state when ℓ_t is high, which is when output is high. If the economy is in the midst of a boom and the state changes,

---

5. Another tractable assumption is that θ_t follows a two-state Markov process between a good state θ_g (expansion) and a bad state θ_b (recession), with $\theta_g > \theta_b$.

beliefs react strongly and quickly to the abundance of new data. This leads to an abrupt downward adjustment in production. If the economy is in a recession, where output and labor are low, data is scarce, and therefore, beliefs and activity are sluggish to respond.

Asymmetric Fluctuations   Abundant data flow when economic activity is high and scarce flow when activity is low can explain why the business cycle is asymmetric. It lengthens recessions and shortens booms. Veldkamp (2005) proposed this mechanism to explain why many asset markets exhibit slow booms and sudden crashes. Van Nieuwerburgh and Veldkamp (2006) exploits it to understand business cycle asymmetries with slow expansions and sudden recessions. Ordoñez (2013) documents that this asymmetry varies across countries and explains the variation with different degrees of financial frictions. In Straub and Ulbricht (2023), the ability of investors to learn about firm-level fundamentals declines during financial crises, which generates negative spillovers from financial distress onto the real economy. In each of these cases, the slow recovery from a recession is a business cycle analog to the data poverty trap discussed in section 9.7.

To make slow recoveries even slower, Fajgelbaum, Schaal, and Taschereau-Dumouchel (2017) propose a theory of self-reinforcing episodes of high uncertainty and low activity. Entry costs prevent firms whose expected productivity is low from revealing any data at all because those firms choose to stay out of the market. Entry costs are a form of irreversible investment, which also introduce an option value of waiting or a "wait-and-see" effect. The real option value to waiting is stronger when uncertainty is higher, which is in recessions. In their setting, recessions last even longer because firms wait to learn more in the aftermath of a recession.

In all of these papers, there is a two-way interaction between the level of economic activity and aggregate uncertainty, which is determined by the amount of data.

9.9 Learning an Asset Market Equilibrium with Data Feedback

Asset markets have their own variety of a data feedback loop. When investors do not know the mapping from prices to fundamentals and must learn the equilibria, their beliefs influence prices as in section 2.6.2. However, since they learn from prices, these prices, in turn, influence their beliefs. A data feedback loop arises.

The theory of internal rationality has explained several asset pricing puzzles. In these models, rational investors with subjective beliefs about price behavior optimally learn from data on past observations of asset prices, dividends, or returns. Next, we present a simplified framework version to highlight the key ideas.

9.9.1 Consumption-Based Asset Pricing

The model's core is the stochastic exchange economy in Lucas (1978), extended with a general probability measure as in Adam and Marcet (2011). Consider a continuum of identical risk-neutral investors indexed by $i \in [0, 1]$ that discount the future at a common rate $\beta < 1$. They choose consumption $c^i \geq 0$ and the number of shares of a risky asset $s^i \leq \bar{s}$ to maximize the expected utility from consumption of a single good:[6]

$$\max_{\{c_t^i \geq 0,\, s_t^i \leq \bar{s}\}_{t=0}^{\infty}} \mathbb{E}_0^{\mathcal{P}^i} \left[\sum_{t=0}^{\infty} \beta^t c_t^i \right]. \tag{9.33}$$

If we let P_t be the ex-dividend risky asset price and D_t the dividend, the budget constraint is

$$P_t s_t^i + c_t^i = s_{t-1}^i (P_t + D_t), \tag{9.34}$$

for given initial holdings $s_{-1}^i = 1$. For each investor i, $\mathbb{E}_0^{\mathcal{P}^i}$ is the time-zero individual subjective expectations under the probability measure $\mathcal{P}^i$. Dividends or endowments grow at an average rate $a > 0$ and are subject to i.i.d. ϵ_{t+1}^D shocks:

$$\frac{D_{t+1}}{D_t} = a + \epsilon_{t+1}^D, \qquad \epsilon_{t+1}^D \sim_{iid} \mathcal{N}\left(0, \sigma_D^2\right), \tag{9.35}$$

with D_0 given. The dividend process is known to investors. Equilibrium is defined in two ways, corresponding to two different belief processes below.

To solve the model, start by substituting the budget constraint (9.34) into the objective (9.33). The objective simplifies to $\mathbb{E}_0^{\mathcal{P}^i} \left[\sum_{t=0}^{\infty} \beta^t (s_{t-1}^i (P_t + D_t) - P_t s_t^i) \right]$. The first-order condition to maximize this objective, concerning stock holdings s_t^i, yields a standard asset-pricing Euler equation but under subjective expectations:

$$P_t = \beta \mathbb{E}_t^{\mathcal{P}^i} \left[P_{t+1} + D_{t+1} \right]. \tag{9.36}$$

---

6. Adam and Marcet (2011) emphasize that an upper bound on stock holdings, $s_t^i < \bar{s}$, helps ensure the existence of a maximum with risk-neutral investors. Adding risk aversion does not qualitatively change the predictions of the model.

9.9.2 Stock Prices under Rational Expectations

Under rational expectations, investors understand they are all identical and have identical beliefs: $\mathcal{P}^i = \mathcal{P}^j = \mathcal{P}$. In this case, the law of iterated expectations applies. This allows us to iterate forward the Euler equation and use a transversality condition $(\lim_{j \to \infty} \beta^j \mathbb{E}[P_{t+j}] = 0)$ to obtain an expression for the equilibrium stock price equal to the expected discounted sum of future dividends:[7]

$$P_t = \sum_{j=1}^{\infty} \beta^j \mathbb{E}[D_{t+j}]. \tag{9.37}$$

Dividing both sides by D_t, substituting the dividend process in (9.35), and computing the infinite sum (note that it starts from $j = 1$), yields:

$$\frac{P_t}{D_t} = \sum_{j=1}^{\infty} \beta^j \mathbb{E}\left[\frac{D_{t+j}}{D_t}\right] = \sum_{j=1}^{\infty} (\beta a)^j = \frac{\beta a}{1 - \beta a}. \tag{9.38}$$

Since the price-to-dividend ratio P_t/D_t is constant, the equilibrium stock price P_t must always remain proportional to dividends. This implies that the implicit model of price growth agents use under rational expectations is

$$\frac{P_{t+1}}{P_t} = \frac{D_{t+1}}{D_t} = a + \epsilon_{t+1}^D. \tag{9.39}$$

The subjective model of price growth in the next section generalizes this solution.

9.9.3 Data Feedback When Learning from Stock Price Data

Next, we depart from rational expectations and relax the assumption that investors know they are identical. This assumption breaks the law of iterated expectations because future expectations computed under others' beliefs $\mathcal{P}^j$ might differ from one's own $\mathcal{P}^i$. Since iterating forward is unfeasible, and prices cannot be backed out from optimality conditions, investors take them as given. Thus, under internal rationality, prices become part of the state-space together with fundamentals.

Risky asset holdings must be characterized by the one-period ahead Euler equation (9.36). We rewrite the Euler equation in terms of stock price and

---

7. To simplify notation, we denote rational expectations without the superscript $\mathbb{E}[\cdot] = \mathbb{E}^{\mathcal{P}}[\cdot]$.

dividend growth rates and solve for the price-to-dividend ratio:

$$\frac{P_t}{D_t} = \frac{\beta a}{1 - \beta \mathbb{E}_t^{\mathcal{P}^i} \left[\frac{P_{t+1}}{P_t} \right]}. \tag{9.40}$$

This general expression emphasizes the role of the beliefs about capital gains. It is not an equilibrium object yet since beliefs are unspecified. Next, we assume investors believe the growth rate of stock prices has permanent b_t and transitory ϵ_{t+1}^p components that cannot be disentangled:[8]

$$\frac{P_{t+1}}{P_t} = b_{t+1} + \epsilon_{t+1}^P \qquad \epsilon_{t+1}^P \sim \mathcal{N}(0, \sigma_P^2) \tag{9.41}$$

$$b_{t+1} = b_t + v_{t+1} \qquad v_{t+1} \sim \mathcal{N}(0, \sigma_v^2). \tag{9.42}$$

Investors face a signal extraction problem as in section 4.2. To learn b_t, they use data on past realizations of stock prices $\mathcal{I}_t = \{P_s : s < t\}$ and Bayesian updating. Since investors are assumed to be Bayesian in their estimates of b_t, we can use the Kalman Filter formulas in (2.46), (2.47), and (2.48). Evaluated at $\rho = 1$ to reflect the random walk assumption, they deliver an estimate for the permanent component of stock price growth $\hat{b}_{t+1} \equiv \mathbb{E}[b_{t+1}|\mathcal{I}_t]$:

$$\hat{b}_{t+1} = \hat{b}_t + K \left(\frac{P_t}{P_{t-1}} - \hat{b}_t \right), \tag{9.43}$$

where K stands for the steady-state Kalman gain. Beliefs evolve according to constant gain learning, which would be optimal if beliefs (9.41) and (9.42) were the true law of motion (Adam, Marcet, and Nicolini, 2016). Substituting the subjective expected price growth $\mathbb{E}_t^{\mathcal{P}^i} [P_{t+1}/P_t] = \hat{b}_{t+1}$ into (9.40) yields a time-varying price-dividend ratio that depends on beliefs:

$$\frac{P_t}{D_t} = \frac{\beta a}{1 - \beta \hat{b}_{t+1}}. \tag{9.44}$$

Since beliefs influence data (prices), which influence beliefs, a data feedback loop arises.[9] Combining the two expressions, we arrive at a second-order

---

8. The specific choice for the subjective model of stock prices is based on two grounds. Theoretically, it generalizes the rational expectations model in (9.39), which is a special case with $\sigma_v^2 = 0$ and the prior $b_0 = a$. Empirically, it is consistent with the large swings in the price-dividend ratio.

9. Typically, the literature uses lagged priced growth P_{t-1}/P_{t-2} in (9.43) so that $\hat{b}_{t+1}$ in (9.44) becomes predetermined at date t. This renders the system recursive and eliminates multiple equilibria.

difference equation in beliefs:

$$\hat{b}_{t+1} = (1 - K)\hat{b}_{t-1} + K \left(\frac{1 - \beta \hat{b}_t}{1 - \beta \hat{b}_{t+1}} \right) (a + \epsilon_t^D). \qquad (9.45)$$

The steady state of this equation corresponds to the rational expectations equilibrium $\hat{b}_t = a$ for all t. Outside the steady state, beliefs move around the rational expectations solution, amplified by the data feedback effect, producing booms and busts.

Revisiting Asset Pricing Puzzles   This asset price data feedback loop explains several asset pricing puzzles. Adam, Marcet, and Nicolini (2016) show that this framework generates realistic amounts of volatility, momentum, and mean reversion in equity prices. Adam, Marcet, and Beutel (2017) consider investors that learn about capital gains and match the empirically strong positive correlation between the price dividend ratio and survey return expectations. Belda (2022) extends their model to incorporate taxes on capital gains and portfolio adjustment costs. Belda argues that the US capital gains tax cuts enacted during the 1980s made asset prices more responsive to changes in investors' beliefs, explaining part of the rise in financial volatility. Belda, Heineken, and Ifrim (2023) extend the model to incorporate heterogeneous expectations and study the feedback loop between stock prices and trading. Winkler (2020) embeds learning-based asset pricing into a business cycle model in which firms face credit constraints that depend partly on their market value. The financial frictions and learning combination amplifies shocks through an additional data feedback loop between asset prices and real activity. Finally, Caines and Winkler (2021) characterize optimal monetary policy with an asset price data feedback loop.

Key Ideas

- The data feedback loop makes firm size diverge: big firms with lots of data grow larger, and data-poor firms grow slowly.
- The stock of data can be a state variable in a dynamic programming problem that describes the evolution and fluctuations of a data economy.
- Data feedback loops can also arise when the data helps firms learn about the equilibrium payoff distribution.

Practice Questions

9.1 Suppose that the productivity function $g(\cdot)$ is not linear.
  (a) Derive a first-order Taylor approximation of $g((a_{it} - a_t^*)^2)$.
  (b) Derive a second-order Taylor approximation of $g((a_{it} - a_t^*)^2)$.
  (c) Under what conditions is equation (9.5) reasonably accurate?
9.2 Suppose a firm can both buy and sell data in the same period. Characterize the optimal amount of data to buy and to sell. How does your answer depend on the price of data π_t?
9.3 If firms can buy or sell data, what is one feature of a firm that would make it a likely data seller?
9.4 Assume $g(\cdot)$ has finite value except at 0, show that $\mathbb{E}[g(\cdot)]$ is bounded above, even if $g(0) \to \infty$ and $\Omega_t \to \infty$.
9.5 What is the variance of the signal that firms get from observing their output? (*Hint: The signal extracted from output is a mixture of normal variables.*)

10

Data Measurement
and Valuation

Data is an asset. It is traded in markets; it is bought and sold. What properties does data have as an asset? Is it cyclical? What does it covary with? Is it a risky asset, or is it a relatively safe asset? We know that the most valuable firms in the economy today are valued primarily for their data. Are these valuations sound? We also know that large swaths of the economy are generating valuable data. But it is not clear that GDP measurement captures this valuable economic activity appropriately.

Answering all these questions begins with measuring the amount and value of a firm's data. This chapter presents methodologies to measure data and its value. The goal is to unify the theory in the previous chapters with viable empirical approaches. No one approach will fit all relevant situations. We will develop an arsenal of tools to value data in different ways: a cost approach, a revenue approach, value function estimation, and using complementary inputs. In order to know how to value data, it is essential to know how to depreciate data.

In the following section, the amount and value of data are used interchangeably. It is natural to equate these two notions of data; because data does not usually have natural units, it makes sense to align data units with the data value. In essence, we are measuring data with the metric that makes one unit of data (however much data) worth one dollar.

Keep in mind that there is no single value for any data set. The data has value to a user that depends on their objective and ability to use it. Section 10.7 will return to the idea of multiple values for the same data and show that, in a financial market context, data has a large private value component: it takes on very different values to different users.

10.1 Measuring Data Depreciation

To measure a stock of data, we need to know how it accumulates and how it depreciates. We start with depreciation and then turn to measuring the accumulation.

New data technologies, like machine learning, AI, or neural networks, are prediction technologies. They use large data sets to predict outcomes. Many predictions take the form of forecasts of future events. To inform the question of how data depreciates, we can look at how data's ability to predict depreciates. Of course, one could simply assume that in each period, a fraction ζ of data is lost due to depreciation. This is akin to how economists typically depreciate capital. However with data, Bayes' Law dictates what this depreciation rate should be. To understand what determines the rate of data depreciation, consider the following simple example.

Suppose we use data with normally distributed noise to forecast an AR(1) process with normally distributed innovations:

$$\theta_{t+1} = \rho\theta_t + \epsilon_{t+1}, \qquad \epsilon_{t+1} \sim \mathcal{N}(0, \sigma_\epsilon^2), \tag{10.1}$$

for $0 < \rho < 1$. This process could represent the return on an asset, a procurement cost, a customer acquisition probability, or the demand for a good.

The prior mean and variance are given by $\mathbb{E}[\theta_t|\mathcal{I}_t]$ and $\mathbb{V}ar[\theta_t|\mathcal{I}_t] = \Omega_t^{-1}$, where $\mathcal{I}_t$ represents whatever information set the agent has at time t. We define Ω with the inverse because this lends itself to interpreting Ω_t as the stock of knowledge. A lower variance estimate or more accurate estimate implies more knowledge about θ_t.

Next, consider today's forecast and the variance of tomorrow's state. Taking the mean and then the variance of both sides of (10.1), we get

$$\mathbb{E}[\theta_{t+1}|\mathcal{I}_t] = \rho\mathbb{E}[\theta_t|\mathcal{I}_t], \tag{10.2}$$

$$\mathbb{V}ar[\theta_{t+1}|\mathcal{I}_t] = \rho^2\Omega_t^{-1} + \sigma_\epsilon^2. \tag{10.3}$$

Equation (10.3) tells us the conditional variance of the state θ_{t+1}, conditional on all information at time t. This conditional variance is not a measure of θ's volatility. Rather, it is a measure of uncertainty. It is the expected squared forecast error: $\mathbb{V}ar[\theta_{t+1}|\mathcal{I}_t] \equiv \mathbb{E}[(\theta_{t+1} - \mathbb{E}[\theta_{t+1}|\mathcal{I}_t])^2|\mathcal{I}_t]$. It reveals how inaccurate our forecasts are. In Bayesian language, this is a prior variance of θ_{t+1}.

If data is used to forecast θ_{t+1} and has normally distributed noise, then Bayes' Law says that we can combine that data and represent it as a signal about tomorrow's state $s_t = \theta_{t+1} + e_t$, with $e_t \sim \mathcal{N}(0, \sigma_s^2)$. In other words, we can represent the information set equivalently as $\mathcal{I}_{t+1} = \{\mathcal{I}_t, s_t\}$. The information the agent will have to make decisions tomorrow is the information available today, plus the signal observed at the end of period t.

When we combine a normal prior belief with a signal that has normally distributed signal noise, Bayes' Law says that the precision of the resulting posterior belief is the prior precision—inverse the inverse of equation (10.3)—plus the signal precision σ_s^{-2}:

$$\Omega_{t+1} = (\rho^2 \Omega_t^{-1} + \sigma_\epsilon^2)^{-1} + \sigma_s^{-2}. \tag{10.4}$$

This equation maps the time-t stock of knowledge Ω_t into time-$t+1$ stock of knowledge. In other words, it is a law of motion for the stock of knowledge. That law of motion says that we take the stock Ω_t, depreciate it by transforming it into $(\rho^2 \Omega_t^{-1} + \sigma_\epsilon^2)^{-1}$ and then add on the flow of new data. That new data flow has total precision σ_s^{-2}. This is similar to a law of motion for a stock of capital: $k_{t+1} = (1 - \zeta)k_t + i_t$, where i_t is new investment. For data, the time-varying depreciation rate is as follows:[1]

$$\zeta_t = 1 - \frac{1}{\rho^2 + \sigma_\epsilon^2 \Omega_t}. \tag{10.5}$$

This depreciation rate teaches us that if the AR(1) process is highly volatile (high σ_ϵ), then the stock of knowledge will depreciate quickly. Data about yesterday's state is less relevant to today's state because the state is changing quickly. Also, we learn that if the AR(1) process is very persistent (high ρ), depreciation is faster. The effect of persistence on knowledge depreciation might seem counterintuitive at first glance. However, it makes sense once we take a long-run view. The unconditional variance of an AR(1) process is $\sigma_\epsilon^2/(1 - \rho^2)$, which is increasing in ρ. A process approaching a random walk ($\rho \to 1$) has a huge unconditional variance because it may drift far away. Thus, past data is not valuable for prediction. Finally, large stocks of knowledge (large Ω_t) depreciate at a faster rate than small stocks. However, in many cases, the depreciation rate can be close to linear. That depends on how volatile and persistent the environment is.

This depreciation rate is measurable. It requires measuring the persistence and volatility of the object the firm is trying to forecast. We can use those estimates to create a depreciation rate for data. The depreciation rate will be context-specific. For example, data about order flow, which is highly volatile, will have a different depreciation rate than data about customer zip codes, which persist for years. To depreciate data, we need to know what the

---

1. In Chapter 9, we considered the depreciation rate as a parameter ζ to simplify the exposition.

data will be used to predict. But once the persistence, volatility, and data stock are known, Bayes' Law can do the rest.

10.2 Value Function Approach

The value function approach uses the same tools macroeconomics uses to value capital and can be applied to value data with some adjustments. The value function for data is

$$V(\Omega_{i,t}) = \max_{k_{i,t}, \ell_{i,t}} A(\Omega_{i,t}) k_{i,t}^{\alpha} \ell_{i,t}^{1-\alpha} - w\ell_{i,t} - rk_{i,t} + \beta V(\Omega_{i,t+1}). \quad (10.6)$$

Firms choose capital $k_{i,t}$ and labor $\ell_{i,t}$. Productivity $A(\Omega_{i,t})$ is a function of data, just like in the data feedback loop models. Productivity multiplies capital and labor. The firm has to pay for labor and capital. Tomorrow, the firm will have a discounted value of the data that it has today. The discount factor is a constant $\beta < 1$, but can be modified to be the risk-less interest rate $1/(1+r)$ or a stochastic discount factor. This expression can be adapted in many ways.

This recursive approach requires us to specify the data's law of motion. Tomorrow's stock of data is today's depreciated stock of data plus the data flow:

$$\Omega_{i,t+1} = (1 - \zeta_{i,t})\Omega_{i,t} + \underbrace{\tau_s \delta_{i,t}}_{\text{data flow}}. \quad (10.7)$$

The depreciation rate $\zeta_{i,t}$ may follow (10.5). A theory of data flows $\delta_{i,t}$ is required here. The flow could be a fraction of transactions $(\delta_{i,t} = z_i y_{i,t})$ as in the data feedback loop from section 9.1. Data purchases and sales can be added, as in section 9.4. Additionally, we can think about using labor inputs to process raw data into structured data and structured data into knowledge, as we will do in section 10.8. We can augment this with many theories of how firms accumulate data.

10.3 Firm Surveys on Data Technology Adoption

Several surveys directly ask firms about their use of big data. One example is the European Investment Bank (EIB) Investment Survey, conducted yearly since 2016 on about 10,000 firms.[2] According to this survey, which asks European firms about their data use and their adoption of digital technologies, 24% of firms have adopted cognitive technologies such as big data analytics and

---

2. "EIB Investment Survey (EIBIS)," European Investment Bank (website), 2024, https://www.eib.org/en/publications-research/economics/surveys-data/eibis/index.htm.

artificial intelligence. This figure varies significantly by country, industry, and firm size (there is more adoption in larger firms).

A second example is the Survey on Information and Communication Technologies in Business, elaborated by the French National Institute of Statistics and Economic Studies (INSEE), which provides detailed information on the type of data used, factors limiting adoption, and data trade.[3] An interesting question asks firms if they use big data for (i) improving marketing or sales management, (ii) developing or improving goods or services, and/or (iii) improving internal production processes. These answers could be helpful in testing the data-driven theories developed in this book.

Since most questions are qualitative, the answers measure the extensive margin of adoption. Merging these types of surveys with firm-level balance sheet information is a promising avenue for studying the interaction between data use and labor productivity (Cathles, Nayyar, and Rückert, 2020), revenue (Galdon-Sanchez, Gil, and Uriz Uharte, 2022), patenting (Wu, Hitt, and Lou, 2020), and investment (Rábano, Rückert, and Weiss, 2023).

Surveys also provide evidence of improved firm predictions. Brynjolfsson and McElheran (2016) designed the first-ever Management and Organizational Practices Survey (MOPS) to investigate the impact of data-driven decision-making. They discovered that increased use of data-driven decision-making is linked to a statistically significant boost in productivity of 3% or more on average. The performance differentials linked with data-driven decision-making for early and late adopters diminished over time, suggesting firm learning and the emergence of organizational complementarities. Goldfarb and Tucker (2019a) emphasized the reduction in five distinct economic costs associated with digital economic activity: search costs, replication costs, transportation costs, tracking costs, and verification costs.

10.4 Using Forecast Data

One way of measuring how much information agents have is to ask them what they believe will happen. Recently, there has been a proliferation in the sources and types of forecast data: unemployed workers' job-finding expectations; senior households' expectations about retirement; households' inflation or housing forecasts; education, development, and health economics expectations; firm-level forecasts of their own revenues, investment plans, and pricing decisions; firms' macroeconomic forecasts and financial market participants' asset market forecasts. The *Handbook of Economic Expectations* (Bachmann,

---

3. "Survey of Information and Communication Technologies in Enterprises," INSEE (website), 2024, https://www.insee.fr/fr/metadonnees/source/serie/s1273.

Topa, and van der Klaauw, 2022) provides a comprehensive review, discussing the measurement and role of these expectations and many others.

To map a forecast series into an amount of data is a straightforward process. First, construct the forecast errors. Errors are the difference between the forecast and the realized variable being forecasted. Next, square these errors and average the squared values. If there are not many observations, a standard degrees-of-freedom adjustment improves the estimate. This is a conditional variance estimator. Invert the variance to obtain a precision estimate. See section 10.7.2 for details of a similar approach in a financial market context.

Analysts and Managers Forecasts   One source of forecast data on firm-level outcomes is the I/B/E/S (Institutional Brokers' Estimate System), which compiles a historical record of forecasts made by stock analysts and managers on the future earnings of publicly traded companies. It covers about 60,000 companies in more than 100 markets and goes back to 1975. The database I/B/E/S Historical Estimates provides third-party analysts' forecasts. The database I/B/E/S Guidance provides managerial forecasts of several firm-specific outcomes, including revenue and profits.

Individual firms' forecasts are useful to gauge secular trends and cross-sectional differences in the use of data. For example, Asriyan and Kohlhas (2023) combine the I/B/E/S Guidance survey with firm-level data from Compustat to document a systematic improvement in the forecasting ability of US public firms over time and show that this aggregate trend can be explained by firms growing larger over time.

Forecast data has also been used to assess time variation in firm-level uncertainty. For instance, Bachmann, Elstner, and Hristov (2017) and Bachmann et al. (2021) document substantial time-variation and cross-sectional heterogeneity in measures of firm-level uncertainty using forecast data of German firms from the Ifo Institute. Similar evidence is documented for the United States in Senga (2018) by merging forecast data from the I/B/E/S and Compustat. Their evidence reveals persistent differences in the degree of firm-level uncertainty in the cross section and across time within the same firm.

Professionals Forecasts   For theories about macroeconomic data, the Survey of Professional Forecasters (SPF) from the Federal Reserve Bank of Philadelphia is a good source of data about beliefs. These forecasts can be combined with realizations of macro outcomes to construct two data measures. One is the cross-sectional dispersion of the forecasts or disagreement. More data is generally associated with less forecast dispersion, although this varies model by model. A second measure is the average mean squared error or average absolute deviation of forecasts from the realization of the forecasted variable.

This is a measure of forecast uncertainty, or its inverse, forecast precision. More data generally increases precision.

Kozeniauskas, Orlik, and Veldkamp (2018) combine the SPF with Blue Chip Economic Indicators to highlight the differences between higher-order uncertainty (forecasters disagreement), macro uncertainty (uncertainty about macro outcomes), and changes in fundamental macro volatility. Giacomini, Skreta, and Turén (2020) and Baley and Turén (2023) use the Bloomberg survey of professional forecasters to establish stylized facts on the dynamics of accuracy, disagreement, and lumpiness of inflation forecasts.

10.5   Cost Approach

A typical approach to valuing most assets is to assume the asset's value is the sum of the costs to obtain the asset. This approach can be applied to data. Firms may purchase data at a cost, and the cost of data can be used as its value or amount. However, this approach can only be applied if the firm purchased the data. Firms often do not purchase data. Instead, they obtain data as a by-product of economic activity. This barter trade may be implicit in all kinds of the firm's transactions, and the value of this data cannot be measured by the cost approach. Customers may be paid for their data in terms of a discounted good. The firm may have charged the customer more had the customer not provided the firm with their data. For example, Amazon may give customers a discount on products in exchange for their data. If we could measure this product discount directly, the cost approach would be a potential method to estimate a single firm's data value or the aggregate value of data in the economy.

Brynjolfsson et al. (2023) estimate the value of free digital goods to consumers: the ten digital goods selected in this study generate a combined total of $2.52 trillion in welfare across these countries—ranging from $1.29 trillion in the US to $13 billion in Romania. For the United States, this represents 5.5% of total US economic output. In another study, Brynjolfsson, Kim, and Oh (2023) measure the consumer surplus of free goods on the internet and find them to be worth about $38 billion per year in the United States, equivalent to approximately 0.29% of annual GDP. Since the price paid for all these digital goods was zero, the discount might be regarded as the entire consumer value of the good. This is a measure of the data value derived from these free goods.

However, this is surely an underestimate of aggregate data value because data is also exchanged for goods that are not free. Free digital goods are a pure barter trade. Data is bartered for goods. However, the discounted price examples represent partial barter trades—cases where consumers paid, in part, with money and, in part, with data. Partial barter trades might involve lower values for the data but are potentially much more widespread.

Even if partial data barter trades could be measured, they are still imperfect because data has a large private value component. Thus, the cost to the firm, in the form of product discounts, may be less than their value for that data. We discuss private values in section 10.7.3.

10.6 Choice Covariance

The next data measurement approach measures covariances between a firm's choices and its payoffs.

Data allows agents to take better actions. We call a firm's action a_t, which we interpret here as a quantity. It can also be a price or any other action. The quantity might covary with the payoff, which is called θ_t. The expected profit a firm gets is equal to the expected quantity times the expected return plus the covariance between quantities and returns.

$$\mathbb{E}[a_t \theta_t] = \mathbb{E}[a_t]\mathbb{E}[\theta_t] + \mathbb{C}ov[a_t, \theta_t]. \qquad (10.8)$$

If a firm has data that predicts θ_t, the firm can choose the a_t that covaries with θ_t. If the firm does not know anything about θ_t, it is not possible for the firm to choose a_t to covary systemically with θ_t. Data makes the covariance between actions and payoffs possible. That is why firms value data because it allows them to take actions that covary with their payoffs.

This idea can be applied in a finance context to portfolio choice. An investor may choose assets that systematically have high returns relative to a benchmark, which is captured by the portfolio alpha. The portfolio alpha is a well-known measure of manager skill. It is also a measure of the information that the manager has. Similarly, Durnev et al. (2003) measure which assets' prices contain more and less information about future earnings by regressing future earnings on asset prices. The idea is that when investors collectively have information about future earnings, they buy when earnings are high, pushing the asset's price up, and sell when earnings are low, pushing the price down. Thus, when the price moves in advance of earnings announcements (in the same direction as the announcement), investors must have information about what that announcement will be. This is used as a proxy for how informed investors are.

Consider a firm using data to determine which product to produce. If the firm wants to maximize its profits, it should produce high-markup products. Data could forecast which products are in high demand and can therefore command high markups. The firm can forecast which shirts everybody is going to want next period and produce more of those shirts. If the firm has precise forecasts of demand for shirts, they can produce exactly the high-demand, high-price shirts every season. Without the data forecasting demand, this production scheme would be impossible. Thus, data should be associated with a high covariance between the production of a shirt and demand for that type of shirt.

The same logic applies to the covariance between advertising revenue and customer click-through. All of these covariances should tell us something about the underlying information that was used to make a decision. This approach may not always be possible when economists cannot observe the actions a firm takes or what its objective is. If we think data has a clear purpose for the firm, then sometimes one can measure covariances between actions and payoffs in order to value data.

In section 11.7.3, the relationship between data and covariance reappears: firms with more data about another country's economy choose output that covaries more with that country's output.

In some instances, covariances are measurable and can be used to estimate data. For example, Klenow and Willis (2007) test inattentiveness models of price setting by asking whether the information revealed in past periods acts as a shock to prices in the current period. Since an inattentive agent does now know about realized shocks until the information set is updated, the shocks only affect price-setting with a lag. They find that lagged shocks affect current prices, consistent with the inattentiveness theory for sticky prices in Reis (2006b). In a similar exercise with asset prices, Hong, Torous, and Valkanov (2007) find that industry information affects the market equity index value with a lag.

Hong, Stein, and Yu (2007) do a case study of Amazon equity. They find that traders writing about and trading on data about the number of clicks on Amazon's website suddenly shifted in the year 2000 to writing about and trading based on earnings announcements. They infer that traders changed the information they used because of the change in the covariance of the stock price with the announcements of earnings fundamentals.

One potential drawback of this approach is that the covariance of the state variable and the action may be what the model is designed to explain. If that is the case, then this approach will not distinguish between competing theories all designed to explain this covariance. However, no agent, in any context, can achieve covariance of a choice variable with a random outcome without sufficient information. Choosing actions that covary without sufficient information is not a measurable strategy. Many theories might explain why covariances are low; various frictions can get in the way. However, observing a covariance places a lower bound on how much data or information an agent must have to achieve that covariance.

10.6.1   Insensitivity to Public Information as a Measure of Data

A measurement idea related to using action covariances is to gauge how much an agent's choice changes when new information is revealed. Information revelations that economists observe are typically public announcements. If the agent has very precise private information, the Bayesian weight on the new public information should be low. The action response should be muted. Conversely, if we observe an agent reacting strongly to new, public information, we can infer that their existing data must have been imprecise.

Kacperczyk and Seru (2007) construct a measure of *reliance on public information* (RPI) to be a proxy for the amount of public information the fund manager uses to manage his portfolio. RPI is the R^2 of the regression of changes in fund managers' portfolio holdings on changes in analysts' forecasts. They claim that managers rely more on public information when they have less private information. This claim is supported by the fact that funds with higher RPI earn lower profits.

10.7   Revenue Approach

The revenue approach focuses on how much firms profit from data. The data value should be the present discounted value of the revenue it generates, adjusted for risk. The key challenge is isolating data revenue from other revenue. When data is the primary source of revenue, the business model is simple, and measurement may be straightforward. However, when data is used for multiple purposes, separating data revenue from other revenue may be difficult.

Another complication that arises is that young, data-intensive firms may operate at a loss. If a firm needs a lot of customers to get more data, and they need to get more data to operate profitably and be more efficient, their main goal early on should be to get as many customers as possible, at whatever cost. For example, Amazon was unprofitable for the first six years of its existence. That makes great sense for a firm in the data feedback loop. The optimal path for a financially unconstrained firm may involve pricing below cost early on. Pricing below cost is a form of costly investment in data and in future transactions that will generate more future data.

What is the value of this data for the firm, given that it is making a loss, quarter after quarter? It is possible to value this data with a clear idea of how data generates future profits. Using a theory is necessary here because a counterfactual is required to value this data. How much would this firm be worth, or how much revenue would it generate, if it did not have the data? We do not have data from the alternative world, where the firm does not have data. Models are necessary to answer those kinds of what if questions.

10.7.1   Application: Firms' Price Setting

In the price-setting model with menu costs and learning about fat-tailed risk by Baley and Blanco (2019) presented in section 4.4.1, one can compute the data value. Consider a constant returns-to-scale production technology and a constant elasticity of substitution (CES) demand with elasticity $\eta > 1$. Recall that $\hat{\theta}$ is a firm's average belief about its price gap (the difference between its current price and a frictionless optimal price) and $\hat{\Sigma}$ is the belief's conditional variance or uncertainty. Then, the expected perperiod gains from access to better data, expressed as a fraction of revenue, can be expressed as:

$$\text{Data value} = \frac{1-\eta}{2}\left[\underbrace{\mathbb{E}[\hat{\Sigma}]}_{\text{Better prediction}} + \underbrace{Var[\hat{\theta}]}_{\text{Eliminating menu costs}}\right]. \quad (10.9)$$

The first term, equal to the average level of uncertainty, reflects the potential gains from better data and prediction. The second term, equal to dispersion in price gaps, reflects the potential gains due to eliminating the menu costs and thus setting prices closer to the optimal one.

10.7.2   Application: Valuing Financial Data

At first glance, valuing data in a financial market with heterogeneous investors requires a seemingly impossible amount of knowledge. To structurally estimate a heterogeneous asset pricing model, one would need to know the characteristics and information sets of every financial market participant. This is not observable information. Farboodi et al. (2022b) develop sufficient statistics that depend on equilibrium returns. These sufficient statistics allow us to compute the value of data for an investor, knowing only that particular investor's characteristics, but without knowing the characteristics of all other investors.

Consider a dynamic, noisy rational expectations model (as in section 6.6), correlated assets, heterogeneous absolute risk aversions to capture different wealth levels, and heterogeneous investment sets. Let R be the set of returns that correspond to assets that the investor can hold according to their strategy or constraints. Three sufficient statistics summarize what an investor needs to know, in addition to his own characteristics, in order to value data. Those statistics are the expected return $\mathbb{E}[R_t]$, the unconditional variance of returns $\mathbb{V}ar[R_t]$, and the variance of returns conditional on the data to be valued, $\mathbb{V}ar[R_t|\mathcal{I}_{it}]$. If the investor already has predictive data, they need to know the conditional mean of returns with the existing data, the conditional variance with the existing data, and the conditional variance with the new data to be valued. For an investor with no price impact, the resulting value of financial data can be expressed as

$$\text{Value of data} = \frac{\rho}{2}\,\mathbb{E}[R_t]'\,(\mathbb{V}ar[R_t|\mathcal{I}_{it}]^{-1} - \mathbb{V}ar[R_t]^{-1})\mathbb{E}[R_t] \quad (10.10)$$

$$+ \frac{\rho}{2}\mathrm{Tr}\left[\mathbb{V}ar[R_t]\mathbb{V}ar[R_t|\mathcal{I}_{it}]^{-1} - I\right].$$

For the formula valuing data with price impact (as in section 7.10), see Farboodi et al. (2022b).

This valuation does not explicitly account for whether the valued data is public, private, or correlated with what others know. Yet, we know the value of information is quite different, depending on who else knows it. This effect seems to be missing. How can the value of financial data not depend on its publicity?

The publicity of data is in (10.10). If many investors know a piece of data, then conditioning on that data should not forecast returns. If everybody knows that Tesla will lose value and have much lower than expected earnings, that information should be fully impounded in today's price. Because Tesla's poor payoff tomorrow is also reflected in the price today, it should not affect Tesla stock's return, which is the ratio of payoff to price. Finance teaches that public information should not predict returns. If a piece of data cannot forecast the return, then including that data in the conditioning information set will not reduce the conditional variance of returns. In other words, adding a regressor with no forecasting power does not shrink forecast errors. If the forecast errors are not expected to fall, the conditional variance $\mathbb{V}ar[R_t|\mathcal{I}_{it}]$ will not be affected, and the piece of data will not improve the expected utility.

The main finding from this estimation exercise is that most of the variation in the value of data comes from investor characteristics, such as wealth, price impact, the existing information that they have, and their frequency of trade. This main point is a point about heterogeneous values at a given moment in time. One could also use this approach to measure changes in information values over time. However, like all sufficient statistic approaches, this one would lose validity over time, if the market structurally changes.

10.7.3   The Private Value Component of Data Assets

Typically, there is not one value for data. Instead, data has different values depending on the investor's characteristics. In other words, data is an asset with an important private value component. In a financial market, if an investor uses the data to manage a high-value portfolio, it has a different value than for an investor that manages a low-value portfolio. An investor who trades in large assets will have a different value for the data than an investor who trades primarily small-cap stocks. Farboodi et al. (2022b) show that, depending on an investor's size, price impact, trading strategy, trading frequency, and existing data, the value of the same data can differ by orders of magnitude.

Because private values for data differ, a revenue-based data value is not the transaction price of data; it is the personal value of data. In financial markets, that value depends on the investor's information, characteristics, and absolute risk aversion. The transaction price depends on the intersection point between the demand and supply curves. The value of data is one investor's point on the demand curve. One should not expect revenue-based data value estimates to coincide with the posted prices of data sets.

Heterogeneity in private valuations for data is important because this means that small changes in the price do not pick up many more customers on the margin—there is a lower price elasticity of demand for data. Much discussion is focused on inelastic demand in financial markets, but data markets are also very inelastic because valuations for data are so different. Furthermore, inelastic demand and price impact in the primary goods or asset market can affect the price elasticity in data markets and vice-versa. Understanding the private values and elasticity of demand for data is important for understanding the nature of competition and welfare.

10.7.4   Estimating Conditional Means and Variances in Practice

How can we put this estimate of the data value into practice? Means and variances are easy-to-measure sufficient statistics. Conditional variance is the key challenge. Conditional variance measures how variable a return is, conditional on what an investor knows. That is an expected squared forecast error. A linear normal Bayesian forecast is the same as an OLS forecast. They are both efficient linear estimators. Conditional variance is the same as an average squared residual from an OLS forecast. First, forecast returns without data and calculate the forecast errors. Second, forecast returns again using a historical sample of the data set of interest and calculate the forecast errors. Take the expected squared forecast errors from the two steps and use those in the formula for the data value in equation (10.10). This gives the value of the risk-adjusted return obtained from data when trading a portfolio.

This approach is valuable because it allows us to measure the value of data to a particular investor without knowing the characteristics or information of other investors in the market. The econometrician needs to know only about the investor for whom the data is being valued.

10.8   Complementary Inputs

Firms use other inputs in conjunction with data. Sometimes, these other inputs are visible, even if the data is not. We consider two such inputs: labor and information technology capital. In one case, the authors used a structural model to make inferences about data that would rationalize that much use of the complementary input. In the other case, the complementary input was a proxy for data.

10.8.1   Imputing Data from Job Postings

In this example, firms that use data need to hire data managers to prepare the data and analysts to work with the data and turn it into action recommendations that we call knowledge. If we can observe how many data managers and analysts a firm hires and how much they are paid, we can say that such a firm must have this much data for such an employment strategy to be rational.

Suppose new knowledge Ω_{it} is produced using structured and analyst data.

$$\Omega_{it} = A_t \theta_i D_{it}^{\alpha} L_{it}^{1-\alpha}. \tag{10.11}$$

This equation represents the process of taking structured data and using it to make action recommendations at the top of the Knowledge Production Triangle in Figure X. Knowledge is the structured data D_{it} and labor input L_{it} multiplied by a firm-specific component to productivity θ_i and an aggregate time-specific component A_t. The time-specific component could arise because new technologies are invented, or machine learning techniques improve over time.

A natural next step might be to model a production process that takes knowledge Ω as an input and produces a final good as an output. However, another approach is to normalize the units of knowledge so that one unit of knowledge is however much generates one additional dollar of revenue. This changes the interpretation of the productivity parameters A_t and θ_i. Those parameters absorb any change in the mapping from knowledge to revenue. At the same time, this approach relieves the researcher from having to model

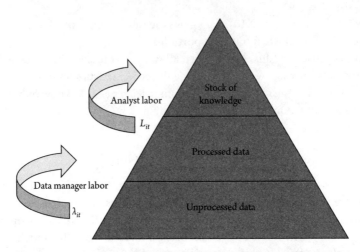

FIGURE X. Knowledge Production Triangle. *Notes*: The figure illustrates the process of combining unprocessed data with data manager labor λ_{it} to generate processed data D_{it}, and the process of combining processed data D_{it} with analyst labor L_{it} to increase the stock of knowledge Ω_{it}.

and estimate a goods or services production function and determine the price of the good or service.

Raw data turns out not to be very useful for analysis unless it is structured for a firm's specific purpose. Many workers are employed as data managers. We can represent the idea that data manager workers λ_{it} prepare new data to be added to the firm's structured data stock D_{it}, and that the data stock depreciates at rate ζ as

$$D_{i,t+1} = (1 - \zeta)D_{it} + \lambda_{it}^{1-\phi}, \tag{10.12}$$

where the exponent $\phi \leq 1$ governs the rate of diminishing marginal returns to data managers. The existing stock of structured data depreciates linearly at rate $\zeta < 1$ (recall section 10.1 for a technique to estimate this depreciation rate). New structured data is added to the existing stock of structured data with data management labor λ_{it}.

A firm's data stock can be estimated by measuring the hiring and wages of these data managers, who deal with raw data, and analysts, who deal with structured data. With a structural model, if we know how many data managers and analysts the firm hires and how much each group is paid, we can make inferences about the extent to which there are diminishing returns to data and how much a firm values its data. If a firm does not value its data very much, it would not hire many data managers or analysts or pay them very much. If the firm values that data a lot, then the firm would hire workers who work with this data in various ways. This structure allows one to impute the value of data for different types of firms and estimate how production functions for knowledge have changed and how different they are with and without machine learning.

Abis and Veldkamp (2024) use this approach, in combination with a dynamic valuation model, and find that the value of data for firms doing financial analysis has been rising enormously over time—it has grown by more than 25% in the 4-year period from 2015 to 2019. Using the model, they tease out three reasons for this growth in data value. First, firms are simply acquiring more data, increasing the value of the data stock. Second, firms are hiring more analysis workers to work with the data. Each worker raises the marginal productivity of data and raises its marginal value. In this sector, data accumulation is not labor-replacing. Third, the estimates reveal that firms are becoming more productive using data. This is particularly true for firms that hire workers with AI or machine learning skills. Each of these three forces accounts for roughly a third of the total increase in data value.

10.8.2   Computers as Data Complements

Another observable complementary input is information technology capital. Bresnahan, Brynjolfsson, and Hitt (2002) have measured firms' IT investments and used it as a proxy for data use. Arvai and Mann (2022) use the intensity of information and communication technology capital as a key input in a structural model to infer how much data firms have. They use the model to speak to the inequality generated by the digital economy.

If we can write down structural models, we can use any complementary input that might be used with the data. For example, if data analysts consume jelly beans, then jelly bean purchases are a complementary input and can inform us about the amount of data analysis and the amount of data at work.

10.8.3   Patents as Data Complements

Gomes, Mihet, and Rishabh (2023) propose a methodology to measure data intensity using patents. Data-intensive firms are identified as those actively engaged in AI innovation, which involves filing AI patents. AI patents are identified using a combination of the US Patent and Trademark Office data set on AI patents (Giczy, Pairolero, and Toole, 2021) and the KPSS patent data set linked to firms (Kogan et al., 2017). Additionally, there are firms that are "close" to patenting firms and mirror their AI innovations. They measure "closeness" in the sense of Hoberg-Phillips, which uses business descriptions in Form 10-K fillings.[4] This measure is separate from IT expenditures. An advantage of this measure is that it can be constructed from publicly available data.

10.9   Measuring Information in Asset Prices

One of the most popular measures of information contained in the prices of financial assets is the price informativeness measure of Bai, Philippon, and Savov (2016). The measure is based on the covariance between firm j's equity price P_{j1} and the earnings of that firm at some future date s, d_{js}. Typically, researchers normalize this covariance by the standard deviation of the equity price to account for the fact that more volatile price series are likely to have higher covariances mechanically. Thus, the s-period ahead price informativeness of an asset j, PINF_{js}, can be expressed as $\mathbb{C}ov(d_{js}; P_{j1}|d_{j0})/StdDev(P_{j1}|d_{j0})$.

Farboodi et al. (2022a) use a dynamic, noisy rational expectations model (as in section 6.6) to reinterpret the price informativeness measure. They show that the model object that corresponds to price informativeness does capture the ability of price to predict future earnings. But to isolate an amount of data implied by this predictive ability, a researcher needs to remove a volatility effect and a growth effect:

$$\text{PINF}_{js} \equiv \underbrace{\frac{\mathbb{C}ov(d_{js}; P_{j1}|d_{j0})}{StdDev(P_{j1}|d_{j0})}}_{} = \underbrace{\frac{\mathbb{V}ar(d_{j1}|d_{j0})}{StdDev(P_{j1}|d_{j0})}}_{\text{volatility}} \underbrace{\frac{g_j}{r-g_j}}_{\text{growth}} \underbrace{\left[1 - \frac{\overline{\Sigma}_j}{\mathbb{V}ar(d_{j1}|d_{j0})}\right]}_{\text{data}},$$

$$(10.13)$$

where r is a riskless rate of return, g_j is the rate of growth of asset j's future cash flows, and $\overline{\Sigma}_j$ is market-wide uncertainty about firm j's next-period cash flow. Technically, $\overline{\Sigma}_j$ is the harmonic mean of the posterior variances of all investors' forecasts of cash flows. If investors are heterogeneous, their posterior precisions should be weighted by their risk tolerance: $\overline{\Sigma}_j = \int (1/\rho_i) \mathbb{V}ar[d_s|\mathcal{I}_{jt}]^{-1}\, di$, where ρ_i is the local absolute risk aversion of investor i. The term that captures investors' data is $\overline{\Sigma}_j$.

By measuring price informativeness, as in Bai, Philippon, and Savov (2016), but then dividing by the two terms labeled "volatility" and "growth," a researcher can recover the amount of data the average investor in asset j

---

4. Hoberg-Phillips text-based industry classifications is available at https://hobergphillips. tuck.dartmouth.edu/.

uses to guide their investment decision. Similarly, Borovička, Hansen, and Scheinkman (2016) propose a methodology to learn about investors' beliefs using Arrow-Debreu securities.

This measure of data captures something quite different from the measures outlined above. This is an aggregate measure of data. It does not measure or value data for one investor. Instead, this measure reveals the aggregate amount of data used by all investors actively trading in the market for firm j's equity. This is not a better or worse measure than the others. It simply answers a different set of questions.

10.9.1   Application: Intangibles Approach

While the previous measure uses asset prices to infer how much data investors have, another use of asset prices is to infer the value of a firm's data. Data is an example of an intangible asset, like patents, goodwill, or customer capital. Some of these items may be conflated with data. A typical approach to valuing intangible assets is to use the ratio of the market value and book value of a firm. Using this approach with data, we might say that the ratio of the market value and book value of the firm reflects the data value:

$$\text{Value of data} = \frac{\text{Market value}}{\text{Book value}}. \tag{10.14}$$

The problem with this approach is that the market-to-book ratio has been used as a proxy for the value of many different intangible assets; this same quantity has been called the value of the firm's branding, patents, or organizational capital. Data may contribute to each of these intangibles, but it is not equivalent to any of them. How can the value of data be separated from the value of other intangible assets and market value?

Data almost never appears separately on a firm's balance sheet, unless the data has been purchased from another entity. If a firm acquires a target firm, the acquirer may attribute some of the value of the target firm to the target's data. In this case, data may show up on the firm's balance sheet as an asset. If the data is generated internally, it will not appear on the firm's balance sheet. The IT equipment used with data may be reported as an asset. But that is not the same as the data itself.

Finally, this approach assumes that equity market participants know exactly how to value data. If data valuation methods are not fully developed, it is unlikely that equity market participants got this value just right and reflected that knowledge in the firm's equity price. Investors might need data valuation guidance as well.

10.9.2   Application: Measuring Capital Misallocation

David, Hopenhayn, and Venkateswaran (2016) measure price information and quantify its effect on resource misallocation, aggregate productivity, and output. They devise a novel empirical strategy that uses a combination of firm-level production and stock market data to estimate firms' data precision. Applying this methodology in the United States, China, and India reveals 7%–10% losses in the United States and 10%–14% output in China and India from imperfect information. Across countries, they find stock prices contribute little to firms' data precision.

10.10   Measuring Public Data: Flows of News

One way to measure information flows is to look at the quantity of information being provided. For example, Graham (1999) counts the amount of coverage assets get in investment newsletters. Fang and Peress (2009) and Veldkamp (2006b) count the number of stories about firms or emerging markets in the popular press. A large empirical finance literature uses analyst coverage of firms to be a proxy for the information investors have. Overall, such information proxies have significant explanatory power for asset prices.

One issue to be aware of with these measures is that information supply is endogenous. It reacts to movements in asset prices and creates movements in asset prices. Veldkamp (2006b) measures the joint relationship between *Financial Times* news stories per week and emerging market prices and returns. Using a different information proxy, Hameed, Morck, and Yeung (2010) show that firm size, trade volume, and earnings predict how many analysts will cover a stock. Brennan and Hughes (1991) model a brokerage commission rate that depends on share price such that there is an incentive for brokers to produce research reports on firms with low share prices. The authors use stock splits, where prices fall dramatically without any bad news, to test the theory. These effects operate not only on individual stocks but also on mutual funds. Kaniel, Starks, and Vasudevan (2007) establish that fund characteristics predict media coverage, predicting capital flows into the fund.

10.11   Age, Hazard Rates, and Tenure to Infer Data Quality

In some settings where data accumulates over time, time-dependent measures are proxies for the amount of data a firm has. While these are not direct measures of data, they have the advantage that they might be easier to observe than some of the more nuanced measures of data.

Price Age   In the price-setting models with learning of section 4.4.1, the age of a price (the time since the price was last changed) is a sufficient statistic for firm uncertainty: young (recently set) prices correspond to firms with uncertain estimates and will likely change soon, whereas older prices (set long ago) correspond to firms with precise estimates and are unlikely to be changed. Data accumulation generates a decreasing hazard rate (probability) of price adjustment. Empirical evidence supports the predictions of the price-setting model with uncertainty cycles and the relationship between idiosyncratic uncertainty and adjustment frequency. Bachmann et al. (2019) document a positive correlation between firm-level uncertainty and price adjustment for German firms. In the United States, Campbell and Eden (2014) document that price changes in the retail sector are more extreme and dispersed for recently changed prices compared to older prices.

Hazard Rates   Not only is the age of a price indicative of uncertainty, but also the rate at which price changes become less frequent can indicate data quality. This is what is known as a decreasing hazard rate.[5] Decreasing hazard rates are a tell-tale sign of signal extraction with adjustment costs in actions. Using the model in section 4.4, the hazard's slope maps to data quality—the signal noise γ—and the implied learning speed. The basic idea is as follows. With high-quality data, the hazard rate declines steeply because learning is fast. Adjustments are unlikely after a few periods of inaction. In contrast, with low-quality data, the hazard rate declines slowly as slow learning keeps the likelihood of making price adjustments high. Data quality is what modulates the hazard rate's slope. Alvarez, Lippi, and Paciello (2011), Baley and Blanco (2019), and Argente and Yeh (2022) apply this idea to calibrate data quality in price-setting models.

Work on labor markets has taken a similar approach. In this case, the relevant hazards measure the likelihood a worker separates from a specific firm, occupation, or industry. Borovičková (2016) uses job separation hazards to infer firms' learning speed. Baley, Figueiredo, and Ulbricht (2022) show that the probability of a worker switching her occupation decreases as the number of jobs held within the same occupation increases and use this occupation-separation hazard to infer how workers use data to learn about their abilities. Hazard rates are also used in Baley and Turén (2023) to assess professional forecasters' learning in a forecasting model with strategic concerns and fixed forecast revision costs.

---

5. Decreasing hazard rates of price adjustment are documented for various data sets, countries, and time periods. See Dhyne et al. (2006), Nakamura and Steinsson (2008), and Alvarez, Borovičková, and Shimer (2021).

Tenure Several papers exploit data on the duration of relationships or *tenure* as a proxy for the amount of data accumulated. Farber and Gibbons (1996) show that the wages of long-tenured workers correlate more with unobserved skills (measured via test scores); Kellogg (2011) shows that the productivity of an oil company and its drilling contractor increases with their joint experience; Botsch and Vanasco (2019) show that loan terms become more correlated with unobserved firm characteristics as the duration of the lender-creditor relationship increases.

Key Ideas

- There are many possible approaches to infer the value of data. None is perfect.
- A hallmark of data is that it enables agents' choices to covary systematically with stochastic payoffs.
- Data can be an input, along with labor, in the creation of knowledge, which is an action recommendation.

Practice Questions

10.1. How does the data depreciation rate depend on the state innovations' variance, σ_ϵ^2? Interpret this relationship.

10.2. How does the data depreciation rate depend on the data stock, Ω_t? Interpret this relationship.

10.3. How does the data depreciation rate depend on the state's persistence, ρ? Interpret this relationship.

10.4. If analyst labor L_{it} in (10.11) exogenously becomes more abundant, should this make data more or less valuable? Why?

10.5. If data-manager labor λ_{it} in (10.12) exogenously becomes more abundant, should this make raw data more or less valuable? Should this make processed or structured data more valuable? Explain your answers.

10.6. If an economist observes a firm choosing to hire more data management labor, should they infer that the firm's raw data is more or less valuable? Why?

10.7. End-of-period consumption for investor i at the end of period t can be represented as

$$c_{i,t+1} = r\bar{w}_{it} + q_{it}'\Pi_{it}$$

where r is the risk-free rate, $\bar{w}_{it}$ is the initial endowment, q_{it} is the portfolio choice of investor, and Π_{it} is profit of securities. Each investor seeks to maximize the following expected utility function

$$\mathbb{E}[U(c_{i,t+1})|\mathcal{I}_{it}] = \rho_i \mathbb{E}[r\bar{w}_{it} + q'_{it}\Pi_{it}|\mathcal{I}_{it}] - \frac{\rho_i^2}{2}\mathbb{V}ar[r\bar{w}_{it}$$

$$+ q'_{it}\Pi_{it}|\mathcal{I}_{it}], \tag{10.15}$$

where ρ_i is the absolute risk aversion of investor i. We further assume that it is a competitive market (there exists an infinite number of investors), and posterior variance of profit is a known quantity. In this setup, derive the ex ante expected utility $\mathbb{E}[U(c_{i,t+1})]$ using the revenue approach.

10.8. Derive the ex ante expected utility in the previous question when an investor has price impact dp/dq_i. (*Hint: See Chapter 7.*)

11

Data Policy and Welfare

Some of the most important policy debates today surround the use and regulation of data and data-intensive firms. The question of what regulations should be adopted is a question of welfare. Therefore, we end by considering the welfare consequences of data, through the lens of the models we have considered thus far. This chapter is not a comprehensive review of all data policy considerations. Rather, it is an exploration of a set of welfare consequences of data that make contact with the issues and frameworks of the book. Because of imperfect competition, nonrivalry, and the ability to make inferences about others, even our simple data economy models may exhibit many forms of inefficient behavior. These inefficiencies teach us about potential harms and the scope for corrective policy actions.

11.1 Privacy

When discussing data and welfare, perhaps the first concern that comes to mind is privacy. The focus of this book is on firms and macroeconomics. Privacy concerns households and requires different tools to analyze comprehensively. We will not attempt to cover the vast literature on data privacy comprehensively. See Goldfarb and Que (2023) for a review of the literature on digital privacy. Instead, we describe a handful of papers that connect with the literature we have discussed and also model privacy concerns.

11.1.1 Data and Manipulation

Much of the concern about the lack of digital privacy is the potential for manipulation. Liu, Sockin, and Xiong (2021) model weak-willed consumers who can be manipulated by advertising, in a way that reduces their welfare. The role of data in this setting is to identify consumers susceptible to such manipulation. Specifically, a platform learns whether each consumer is interested in a particular good and whether they have behavioral susceptibilities that sellers could exploit. In this setting, a data externality arises: when mildly weak-willed consumers share their data, it makes it easier for sellers to target the most weak-willed consumers. The combination of the behavioral problems of susceptible consumers and the information externality makes privacy regulations like the European Union's General Data Protection Regulation (GDPR) and the California Consumer Privacy Act (CCPA) optimal. The data externality in Liu, Sockin, and Xiong (2021) shares some similarities with the preference information externalities in Acemoglu et al. (2022) and Bergemann, Bonatti, and Gan (2022). However, in this context where consumers can be manipulated, the externality is more serious and likely to be welfare-reducing.

For more on the psychology and microeconomics of data, manipulation and the related problem of digital addiction, see Matz et al. (2017) and Fletcher et al. (2023).

11.1.2 Statistical Inference Externalities

By providing their data to a platform, users reveal information about others with similar characteristics. For example, if one buyer is similar to her neighbors, then her transaction reveals information. If privacy is one's ability to keep their information private, the user's transaction and the resulting information leakage compromise the neighbor's privacy.

Acemoglu et al. (2022) develop a model of data markets that captures this privacy externality. A platform wants to estimate the type of each user and offers to pay each user for their personal data. Personal data reveals information about a person's type. Each user's personal data is correlated with other users' data. The authors find that (i) too much data is shared relative to the socially efficient outcome; (ii) prices of data will not reflect users' valuation of privacy; and (iii) competition between platforms does not solve this problem. The results also highlight the advantages of data, such as improved resource allocation and innovation.

These findings inform privacy measurement. One interpretation is that data markets could produce an excessive amount of data when privacy concerns are present. The fact that users are willing to share their personal data for minimal benefit might be interpreted as evidence that users place little value on their privacy. A second viewpoint challenges this interpretation and shows that prices may understate users' valuation of privacy because users have fewer incentives to protect their data when it is exposed by others. The model below is a simplified version of Acemoglu et al. (2022).

Setup There is a single platform with n users. Each user i has a type x_i, and data $s_i = x_i + z_i$ that is informative about their type. We assume $(x_1, \ldots, x_n)$

has a joint normal distribution of $\mathcal{N}(0, \Sigma)$, and each $z_i \sim \mathcal{N}(0, 1)$. Let σ_i^2 be the variance of user i's type. An essential element of this model is the correlation structure of users' types (through Σ), which provides a foundation for the data-sharing externality. Each user chooses an action a_i, which is whether to share their data ($a_i = 1$) or not ($a_i = 0$). The vector of actions for all users is denoted $a = (a_1, \ldots, a_n)$. Let S_a be the vector of data for all individuals who choose to share their data.

Leaked information for user i given an action profile a is defined as follows:

$$\mathcal{I}_i(a) = \sigma_i^2 - \min_{\hat{x}_i} \mathbb{E}\left[(x_i - \hat{x}_i(S_a))^2\right], \qquad (11.1)$$

where $\hat{x}_i(S_a)$ can be interpreted as the best predictor of i's type x_i, given data S_a. This expression captures how much the shared data decreases the platform's mean squared error of their forecast of the user's type. The first term reflects the mean squared error if no data were shared.

Platforms need to induce users to use them and reveal their data. They do that by paying p_i to agent i, if they use the platform. In reality, this could take the form of a discount on the platform services, such as free shipping. If the transfer p_i took the form of a discount rather than a monetary payment, then this would be a partial data barter, as in section 9.5.

The platform chooses the vector of prices p, with ith entry p_i, to maximize the total amount of information leaked about each user, minus the cost paid for their data:

$$U(a, p) = \sum_i \mathcal{I}_i(a) - \sum_{a_i=1} p_i. \qquad (11.2)$$

User i chooses a_i, to share data with the platform or not, to maximize the price paid to them, minus their privacy cost. The privacy cost depends on a parameter v_i, which governs how much they value their privacy, times the amount of information leakage. If a platform user shares their data, then the total amount of information leaked about them is $\mathcal{I}_i(a_i = 1, a_{-i})$ and their privacy cost is $v_i \mathcal{I}_i(a_i = 1, a_{-i})$. However, they get paid p_i for their data. If a user does not share data, they do not get paid, and $\mathcal{I}_i(a_i = 0, a_{-i})$ units of information is still leaked about them by other platform users. Thus, the payoff of user i is

$$u_i(a_i, a_{-i}, p_i) = \begin{cases} p_i - v_i \mathcal{I}_i(a_i = 1, a_{-i}) & \text{if } a_i = 1 \\ - v_i \mathcal{I}_i(a_i = 0, a_{-i}) & \text{if } a_i = 0. \end{cases} \qquad (11.3)$$

Each user chooses $a_i = \{0, 1\}$, whether or not to share their data, given prices. An equilibrium always exists but may not be unique.

The main result is that the equilibrium is inefficient. Define "high-value users" as those with a high value of privacy, $v_i > 1$. Define "low-value users" as those with $v_i \leq 1$. If high-value users' privacy preferences were not correlated with others' preferences, then the equilibrium would be efficient. In this case, those who reveal their information do not inform the platform about others' characteristics. However, when one's actions reveal information about others, the welfare cost to others is not fully internalized by buyers. The presence of such externalities typically make the equilibrium inefficient.

The equilibrium price for user i's data is the amount by which user i's data increases the platform's information, adjusted by the user's value of privacy. Equilibrium prices are weakly decreasing in the correlation between any two users' data and decreasing in the number of users that share their data. These results capture the idea that prices understate users' demand for privacy when others leak their information.

Multiplatform Results   One might think that, if only there were competition between multiple platforms, users would be better compensated for their data, and efficiency would be restored. This is not the case. A new problem arises. To prevent data revelation to any one platform, users spread their transactions across many platforms. This compromises the efficiency benefits from network effects arising from having all users on one platform.

11.1.3 Cyber Risk

Jamilov, Rey, and Tahoun (2021) use computational linguistics to introduce a novel measure of firm-level cyber-risk exposure based on quarterly earnings conference calls of listed firms. Cyber-risk exposure predicts cyberattacks, affects stock returns and profits, and is priced in the equity options market. Cyber risks spill over across firms and pass through from firm to the sectoral level. The authors' back-of-the-envelope calculations suggest that the global cost of cyber risk is over $200 billion annually.

Gomes, Mihet, and Rishabh (2023) highlight the dual role of data as a business optimization tool and a cybercrime target. Cybercrime risk leads to reduced knowledge stocks, decreased productivity, and slower growth for all firms. Cybercrime risk mitigates some of the adverse effects as it ex ante prompts data-savvy firms to pursue digital innovation that enhances productivity in other domains. Using data on firms' investments in cyber-protection, the authors find increased innovation rates in response to higher cybercrime risk, driven primarily by data-savvy firms and firms that intensively pursue in-house cybersecurity protection rather than third-party cybersecurity delegation.

11.1.4 Privacy Externalities That Affect Production

Jones and Tonetti (2020) focus on property rights and how using nonrival data can affect firms' production efficiency. Recall from section 9.2.2 that firms can obtain data from their own production ($y_{i,t}$) and from other firms' production $y_{j,t}$. Other firms' data is not as relevant and might not be shared. Both are captured by the nonrivalry parameter $(1 - \iota)$:

$$\Omega_{i,t} = (1 - \zeta)\Omega_{i,t-1} + y_{i,t} + \int_{i \neq j} (1 - \iota)y_{j,t}\, dj. \qquad (11.4)$$

The nonrivalry rate $(1 - \iota)$ depends on the data privacy environment. If firms are not allowed to or choose not to sell data or share data with other firms, then $(1 - \iota) = 0$. Higher $(1 - \iota)$ benefits firms' productivity. At the same time, more data sharing increases the probability of a firm being displaced by new entrants. In an equilibrium where firms own the data, they hoard their data because they fear entrant competition. Hoarding is an inefficient use of data, which lowers aggregate productivity. In contrast, if consumers have data property rights, they balance their concerns for privacy against the economic gains of data sharing. They choose more data sharing than firms would, fostering competition and increasing welfare.

If firms or platforms have market power and users value privacy, additional externalities arise. Digital consumers do not internalize how revealing their data impacts others. Cong and Mayer (2022) identify three externalities: (i) sharing data allows firms to improve service quality for all users; (ii) data enables market concentration (as in Chapter 7); and (iii) the amount of data shared affects platforms' incentives to invest in data infrastructure. These externalities can cause inefficient over- or under-collection of data. Cong and Mayer (2022) also evaluate privacy policies and data-sharing initiatives. Most policies cannot simultaneously address the market concentration and misaligned incentive inefficiencies. However, a user union for platform customers jointly remedies these problems.

Quan (2023) considers privacy policies that allow users to opt out of sharing their data in a transaction. Using a calibrated structural model, the author measures the value of privacy and the effect of withholding data on service quality. These values are calibrated to match the change in consumers' app ratings and firms' investment decisions following the implementation of the European Union's GDPR. The author finds that privacy regulations lead to the under-provision of data and a substantial decline in service quality. While privacy-conscious consumers gain from regulation, the average consumer is made worse off.

11.2   Data Barter

Rules about whether consumers can, must, or choose to share data can affect the prices of traded goods and services. There are two broad categories of price effects. One category is the effect on the average price or a single, uniform price that is charged to all customers. We call this the data barter effect. The other category is about how data enables firms to charge personalized prices. Personalized pricing is also called price discrimination. We briefly discuss each type of effect in this section and the next.

If customers choose not to share their data when purchasing a product, it changes the value of the transaction for the seller. This affects product prices. Not sharing data may mean that the customer does not allow the seller to resell their data to a third party. Alternatively, it could mean that the seller cannot use any information about the transaction for any purpose after the transaction is complete. In either case, the data has less value to the seller than it would if its use were unrestricted. Section 9.5 shows how this valuable data substitutes for monetary payment in a data economy. That implies that if the data is not transferred, the price the seller requires to engage in the transaction is higher. Thus, the concept of data barter implies that privacy regulations will increase the prices of all kinds of goods and services, not just digital ones.

Walker (2001) argues that protecting buyers' privacy will increase the price of goods and reduce the volume of goods and services sold. This is consistent with data barter. They conclude that the welfare of consumers who value privacy highly may increase. But this increase comes at the expense of consumers who are more indifferent to privacy. Those consumers lose utility because they have to pay higher prices. The friction at work is that firms are restricted to charging one price to all customers. Since sharing data is like paying a higher price, restricting data sharing, or even just giving consumers the right to not share, raises the single price paid by all. If firms could set a price for a transaction with privacy and another price for a transaction without privacy, this negative externality on nonprivacy-conscious consumers would be resolved.

11.3   Price-Discrimination and Product Personalization

Most digital businesses charge a uniform price to all customers. However, one concern about big data is that it allows firms to charge different prices to different consumers. Kehoe, Larsen, and Pastorino (2022) explore what the welfare consequences would be if firms did personalize prices. Specifically, they model firms that can track the history of a consumer's purchases and product experiences and set a price that depends on this information. Firms compete in prices and product varieties in a dynamic game with Bertrand competition. They assume that consumers' purchase histories and experiences are public information. When setting a price, firms consider demand and strategically manage the information flow to consumers. Surprisingly, introducing price discrimination benefits most consumers. Consumers with similar preferences for different brands benefit the most because price competition intensifies. With intense firm competition, the market is efficient, even though prices are discriminatory.

Bergemann, Bonatti, and Gan (2022) study an economy where a monopolistic intermediary acquires data about customers with correlated preferences and sells that data to firms. The firms use the data to personalize the prices of their products. Consumers benefit from data sharing only if they learn about their own preferences from others' data. Otherwise, consumers lose out. In contrast, producers always benefit. For social welfare, such data sales are inefficient unless they help customers determine their product preferences.

An active literature in microeconomic theory explores topics such as the strategic aspects of consumer data disclosure (Ichihashi, 2020), the value of data to a platform, information design, and the efficiency of data markets (Galperti and Perego, 2023), all in a context where firms use data for price discrimination. This work involves different theoretical tools and is beyond the scope of this book. See Bergemann and Bonatti (2019) for a review of this literature.

11.4   Firm Data Externalities

Firms' use of data also creates external effects that could warrant policy action. We consider two such effects.

11.4.1   Business Stealing

When data can be used for marketing or other forms of capturing or "stealing" business from one's rivals, firms' use of data harms other firms' profits. With such an externality, firms' choices will be socially inefficient. We will leave it to a growing microeconomics literature to discuss the mechanisms by which one firm can use data to cannibalize others' business. Here, we show how to incorporate a stylized representation of this type of activity in our macroeconomic framework.

In the data feedback model from Chapter 9, where we use data as a tool for prediction, business stealing can be represented by augmenting equation (9.4). Originally, the equation expressed the quality of a good as a decreasing function of the forecast errors that a firm makes. This represented the idea that firms use data to adopt more efficient or effective business practices. For example, if the firm forecasts consumer tastes incorrectly, their goods would be ill-suited to the market and would be less valuable. To capture the idea of business stealing, we add a quality externality. The externality, the third term in (11.5), makes a firm worse off if its competitors make better predictions. This captures the idea that a firm is better off when its competitors make mistakes:

$$A_{i,t} = \bar{A} - \left[\left(a_{i,t} - \theta_t - \epsilon_{a,i,t} \right)^2 - b \int_{j=0}^{1} \left(a_{j,t} - \theta_t - \epsilon_{a,j,t} \right)^2 dj \right]$$

$$\text{for } b \in [0, 1]. \tag{11.5}$$

In this representation, mistakes are choices of $a_{j,t}$ that are far away from $\theta_t - \epsilon_{a,j,t}$. Moving b between 0 and 1 regulates how much data enhances welfare. The model without any externality is represented by $b = 0$. In this case, equations (11.5) and (9.4) are identical. If $b > 0$, a firm's quality depends on the difference between the precision of its prediction and the average precision of the predictions of all other firms. One interpretation is that firms are competing for customers and gain a larger market share when others target their advertisements poorly. When $b = 1$, data has no social value. The aggregate losses from business stealing entirely offset the productivity gains from data: $\int A_{i,t} \, di = \bar{A}$.

The business stealing externality does not change firms' choices because the last term does not enter a firm's first-order condition.[1] However, it does influence welfare through the aggregate quality of goods.

11.4.2 Advertising and Welfare

Advertising is not simply a way for one business to steal customers from another. Advertising also provides product information to customers and, if done well, might even entertain them.

Greenwood, Ma, and Yorukoglu (2021) embed this more positive notion of advertising in a general equilibrium model to explore its welfare consequences. They develop a modernized version of Butters's (1978) information-based advertising model in which traditional and digital advertising entertain and inform people. This affects the equilibrium price distribution for the goods being advertised.

---

1. To see why, note that firm i has zero mass in the integral $\int_{j=0}^{1} \left(a_{j,t} - \theta_t - \epsilon_{a,j,t} \right)^2 dj$. So i's actions have a negligible effect on that term. So the derivative of the integral term, with respect to i's choice variables, is zero. If the term has zero effect on the first-order condition, it does not affect the firm's choices. This externality formulation is inspired by Morris and Shin (2002).

Their equilibrium is inefficient because free media goods are undersupplied, and some advertising is sent to consumers who cannot afford to buy the goods at the posted price. Furthermore, when they calibrate the model to the US macro data, they find that advertising significantly increases welfare.

11.5 Labor Market Effects

Artificial intelligence is like the Industrial Revolution, but for knowledge production instead of industrial goods production. Before AI, knowledge workers used enormous amounts of labor and modest data sets to analyze the relevant information and recommend profitable actions. AI uses data much more intensively and requires less labor on the part of a user to analyze that data.

While data holds much promise to improve efficiency, labor still appears essential. Although several studies claim that data impacted economic activity, others find that data alone did not add any value to companies. According to Lambrecht and Tucker (2015), big data is not inimitable or rare, as substitutes exist. Instead of just amassing big data to gain a competitive advantage, firms must focus on building both the tools and organizational expertise to enable them to use big data to provide value to customers in new ways.

11.5.1 Changes in Labor Share

One way to think about labor replacement is that new data technologies have increased the data intensity of production. Suppose the production function is

$$Y = AD^{\alpha}L^{1-\alpha}, \tag{11.6}$$

where A is productivity, D is data, L is labor, and Y is output. Then, this shift to data as a more important factor is represented as an increase in the exponent α. This is similar to how economic historians think about the Industrial Revolution. The Industrial Revolution was an increase in the capital intensity of production. Using an analogous production function with capital instead of data, $Y = AK^{\alpha}L^{1-\alpha}$, historians estimate that α rose between 5%–12%. This did not undermine the demand for labor. Instead, large numbers of workers were employed in the new factories, producing more goods than ever before.

Using modern data from job posting websites, one can estimate a separate production function for firms that hire workers with AI skills and those that do not to determine how much the labor share changes. Estimating the model from section 10.8 to impute data and control for firm and time fixed effects, Abis and Veldkamp (2024) find that the data share in knowledge production is 5% higher for financial firms that use AI compared to firms that don't. In other words, AI appears to make labor a less important input into production in the firms that adopt it. However, labor demand does not fall in these firms. Instead, AI-adopting firms hire more workers and produce more knowledge and more profit than their non-AI counterparts.

This change in production technology has clear consequences for the distribution of wealth. In recent years, most of the gains in US income have gone to a small group of people. Although technology is not the sole factor, Mitchell and Brynjolfsson (2017) argue that it is the main force. Benzell and Brynjolfsson (2019) developed a model to explain why regular labor and capital haven't reaped the benefits of digitalization while a few superstars have made enormous riches.

11.5.2 Labor Displacement

New data technologies hold the promise of better prediction and enhanced efficiency. However, one of the concerns of economists and policymakers is that technologies like AI will displace human labor.

Korinek and Stiglitz (2021) build a model where AI allows capital to replace labor. They explore the distributive and welfare consequences of such a change. Similarly, Frank et al. (2019) predict the demise of labor. However, the evidence on whether AI really does replace labor is mixed.[2]

Frank et al. (2019) argue that AI and automation could completely replace labor and will alter all jobs to some extent. They suggest that the lack of data on workplace duties and abilities limits feasible solutions to the problem of technological transformation and the future of work.

However, there are other studies suggesting an ambiguous effect of digital technology on labor replacement. For example, workers whose core skill is not making a prediction, such as brain surgeons, may discover that automated prediction increases the value of their profession. The relative importance of AI's pressures on individual employees will be determined by the degree to which their core skill is based on prediction. The majority of AI applications have multiple forces that affect jobs, both increasing and decreasing labor demand. Therefore, the net effect is an empirical question that will vary depending on the application and industry (Agrawal, Gans, and Goldfarb, 2019).

2. Babina et al. (2024) examine how firms use AI in production and find that it primarily supports product innovation. Acemoglu et al. (2020) identify industries, firms, or regions that are more exposed to machine learning technology and explore their labor growth relative to similar, unexposed regions or industries. They find that AI exposure predicts a shift in hiring from non-AI positions. However, the net effect on hiring is not distinguishable from zero.

11.5.3 Insuring against the Risk of Skill Obsolescence

Baley et al. (2024) study the labor market and welfare effects stemming from the risk of skill obsolescence—also known as "turbulence" risk—due to the emergence of new technologies.[3] For instance, Chat GPT and other natural language processing tools will likely pose risks for translators, copywriters, and professors, just as robotization and automation posed risks to manufacturing workers in the 1980s and 1990s. In a world with imperfect insurance markets and labor market frictions, how do workers insure against (and cope with) the risk of skill obsolescence?

In their model, employed workers self-insure against the risk of losing their skills by accumulating wealth—a standard precautionary savings motive—and unemployed workers may choose to direct their search to jobs that pay little but are easier to get—a novel precautionary search motive (Eeckhout and Sepahsalari, 2023). Workers in high-paying occupations who suffer involuntary job loss and skill obsolescence may be able to recover their predisplacement earnings if they have sufficiently high wealth when displaced, as wealth allows them to wait for good job offers or pay for retraining. An identical worker, except for having low wealth at displacement, may end up in a low-paying occupation and suffer a long-term scar on their earnings. Thus, the individual and aggregate consequences of increased turbulence risk depend on the risk incidence across the wealth distribution.

11.6 Public Data and Welfare

Goldstein, Yang, and Zuo (2020) show how improved digital dissemination of financial data can boost firm growth. Following the implementation of the EDGAR (Electronic Data Gathering, Analysis, and Retrieval) system in the US Securities and Exchange Commission from 1993 to 1996, there was a rise in equity prices, which made it cheaper for firms to raise equity capital. The authors measure a 10% average increase in the level of corporate investment following EDGAR. At the same time, EDGAR disclosures appear to crowd out investors' private information acquisition and reduce managerial learning from stock prices. This crowd-out effect was especially strong for high-growth firms.

This section examines the choice of how much data to disclose to others. Typically, the agent deciding whether or not to disclose is a central bank or

---

3. For other work studying turbulence risk, see Ljungqvist and Sargent (1998, 2007); and Baley, Ljungqvist, and Sargent (2023, 2024).

a government statistical agency seeking to maximize social welfare. The government agency is choosing whether or not to reveal a piece of data (or how much data to reveal) to the public.

We usually think of more information as welfare-improving because it facilitates efficient market outcomes. However, recent literature has questioned this wisdom. This section examines reasons why revealing information might be socially costly. The data to be revealed would be a public signal. The publicity is important because public signals convey information, not just about an unknown state but also about what other agents know. Thus, providing public data can facilitate coordination. In fact, it might enable too much coordination, relative to a social optimum, in settings with coordination externalities. Another drawback is that public information releases can deter agents from acquiring or transmitting private information. A third issue is that more information can cause beliefs and, therefore, market prices to be more volatile.

11.6.1 Coordination and Overreaction to Public Data

Recall the exogenous-information "mean-field game" from section 5.2. The optimal action was

$$a_i = \mu_\theta + \frac{\alpha_s(1-r)}{1-\alpha_s r}(s_i - \mu_\theta) + \frac{\alpha_z}{1-\alpha_s r}(z - \mu_\theta). \qquad (11.7)$$

Notice how an increase in the value of the private data s_i affects the optimal action differently from an increase in the value of the public data z. In particular, if $r > 0$, and the relative precisions of private data and public data are equal $(\alpha_s = \alpha_z)$, then an increase in the public data affects the action more. The effect of an increase in private data is scaled down by $(1 - r)$. The greater the complementarity, the less agents care about private relative to public data. Also, because $\alpha_z/(1 - \alpha_s r)$ rises in r, stronger complementarity makes agents' actions more sensitive to public information.

Public data carries two types of information: it tells the agents something about the state θ, and it tells them something about what others' beliefs are, which affects the average action a. In contrast, private data tells the agent something about the state but nothing about what others know. So when agents want to coordinate their actions with others' actions $(r > 0)$, public data is more useful for that purpose, so they weigh it more. If agents want to take actions different from what others do $(r < 0)$, giving more weight to private data achieves that goal.

11.6.2   Social Cost of Public Data

The overreaction to public data, relative to private data, can make additional public information welfare-reducing (Morris and Shin, 2002). To make this point, we need to change the utility function in (5.6) by adding a new term:[4]

$$\mathcal{L}_i = \mathbb{E}\left[(1-r)(a_i - \theta)^2 + r(a_i - a)^2 - \underbrace{r \int_0^1 (a_j - a)^2 \, dj}_{\text{externality}} \Big| \mathcal{I}_i\right]. \quad (11.8)$$

The last term, the newly added one, depends only on the actions that other players take. Since each agent has zero mass, he does not affect the value of this integral. Thus, the last term is irrelevant to the agents' decision problem. The optimal action a_i is the same as in section 5.2. The role of this last term is to introduce a payoff externality that affects social welfare.

Social welfare is defined as the integral over all individuals' welfare: $\mathcal{L} \equiv \int_0^1 \mathcal{L}_i \, di$. When we evaluate this integral, the second and third terms of utility cancel each other out:

$$\mathcal{L} = \mathbb{E}\left[(1-r) \int_0^1 (a_i - \theta)^2 \, di \Big| \mathcal{I}_i\right]. \quad (11.9)$$

This tells us that social welfare is only improved when agents' actions are closer to the state θ. Thus, coordination offers private benefits but no social benefits. To the extent that agents' desire to coordinate trades off with their desire to take actions close to θ, coordination is socially costly. This insight—that coordination is socially costly—is key to understanding Morris and Shin's result. Because public information facilitates coordination, it will turn out to be social welfare-reducing as well.

Substituting the optimal actions from (11.7) into the welfare function (11.9), and taking the integral over agents' private signals yields

$$\mathcal{L} = \frac{1-r}{(1-\alpha_s r)^2} \left[(1 - \alpha_s - \alpha_z)^2 \mathbb{E}[(\mu_\theta - \theta)^2] + \alpha_s^2 (1-r)^2 \right.$$
$$\left. \int_0^1 \mathbb{E}[(s_i - \theta)^2] \, di + \alpha_z^2 \mathbb{E}[(z - \theta)^2]\right]. \quad (11.10)$$

---

4. The utility function in (5.6) also differs in that losses arise when actions deviate from a single target that jointly reflects the state and the average action; in contrast, the payoff in (11.8) separately penalizes deviations to the state and the target. Nevertheless, the optimal policies under both payoffs are identical.

Using the fact that the error in priors $(\mu_\theta - \theta)$ and the signal noises $(z - \theta)$ and $(s_i - \theta)$ are mutually independent, we replace $\mathbb{E}[(\mu_\theta - \theta)^2]$ and $\mathbb{E}[(z - \theta)^2]$ with τ_θ^{-1} and τ_z^{-1}. Then, we substitute $\tau_s^{-1} = \int_0^1 (s_i - \theta)^2 \, di$ (the proof of this equality is left as an exercise), replace the relative precisions $\alpha_s = \hat{\Sigma}\tau_s$ and $\alpha_z = \hat{\Sigma}\tau_z$, and rearrange to get:

$$\mathcal{L} = (1 - r)\left[-\frac{\tau_\theta + (1 - r)^2 \tau_s + \tau_z}{(\tau_\theta + (1 - r)\tau_s + \tau_z)^2} \right]. \qquad (11.11)$$

Finally, we take a partial derivative with respect to the precision of public data τ_z

$$\frac{\partial \mathcal{L}}{\partial \tau_z} = (1 - r)\left[\frac{-\tau_\theta - (1 - 2r)(1 - r)\tau_s - \tau_z}{(\tau_\theta + (1 - r)\tau_s + \tau_z)^3} \right]. \qquad (11.12)$$

When $0 < r < 1$, this expression is positive if and only if $(\tau_\theta + \tau_z)/\tau_s > (2r - 1)(1 - r)$.

This tells us that if public information (which includes both the common prior and the public data because both are common knowledge) is sufficiently precise, then adding more public information improves welfare. Furthermore, when coordination motives are not very strong $(r < 1/2)$, then public information is always welfare-improving. But in cases where agents have a strong desire to coordinate and the existing public information is noisy, adding to the precision of public information can cause agents to put too much weight on it. They coordinate at the expense of choosing actions that are further away from the true state, on average. Because social welfare is linked to the distance of actions from the true state, these are situations where public information is socially costly.

Application: Central Bank Transparency A classic issue in macroeconomics is the role of transparency in central bank practices and policies. Conventional wisdom suggests that more central bank data provision is desirable as it helps the public make more informed decisions. Morris and Shin (2002) have warned against such conventional wisdom. Subsequent research has, however, found that these detrimental effects are outweighed by the "conventional" benefits of transparency (Hellwig, 2005; Roca, 2010).

Candian (2021) shows the case for maximal data in closed economies can be overturned in open economies that face financial market imperfections. The paper considers a dispersed-information open-economy model with noisy public signals (central bank data announcements). The volatility of welfare-relevant gaps is nonmonotonic in the precision of public data because public information entails both an information effect (more information about fundamentals) and a crowding out effect (agents coordinate too much on noisy public signals). In complete international financial markets, public data always improves welfare and complete transparency is optimal. However, with incomplete markets, more accurate public signals can decrease welfare, by exacerbating the cost of cross-country demand imbalances.

11.6.3   Substitutable Public and Private Data

Public data could be socially costly in that it inhibits the transmission of private data. Whereas the previous two sections built externalities into agents' payoffs, this argument relies on data externalities. It stipulates how information used to form actions affects other agents' ability to learn from those actions.

In Amador and Weill (2012), increasing the precision of public data causes agents to weigh it more heavily and private data less heavily in their actions. Because actions are observed with some noise, a smaller private data component makes actions less informative about what private data others know. Because information diffuses only when actions reveal private data that the observer did not already know, more public data eventually makes agents less informed. In short, public data crowds out private data. The following is a two-period model that illustrates the effect that Amador and Weill (2012) build into an infinite-horizon, continuous-time model.

Setup   Consider a continuum of agents indexed by i with payoffs that depend on the agent's action in the first and second periods, a_{1i} and a_{2i}, and an unknown state θ:

$$\mathcal{L}_i = -(a_{1i} - \theta)^2 - (a_{2i} - \theta)^2. \tag{11.13}$$

Prior beliefs are diffuse. Before taking their first action, each agent observes a private signal s_{1i} and a public signal z_1 of θ, with precisions τ_{s_1} and τ_{z_1} respectively:

$$s_{1i} = \theta + \eta_{1i}, \quad \eta_{1i} \sim_{iid} \mathcal{N}(0, \tau_{s_1}^{-1}) \tag{11.14}$$

$$z_1 = \theta + \eta_1, \quad \eta_1 \sim \mathcal{N}(0, \tau_{z_1}^{-1}). \tag{11.15}$$

After taking their first action, but before taking their second action, each agent observes endogenous private and public data signals about the average first action $a_1 \equiv \int a_{1i}\, di$:

$$s_{2i} = a_1 + \eta_{2i}, \quad \eta_{2i} \sim_{iid} \mathcal{N}(0, \tau_{s_2}^{-1}) \tag{11.16}$$

$$z_2 = a_1 + \eta_2, \quad \eta_2 \sim \mathcal{N}(0, \tau_{z_2}^{-1}). \tag{11.17}$$

DATA POLICY AND WELFARE 253

Thus, the agent's problem is to choose a_{1i}, given their time-1 information set $\{s_{1i}, z_1\}$ and to choose a_{2i}, given their time-2 information set $\{s_{1i}, z_1, s_{2i}, z_2\}$ to maximize (11.13).

Equilibrium Outcomes   The key result is that more precise initial public information (τ_{z_1}) lowers the precision of subsequent signals $(\tau_{s_2}$ and $\tau_{z_2})$. This is the crowding-out effect. The reason this happens is that agents who have more precise public information put less weight on their private information when choosing their first-period action. This makes the average first-period action a_1 and subsequent actions less informative. In an infinite-horizon model, Amador and Weill show that more initial public information eventually leads agents to have less total information. The conclusion is ironic: giving agents more public information can cause them to be less well-informed.

Amador and Weill (2010) embed this mechanism in a cash-in-advance model where households observe the prices of goods but cannot disentangle productivity from money supply shocks. When the central bank provides more precise public information about the money supply (or productivity), households' production and purchasing decisions depend less on their private information and more on public information. This can make prices less informative.

Drenik and Perez (2020) exploit a historical episode—the manipulation of inflation statistics in Argentina—to show that a reduction in public signal precision τ_z increased the weight γ_s on private signals when forecasting inflation and generated a more significant cross-sectional price dispersion. Higher dispersion, in turn, reduces the effectiveness of the monetary policy.

11.6.4 Complementary Public and Private Data

While the idea that public data crowds out private data is intuitively appealing, it is possible to generate the reverse conclusion. In Gosselin, Lotz, and Wyplosz (2008), disclosing public data facilitates the transmission of private data.

The interpretation of their result is that when a central bank publicly releases its information, it eliminates the need for price-setters to second-guess what the bank knows. As a result, price-setters only base prices on their information about fundamentals, not on their information about central bank beliefs. This makes prices more informative to the central bank, who can use that information to set better policy. In essence, releasing public information turns Federal Reserve watchers into inflation watchers.

In Duffie, Malamud, and Manso (2009), agents publicly reveal their posterior beliefs to others. Because they reveal beliefs and not actions, others can always extract all the new information. The Amador and Weill (2012) agents observe each others' actions, which gives them noisy data about what new information the other agent knows. The signal-to-noise ratio of another agent's action depends on how much public data that agent knows. So, data information can make actions less informative in Amador and Weill (2012), while in Duffie, Malamud, and Manso (2009), agents who have more data reveal more to others.

11.7   Data and Risk-Sharing

Data technologies facilitate self-risk management, making it easier to face uncertainty. More information about future random events leads to better individual decisions and, therefore, higher welfare. However, households and firms do not live in isolation. They interact in many ways with others through markets. They supply labor, consume goods, and trade in asset markets. Risk-sharing refers to situations when companies or individuals transfer individual risks to a third party through their actions, to cover the potential loss from uncertain events. Risk-sharing arrangements are useful to hedge and minimize risk. Insurance contracts are risk-sharing instruments. The use of risk-sharing strategies through markets, together with self-risk management, has welfare consequences.

The relationship between data and risk-sharing is nuanced. On the one hand, data increases asset price volatility. On the other hand, data inhibits risk-sharing. These opposing effects of data affect its value and have important welfare consequences.

11.7.1   Data Increases Asset Price Volatility

More data makes expected asset values more volatile. This is an effect of risk, not of risk-sharing. But it will be an important force in our risk-sharing results. To see why data creates price volatility, consider an agent i who has an information set $\mathcal{I}$ and forms the expectation about an asset with stationary value v:

$$v = \mathbb{E}[v|\mathcal{I}] + e, \tag{11.18}$$

where $e \equiv v - \mathbb{E}[v|\mathcal{I}]$ is the expectation error. If the agent's beliefs are unbiased, then $\mathbb{E}[e] = 0$, and there is zero correlation between e and $\mathbb{E}[v|\mathcal{I}]$. Taking the unconditional variance of both sides of this equation we obtain

$$\mathbb{V}ar[v] = \mathbb{V}ar[\mathbb{E}[v|\mathcal{I}]] + \mathbb{V}ar[e]. \tag{11.19}$$

Getting more precise information means that the variance of the expectation error $\mathbb{V}ar[e]$ is smaller. Since the unconditional variance of asset payoffs is exogenous, for the equality to hold, it must be that more precise information raises $\mathbb{V}ar[\mathbb{E}[v|\mathcal{I}]]$. Thus, if asset prices are determined by a representative investor's expected value of an asset, then giving that investor more precise data (be it public or private information) will increase the variance of the asset price.

11.7.2 The Hirshleifer Effect

Data availability in advance of trading limits risk-sharing opportunities in the economy, reducing welfare. The argument for why uncertainty facilitates risk-sharing is well understood in finance and is often called the "Hirshleifer effect." Hirshleifer (1971) considers the example of two bettors, each with a ticket on an identical but independent lottery. The bettors can diversify their risk by splitting the two claims so that both get half the winnings if either lottery pays off. Now, suppose that both bettors observe noisy signals about the outcome of each lottery. The bettor whose claim is on the lottery with the more favorable signal would want to keep a larger claim on his own lottery. The signal reduces uncertainty about both lottery outcomes but, at the same time, undermines risk-sharing. The only way both bettors will consistently share all their risk is if they know nothing about the lottery outcomes.

11.7.3 Data Undermining Risk-Sharing in Goods Markets

A different version of the Hirshleifer effect arises in international trade. In international trade, it is well known that fluctuations in the relative price of goods, also known as the terms of trade, help countries to share aggregate risk. Baley, Veldkamp, and Waugh (2020) show how data causes countries' exports to covary more with each other, causing the relative price to move less, which undermines the ability of the relative price to share risk across countries. Whether data increases or decreases welfare depends on the complementarity or substitutability encoded in agents' preferences. Next, we present the key elements of their analysis.

Setup There are two large markets, labeled x and y, and a continuum of entrepreneurs within each market. Entrepreneurs like to consume two goods, x and y, which are market-differentiated: $U(c_x, c_y)$. Each entrepreneur in the x market has an idiosyncratic endowment of z_x units of good x, where $\ln z_x \sim \mathcal{N}(\mu_x, \sigma_x^2)$. Entrepreneurs in the y market have an idiosyncratic endowment of z_y units of good y, where $\ln z_y \sim \mathcal{N}(\mu_y, \sigma_y^2)$. Given their endowments, entrepreneurs choose how much to sell of their own goods in exchange for other goods to maximize their utility.

Risks and Information Structure   The means of the endowment distributions are independent random variables: $\mu_x \sim \mathcal{N}(m_x, s_x^2)$ and $\mu_y \sim \mathcal{N}(m_y, s_y^2)$. μ_x and μ_y are aggregate shocks because they represent the average endowment realization for each market. Endowment shocks are the source of uncertainty in the model. They could equivalently be quality or preference shocks.

At the beginning of the period, agents in market x observe their own endowment z_x and the mean of their own market's endowment μ_x. Likewise, agents in market y observe z_y and μ_y. Entrepreneurs know the distribution from which average productivity is drawn and the cross-sectional distribution of outcomes. In other words, $m_x, m_y, s_x, s_y, \sigma_x$ and σ_y are common knowledge.

Agents in each market receive data signals about the other countries' aggregate endowment realization. Specifically, agents in market x observe a signal about the y-endowment

$$\tilde{m}_y = \mu_y + \eta_y, \qquad \eta_y \sim \mathcal{N}(0, \tilde{s}_y^2). \qquad (11.20)$$

Similarly, agents in market y observe a signal about the x-endowment

$$\tilde{m}_x = \mu_x + \eta_x, \qquad \eta_x \sim \mathcal{N}(0, \tilde{s}_x^2). \qquad (11.21)$$

Thus, agents in each market receive imprecise but unbiased data about fundamentals in the other market. How precise or imprecise the data signal is will depend on the noise variance, $\tilde{s}_x^2$ and $\tilde{s}_y^2$. Let $\mathcal{I}_x$ and $\mathcal{I}_y$ denote the information sets of entrepreneurs in each market.

Bayesian Updating   Entrepreneurs in each market combine their signals with their prior knowledge of the endowment distribution to form posterior beliefs. Agents must form posterior beliefs over two outcomes: first-order beliefs, which are beliefs about the endowment realization in the foreign market, and second-order beliefs, which are home market beliefs about the foreign market's beliefs about themselves. Characterizing first- and second-order beliefs is sufficient to characterize optimal actions.[5]

To compute market x's first-order beliefs about market y's endowment distribution, note that by Bayes' Law, the posterior probability distribution is normal with mean $\hat{m}_y$ and variance $\hat{s}_y^2$ given by

$$F(\mu_y | \mathcal{I}_x) = \Phi\left(\frac{\mu_y - \hat{m}_y}{\hat{s}_y}\right) \quad \text{with} \quad \hat{m}_y = \frac{s_y^{-2} m_y + \tilde{s}_y^{-2} \tilde{m}_y}{s_y^{-2} + \tilde{s}_y^{-2}}, \quad \hat{s}_y^2 = \frac{1}{s_y^{-2} + \tilde{s}_y^{-2}}.$$
$$(11.22)$$

---

5. All higher orders of beliefs can matter for choices. However, because only two shocks are observed by each market, the first two orders of beliefs are sufficient to characterize the entire hierarchy.

The posterior mean is a precision weighted average of the signal and unconditional mean; Φ is the standard normal distribution. Similarly, one computes market y's beliefs.

The timing protocol is as follows: First, agents see their endowments and receive data about the foreign market's endowments. Agents then make sale decisions. Thus, they are selling before knowing the actual price p. This timing protocol allows information frictions to matter: uncertainty about the other market's endowment gives rise to aggregate uncertainty about the terms of trade, and this uncertainty, in turn, feeds back into the decision to trade.

Solution   Given their information sets, agents chose how much to sell, t_x or t_y. In return, they receive the other market's goods at a relative price p, denominated in units of y good. For example, an agent who sells t_x units of the x goods receives pt_x units of y for immediate consumption. There is no secondary resale market or storage, and we restrict sales and consumption to be nonnegative. This implies that market x's budget set is $c_x \in [0, z_x - t_x]$, $c_y \in [0, pt_x]$ and market y's budget set is $c_x \in \left[0, t_y/p\right]$, $c_y \in [0, z_y - t_y]$.

Since every unit of x sales must be paid for with y sales, and conversely, every unit of y sales must be paid for with x sales, the only price that clears the market is the ratio of aggregate sales:

$$p(\mu_x, \mu_y, \hat{m}_x, \hat{m}_y) = \frac{T_y(\mu_y, \hat{m}_x)}{T_x(\mu_x, \hat{m}_y)} \tag{11.23}$$

where aggregate sales in market x are $T_x(\mu_x, \hat{m}_y) = \int t_x(z_x, \mu_x, \hat{m}_y) \, dF(z_x|\mu_x)$ and aggregate sales in market y are $T_y(\mu_y, \hat{m}_x) = \int t_y(z_y, \mu_y, \hat{m}_x) \, dF(z_y|\mu_y)$.

Risk-Sharing through Prices   When a market gets a positive or negative productivity shock z, movements in the price p in (11.23) provide partial insurance of that risk. If country x productivity is low (μ_x is low), then country x's exports will be low as well (low T_x). But if x goods are scarce, their price will be high (a low T_x results in a high relative price p in (11.23)). That high price of x goods raises country x's revenue from selling their goods. While the negative productivity shock lowers revenue, the high relative price raises revenue, helping to smooth the effect of the shock on the market's consumption. This insurance mechanism through terms of trade is well-known from Cole and Obstfeld (1991).

Data undermines this risk-sharing mechanism because it leads markets to coordinate production. To see why, note that data allows production choices to covary more with the outcomes each market is learning about. We know this from section 10.6. In this case, that means that more data for market y

allows y's sales to covary more with the productivity of market x; data raises $\mathbb{C}ov[T_y, \mu_x]$. Since market x already knew their own productivity, their sales already covaried with their own productivity, $\mathbb{C}ov[T_x, \mu_x] > 0$. Thus, data makes market y sales covary more with market x sales; it raises $\mathbb{C}ov[T_y, T_x]$. In this setting, more data is bringing markets closer to symmetric information and allowing their choices to be more coordinated.

When sales across markets covary more, the price fluctuates less. In (11.23), the price is the ratio of the sales in the two markets. If these sales move proportionately, the price does not change. When sales have lots of independent variation, this price will fluctuate greatly. So data raises sales covariance, which causes the market price to move less: high $\mathbb{C}ov[T_y, T_x]$ lowers $\mathbb{V}ar[p]$. Recall that the insurance role of prices depends on price moving sufficiently when productivity changes. Thus, when data causes the market clearing price to be more stable, it undermines the risk-sharing role of the price.

It is possible in this setting for more data to reduce welfare by undermining risk-sharing, as in Hirshleifer (1971). This result depends on the properties of preferences. Baley, Veldkamp, and Waugh (2020) characterize a class of preferences for which more data increases or decreases welfare. In particular, if the expected utility takes a CES form $\mathbb{E}[c_x^\eta + c_y^\eta]$ with $\eta < 1$, then data increases risk-sharing when goods are highly complementary ($\eta < 0$). In contrast, data decreases risk-sharing when goods are highly substitutable ($\eta > 0$).

Eckwert and Zilcha (2003) have some of these forces at work as well. They argue that data has a positive value in a production economy if the data predicts nontradable risks; data that predicts tradable risks may have negative value if the consumers are highly risk averse.

11.7.4 Data, Risk-Sharing, and Risk-Hedging

Data has two competing effects on risk. The first effect is that data limits risk-sharing opportunities, as in Hirshleifer (1971) and Baley, Veldkamp, and Waugh (2020), discussed in the previous section. The second effect is that data allows firms to anticipate shocks and allocate resources to mitigate or hedge the risk. For example, a firm that knows a recession is coming might cut its investment to survive; an investor who knows that Apple stock is likely to have low future payoffs can sell some of that stock to reduce exposure. We discuss the competing effects of risk-sharing and hedging on welfare using a simplified version of the framework developed by Gaballo and Ordoñez (2023).

Setup The risk in this model comes from an uncertain rate at which raw capital is transformed into intermediate capital. Each firm's raw capital has a different random realization of this transformation rate. Data predicts this rate.

Since raw capital can be traded, firms can share risk by buying raw capital from many other firms and diversifying this risk. When firms know each others' rates of transformation, firms with high-productivity raw capital will sell less of it and less risk will be shared. However, when firms have data to predict the capital transformation productivity shocks, they can choose to hire labor that is efficiently aligned with the amount of intermediate capital they will have. The model is designed to explore the net effect of these forces on welfare.

Preferences and Technology The economy lasts for one period. There is a continuum of entrepreneurs, indexed by $i \in [0, 1]$, who perform four roles: consumer, producer, buyer, and seller. The entrepreneur has preferences over consumption c_i and labor ℓ_i given by

$$u(c_i, \ell_i) = \frac{c_i^{1-\sigma}}{1-\sigma} - \frac{1}{\gamma}\ell_i^{\gamma}, \tag{11.24}$$

where $\sigma > 0$ is the coefficient of relative risk aversion and $\gamma > 1$ is the inverse (Frisch) elasticity of labor supply to the wage rate. Producing consumption goods requires *intermediate* capital, k_i. These goods are produced with a constant returns-to-scale technology[6]

$$y_i = \ell_i^{\alpha} \hat{k}_i^{1-\alpha}, \quad \text{with} \quad \hat{k}_i = e^{k_i}. \tag{11.25}$$

Raw and Intermediate Capital Entrepreneur i is endowed with one unit of *raw* capital. Intermediate capital k_i is obtained from raw capital in two ways. The first way is using a fixed fraction β_i of its own raw capital[7] that transforms into intermediate capital at a random rate $(\bar{\theta} + \theta_i)$, with $\theta_i \sim \mathcal{N}(0, 1)$:

$$k(\beta_i) = (\bar{\theta} + \theta_i)\beta_i. \tag{11.26}$$

The second way is purchasing a fraction β_{ij} from entrepreneur j's raw capital at a noncontingent price R_j. Firms j's raw capital, even when used by firm i, transforms into intermediate capital at j random rate $\theta_j \sim \mathcal{N}(0, 1)$ with $\mathbb{E}[\theta_i, \theta_j] = 0$:

$$k(\beta_{ij}) = (\bar{\theta} + \theta_j)\beta_{ij} - \frac{\varphi}{2}\beta_{ij}^2 - R_j\beta_{ij}. \tag{11.27}$$

Using other entrepreneurs' raw capital incurs a transaction cost as well as the equilibrium price R_j. The quadratic transaction cost is necessary to keep

---

6. The exponential transformation of intermediate capital into final capital makes agents display constant absolute risk aversion (CARA) with respect to intermediate capital despite constant relative risk aversion (CRRA) with respect to consumption goods. This useful trick is for analytical tractability and does not change the qualitative predictions of the model.

7. Raw capital supply $1 - \beta_i$ is assumed to be fixed; it is a choice in the paper.

β_{ij} choices bounded. The equilibrium price is there to clear the raw capital market.

Trading and Market Equilibrium   Given productivity realizations $\{\theta_i\}_{i\in[0,1]}$, a market equilibrium is the cross-sectional allocation $\{\hat{k}_i, c_i\}_{i\in[0,1]}$ and raw capital prices $\{R_i\}_{i\in[0,1]}$ such that for all entrepreneurs i: (i) the labor choice $\{\ell_i\}_{i\in[0,1]}$ and the purchase of raw capital $\{\beta_{ij}\}_{j\neq i, i\in[0,1]}$ maximize expected utility $\mathbb{E}_i[u(c_i, \ell_i)]$, and (ii) markets clear

$$\int_{J(i)} \beta_{ij}\, dj = 1 - \beta_i, \qquad (11.28)$$

where $J(i) \equiv [0,1]\setminus\{i\}$. In other words, all the capital of type i bought by all other entrepreneurs $j \neq i$ should equal the total capital sold by i. The expectation $\mathbb{E}_i[\cdot]$ is conditional on the data set of entrepreneur i.

To solve the model, first find the optimal labor supply, then solve for the optimal raw capital choices. Then, explore the welfare effect of data by substituting the optimal choices and computing ex ante utility for different assumptions about data.

Optimal Labor Supply and Risk-Hedging   The entrepreneur i supplies labor optimally (based on the available amount of data) according to

$$\ell_i^* = \mathbb{E}_i[K_i]^{\frac{\phi}{\gamma}}, \qquad (11.29)$$

where we define $K_i \equiv \alpha e^{(1-\alpha)(1-\sigma)k_i}$ and $\phi \equiv \frac{1}{1-\frac{\alpha}{\gamma}(1-\sigma)} > 0$. The role of data for the labor choice is captured through the expectations operator. With no data, agents can only choose labor based on expected capital. With abundant data, agents can choose labor based on a precise forecast of k_i. Data allows firms to adjust production for anticipated shocks. This is risk-hedging.

Raw Capital Trade and Risk-Sharing   Firm i sells a fraction β_i of its own raw capital and earns $(1-\beta_i)R_i$ units of intermediate capital in return. The firm gets $(\bar{\theta}+\theta_i)\beta_i$ from transforming its own raw capital into intermediate capital. Finally, the firm gets $\int_0^1 k(\beta_{ij})dj$ units of intermediate capital from its purchases of other firms' raw capital. Adding these three and using (11.27) to substitute for $k(\beta_{ij})$ yields the amount of intermediate capital available to agent i for production:

$$k_i = (\bar{\theta}+\theta_i)\beta_i + (1-\beta_i)R_i + \int_0^1 k(\beta_{ij})\, dj. \qquad (11.30)$$

The derivative of the expectation of profits (11.27) with respect to β_{ij} implies entrepreneur i's optimal demand of agent j's raw capital is

$$\beta_{ij}^* = \frac{\bar{\theta} + \mathbb{E}_i[\theta_j] - R_j}{\varphi}. \tag{11.31}$$

The numerator is the expected net return of j's raw capital, expressed in units of intermediate capital. The denominator is the adjustment cost parameter, which must be $\varphi > 0$ for capital choices to be bounded. This expression resembles the optimal portfolio choice from Chapter 6, where the quadratic adjustment cost takes the place of risk—also a quadratic function of the portfolio choice—in the denominator.

Consider a symmetric equilibrium in which all agents supply the same amount of raw capital ($\beta_i = \beta$, for all i) and all agents have the same information ($\mathbb{E}_i[\theta_j] = \mathbb{E}_j[\theta_j]$). Equating supply (11.28) and demand (11.31) determines the competitive per unit price of agent j's raw capital:

$$R_j = \bar{\theta} + \mathbb{E}_i[\theta_j] - \varphi(1 - \beta). \tag{11.32}$$

Since the price of raw capital from seller j depends on what buyers know about θ_j, the more i knows, the more volatile the price R_j. As in section 11.7.1, data generate price volatility. Thus, data generates ex ante uncertainty about firms's raw capital revenue. This is data undermining risk-sharing. If agents had no information about the shocks θ_j, all raw capital prices would be equal. Some capital would be better and some worse, but this risk would be diversified by the purchasers and not borne by the sellers, who get the uniform price.

Substituting the price (11.32) into optimal capital demand (11.31) reveals that $\beta_{ij}^* - (1 - \beta)$, which clear the market. Substituting this into the payoff (11.27) and integrating over all firms j reveals that firm i's profits from purchasing other firms' capital is:

$$\int_0^1 k(\beta_{ij})\,dj = \frac{\varphi}{2}(1 - \beta)^2. \tag{11.33}$$

Notice that there are no random variables on the right side. This tells us that the profits from purchasing other firms' capital are deterministic. In other words, raw capital markets can fully diversify all firm-specific risk. This is the benefit of risk-sharing.

Substituting back prices (11.32) and profits (11.33) into intermediate capital (11.30) yields an expected amount of intermediate capital available to firm i that is $\mathbb{E}_i[k_i] = \bar{\theta} - \varphi(1 - \beta)^2 + \frac{\varphi}{2}(1 - \beta)^2$. This expected amount of capital does not depend on how much data firms have. What data does do is change the variance of capital. Data changes the risks firms face. These risks matter because utility is concave and thus agents are risk averse.

Welfare   To determine the welfare consequences of firms' data, substitute the optimal capital and labor choices in the production function (11.25), equate output and consumption ($y_i = c_i$), and substitute consumption and labor in the utility function (11.24). Finally, take an expectation over utility and compare this expression in the case where firms do or do not have data.

Whether data improves welfare or not depends on the value of the risk-aversion coefficient σ. When $\sigma \leq 1$, there is no trade-off: full information always dominates. This is because without risk aversion, there is no benefit to diversification. However, there is still an efficiency benefit to choosing labor that is well-aligned with the firm's intermediate capital stock. This is best achieved when the firm has the maximum possible data. When $\sigma > 1$, full information is only optimal if $\beta_i^2 > \phi$. If the firm expects to retain a large share of its own capital (high β_i), then data is valuable because it helps the firm choose an efficient amount of labor. The loss of diversification is not too costly because when firms retain a large fraction of raw capital, they trade relatively little. Thus the benefits to diversifying the income traded capital are small.

In Gaballo and Ordoñez (2023), firms can choose whether or not they want to buy data. Data externalities arise because one firm's decision to acquire data undermines the ability of other firms to diversify risk. When selling raw capital is riskier, firms retain more raw capital. Retaining more raw capital makes adjusting labor optimally more important, which raises the value of data for other firms. This mechanism creates too much data production relative to the social optimum.

Key Ideas

- Data privacy regulations raise the welfare of some agents but may harm others. Harms come from higher prices, lower service quality, and greater uncertainty.
- New data technologies may be lowering labor's share of total income while raising the fraction of income paid to the owners of data. It is still possible that everyone gains.
- Data can help agents hedge risk but undermine their ability to share risks.

Practice Questions

11.1 In the Acemoglu et al. (2022) model from 11.1.2, characterize the firm's profit-maximizing price.

11.2 In the model of 11.6.2, prove that $\int_0^1 \mathbb{E}[(s_i - \theta)^2 \, di] = \tau_s^{-1}$.

11.3 In the model of 11.6.2, derive equation (11.11) from equation (11.10).

11.4 In the model of 11.6.2, suppose that $r < 0$ so that actions are strategic substitutes. Can public information still be socially costly?

11.5 In the model of 11.6.2, suppose that $r < 0$ so that actions are strategic substitutes. Can private information be socially costly?

11.6 In the model of 11.6.3, derive the optimal first-period action a_{1i} and the average action a.

11.7 In the model of 11.6.3, what information is conveyed by the data point z_{2i}? What makes this data more or less informative?

Conclusion

New data technologies are revolutionizing the way we process and analyze data. At their core, these new technologies solve prediction problems. Algorithms that use large data sets to predict the language we want to use, business trends, or the efficacy of new drugs play an increasingly important economic role. Therefore, our study of data economics starts with understanding types of prediction problems and their economic effects. The first half of our book is devoted to categorizing the different types of prediction problems and providing theoretical tools that can be used to describe and solve them. Many of these tools have not yet been applied to study data economics, making this book a valuable resource for researchers looking to match the right tool with the right question. By providing a reference manual for prediction problems, we aim to empower researchers to tackle complex data economics questions and generate new insights into this rapidly evolving field.

The second part of the book delves deeper into the workings of the data economy, exploring ideas and models that can help formalize our understanding of this field. One of the key concepts discussed is the data feedback loop, which describes the cycle of increasing returns that arises when a firm accumulates more data and becomes more efficient, profitable, and produces even more data. This feedback loop enables the emergence of large, superstar firms, which are incredibly efficient but their existence can lead to concerns about market concentration and market power. To address these issues, economists need to use models to predict the outcomes of policies that have not yet been tried.

Another important idea discussed in the book is that data markets may not function like traditional markets. This is because data is nonrival. It can leak out through the information conveyed by one's actions, and others' use of data can reduce its value, a force we call strategic substitutability. Understanding how these forces play out will be important for businesses that participate in data markets, for policymakers that might want to regulate data markets, and for academics to make sense of the data-related empirical evidence they collect.

Data platforms are an integral part of the data ecosystem. These platforms can facilitate or disrupt the data feedback loop as they observe data from buyers and sellers and may deliver some form of that data back to both parties as product recommendations, sales statistics, or consumer trends. Platforms may also use the information they gather to compete in markets or to sell advertising. While these seemingly complex problems can be difficult to model, the book proposes a linear framework that can help simplify these issues and provide insights into how data platforms affect markets and the aggregate economy.

The value of data as an asset for firms is a central topic in the study of data economics. To piece together a clearer picture of the value of data, economists and researchers will need to use many different approaches. These approaches may include cost accounting, revenue forecasting, measuring the value of complementary inputs, using prices to infer data value, and calibrating an aggregate, recursive, dynamic model. By combining these approaches, researchers can gain a more comprehensive understanding of the value of data and how it can be used to drive economic growth and innovation.

Data regulation is an active area of policy experimentation in many countries. The last section of the book considers welfare, the basis for sound policies. An important area of concern has been data firms' market power. When firms barter—or partially barter—data for goods and services and when they use data to resolve risk, measuring market power is challenging. One challenge is the implicit price of a barter trade. Another challenge is that reducing risk and reducing market power have similar effects on firms' decisions, making it difficult to interpret changes in measures of market power without direct evidence about data and changes in subjective risk.

While the collection and use of data can bring about many benefits, such as increased efficiency and better-targeted products and services, there are also concerns about potential harms, such as discrimination, loss of autonomy, and breaches of personal privacy. As more and more data is collected and analyzed, policymakers will need to consider these trade-offs. This book did not discuss privacy, not because it is unimportant, but because, at this time, there is little theoretical work to guide our thinking and inform our measurement of the costs of privacy. But this is an important area for future research, both at the micro and macro levels of analysis.

When considering data policy, it is crucial to account for the impact of data on risk. Data, as digital information for prediction, can greatly reduce uncertainty or subjective risk. Social costs of risk are substantial, as evidenced by the premium that investors demand for bearing risk in the equity market, which is typically twice as large as the riskless return. Therefore, the value of risk reduction provided by data should not be overlooked. By properly modeling and measuring the risk-reduction benefits of data, policymakers can make more-informed decisions.

This book provides a range of theoretical and analytical tools to help us better understand the data economy and develop effective policies to promote competition, efficiency, and welfare. By building on the foundational ideas and models presented in the book, we hope readers can contribute their own novel ideas to deepen our collective understanding of the rapidly evolving data economy.

Mathematical Appendix

This chapter reviews the basic concepts and mathematical tools needed to understand the material in this book. It does not attempt to be comprehensive. We provide additional references to each topic for the interested reader.

A.1 Densities

Uniform Let $x \sim \mathcal{U}[a, b]$ be a continuous uniform random variable defined on the interval $[a, b]$ with mean $\mathbb{E}[x] = (a + b)/2$ and variance $\mathbb{V}ar[x] = (b - a)^2/12$. Then, its density is

$$f(x) = \frac{1}{b - a}. \tag{A.1}$$

Normal Let $x \sim \mathcal{N}(\mu, \sigma^2)$ be a normal random variable, defined over $(-\infty, \infty)$, with mean $\mathbb{E}[x] = \mu$ and variance $\mathbb{V}ar[x] = \sigma^2$. Then, its density is

$$f(x) = \frac{1}{\sqrt{2\pi\sigma^2}} e^{-\frac{1}{2}\frac{(x-\mu)^2}{\sigma^2}}. \tag{A.2}$$

Gamma Let $x \sim Gamma(\alpha, \beta)$ be a gamma random variable, defined over $(0, \infty)$, with mean $\mathbb{E}[x] = \alpha/\beta$ and variance $\mathbb{V}ar[x] = \alpha/\beta^2$, where $\alpha, \beta > 0$. Then, its density is

$$f(x) = \frac{x^{\alpha-1} e^{-\beta x} \beta^\alpha}{\Gamma(\alpha)}, \tag{A.3}$$

where the normalization constant $\Gamma(\gamma) = \int_0^\infty t^{\gamma-1} e^{-t} \, dt$ is the gamma function.

Beta Let $x \sim Beta(\alpha, \beta)$ be a Beta random variable defined on the interval $[0, 1]$, with mean $\mathbb{E}[x] = \alpha/(\alpha + \beta)$ and variance $\mathbb{V}ar[x] = \alpha\beta/[\alpha + \beta]^2(\alpha + \beta + 1)$. Then, its density is

$$f(x) = \frac{1}{B(\alpha, \beta)} x^{\alpha-1}(1-x)^{\beta-1}, \qquad (A.4)$$

where $B(\alpha, \beta) = \Gamma(\alpha + \beta)/\Gamma(\alpha)\Gamma(\beta)$ is a normalization constant.

A.2 Jensen's Inequality

Let $X \subset \mathbb{R}$ be a convex set of the real numbers, and let x be an integrable random variable taking values in X.

Jensen's Inequality for Convex Functions   The function $f : X \to R$ is *convex* if

$$f(\alpha x_1 + (1-\alpha)x_2) \leq \alpha f(x_1) + (1-\alpha)f(x_2) \quad \forall x_1, x_2 \in X, \quad \forall \alpha \in [0, 1].$$
$$(A.5)$$

If f is convex, then the following inequality holds:

$$f(\mathbb{E}[x]) \leq \mathbb{E}[f(x)]. \qquad (A.6)$$

The function of the average is below the average of the function.

Jensen's Inequality for Concave Functions   The function $f : X \to R$ is *concave* if

$$f(\alpha x_1 + (1-\alpha)x_2) \geq \alpha f(x_1) + (1-\alpha)f(x_2) \quad \forall x_1, x_2 \in X, \quad \forall \alpha \in [0, 1].$$
$$(A.7)$$

If f is convex, then the following inequality holds:

$$f(\mathbb{E}[x]) \geq \mathbb{E}[f(x)]. \qquad (A.8)$$

That is, the function of the average is above the average of the function.

A.3 Preferences and Approximations

We present commonly used preferences and useful approximations.

A.3.1 CARA Preferences

A utility function $U(y)$ represents preferences with constant absolute risk aversion (CARA) if the number $\rho \equiv -u''(y)/u'(y)$ is constant.

Exponential   Exponential utility belongs to the CARA family and takes the form

$$U(y) = -\mathbb{E}[\exp(-\rho y)], \qquad (A.9)$$

where ρ is a constant representing the degree of risk preference. If $\rho > 0$, the agent is risk averse; if $\rho = 0$, the agent is neutral; and if $\rho < 0$, the agent is risk loving. Note that maximizing this objective means minimizing $\mathbb{E}[\exp(-\rho y)]$.

Mean-Variance   In the case that y is normally distributed, then by (A.16) we have that exponential preferences can be written as

$$U(y) = -\exp\left(-\rho\mathbb{E}[y] + \frac{\rho^2}{2}\mathbb{V}ar[y]\right). \tag{A.10}$$

Furthermore, since the exponential transformation is a monotonically increasing function, minimizing the exponential of the argument is the same as minimizing the argument itself. Therefore, many settings maximize an objective that takes the form

$$U(y) = \mathbb{E}[y] - \frac{\rho}{2}\mathbb{V}ar[y]. \tag{A.11}$$

These are mean-variance preferences. In a one-period problem, the exponential and mean-variance preferences are equivalent.

A.3.2   Two-Stage Preferences

In setups with information choice, two stages naturally arise.

$$U_1(y) = \mathbb{E}_1[U_2(y)], \tag{A.12}$$

where we denote expectations conditional on time t information as $\mathbb{E}_t[\cdot]$.

With exponential preferences in period 2, the period-1 utility reads:

$$U_1(y) = -\mathbb{E}_1\left[\mathbb{E}_2[\exp(-\rho y)]\right]. \tag{A.13}$$

With mean-variance preferences in period 2, the period-1 utility reads:

$$U_1(y) = \mathbb{E}_1\left[\rho\mathbb{E}_2[y] - \frac{\rho^2}{2}\mathbb{V}ar_2[y]\right] = -\mathbb{E}_1\left[\ln\left(\mathbb{E}_2[\exp(-\rho y)]\right)\right], \tag{A.14}$$

where the second equality applies to normal variables as in (A.10).

Early Resolution of Uncertainty   Comparing (A.13) and (A.14) shows that with two periods the equivalence between exponential and mean-variance breaks down. Exponential utility conforms with the expected utility framework, in which the law of iterated expectations applies, i.e., $\mathbb{E}_1[\mathbb{E}_2[\cdot]] = \mathbb{E}_1[\cdot]$, and thus the exact date of the resolution of uncertainty does not matter. In contrast, mean-variance is the expectation of the log of exponential utility, and it represents preferences for early resolution of uncertainty. This utility formulation is related to Epstein and Zin (1989) preference for early resolution of uncertainty. These preferences are also used in Wilson (1975).

A.4   Skewed Variables

Skewness is a measure of the asymmetry of the distribution of a random variable around its mean and is defined as the third centralized and standardized moment:

$$Skew(y) = \mathbb{E}\left[\left(\frac{y - \mathbb{E}[y]}{\sqrt{\mathbb{V}ar[y]}}\right)^3\right]. \tag{A.15}$$

Normal random variables are symmetric and thus have zero skewness.

A.4.1   Building Skewed Random Variables

One useful way to build a skewed variable is by representing it as a nonlinear transformation of a normal variable. Let g be a continuous and monotonic function and $x \sim \mathcal{N}(0, 1)$ be a standard normal variable. Then $y \equiv g(x)$ is positively skewed if g is convex $(g'' > 0)$ and is negatively skewed if g is concave $(g'' < 0)$. Note that these are sufficient conditions but are stronger than what is necessary.

Two well-known examples are lognormal and chi-square.

Mean of Lognormal   Let $x \sim \mathcal{N}(\mathbb{E}[x], \mathbb{V}ar[x])$ be a normal random variable. Now let $y \equiv \exp(\alpha x)$. Then y is a lognormal random variable with mean

$$\mathbb{E}[\exp \alpha x] = \exp\left(\alpha \mathbb{E}[x] + \frac{\alpha^2}{2}\mathbb{V}ar[x]\right). \tag{A.16}$$

Mean of Noncentral Chi-Square   Let $x \sim \mathcal{N}(\mathbb{E}[x], \mathbb{V}ar[x])$ be a normal random variable. Now let $y \equiv x'x$. Then y is a noncentral chi-square random variable with mean

$$\mathbb{E}[x'x] = \text{Tr}(\mathbb{V}ar[x]) + \mathbb{E}[x]'\mathbb{E}[x], \tag{A.17}$$

where $\text{Tr}(A)$ denotes the trace of matrix A and equals the sum of its diagonal elements.

A.4.2   Expected Utility with Skewed Payoffs

Let y be a skewed random variable with cumulative distribution function (CDF) denoted by F, and let $U(y)$ be a utility function. We want to compute the expected utility

$$\mathbb{E}[U(y)|\mathcal{I}] = \int U(y)\, dF(y). \tag{A.18}$$

As above, we can represent $y = g(x)$ as a transformation of a standard normal random variable $x \sim \mathcal{N}(0, 1)$, where g is a continuous and one-to-one mapping. Thus, we can rewrite the expected utility taking the expectation over the normal random variable. Recall the change of variables rule from calculus: If $y = g(x)$, then $\int f(y)\, dy = \int f(g(x))g'(x)\, dx$ for any function f. Applying this rule allows us to write expected utility as

$$\mathbb{E}[U(y)|\mathcal{I}] = \int U(g(x))g'(x)\, d\Phi(x), \qquad (A.19)$$

where Φ is the standard normal CDF. Given this expression for expected utility, we now take a second-order Taylor approximation of the argument of the integral around the mean of x, which is $x = 0$:

$$U(x) \approx U(g(0))g'(0) + \left[U'(g(0))g'(0) + U(g(0))g''(0)\right] x \qquad (A.20)$$

$$+ \frac{1}{2}\left[U''(g(0))g'(0) + 2U'(g(0))g''(0) + U(g(0))g'''(0)\right] x^2.$$

Since the level of a utility function does not affect choices in any way, we can normalize our utility function such that $U(g(0)) = 0$. If we do that, utility simplifies to

$$U(x) \approx U'(g(0))g'(0)x + \frac{1}{2}\left[U''(g(0))g'(0) + 2U'(g(0))g''(0)\right] x^2.$$

Assuming U and g are strictly increasing at the median value of $y = g(0)$, we can divide through by $U'(g(0))g'(0) > 0$ and obtain:

$$U(x) \approx x - \frac{1}{2}\left(\frac{U''(g(0))}{U'(g(0))} - 2\frac{g''(0)}{g'(0)}\right) x^2.$$

If we now integrate over x and condition on any information about x, we get

$$\mathbb{E}[U(y)|\mathcal{I}] \approx \mathbb{E}[x|\mathcal{I}] - \frac{1}{2}\mathrm{Var}[x|\mathcal{I}]\left(\underbrace{\frac{U''(g(0))}{U'(g(0))}}_{\substack{\text{preference} \\ \text{convexity}}} - 2\underbrace{\frac{g''(0)}{g'(0)}}_{\substack{\text{payoff} \\ \text{convexity}}}\right) \qquad (A.21)$$

The first term in the parenthesis that multiplies the variance, $\rho \equiv U''(g(0))/U'(g(0))$, is simply the coefficient of absolute risk aversion evaluated at the median of y. The second term $\mathcal{S} \equiv g''(0)/g'(0)$ reflects the skewness of g at the median of y. Substituting these definitions:

$$\mathbb{E}[U(y)] \approx \mathbb{E}[x|\mathcal{I}] - \frac{1}{2}\mathrm{Var}[x|\mathcal{I}]\,(\rho - 2\mathcal{S}). \qquad (A.22)$$

The previous expression shows that when y is positively skewed, $\mathcal{S} > 0$, then it is as if preferences are less risk averse. When y is negatively skewed, $\mathcal{S} < 0$, the double negative adds to the risk adjustment, and it is as if preferences are more risk averse.

A.5   Eigendecompositions

A symmetric matrix A is positive semi-definite if $v'Av \geq 0$ for every nonzero vector v (it is positive definite if the strict inequality holds).

An *eigenvector v* of a square matrix A is a nonzero vector such that

$$Av = \lambda v. \tag{A.23}$$

where λ is called the *eigenvalue*.

The following properties of matrix algebra are used extensively:

(i) Any square, symmetric positive semi-definite matrix Σ can be decomposed into its eigenvalues and eigenvectors.

$$\Sigma = \Gamma \Lambda \Gamma'.$$

The eigenvalue matrix Λ is diagonal.

(ii) Eigenvector matrices are idempotent:

$$\Gamma'\Gamma = I. \tag{A.24}$$

This implies that for any columns i, j of the eigenvector matrix, $\Gamma_i'\Gamma_i = 1$ and $\Gamma_i'\Gamma_j = 0$ for $i \neq j$.

(iii) Sums of matrices with the same eigenvectors have the same eigenvectors. If $\Sigma = \Gamma \Lambda \Gamma'$ and $\tilde{\Sigma} = \Gamma \tilde{\Lambda} \Gamma'$ are eigendecompositions, then

$$\Sigma + \tilde{\Sigma} = \Gamma (\Lambda + \tilde{\Lambda}) \Gamma'. \tag{A.25}$$

(iv) Products of matrices with the same eigenvectors have the same eigenvectors. If $\Sigma = \Gamma \Lambda \Gamma'$ and $\tilde{\Sigma} = \Gamma \tilde{\Lambda} \Gamma'$ are eigendecompositions, then

$$\Sigma \tilde{\Sigma} = \Gamma (\Lambda \tilde{\Lambda}) \Gamma'. \tag{A.26}$$

(v) Inverting a matrix preserves its eigenvectors. If $\Sigma = \Gamma \Lambda \Gamma'$ then

$$\Sigma^{-1} = \Gamma \Lambda^{-1} \Gamma'. \tag{A.27}$$

(vi) The determinant is the product of its eigenvalues. If $\Sigma = \Gamma \Lambda \Gamma'$ then

$$|\Sigma| = \prod_i \Lambda_{ii}. \tag{A.28}$$

This implies that $|\Sigma^{-1}| = |\Sigma|^{-1}$.

(vii) The trace of a matrix is defined as the sum of its diagonal elements. It is also equal to the sum of its eigenvalues.

$$\mathrm{Tr}(\Sigma) = \sum_i \Lambda_{ii}. \tag{A.29}$$

A.6 Brownian Motion

Wiener process A Wiener process W_t is a continuous-time stochastic process characterized by four properties:

(i) $W_0 = 0$.
(ii) W_t has continuous sample paths.
(iii) W_t has independent and stationary increments.
(vi) Increments are normal: $W_t - W_s \sim \mathcal{N}(0, t - s)$ for $0 \leq s \leq t$.

Brownian Motion A Brownian motion X_t or diffusion with constant drift μ and constant variance σ^2 satisfies the stochastic differential equation

$$X_t = \mu t + \sigma W_t, \tag{A.30}$$

where W_t is a Wiener process. Equivalently, it can be written in differentials as

$$dX_t = \mu\, dt + \sigma\, dW_t. \tag{A.31}$$

It is a Wiener process where increments have mean $\mu(t - s)$ and variance $\sigma^2(t - s)$.

Ito's Lemma Let $f(t, X)$ be a continuous and twice-differentiable scalar function of a Brownian motion $dX_t = \mu\, dt + \sigma\, dW_t$. Then

$$df = \left(\frac{\partial f}{\partial t} + \mu \frac{\partial f}{\partial x} + \frac{\sigma^2}{2} \frac{\partial^2 f}{\partial x^2} \right) dt + \sigma \frac{\partial f}{\partial x}\, dW_t. \tag{A.32}$$

REFERENCES

ABEL, A. B., EBERLY, J. C. and PANAGEAS, S. (2013). Optimal inattention to the stock market with information costs and transactions costs. *Econometrica*, **81** (4), 1455–1481.

ABIS, S. and VELDKAMP, L. (2024). The changing economics of knowledge production. *Review of Financial Studies*, **37** (1), 89–118.

ACEMOGLU, D., AUTOR, D., HAZELL, J. and RESTREPO, P. (2020). *AI and Jobs: Evidence from Online Vacancies.* National Bureau of Economic Research Working Paper 28257.

ACEMOGLU, D., MAKHDOUMI, A., MALEKIAN, A. and OZDAGLAR, A. (2022). Too much data: Prices and inefficiencies in data markets. *American Economic Journal: Microeconomics*, **14** (4), 218–256.

ACHARYA, S. and WEE, S. L. (2020). Rational inattention in hiring decisions. *American Economic Journal: Macroeconomics*, **12** (1), 1–40.

ADAM, K. and MARCET, A. (2011). Internal rationality, imperfect market knowledge and asset prices. *Journal of Economic Theory*, **146** (3), 1224–1252.

ADAM, K., MARCET, A. and BEUTEL, J. (2017). Stock price booms and expected capital gains. *American Economic Review*, **107** (8), 2352–2408.

ADAM, K., MARCET, A. and NICOLINI, J. P. (2016). Stock market volatility and learning. *Journal of Finance*, **71** (1), 33–82.

ADMATI, A. (1985). A noisy rational expectations equilibrium for multi-asset securities markets. *Econometrica*, **53** (3), 629–657.

AFROUZI, H., DRENIK, A. and KIM, R. (2023). *Concentration, Market Power, and Misallocation: The Role of Endogenous Customer Acquisition.* National Bureau of Economic Research. Working Paper 31415.

AFROUZI, H. and YANG, C. (2021a). Dynamic rational inattention and the Phillips curve. CESifo. Working Paper 8840.

AFROUZI, H. and YANG, C. (2021b). *Selection in Information Acquisition and Monetary Non-Neutrality.* Columbia University. Working Paper.

AGHION, P., BERGEAUD, A., BOPPART, T., KLENOW, P. J. and LI, H. (2019). *A Theory of Falling Growth and Rising Rents.* National Bureau of Economic Research. Working Paper 26448.

AGRAWAL, A., GANS, J. and GOLDFARB, A. (2018). *Prediction Machines: The Simple Economics of Artificial Intelligence.* Harvard Business Review Press.

AGRAWAL, A., GANS, J. S. and GOLDFARB, A. (2019). Artificial intelligence: The ambiguous labor market impact of automating prediction. *Journal of Economic Perspectives*, **33** (2), 31–50.

275

AKCIGIT, U. and ATES, S. T. (2021). Ten facts on declining business dynamism and lessons from endogenous growth theory. *American Economic Journal: Macroeconomics*, **13** (1), 257–298.

ALVAREZ, F., BOROVIČKOVÁ, K. and SHIMER, R. (2021). *Consistent Evidence on Duration Dependence of Price Changes*. National Bureau of Economic Research. Working Paper 29112.

ALVAREZ, F., GUISO, L. and LIPPI, F. (2012). Durable consumption and asset management with transaction and observation costs. *American Economic Review*, **102** (5), 2272–2300.

ALVAREZ, F., LIPPI, F. and PACIELLO, L. (2011). Optimal price setting with observation and menu costs. *Quarterly Journal of Economics*, **126** (4), 1909–1960.

ALVAREZ, F., LIPPI, F. and PACIELLO, L. (2016). Monetary shocks in models with inattentive producers. *Review of Economic Studies*, **83** (2), 421–459.

ALVAREZ, F., LIPPI, F. and PACIELLO, L. (2017). Monetary shocks in models with observation and menu costs. *Journal of the European Economic Association*, **16** (2), 353–382.

AMADOR, M. and WEILL, P.-O. (2010). Learning from prices: Public communication and welfare. *Journal of Political Economy*, **118**, 866–907.

AMADOR, M. and WEILL, P.-O. (2012). Learning from private and public observations of others' actions. *Journal of Economic Theory*, **147** (3), 910–940.

ANDRADE, P. and LE BIHAN, H. (2013). Inattentive professional forecasters. *Journal of Monetary Economics*, **60** (8), 967–982.

ANGELETOS, G.-M. and SASTRY, K. (2019). *Inattentive Economies*. National Bureau of Economic Research, Working Paper 26413.

ANTONOVICS, K. and GOLAN, L. (2012). Experimentation and job choice. *Journal of Labor Economics*, **30** (2), 333–366.

ARGENTE, D., FITZGERALD, D., MOREIRA, S. and PRIOLO, A. (2021). How do entrants build market share? The role of demand frictions. SSRN. Working Paper.

ARGENTE, D., and YEH, C. (2022). Product life cycle, learning, and nominal shocks. *Review of Economic Studies*, **89** (6), 2992–3054.

ARKOLAKIS, C. (2010). Market penetration costs and the new consumers margin in international trade. *Journal of Political Economy*, **118**, 1151–1199.

ARKOLAKIS, C., PAPAGEORGIOU, T. and TIMOSHENKO, O. A. (2018). Firm learning and growth. *Review of Economic Dynamics*, **27**, 146–168.

ARROW, K. (1962). Economic welfare and the allocation of resources for invention. In *The Rate and Direction of Inventive Activity: Economic and Social Factors*, 609–626. National Bureau of Economic Research. Princeton University Press.

ARVAI, K. and MANN, K. (2022). Consumption inequality in the digital age. Available at SSRN 3992247.

ASRIYAN, V. and KOHLHAS, A. (2023). Macroeconomics of firm forecasts. CREi Working Paper.

ATKESON, A. and BURSTEIN, A. (2007). Pricing-to-market in a Ricardian model of international trade. National Bureau of Economic Research. Working Paper 12861.

AUCLERT, A., ROGNLIE, M. and STRAUB, L. (2020). *Micro Jumps, Macro Humps: Monetary Policy and Business Cycles in an Estimated HANK Model*. National Bureau of Economic Research. Working Paper 26647.

BABINA, T., FEDYK, A., HE, A. and HODSON, J. (2024). Artificial intelligence, firm growth, and product innovation. *Journal of Financial Economics*, **151**, 103745.

BACHMANN, R., BORN, B., ELSTNER, S. and GRIMME, C. (2019). Time-varying business volatility and the price setting of firms. *Journal of Monetary Economics*, **101**, 82–99.

BACHMANN, R., CARSTENSEN, K., LAUTENBACHER, S. and SCHNEIDER, M. (2021). *Uncertainty and Change: Survey Evidence of Firms' Subjective Beliefs*. National Bureau of Economic Research. Working Paper.

BACHMANN, R., ELSTNER, S. and HRISTOV, A. (2017). Surprise, surprise: Measuring firm-level investment innovations. *Journal of Economic Dynamics and Control*, **83**, 107–148.

BACHMANN, R. and MOSCARINI, G. (2011). Business cycles and endogenous uncertainty. In *2011 Meeting Papers*, Society for Economic Dynamics. Vol. 36, pp. 82–99.

BACHMANN, R., TOPA, G. and VAN DER KLAAUW, W. (2022). *Handbook of Economic Expectations*. Elsevier.

BAI, J., PHILIPPON, T. and SAVOV, A. (2016). Have financial markets become more informative? *Journal of Financial Economics*, **122** (3), 625–654.

BAKSHI, G. and SKOULAKIS, G. (2010). Do subjective expectations explain asset pricing puzzles? *Journal of Financial Economics*, **98** (3), 462–477.

BALEY, I. and BLANCO, A. (2019). Firm uncertainty cycles and the propagation of nominal shocks. *American Economic Journal: Macroeconomics*, **11** (1), 276–337.

BALEY, I., FIGUEIREDO, A., MANTOVANI, C. and SEPAHSALARI, A. (2024). Self-insurance in turbulent labor markets. Pompeu Fabra University. Working Paper.

BALEY, I., MANTOVANI, C. and ULBRICHT, R. (2022). Mismatch cycles. *Journal of Political Economy*, **130**, 2943–2984.

BALEY, I., LJUNGQVIST, L. and SARGENT, T. J. (2023). Cross-phenomenon restrictions: Unemployment effects of layoff costs and quit turbulence. *Review of Economic Dynamics*, **50**, 43–60.

BALEY, I., LJUNGQVIST, L. and SARGENT, T. J. (2024). Returns to labor mobility. *Economic Journal*, Forthcoming.

BALEY, I., and TURÉN, J. (2023). Lumpy forecasts. Pompeu Fabra University. Working Paper.

BALEY, I., VELDKAMP, L. and WAUGH, M. (2020). Can global uncertainty promote international trade? *Journal of International Economics*, **126**, 103347.

BALL, L., MANKIW, N. G. and REIS, R. (2005). Monetary policy for inattentive economies. *Journal of Monetary Economics*, **52** (4), 703–725.

BALL, L., and ROMER, D. (1990). Real rigidities and the non-neutrality of money. *Review of Economic Studies*, **57**, 183–203.

BALVERS, R. J. and COSIMANO, T. F. (1990). Actively learning about demand and the dynamics of price adjustment. *Economic Journal*, **100** (402), 882–898.

BARRO, R. J. (1972). A theory of monopolistic price adjustment. *Review of Economic Studies*, **39** (1), 17–26.

BARTOŠ, V., BAUER, M., CHYTILOVÁ, J. and MATĚJKA, F. (2016). Attention discrimination: Theory and field experiments with monitoring information acquisition. *American Economic Review*, **106** (6), 1437–1475.

BASLANDZE, S., GREENWOOD, J., MARTO, R. and MOREIRA, S. (2023). *The expansion of product varieties in the new age of advertising.* Economie d'Avant Garde, Working Paper.

BEGENAU, J., FARBOODI, M. and VELDKAMP, L. (2018). Big data in finance and the growth of large firms. *Journal of Monetary Economics,* **97**, 71–87.

BELDA, P. (2022). Capital gains taxation, learning and bubbles. Work in progress.

BELDA, P., HEINEKEN, J. and IFRIM, A. (2023). Heterogeneous expectations and stock market cycles. Preliminary version.

BENZELL, S. G. and BRYNJOLFSSON, E. (2019). *Digital abundance and scarce genius: Implications for wages, interest rates, and growth.* National Bureau of Economic Research. Working Paper 25585.

BERGEMANN, D. and BONATTI, A. (2019). Markets for information: An introduction. *Annual Review of Economics,* **11**, 85–107.

BERGEMANN, D., and BONATTI, A. (2022). *Data, Competition, and Digital Platforms.* MIT Sloan Research Paper 6588-21

BERGEMANN, D., and BONATTI, A. and GAN, T. (2022). The economics of social data. *RAND Journal of Economics,* **53** (2), 263–296.

BERGEMANN, D., and VALIMAKI, J. (2008). Bandit problems. In *The New Palgrave Dictionary of Economics,* ed. M. Vernengo, E. P. Caldentey, and B. J. Rosser Jr., 336–340. Palgrave Macmillan.

BERMAN, N., REBEYROL, V. and VICARD, V. (2019). Demand learning and firm dynamics: evidence from exporters. *Review of Economics and Statistics,* **101** (1), 91–106.

BERNARD, A. B., DHYNE, E., MAGERMAN, G., MANOVA, K. and MOXNES, A. (2022). The origins of firm heterogeneity: A production network approach. *Journal of Political Economy,* **130** (7).

BERNARDO, J. M. and SMITH, A. F. (2009). *Bayesian Theory.* Vol. 405 *of Wiley Series in Probability and Statistics.* John Wiley & Sons.

BERTOCCHI, G. and SPAGAT, M. (1998). Growth under uncertainty with experimentation. *Journal of Economic Dynamics and Control,* **23** (2), 209–231.

BERTOLI, S., MORAGA, J. F.-H. and GUICHARD, L. (2020). Rational inattention and migration decisions. *Journal of International Economics,* **126**, 103364.

BILLINGSLEY, P. (1995). *Probability and Measure.* John Wiley & Sons. 3rd ed.

BILS, M. (1989). Pricing in a customer market. *Quarterly Journal of Economics,* **104**, 699–718.

BLOOM, N. (2009). The impact of uncertainty shocks. *Econometrica,* **77** (3), 623–685.

BOERMA, J. and KARABARBOUNIS, L. (2021). *Reparations and Persistent Racial Wealth Gaps.* National Bureau of Economic Research. Working Paper 28468

BONOMO, M. and CARVALHO, C. (2004). Endogenous time-dependent rules and inflation inertia. *Journal of Money, Credit and Banking,* **36** (6), 1015–1041.

BONOMO, M. and CARVALHO, C., GARCIA, R., MALTA, V. and RIGATO, R. (2023). Persistent monetary non-neutrality in an estimated menu-cost model with partially costly information. *American Economic Journal: Macroeconomics,* **15** (2), 466–505.

BORNSTEIN, G. (2020). *Entry and Profits in an Aging Economy: The Role of Consumer Inertia.* Working Paper.

BOROVIČKA, J., HANSEN, L. P. and SCHEINKMAN, J. A. (2016). Misspecified recovery. *Journal of Finance,* **71** (6), 2493–2544.

BOROVIČKOVÁ, K. (2016). *Job Flows, Worker Flows and Labor Market Policies*. New York University. Working Paper.

BOTSCH, M. and VANASCO, V. (2019). Learning by lending. *Journal of Financial Intermediation*, 37, 1–14.

BOYARCHENKO, N., LUCCA, D. O. and VELDKAMP, L. (2021). Taking orders and taking notes: Dealer information sharing in treasury auctions. *Journal of Political Economy*, 129 (2), 607–645.

BRENNAN, M. and HUGHES, P. (1991). Stock prices and the supply of information. *Journal of Finance*, 46 (5), 1665–1691.

BRESNAHAN, T. F., BRYNJOLFSSON, E. and HITT, L. M. (2002). Information technology, workplace organization, and the demand for skilled labor: Firm-level evidence. *Quarterly Journal of Economics*, 117 (1), 339–376.

BRONNENBERG, B. J., DUBÉ, J.-P. H. and GENTZKOW, M. (2012). The evolution of brand preferences: Evidence from consumer migration. *American Economic Review*, 102 (6), 2472–2508.

BROWN, Z. Y. and JEON, J. (2019). *Endogenous Information Acquisition and Insurance Choice*. University of Michigan and Boston University. Working Paper.

BRUNNERMEIER, M. and PAYNE, J. (2022). *Platforms, tokens, and interoperability*. Princeton University. Working Paper.

BRYNJOLFSSON, E., COLLIS, A., LIAQAT, A., KUTZMAN, D., GARRO, H., DEISENROTH, D., WERNERFELT, N. and LEE, J. J. (2023). *The Digital Welfare of Nations: New Measures of Welfare Gains and Inequality*. National Bureau of Economic Research, Working Paper 31670.

BRYNJOLFSSON, E., KIM, S. T. and OH, J. H. (2023). The attention economy: Measuring the value of free goods on the internet. *Information Systems Research*.

BRYNJOLFSSON, E., and MCELHERAN, K. (2016). *Data in Action: Data-Driven Decision Making in US Manufacturing*. US Census Bureau Center for Economic Studies. Working Paper CES-16-06. Rotman School of Management. Working Paper 2722502.

BUERA, F. J., MONGE-NARANJO, A. and PRIMICERI, G. E. (2011). Learning the wealth of nations. *Econometrica*, 79 (1), 1–45.

BULLARD, J. and MITRA, K. (2002). Learning about monetary policy rules. *Journal of Monetary Economics*, 49 (6), 1105–1129.

BURDETT, K. and COLES, M. G. (1997). Steady state price distributions in a noisy search equilibrium. *Journal of Economic Theory*, 72 (1), 1–32.

BURDETT, K. and JUDD, K. L. (1983). Equilibrium price dispersion. *Econometrica: Journal of the Econometric Society*, 51 (4), 955–969.

BUTTERS, G. R. (1978). Equilibrium distributions of sales and advertising prices. In *Uncertainty in Economics*, ed. P. Diamond and M. Rothschild, 493–513, Elsevier.

CAGETTI, M., HANSEN, L., SARGENT, T. and WILLIAMS, N. (2002). Robustness and pricing with uncertain growth. *Review of Financial Studies*, 15 (2), 363–404.

CAINES, C. and WINKLER, F. (2021). Asset price beliefs and optimal monetary policy. *Journal of Monetary Economics*, 123, 53–67.

CALVO, G. (1983). Staggered prices in a utility maximizing framework. *Journal of Monetary Economics*, 12 (3), 383–398.

CAMPBELL, J. R. and EDEN, B. (2014). Rigid prices: Evidence from US scanner data. *International Economic Review*, **55** (2), 423–442.

CANDIAN, G. (2019). Information frictions and real exchange rate dynamics. *Journal of International Economics*, **116**, 189–205.

CANDIAN, G. (2021). Central bank transparency, exchange rates, and demand imbalances. *Journal of Monetary Economics*, **119**, 90–107.

CARROLL, C. D., CRAWLEY, E., SLACALEK, J., TOKUOKA, K. and WHITE, M. N. (2020). Sticky expectations and consumption dynamics. *American Economic Journal: Macroeconomics*, **12** (3), 40–76.

CATHLES, A., NAYYAR, G. and RÜCKERT, D. (2020). *Digital Technologies and Firm Performance: Evidence from Europe*. European Investment Bank. Working Paper 2020/06.

CAVENAILE, L., CELIK, M. A., PERLA, J. and ROLDAN-BLANCO, P. (2023). A theory of dynamic product awareness and targeted advertising. Working paper.

CHAHROUR, R., NIMARK, K. and PITSCHNER, S. (2021). Sectoral media focus and aggregate fluctuations. *American Economic Review*, **111** (12), 3872–3922.

CHAMLEY, C. (2004). *Rational Herds: Economics Models of Social Learning*. Cambridge University Press.

CHEN, C., SENGA, T., SUN, C. and ZHANG, H. (2023). Uncertainty, imperfect information, and expectation formation over the firm's life cycle. *Journal of Monetary Economics*, **140**, 60–77.

CHEN, D. (2022). *The Market for Attention*. Princeton University. Working Paper.

CHEREMUKHIN, A., RESTREPO-ECHAVARRIA, P. and TUTINO, A. (2020). Targeted search in matching markets. *Journal of Economic Theory*, **185**, 104956.

CHIAVARI, A. (2023). *The Macroeconomics of Rising Returns to Scale*. Working Paper.

CHRISTIANO, L. J., EICHENBAUM, M. and EVANS, C. L. (2005). Nominal rigidities and the dynamic effects of a shock to monetary policy. *Journal of Political Economy*, **113** (1), 1–45.

COGLEY, T. and SARGENT, T. J. (2005). The conquest of US inflation: Learning and robustness to model uncertainty. *Review of Economic Dynamics*, **8** (2), 528–563.

COHEN, L. and FRAZZINI, A. (2008). Economic links and predictable returns. *Journal of Finance*, **63** (4), 1977–2011.

COIBION, O., GEORGARAKOS, D., GORODNICHENKO, Y., KENNY, G. and WEBER, M. (2021). *The Effect of Macroeconomic Uncertainty on Household Spending*. National Bureau of Economic Research. Working Paper 28625.

COIBION, O. and GORODNICHENKO, Y. (2012). What can survey forecasts tell us about information rigidities? *Journal of Political Economy*, **120** (1), 116–159.

COIBION, O., and GORODNICHENKO, Y. and KUMAR, S. (2018). How do firms form their expectations? New survey evidence. *American Economic Review*, **108** (9), 2671–2713.

COIBION, O., and GORODNICHENKO, Y. and WEBER, M. (2019). *Monetary Policy Communications and their Effects on Household Inflation Expectations*. National Bureau of Economic Research. Working Paper 25482.

COLE, H. and OBSTFELD, M. (1991). Commodity trade and international risk sharing: How much do financial markets matter? *Journal of Monetary Economics*, **28**, 3–24.

COLE, H. L., NEUHANN, D. and ORDOÑEZ, G. (2022). *Information Spillovers and Sovereign Debt: Theory Meets the Eurozone Crisis*. National Bureau of Economic Research. Working Paper 30216.

COLLIN-DUFRESNE, P., JOHANNES, M. and LOCHSTOER, L. A. (2016). Parameter learning in general equilibrium: The asset pricing implications. *American Economic Review*, **106** (3), 664–98.

CONG, L. W. and MAYER, S. (2022). *Antitrust and User Union in the Era of Digital Platforms and Big Data*. Competition Policy International. Working Paper. Available at SSRN.

CONG, L. W., XIE, D. and ZHANG, L. (2021). Knowledge accumulation, privacy, and growth in a data economy. *Management Science*, **67** (10), 6480–6492.

CONLEY, T. G. and UDRY, C. R. (2010). Learning about a new technology: Pineapple in Ghana. *American Economic Review*, **100** (1), 35–69.

COVER, T. M. and THOMAS, J. A. (1991). Entropy, relative entropy and mutual information. *Elements of Information Theory*, **2** (1), 12–13.

CRÉMER, J., CRAWFORD, G. S., DINIELLI, D., FLETCHER, A., HEIDHUES, P., SCHNITZER, M., SCOTT MORTON, F. M. and SEIM, K. (2021). *Fairness and Contestability in the digital Markets Act*. Working Paper. Available at SSRN.

DASGUPTA, K. and MONDRIA, J. (2018). Inattentive importers. *Journal of International Economics*, **112**, 150–165.

DAVID, J. M., HOPENHAYN, H. A. and VENKATESWARAN, V. (2016). Information, misallocation, and aggregate productivity. *Quarterly Journal of Economics*, **131** (2), 943–1005.

DHYNE, E., ALVAREZ, L. J., LE BIHAN, H., VERONESE, G., DIAS, D., HOFFMANN, J., JONKER, N., LUNNEMANN, P., RUMLER, F. and VILMUNEN, J. (2006). Price changes in the Euro area and the United States: Some facts from individual consumer price data. *Journal of Economic Perspectives*, **20** (2), 171–192.

DIAMOND, D. W. and VERRECCHIA, R. E. (1981). Information aggregation in a noisy rational expectations economy. *Journal of Financial Economics*, **9** (3), 221–235.

DINLERSOZ, E. M. and YORUKOGLU, M. (2012). Information and industry dynamics. *American Economic Review*, **102** (2), 884–913.

DIXIT, A. (1991). Analytical approximations in models of hysteresis. *Review of Economic Studies*, **58** (1), 141–151.

DOPPELT, R. (2016). *The Hazards of Unemployment*. Working Paper.

DRENIK, A. and PEREZ, D. J. (2020). Price setting under uncertainty about inflation. *Journal of Monetary Economics*, **116**, 23–38.

DROZD, L. A. and NOSAL, J. B. (2012). Understanding international prices: Customers as capital. *American Economic Review*, **102** (1), 364–395.

DUFFIE, D., MALAMUD, S. and MANSO, G. (2009). Information percolation with equilibrium search dynamics. *Econometrica*, **77**, 1513–1574.

DURNEV, A., MORCK, R., YEUNG, B. and ZAROWIN, P. (2003). Does greater firm-specific return variation mean more or less informed stock pricing? *Journal of Accounting Research*, **41** (5), 797–836.

DZIUDA, W. and MONDRIA, J. (2012). Asymmetric information, portfolio managers, and home bias. *Review of Financial Studies*, **25** (7), 2109–2154.

EASTERLY, W. (2002). *The Elusive Quest for Growth: Economists' Adventures and Misadventures in the Tropics*. MIT Press.

ECKERT, F., GANAPATI, S. and WALSH, C. (2022). *Urban-Biased Growth: A Macroeconomic Analysis*. National Bureau of Economic Research. Working Paper 30515.

ECKWERT, B. and ZILCHA, I. (2003). Incomplete risk sharing arrangements and the value of information. *Economic Theory*, **21**, 43–58.

EDERER, F. and PELLEGRINO, B. (2022). *A Tale of Two Networks: Common Ownership and Product Market Rivalry*. National Bureau of Economic Research. Working Paper 30004.

EECKHOUT, J. and SEPAHSALARI, A. (2023). The effect of asset holdings on worker productivity. *Review of Economic Studies*, **24**, 872–906.

EECKHOUT, J. and VELDKAMP, L. (2022). *Data and Market Power*. CEPR. Discussion Paper.

EINAV, L., KLENOW, P. J., LEVIN, J. D. and MURCIANO-GOROFF, R. (2021). *Customers and Retail Growth*. National Bureau of Economic Research. Working Paper 29561.

ELLIOTT, R., AGGOUN, L. and MOORE, J. (1995). *Hidden Markov Models: Estimation and Control*. Springer.

EPSTEIN, L. and ZIN, S. (1989). Substitution, risk aversion, and the temporal behavior of consumption and asset returns: A theoretical framework. *Econometrica*, **57**, 937–969.

EUSEPI, S. and PRESTON, B. (2011). Expectations, learning, and business cycle fluctuations. *American Economic Review*, **101** (6), 2844–2872.

EVANS, G. W. and HONKAPOHJA, S. (1996). Least squares learning with heterogeneous expectations. *Economics Letters*, **53** (2), 197–201.

EVANS, G. W. and HONKAPOHJA, S. (2001). *Learning and Expectations in Macroeconomics*. Princeton University Press.

EVANS, G. W., HONKAPOHJA, S. SARGENT, T. J. and WILLIAMS, N. (2013). Bayesian model averaging, learning and model selection. *Macroeconomics at the Service of Public Policy*, **6**, 99–119.

FAJGELBAUM, P. D., SCHAAL, E. and TASCHEREAU-DUMOUCHEL, M. (2017). Uncertainty traps. *Quarterly Journal of Economics*, **132** (4), 1641–1692.

FANG, L. and PERESS, J. (2009). Media coverage and the cross-section of stock returns. *Journal of Finance*, **64** (5), 2023–2052.

FARBER, H. S. and GIBBONS, R. (1996). Learning and wage dynamics. *Quarterly Journal of Economics*, **111** (4), 1007–1047.

FARBOODI, M., MATRAY, A., VELDKAMP, L. and VENKATESWARAN, V. (2022a). Where has all the data gone? *Review of Financial Studies*, **35** (7), 3101–3138.

FARBOODI, M., SINGAL, D., VELDKAMP, L. and VENKATESWARAN, V. (2022b). *Valuing Financial Data*. National Bureau of Economic Research. Working Paper 29894.

FARBOODI, M. and VELDKAMP, L. (2020). Long-run growth of financial data technology. *American Economic Review*, **110** (8), 2485–2523.

FARBOODI, M. and VELDKAMP, L. (2021). *A Growth Model of the Data Economy*. National Bureau of Economic Research. Working Paper 28427.

FERNANDES, A. P. and TANG, H. (2014). Learning to export from neighbors. *Jornal of International Economics*, **94** (1), 67–84.

FIGUEIREDO, A. (2020). *Information Frictions in Education and Inequality*. Working Paper.

FISHMAN, A. and ROB, R. (2003). Consumer inertia, firm growth and industry dynamics. *Journal of Economic Theory*, **109** (1), 24–38.

FITZGERALD, D., HALLER, S. and YEDID-LEVI, Y. (2016). *How Exporters Grow*. National Bureau of Economic Research. Working Paper 21935.

FLETCHER, A., CRAWFORD, G. S., CRÉMER, J., DINIELLI, D., HEIDHUES, P., LUCA, M., SALZ, T., SCHNITZER, M., MORTON, F. M. S., SEIM, K., et al. (2023). Consumer protection for online markets and large digital platforms. *Yale Journal on Regulation*, **40** (3), 875–914.

FOGLI, A. and VELDKAMP, L. (2011). Nature or nurture? Learning and the geography of female labor force participation. *Econometrica*, **79** (4), 1103–1138.

FOSTER, L., HALTIWANGER, J. and SYVERSON, C. (2008). Reallocation, firm turnover, and efficiency: Selection on productivity or profitability? *American Economic Review*, **98** (1), 394–425.

FRANK, M. R., AUTOR, D., BESSEN, J. E., BRYNJOLFSSON, E., CEBRIAN, M., DEMING, D. J., FELDMAN, M., GROH, M., LOBO, J., MORO, E., et al. (2019). Toward understanding the impact of artificial intelligence on labor. *Proceedings of the National Academy of Sciences*, **116** (14), 6531–6539.

FUSTER, A., PEREZ-TRUGLIA, R., WIEDERHOLT, M. and ZAFAR, B. (2022). Expectations with endogenous information acquisition: an experimental investigation. *Review of Economics and Statistics*, **404** (5), 1059—1078.

GABAIX, X. and LAIBSON, D. (2001). The 6D bias and the equity-premium puzzle. *NBER macroeconomics annual*, **16**, 257–312.

GABALLO, G. and ORDOÑEZ, G. (2023). Information technologies and safe assets. Working Paper.

GALDON-SANCHEZ, J. E., GIL, R. and URIZ UHARTE, G. (2022). *The Value of Information in Competitive Markets: The Impact of Big Data on Small and Medium Enterprises*. Working Paper. Available at SSRN 4022675.

GALENIANOS, M. (2013). Learning about match quality and the use of referrals. *Review of Economic Dynamics*, **16** (4), 668–690.

GALPERTI, S. and PEREGO, J. (2023). Privacy and the value of data. *AEA Papers and Proceedings*, **113**, 197–203.

GAMBACORTA, L., GAMBACORTA, R. and MIHET, R. (2023). FinTech, Investor Sophistication, and Financial Portfolio Choices. *Review of Corporate Finance Studies*, **12** (4), 834–866.

GAN, J. and RIDDIOUGH, T. J. (2008). Monopoly and information advantage in the residential mortgage market. *Review of Financial Studies*, **21** (6), 2677–2703.

GERTLER, M. and LEAHY, J. (2008). A Phillips curve with an Ss foundation. *Journal of Political Economy*, **116** (3), 533–572.

GHOFRANI, E. (2021). *Learning with Uncertainty's Uncertainty*. Pompeu Fabra University. Working Paper.

GIACOMINI, R., SKRETA, V. and TURÉN, J. (2020). Heterogeneity, inattention, and Bayesian updates. *American Economic Journal: Macroeconomics*, **12** (1), 282–309.

GICZY, A., PAIROLERO, N. and TOOLE, A. (2021). Identifying artificial intelligence (AI) invention: A novel AI patent dataset. *Journal of Technology Transfer*, **47**, 476–505.

GILCHRIST, S., SCHOENLE, R., SIM, J. and ZAKRAJŠEK, E. (2017). Inflation dynamics during the financial crisis. *American Economic Review*, **107** (3), 785–823.

GOLDFARB, A. and QUE, V. F. (2023). The economics of digital privacy. *Annual Review of Economics*, **15**, 267–286.

GOLDFARB, A. and TUCKER, C. (2019a). Digital economics. *Journal of Economic Literature*, **57** (1), 3–43.

GOLDFARB, A. and TUCKER, C. (2019b). Digital marketing. In *Marketing and Economics*, ed. J.-P. Dubé and P. E. Rossi, 259–290. Vol. 1 of *Handbook of the Economics of Marketing*, Elsevier.

GOLDSTEIN, I., YANG, S. and ZUO, L. (2020). *The Real Effects of Modern Information Technologies: Evidence from the EDGAR Implementation*. National Bureau of Economic Research. Working Papers 27529.

GOLOSOV, M., LORENZONI, G. and TSYVINSKI, A. (2014). Decentralized trading with private information. *Econometrica*, **82** (3), 1055–1091.

GOLOSOV, M., and LUCAS, R. E. (2007). Menu costs and Phillips curves. *Journal of Political Economy*, **115** (2), 171–199.

GOMES, O., MIHET, R. and RISHABH, K. (2023). *Cyber Risk-Driven Innovation in the Modern Data Economy*. Swiss Finance Institute. Research Paper 23–86.

GONZALEZ, F. M. and SHI, S. (2010). An equilibrium theory of learning, search, and wages. *Econometrica*, **78** (2), 509–537.

GORODNICHENKO, Y. (2008). *Endogenous Information, Menu Costs and Inflation Persistence*. National Bureau of Economic Research. Working Paper 14184.

GOSSELIN, P., LOTZ, A. and WYPLOSZ, C. (2008). When central banks reveal their interest rate forecasts: Alignment of expectations vs. creative opacity. *International Journal of Central Banking*, **4** (3), 145–185.

GOURIO, F. and RUDANKO, L. (2014). Customer capital. *Review of Economic Studies*, **81** (3), 1102–1136.

GOYAL, S. (2011). Learning in networks. In *Handbook of Social Economics*, ed. J. Benhabib, A. Bisin, and M. O. Jackson, 679–727. Elsevier.

GRAHAM, J. (1999). Herding among investment newsletters: Theory and evidence. *Journal of Finance*, **54**, 1.

GREENE, W. H. (2003). *Econometric Analysis*. 5th ed. Pearson Education.

GREENWOOD, J., MA, Y. and YORUKOGLU, M. (2021). *"You Will": A Macroeconomic Analysis of Digital Advertising*. National Bureau of Economic Research. Working Paper 28537.

GROES, F., KIRCHER, P. and MANOVSKII, I. (2014). The U-shapes of occupational mobility. *Review of Economic Studies*, **82** (2), 659–692.

GROSSMAN, S. and STIGLITZ, J. (1980). On the impossibility of informationally efficient markets. *American Economic Review*, **70** (3), 393–408.

GUESNERIE, R. (2011). Expectational coordination failures and market outcomes' volatility. Working Paper.

GUTIÉRREZ-DAZA, A. (2022). *Inattentive Inflation Expectations*. Pompeu Fabra University. Working Paper.

HADDAD, V., HUEBNER, P. and LOUALICHE, E. (2021). *How Competitive Is the Stock Market? Theory, Evidence from Portfolios, and Implications for the Rise of Passive Investing*. University of California, Los Angeles. Working Paper.

HALL, R. E. (2008). *General Equilibrium with Customer Relationships: A Dynamic Analysis of Rent-Seeking*. Working Paper.

HAMEED, A., MORCK, R. and YEUNG, B. (2010). *Information Markets, Analysts and Comovement in Stock Returns*. Alberta School of Business. Working Paper.

HAMILTON, J. D. (2010). Regime switching models. In *Macroeconometrics and Time Series Analysis*, ed. S. N. Durlauf and L. E. Blume, 202–209. Palgrave Macmillan.

HASSAN, T. A. and MERTENS, T. M. (2017). The social cost of near-rational investment. *American Economic Review*, **107** (4), 1059–1103.

HÉBERT, B. and LA'O, J. (2023). Information acquisition, efficiency, and non-fundamental volatility. *Journal of Political Economy*, **131** (10).

HÉBERT, B. and WOODFORD, M. (2021). Neighborhood-based information costs. *American Economic Review*, **111** (10), 3225–3255.

HELLWIG, C. (2005). *Heterogeneous Information and the Benefits of Public Information Disclosures*. Working Paper.

HELLWIG, C., KOHLS, S. and VELDKAMP, L. (2012). Information choice technologies. *American Economic Review*, **102** (3), 35–40.

HELLWIG, C. and VELDKAMP, L. (2009). Knowing what others know: Coordination motives in information acquisition. *Review of Economic Studies*, **76**, 223–251.

HELLWIG, C. and VENKATESWARAN, V. (2009). Setting the right prices for the wrong reasons. *Journal of Monetary Economics*, **56**, S57–S77.

HERSKOVIC, B. and RAMOS, J. (2020). Acquiring information through peers. *American Economic Review*, **110** (7), 2128–2152.

HIRSHLEIFER, J. (1971). The private and social value of information and the reward to inventive activity. *American Economic Review*, **61** (4), 561–574.

HONG, H., STEIN, J. and YU, J. (2007). Simple forecasts and paradigm shifts. *Journal of Finance*, **62** (3), 1207–1242.

HONG, H., TOROUS, W. and VALKANOV, R. (2007). Do industries lead stock markets? *Journal of Financial Economics*, **83** (2), 367–396.

ICHIHASHI, S. (2020). Dynamic privacy choices. In *Proceedings of the 21st ACM Conference on Economics and Computation*, pp. 539–540.

JAMES, G., WITTEN, D., HASTIE, T., TIBSHIRANI, R. and TAYLOR, J. (2023). Statistical learning. In *An Introduction to Statistical Learning: with Applications in Python*, 15–67. Springer.

JAMILOV, R., REY, H. and TAHOUN, A. (2021). *The Anatomy of Cyber Risk*. National Bureau of Economic Research. Working Paper 28906.

JONES, C. I. and TONETTI, C. (2020). Nonrivalry and the economics of data. *American Economic Review*, **110** (9), 2819–2858.

JOVANOVIC, B. (1979). Job matching and the theory of turnover. *Journal of Political Economy*, **87** (5), 972–990.

JOVANOVIC, B. (1984). Matching, turnover, and unemployment. *Journal of Political Economy*, **92** (1), 108–122.

JOVANOVIC, B. and NYARKO, Y. (1996). Learning by doing and the choice of technology. *Econometrica*, **64**, 1299–1310.

JUDD, K. L. (2023). *Numerical Methods in Economics*. MIT Press.

JURADO, K. (2023). Rational inattention in the frequency domain. *Journal of Economic Theory*, **208**, 105604.

KACPERCZYK, M., NOSAL, J. and STEVENS, L. (2019). Investor sophistication and capital income inequality. *Journal of Monetary Economics*, **107**, 18–31.

KACPERCZYK, M., NOSAL, J. and SUNDARESAN, S. (2023). *Market Power and Price Informativeness*. Working Paper. Available at SSRN 3230005.

KACPERCZYK, M. and SERU, A. (2007). Fund manager use of public information: New evidence on managerial skills. *Journal of Finance*, **62** (2), 485–528.

KACPERCZYK, M., VAN NIEUWERBURGH, S. and VELDKAMP, L. (2016). A rational theory of mutual funds' attention allocation. *Econometrica*, **84** (2), 571–626.

KANIEL, R., STARKS, L. and VASUDEVAN, V. (2007). *Headlines and Bottom Lines: Attention and Learning Effects From Media Coverage of Mutual Funds*. Working Paper.

KAPLAN, G. and MENZIO, G. (2015). The morphology of price dispersion. *International Economic Review*, **56** (4), 1165–1206.

KARATZAS, I. and SHREVE, S. (1991). *Brownian Motion and Stochastic Calculus*. 2nd ed. Springer.

KEHOE, P. J., LARSEN, B. J. and PASTORINO, E. (2022). *Dynamic Competition in the Era of Big Data*. Stanford University. Working Paper.

KELLER, G. and RADY, S. (1999). Optimal experimentation in a changing environment. *Review of Economic Studies*, **66** (3), 475–507.

KELLOGG, R. (2011). Learning by drilling: Interfirm learning and relationship persistence in the Texas oilpatch. *Quarterly Journal of Economics*, **126** (4), 1961–2004.

KELLY, D. L. and KOLSTAD, C. D. (1999). Bayesian learning, growth, and pollution. *Journal of Economic Dynamics and Control*, **23** (4), 491–518.

KHAW, M. W., STEVENS, L. and WOODFORD, M. (2017). Discrete adjustment to a changing environment: Experimental evidence. *Journal of Monetary Economics*, **91**, 88–103.

KIRPALANI, R. and PHILIPPON, T. (2020). *Data Sharing and Market Power with Two-Sided Platforms*. National Bureau of Economic Research. Working Paper 28023.

KLEMPERER, P. (1987). Markets with consumer switching costs. *Quarterly Journal of Economics*, **102**.

KLEMPERER, P. (1995). Competition when consumers have switching costs: An overview with applications to industrial organization, macroeconomics, and international trade. *Review of Economic Studies*, **62** (4), 515–539.

KLENOW, P. J. and WILLIS, J. L. (2007). Sticky information and sticky prices. *Journal of Monetary Economics*, **54**, 79–99.

KLESHCHELSKI, I. and VINCENT, N. (2009). Market share and price rigidity. *Journal of Monetary Economics*, **56** (3), 344–352.

KOGAN, L., PAPANIKOLAOU, D., SERU, A. and STOFFMAN, N. (2017). Technological innovation, resource allocation, and growth. *Quarterly Journal of Economics*, **132** (2), 665–712.

KOIJEN, R. S. and YOGO, M. (2019). A demand system approach to asset pricing. *Journal of Political Economy*, **127** (4), 1475–1515.

KOLANOVIC, M. and KRISHNAMACHARI, R. T. (2017). Big data and AI strategies: Machine learning and alternative data approach to investing. *JP Morgan Global Quantitative & Derivatives Strategy Report*.

KORINEK, A. and STIGLITZ, J. (2021). *Artificial Intelligence, Globalization, and Strategies for Economic Development*. National Bureau of Economic Research. Working Papers 28453.

KŐSZEGI, B. and MATĚJKA, F. (2020). Choice simplification: A theory of mental budgeting and naive diversification. *Quarterly Journal of Economics*, **135** (2), 1153–1207.

KOZENIAUSKAS, N. and LYON, S. (2023). Demand learning, customer capital, and exporter dynamics. Working Paper.

KOZENIAUSKAS, N., ORLIK, A. and VELDKAMP, L. (2018). What are uncertainty shocks? *Journal of Monetary Economics*, **100**, 1–15.

KOZLOWSKI, J., VELDKAMP, L. and VENKATESWARAN, V. (2020). The tail that wags the economy: Beliefs and persistent stagnation. *Journal of Political Economy*, **128** (8), 2839–2879.

KUCHLER, T. and STROEBEL, J. (2021). Social Finance. *Annual Review of Financial Economics*, **13** (1), 37–55.

KYLE, A. S. (1989). Informed speculation with imperfect competition. *Review of Economic Studies*, **56** (3), 317–355.

LAMBRECHT, A., GOLDFARB, A., BONATTI, A., GHOSE, A., GOLDSTEIN, D. G., LEWIS, R., RAO, A., SAHNI, N. and YAO, S. (2014). How do firms make money selling digital goods online? *Marketing Letters*, **25** (3), 331–341.

LAMBRECHT, A. and TUCKER, C. E. (2015). *Can Big Data Protect a Firm from Competition?* Working Paper. Available at SSRN 2705530.

LASRY, J.-M. and LIONS, P.-L. (2007). Mean field games. *Japanese Journal of Mathematics*, **2** (1), 229–260.

LENOIR, C., MARTIN, J. and MEJEAN, I. (2023). Search frictions in international goods markets. *Journal of the European Economic Association*, **21** (1), 326–366.

LIPSTER, R. and SHIRYAEV, A. (2001). *Statistics of Random Processes II*. 2nd ed. Springer.

LIU, J., SOCKIN, M. and XIONG, W. (2021). *Data Privacy and Consumer Vulnerability*. Princeton University. Working Paper.

LJUNGQVIST, L. and SARGENT, T. J. (1998). The European unemployment dilemma. *Journal of Political Economy*, **106** (3), 514–550.

LJUNGQVIST, L. and SARGENT, T. J. (2007). Understanding European unemployment with matching and search-island models. *Journal of Monetary Economics*, **54** (8), 2139–2179.

LJUNGQVIST, L. and SARGENT, T. J. (2018). *Recursive Macroeconomic Theory*. MIT Press.

LÓPEZ-MOCTEZUMA, G. (2023). *Sequential Deliberation in Collective Decision-Making: The case of the FOMC*. Tech. rep., Caltech Working Paper.

LÓPEZ-MOCTEZUMA, G. and JOHNSON, B. (2023). *Social Learning behind Closed Doors: Evidence from Seniority Voting in the US Supreme Court*. California Institute of Technology. Working Paper.

LORENZONI, G. (2009). A theory of demand shocks. *American Economic Review*, **99** (5), 2050–2084.

LUCAS, R. (1988). On the mechanics of economic development. *Journal of Monetary Economics*, **22**, 3–42.

LUCAS, R. E. (1972). Expectations and the neutrality of money. *Journal of Economic Theory*, **4** (2), 103–124.

LUCAS, R. E. (1973). Some international evidence on output-inflation tradeoffs. *American Economic Review*, **63** (3), 326–334.

LUCAS, R. E. (1978). Asset prices in an exchange economy. *Econometrica: Journal of the Econometric Society*, **46** (6), 1429–1445.

LUENBERGER, D. G. (1997). *Optimization by Vector Space Methods*. John Wiley & Sons.

LUO, Y. (2008). Consumption dynamics under information processing constraints. *Review of Economic Dynamics*, **11** (2), 366–385.

Luo, Y., Nie, J. and Young, E. R. (2015). Slow information diffusion and the inertial behavior of durable consumption. *Journal of the European Economic Association*, **13** (5), 805–840.

Luttmer, E. G. (2006). *Consumer Search and Firm Growth*. Federal Reserve Bank of Minneapolis. Working Paper.

Maćkowiak, B., Matějka, F. and Wiederholt, M. (2018). Dynamic rational inattention: Analytical results. *Journal of Economic Theory*, **176**, 650–692.

Maćkowiak, B., Matějka, F. and Wiederholt, M. (2023). Rational inattention: A review. *Journal of Economic Literature*, **61** (1), 226–273.

Maćkowiak, B. and Wiederholt, M. (2009). Optimal sticky prices under rational inattention. *American Economic Review*, **99** (3), 769–803.

Maćkowiak, B. and Wiederholt, M. (2015). Business cycle dynamics under rational inattention. *Review of Economic Studies*, **82** (4), 1502–1532.

Maćkowiak, B. and Wiederholt, M. (2023). Rational inattention and the business cycle effects of productivity and news shocks. Working Paper.

Mamon, R. S. and Elliott, R. J. (2007). *Hidden Markov Models in Finance*. Springer.

Mankiw, G. and Reis, R. (2002). Sticky information versus sticky prices: A proposal to replace the New Keynesian Phillips curve. *Quarterly Journal of Economics*, **117**, 1295–1328.

Marcet, A. and Sargent, T. J. (1989). Convergence of least squares learning mechanisms in self-referential linear stochastic models. *Journal of Economic theory*, **48** (2), ' 337–368.

Matějka, F. and McKay, A. (2012). Simple market equilibria with rationally inattentive consumers. *American Economic Review*, **102** (3), 24–29.

Matějka, F. and Tabellini, G. (2021). Electoral competition with rationally inattentive voters. *Journal of the European Economic Association*, **19** (3), 1899–1935.

Matz, S. C., Kosinski, M., Nave, G. and Stillwell, D. J. (2017). Psychological targeting as an effective approach to digital mass persuasion. *Proceedings of the National Academy of Sciences*, **114** (48), 12714–12719.

Medrano, L. and Vives, X. (2004). Regulating insider trading when investment matters. *Review of Finance*, **8**, 199–277.

Melcangi, D. and Turen, J. (2023). Subsidizing startups under imperfect information. *Journal of Monetary Economics*, **139**, 93–109.

Menzio, G. (2023). Optimal product design: Implications for competition and growth under declining search frictions. *Econometrica*, **91** (2), 605–639.

Menzio, G. and Shi, S. (2011). Efficient search on the job and the business cycle. *Journal of Political Economy*, **119** (3), 468–510.

Miao, J., Wu, J. and Young, E. (2019). *Multivariate Rational Inattention*. Boston University. Working Paper 2019-07.

Midrigan, V. (2011). Menu cost, multiproduct firms, and aggregate fluctuations. *Econometrica*, **79** (4), 1139–1180.

Mihet, R. (2021). *Financial Technology and the Inequality Gap*. Swiss Finance Institute. Research Paper Series 21-04.

Miller, R. A. (1984). Job matching and occupational choice. *Journal of Political Economy*, **92** (6), 1086–1120.

MINNITI, M. and BYGRAVE, W. (2001). A dynamic model of entrepreneurial learning. *Entrepreneurship Theory and Practice*, **25** (3), 5–16.

MIRMAN, L. J., SAMUELSON, L. and URBANO, A. (1993). Monopoly experimentation. *International Economic Review*, **34** (3), 549–563.

MITCHELL, T. and BRYNJOLFSSON, E. (2017). Track how technology is transforming work. *Nature*, **544** (7650), 290–292.

MITRA, K., EVANS, G. W. and HONKAPOHJA, S. (2013). Policy change and learning in the RBC model. *Journal of Economic Dynamics and Control*, **37** (10), 1947–1971.

MITRA, K., EVANS, G. W. and HONKAPOHJA, S. (2019). Fiscal policy multipliers in an RBC model with learning. *Macroeconomic Dynamics*, **23** (1), 240–283.

MONDRIA, J. (2010). Portfolio choice, attention allocation, and price comovement. *Journal of Economic Theory*, **145** (5), 1837–1864.

MORLACCO, M. and ZEKE, D. (2021). Monetary policy, customer capital, and market power. *Journal of Monetary Economics*, **121**.

MORRIS, S. and SHIN, H. (1998). Unique equilibrium in a model of self-fulfilling currency attacks. *American Economic Review*, **88** (3), 587–597.

MORRIS, S. and SHIN, H. S. (2002). Social value of public information. *American Economic Review*, **92** (5), 1521–1534.

MORTON, F. M. S. and DINIELLI, D. C. (2020). *Roadmap for a Digital Advertising Monopolization Case Against Google*. Omidyar Network. Working Paper.

MOSCARINI, G. (2001). Excess worker reallocation. *Review of Economic Studies*, **68** (3), 593–612.

MUTH, J. F. (1961). Rational expectations and the theory of price movements. *Econometrica*, **29** (3), 315–335.

MYATT, D. P. and WALLACE, C. (2012). Endogenous information acquisition in coordination games. *Review of Economic Studies*, **79** (1), 340–374.

NAGYPÁL, É. (2007). Learning by doing vs. learning about match quality: Can we tell them apart? *Review of Economic Studies*, **74** (2), 537–566.

NAKAMURA, E. and STEINSSON, J. (2008). Five facts about prices: a reevaluation of menu cost models. *Quarterly Journal of Economics*, **123** (4), 1415–1464.

NAKAMURA, E. and STEINSSON, J. (2011). Price setting in forward-looking customer markets. *Journal of Monetary Economics*, **58** (3), 220–233.

NEAL, D. (1999). The complexity of job mobility among young men. *Journal of Labor Economics*, **17** (2), 237–261.

NERLOVE, M. (1958). Adaptive expectations and cobweb phenomena. *Quarterly Journal of Economics*, **72** (2), 227–240.

NIMARK, K. P. (2014). Man-bites-dog business cycles. *American Economic Review*, **104** (8), 2320–2367.

NIMARK, K. P. and PITSCHNER, S. (2019). News media and delegated information choice. *Journal of Economic Theory*, **181**, 160–196.

ØKSENDAL, B. (2007). *Stochastic Differential Equations*. 6th ed. Springer.

ØKSENDAL, B. K. and SULEM, A. (2010). *Applied Stochastic Control of Jump Diffusions*. Springer.

ORDOÑEZ, G. (2013). The asymmetric effects of financial frictions. *Journal of Political Economy*, **121** (5), 844–895.

ORLIK, A. and VELDKAMP, L. (2014). *Understanding uncertainty shocks and the role of black swans*. National Bureau of Economic Research. Working Paper 20445.

PACIELLO, L., POZZI, A. and TRACHTER, N. (2019). Price dynamics with customer market. *International Economic Review*, **60** (1), 413–446.

PACIELLO, L., and WIEDERHOLT, M. (2014). Exogenous information, endogenous information, and optimal monetary policy. *Review of Economic Studies*, **81** (1), 356–388.

PAPAGEORGIOU, T. (2014). Learning your comparative advantages. *Review of Economic Studies*, **81** (3), 1263–1295.

PÁSTOR, L., TAYLOR, L. A. and VERONESI, P. (2009). Entrepreneurial learning, the IPO decision, and the post-IPO drop in firm profitability. *Review of Financial Studies*, **22** (8), 3005–3046.

PÁSTOR, L. and VERONESI, P. (2012). Uncertainty about government policy and stock prices. *Journal of Finance*, **67** (4), 1219–1264.

PASTORINO, E. (2023). Careers in firms: The role of learning about ability and human capital acquisition. *Journal of Political Economy*. Forthcoming.

PELLEGRINO, B. (2023). *Product Differentiation and Oligopoly: A Network Approach*. CESifo. Working Paper.

PERESS, J. (2004). Wealth, information acquisition, and portfolio choice. *Review of Financial Studies*, **17** (3), 879–914.

PHELPS, E. S. (1970). Introduction: The new microeconomics in employment and inflation theory. In *Microeconomic Foundations of Employment and Inflation Theory*, 1–23. W. W. Norton.

PHELPS, E. S. and WINTER, S. G. (1970). Optimal price policy under atomistic competition. In *Microeconomic Foundations of Employment and Inflation Theory*, 309–337. W. W. Norton.

PORCHER, C. (2020). *Migration with Costly Information*. Princeton University. Working Paper.

PRAT, A. and VALLETTI, T. M. (2022). Attention oligopoly. *American Economic Journal: Microeconomics*, **14** (3), 530–557.

PRESCOTT, E. C. (1972). The multi-period control problem under uncertainty. *Econometrica*, **40** (6), 1043–1058.

PRIES, M. and ROGERSON, R. (2005). Hiring policies, labor market institutions, and labor market flows. *Journal of Political Economy*, **113** (4), 811–839.

PRIMICERI, G. E. (2006). Why inflation rose and fell: Policy-makers' beliefs and US postwar stabilization policy. *Quarterly Journal of Economics*, **121** (3), 867–901.

QUAN, J. (2023). *Tracing Out International Data Flow: The Value of Data and Privacy*. Working Paper. Available at SSRN 4185169.

RÁBANO, A., RÜCKERT, D. and WEISS, C. (2023). *Firms and Big Data*. European Investment Bank. Working Paper.

RACHEL, L. (2021). Leisure-enhancing technological change. London School of Economics. Working Paper.

RADNER, R. and VAN ZANDT, T. (1995). Information processing in firms and returns to scale. In *The Economics of Informational Decentralization: Complexity, Efficiency, and Stability*, ed. J. O. Ledyard, 243–280. Springer.

RADNER, R. and VAN ZANDT, T. (2001). Real-time decentralized information processing and returns to scale. *Economic Theory*, **17**, 497–544.

RAVN, M., SCHMITT-GROHÉ, S. and URIBE, M. (2006). Deep habits. *Review of Economic Studies*, **73** (1), 195–218.

REIS, R. (2006a). Inattentive consumers. *Journal of Monetary Economics*, **53** (8), 1761–1800.

REIS, R. (2006b). Inattentive producers. *Review of Economic Studies*, **73** (3), 793–821.

ROCA, M. M. (2010). *Transparency and Monetary Policy with Imperfect Common Knowledge*. International Monetary Fund. Working Paper.

ROCHET, J.-C. and TIROLE, J. (2003). Platform competition in two-sided markets. *Journal of the European Economic Association*, **1** (4), 990–1029.

ROCHET, J.-C. and TIROLE, J. (2006). Two-sided markets: A progress report. *RAND Journal of Economics*, **37** (3), 645–667.

ROLDAN-BLANCO, P. and GILBUKH, S. (2021). Firm dynamics and pricing under customer capital accumulation. *Journal of Monetary Economics*, **118**, 99–119.

ROMER, P. (1990). Endogenous technological change. *Journal of Political Economy*, **98**, 71–102.

ROSEN, S. (1981). The economics of superstars. *American Economic Review*, **71** (5), 845–858.

ROSENQUIST, J. N., MORTON, F. M. S. and WEINSTEIN, S. N. (2021). Addictive technology and its implications for antitrust enforcement. *North Carolina Law Review*, **100** (2), 431.

ROSS, S. (1976). The arbitrage theory of capital asset pricing. *Journal of Economic Theory*, **13**, 341–360.

ROTEMBERG, J. J. and WOODFORD, M. (1991). Markups and the business cycle. *NBER Macroeconomics Annual*, **6**, 63–129.

ROTHSCHILD, M. (1974). A two-armed bandit theory of market pricing. *Journal of Economic Theory*, **9** (2), 185–202.

RUDANKO, L. (2022). Price Setting with Customer Capital: Uniform Pricing, Sales and Rigidity. Federal Reserve Bank of Philadelphia. Working Paper 22–31.

SARGENT, T., WILLIAMS, N. and ZHA, T. (2006). Shocks and government beliefs: The rise and fall of American inflation. *American Economic Review*, **96** (4), 1193–1224.

SENGA, T. (2018). *A New Look at Uncertainty Shocks: Imperfect Information and Misallocation*. Queen Mary University of London. Working Paper 763.

SHANNON, C. E. (1948). Mathematical theory of communication. *Bell System Technology Journal*, **27**, 379–423 and 623–656.

SHEN, S. (2023). *Customer Acquisition, Rising Concentration, and US Productivity Dynamics*. Working Paper.

SHIMER, R. (2005). The cyclical behavior of equilibrium unemployment and vacancies. *American Economic Review*, **95** (1), 25–49.

SIMS, C. (2003). Implications of rational inattention. *Journal of Monetary Economics*, **50** (3), 665–90.

SIMS, C. A. (2010). Rational inattention and monetary economics. In *Handbook of Monetary Economics*, Vol. 3, ed. B. M Friedman and M. Woodford, 155–181. Elsevier.

STEINER, J., STEWART, C. and MATĚJKA, F. (2017). Rational inattention dynamics: Inertia and delay in decision-making. *Econometrica*, **85** (2), 521–553.

STEVENS, L. (2020). Coarse pricing policies. *Review of Economic Studies*, **87** (1), 420–453.

STRAUB, L. and ULBRICHT, R. (2023). *Endogenous Uncertainty and Credit Crunches*. Working Paper. Available at SSRN 2668078.

Svensson, L. E. and Williams, N. M. (2007). *Bayesian and Adaptive Optimal Policy under Model Uncertainty*. National Bureau of Economic Research. Working Paper 13414.

Tambe, P., Hitt, L., Rock, D. and Brynjolfsson, E. (2020). *Digital Capital and Superstar Firms*. National Bureau of Economic Research. Working Paper 28285.

Timoshenko, O. A. (2015). Product switching in a model of learning. *Journal of International Economics*, **95** (2), 233–249.

Topa, G. (2001). Social interactions, local spillovers and unemployment. *Review of Economic Studies*, **68** (2), 261–295.

Topa, G. (2011). Chapter 22: Labor markets and referrals. In *Handbook of Social Economics*, Vol. 1, ed. J. Benhabib, A. Bisin, and M. O. Jackson, 1193–1221. Elsevier.

Turen, J. (2023). State-dependent attention and pricing decisions. *American Economic Journal: Macroeconomics*, **15** (2), 161–189.

Van Nieuwerburgh, S. and Veldkamp, L. (2006). Learning asymmetries in real business cycles. *Journal of Monetary Economics*, **53** (4), 753–772.

Van Nieuwerburgh, S. and Veldkamp, L. (2010). Information acquisition and portfolio under-diversification. *Review of Economic Studies*, **77** (2), 779–805.

Veldkamp, L. (2005). Slow boom, sudden crash. *Journal of Economic Theory*, **124** (2), 230–257.

Veldkamp, L. (2006a). Information markets and the comovement of asset prices. *Review of Economic Studies*, **73** (3), 823–845.

Veldkamp, L. (2006b). Media frenzies in markets for financial information. *American Economic Review*, **96** (3), 577–601.

Veldkamp, L. (2011). *Information Choice in Macroeconomics and Finance*. Princeton University Press. Working Paper.

Veldkamp, L. and Wolfers, J. (2007). Aggregate shocks or aggregate information? Costly information and business cycle comovement. *Journal of Monetary Economics*, **54**, 37–55.

Venkateswaran, V. (2014). *Heterogeneous Information and Labor Market Fluctuations*, Working Paper.

Walker, K. (2001). The costs of privacy. *Harvard Journal of Law and Public Policy*, **25**, 87.

Wang, J. (1993). A model of intertemporal asset prices under asymmetric information. *Review of Economic Studies*, **60**, 249–282.

Wee, S. L. (2016). *Delayed Learning and Human Capital Accumulation: The Cost of Entering the Job Market during a Recession*. Working Paper.

Weitzman, L., Martin (2007). Subjective expectations and asset-return puzzles. *American Economic Review*, **97** (4), 1102–1130.

Wieland, V. (2000). Monetary policy, parameter uncertainty and optimal learning. *Journal of Monetary Economics*, **46** (1), 199–228.

Willems, T. (2017). Actively learning by pricing: A model of an experimenting seller. *Economic Journal*, **127** (604), 2216–2239.

Wilson, R. (1975). Informational economies of scale. *Bell Journal of Economics*, **6**, 184–95.

Winkler, F. (2020). The role of learning for asset prices and business cycles. *Journal of Monetary Economics*, **114**, 42–58.

WONHAM, W. M. (1964). Some applications of stochastic differential equations to optimal non-linear filtering. *Journal of the Society for Industrial and Applied Mathematics, Series A: Control,* **2** (3), 347–369.

WOODFORD, M. (2003). Imperfect common knowledge and the effects of monetary policy. In *Knowledge, Information, and Expectations in Modern Macroeconomics: In Honor of Edmund S. Phelps,* ed. P. Aghion, R. Frydman, J. Stiglitz, and M. Woodford, 25–58. Princeton University Press

WOODFORD, M. (2009). Information-constrained state-dependent pricing. *Journal of Monetary Economics,* **56**, S100–S124.

WU, L. (2020). *Partially Directed Search in the Labor Market. Working Paper.*

WU, L., HITT, L. and LOU, B. (2020). Data analytics, innovation, and firm productivity. *Management Science,* **66** (5), 2017–2039.

YANG, C. (2020). *Rational Inattention, Menu Costs, and Multi-Product Firms: Micro Evidence and Aggregate Implications.* Federal Reserve Board. Working Paper.

ZINGALES, L. (2017). Towards a political theory of the firm. *Journal of Economic Perspectives,* **31** (3), 113–130.

INDEX